DEVOLVING IDENTITIES

I should like to dedicate this book to my friends in
the North and my family in the South: in particular,
my parents Hazel and Garfield Pearce

Devolving Identities: Feminist Readings in Home and Belonging

edited by
Lynne Pearce

Studies in European Cultural Transition

Volume Eight

General Editors: Martin Stannard and Greg Walker

Ashgate

Aldershot • Burlington USA • Singapore • Sydney

Published by
Ashgate Publishing Limited
Gower House
Croft Road
Aldershot
Hants GU11 3HR
England

Ashgate Publishing Company
131 Main Street
Burlington
Vermont 05401-5600
USA

Ashgate website: http://www.ashgate.com

British Library Cataloguing-in-Publication data

Devolving Identities: feminist readings in home and belonging. – (Studies in European cultural transition; v. 8)
1. Nationalism in literature 2. Nationalism – Great Britain 3. English literature – 19th century – History and criticism 4. English literature – 20th century – History and criticism 5. Feminist literary criticism
I. Pearce, Lynne
820.9'358

Library of Congress Cataloging-in-Publication data

Devolving Identities: feminist readings in home and belonging / edited by Lynne Pearce.
(Studies in European cultural transition; v. 8)
Includes bibliographical references and index.
1. English literature – Women authors – History and criticism. 2. Feminism and literature – Great Britain – History – 20th century. 3. Women and literature – Great Britain – History – 20th century. 4. English literature – 20th century – History and criticism. 5. Identity (Psychology) in literature. 6. Group identity in literature. 7. Home in literature.
I. Pearce, Lynne. II. Series.
PR478.F45 D48 2000
820.9'9287'0904–dc21 00-038978
CIP

ISBN 0 7546 0074 2

Typeset by N^{2}productions and printed on acid-free paper and bound in Great Britain by

Printed and bound in Great Britain by MPG Books Ltd, Bodmin, Cornwall

Contents

General Editors' Preface

The European dimension of research in the humanities has come into sharp focus over recent years, producing scholarship which ranges across disciplines and national boundaries. Until now there has been no major channel for such work. This series aims to provide one, and to unite the fields of cultural studies and traditional scholarship. It will publish the most exciting new writing in areas such as European history and literature, art history, archaeology, language and translation studies, political, cultural and gay studies, music, psychology, sociology and philosophy. The emphasis will be explicitly European and interdisciplinary, concentrating attention on the relativity of cultural perspectives, with a particular interest in issues of cultural transition.

Martin Stannard
Greg Walker

University of Leicester

Acknowledgements

Despite its denomination as an 'edited collection' this volume has been produced in the spirit of genuine co-authorship, and my first thanks must therefore be to all the contributors who have entered into dialogue both with myself and each other with such enthusiasm and dedication: thank you all for the emotional as well as the intellectual labour that I know has gone into many of these chapters.

Other thanks are due to: Rowena Murray and Jackie Jones for helping me conceptualize the project and develop the proposal; to the editors of this Series, and to Ashgate Publishing, for giving it their support; to Ruth McElroy whose 'Sexing the Nation' conference held at Cheltenham and Gloucester College of Higher Education in 1998 brought many of the contributors together for the first time; to all those who have acted as the book's unofficial 'readers' – namely, Tony Pinkney, John Urry, Beverley Skeggs and (most rigorously!) Hilary Hinds; to Rachel Dyer who acted as an unofficial research assistant whilst I was based in Scotland; to Anne Stewart for all her help with the mailings and final stages of MS production; to Mike Greaney for compiling the Index; and finally to my 'friends in the North' – both sides of the Border! – but in particular, to the people of Taynuilt for making me so welcome in my 'destination' home.

Introduction

Devolution and the Politics of Re/location

Lynne Pearce

As its title suggests, this volume marks the impact of devolutionary politics on the female subject's changing sense of 'home and belonging'. Whilst firmly located within the broader context of the major social and cultural upheavals taking place across Europe at the present time, these essays focus specifically on the situation in the British Isles, with feminist academics from England, Scotland, Wales, Northern Ireland and Eire re/negotiating issues of gender, class, ethnicity, and national/regional identity through their readings of two literary/cultural texts: an approach and methodology that pays tribute to the central role of imagination and 'story-telling' in the the formation of both subjects and communities.[1]

My decision to revisit the complex, and often strained, relationship between gender and national/regional identity is in direct response to the the radical constitutional reforms currently being wrought by the British government's devolution policy. As I will explain in the next section, this 'commitment' to the devolution of limited political and economic power from Westminster to the various nations and regions that comprise the United Kingdom is far from new, but the opening of both the Scottish Parliament and the National Assembly for Wales this year (1999), together with the somewhat hasty and pre-emptive establishment of the Northern Ireland assembly in 1998, has moved the process on to a new footing. Although greeted with scepticism by some, the Scottish and Welsh referenda of 1997, and the elections of 1999, produced a significant groundswell of optimism in large numbers of individuals and interest-groups who hoped and believed that the long-awaited decentralization of government power would herald a 'new dawn'.[2] These groups and individuals have, of course, included

1 See Benedict Anderson, *Imagined Communities: Reflections on the Origin and Spread of Nationalism* [1983] (London: Verso, 1998) and Homi K. Bhabha, ed. *Nation and Narration* (London and New York: Routledge, 1990).

2 The referenda of September 1997 asked the citizens of Scotland and Wales to vote on whether or not they wanted constitutional reform which would grant their countries a limited form of devolved government. In Scotland, this would take the form of a full Scottish parliament (the previous one having been 'closed' by the Act of Union in 1707), and in Wales, a national assembly with more limited opportunities for independent legislation. The people of Scotland were asked to vote on two issues: first, the establishment

women, but the fact that feminist issues have rarely been a central part of the devolutionary debate is, indeed, one of the reasons this volume has needed to be written. In what way, or to what extent, is this re-drawing of the British constitutional map going to impact on women's lives? Will a new emphasis on 'the local' help one of the sectors of society most discriminated against by centralized government? Can a feminist consciousness make a significant impact on how the new parliaments and assemblies are run (e.g., less hierarchical/combative structures of 'debate')? Or should we simply expect the patriarchal structures of government to get reproduced on a more local scale? More to the point, perhaps, is the question of whether or not the women of the British Isles care very much about national/regional politics *at all*. On this crucial issue, the contributors to this volume are admittedly very mixed and, on occasion, perceptibly *dis*interested in what devolution might 'mean for them', as well as being wary of an over-involvement in the discourses of 'neo-nationalism'.[3] There are, of course, good historical reasons for these silences which I will return to a little later, but the vital – if superficially contradictory – corollary is that the same contributors all have *plenty* to say about 'home and belonging' in a less explicitly political sense. This is not to say that their engagements are apolitical, of course – anything but: the difference is simply that for this small sample of feminist academics drawn from 'the four corners' of the British Isles, the significance of nation, region, and community is 'known', and mediated, through a sense of place that is ontological rather than overtly ideological. Whilst this distinction could, of course, quickly slide into a typical, and unwelcome, stereotyping of the female psyche, a good deal of recent theorizing around 'the politics of location' supports the view that these alternative ways of 'knowing our place' are entirely valid

---

of an independent parliament; second, whether that parliament should be given tax-raising powers independent of Westminster (hence the prominent 'Yes Yes' campaign mounted by Labour and the SNP). The details of what aspects of government legislation should be devolved to the new parliament/assembly, and which should remain under the jurisdiction of the Westminster parliament have yet to be fully resolved, but it was agreed (in principle) that all legislation should be devolved to Scotland *except* foreign policy, defence, social security, macro-economic policy and the constitution. (This is, of course, a fairly substantive 'except'!) In other words, and the tax levy notwithstanding, we have still to see exactly *how* 'independent' the newly devolved Scottish parliament will be (and whether the Welsh Assembly, without actual policy-making legislation) proves any more than a debating chamber.

On this point, it should be remembered that the people of the North of Ireland have also voted 'yes' for a 'regional assembly' as part of their acceptance of the 'Good Friday Agreement' (this referendum was held 23 May 1998). On 25 June 1998 108 members were elected to this assembly but, after a hostile opening session, it has yet to meet on a regular basis.

[3] It is worth noting that, in my original 'proposal' for this volume, I invited all contributors to reflect directly upon what 'devolution meant for them'.

ones.[4] Once again, this is something I will return to, but for the moment I will simply note that amongst those to draw a productive distinction between the discourses of nationalism on the one hand, and the discourses of 'home and belonging' on the other, is Edward Said, who has written:

> Patriotism is best thought of as an obscure dead language, learned pre-historically but almost forgotten and almost unused since. Nearly everything normally associated with it – wars, rituals of nationalistic loyalty, sentimentalized (or invented) traditions, parades, flags, etc – is quite dreadful ... Thinking affectionately about home is all I'll go along with.[5]

In a similar vein, I might conclude that thinking about national and regional identity and UK devolution through a rigorous (and not always 'affectionate'!) sense of home is all a good many of my contributors have been 'prepared to go along with'. Where we were born, where we now live, where we might have lived 'in between', are matters of vital importance to recent generations of (increasingly mobile) British and Irish citizens, but how we 'know' those locations, and how those locations can be articulated alongside other aspects of our identity, is not something that can necessarily be arrived at through our sense of 'nationhood', however complex.

It is partly in response to the huge challenge we face when asked to define and evaluate our sense of national and regional identity, meanwhile, that I invited the contributors to this volume to use literary or other texts as 'springboards' for their discussions. As several critics and theorists before me have noted, one of the reasons why fiction and poetry are so useful and important in this particular political context is that both 'homes' and 'nations' – despite being defined in very precise territorial terms – nevertheless exist, first and foremostly, as 'acts of the imagination'.[6] It stands to reason, therefore, that a good deal of 'nation-building' goes on in the cultural realm, and that it is through our engagement of an ever more diverse range of cultural products and 'texts' that we are interpellated as nationally, or regionally, defined subjects. Put crudely, literary and other texts (I am thinking particularly of film and popular music) are instrumental in defining/shaping our locational identity: a 'truism' that literary scholars like Murray Pittock

---

4 This idea will be developed at length in subsequent sections of the Introduction, but see in particular Doreen Massey, *Space, Place and Gender* (Oxford: Polity, 1994) and Elspeth Probyn, *Outside Belongings* (London: Routledge, 1996).

5 Edward Said, *The Nation* 22, 15 July (1991), p. 116. Cited by Rosemary Marangoly George, *The Politics of Home* (Cambridge: Cambridge University Press, 1996), p. 201. Further page references to the latter volume will be given after quotations in the text.

6 See Anderson, *Imagined Communities* (note 1 above) and followers like Andrew Parker et al, *Nationalisms and Sexualities* (London: Routledge, 1994).

believe a pro-independence party like the SNP have ignored at their peril.[7] Less instrumentally, however, I would suggest that 'texts of the imagination' are also the means by which we, as subjects, can explore, test, assume, or reject different versions of national or regional locatedness; they are the spaces/places where we can inhabit nations and cultures that may not yet exist (for good or bad) in 'the real world'.[8]

As I will explain more thoroughly in a later section, the literary and other texts examined in this volume are therefore a 'means' rather than an 'end'. This is most definitely *not* a book 'about' the national and regional literatures of the British Isles (unlike Ian Bell's *Peripheral Visions* (1995), for instance) although it is hoped that it will have a supplementary role to play in making visible a fair number of non-canonical texts that have hitherto been ignored or forgotten.[9] What the discussions will reveal, however, is the way in which some of the nations and regions which presently comprise the British Isles are better served in terms of a legitimated 'indigenous' literature than others, and how this most decidedly *does* impact upon the way the contributors are able to see and talk about their sense of 'home and belonging'. It is precisely at this point, indeed, that we see that UK devolution has a cultural as well as a socio-political face, and that this has already had a significant impact on the impending 'break-up of Britain'.[10] (The huge 1990s boom in all areas of the Scottish arts and media is probably the most striking example of this, although the recent success of Welsh rock bands is testimony to a similar ground-swell there.) Indeed, another of the 'hard facts' faced by my contributors is that it is currently much easier to explore the complex intersection of gender/nationhood through writers from the so-called 'Celtic margins' than through those from 'middle-England' – simply because these issues are being *consciously* dealt with in their texts.[11] Whilst contemporary women writers from

---

7 See Murray Pittock, *The Invention of Scotland: The Stuart Myth and The Scottish Identity, 1638 to the Present* (London and New York: Routledge, 1991): 'The SNP is too dependent upon the political issues of the day for its support ... [its] concentration on economic matters is often in danger of rendering it a regionalist pressure-group rather than a nationalist party ... Few, if any, modern European nationalist parties have been successful without cultural nationalist priorities' (pp. 158–9).

8 Space/place: the differential meaning of and/or articulation of these two terms is discussed in note 1 to Chapter 8.

9 Ian A. Bell, *Peripheral Visions: Images of Nationhood in Contemporary British Fiction* (Cardiff: University of Wales Press, 1995).

10 See Tom Nairn, *The Break-Up of Britain* [1977] (London: Verso, 1981). The 'cultural face' of devolution has more recently hit the headlines with the lauch of a new Scottish 'Newsnight' which will 'break away' from its London counterpart every night for the last 20 minutes or so of programme time. (*Newsnight* is the UK's most highly-rated TV news programme.) This 'compromise' is seen by many as symptomatic of the fact that all that devolution has delivered to date is a new 'regionalism'. See Rob Brown, 'A broadcasting Culloden?', *Sunday Herald*, 'Seven Days', 29 August 1999, p. 1.

11 I should note here, however, that my suggestion (in an earlier draft) that it is subsequently 'easier' to identify as a 'Scottish feminist' at the present time than as an

the peripheries have struggled hard to negotiate and align the different aspects of their marginalization, the writers from the centre seem, by and large, not to know where to begin.[12] Fortunately, the same cannot be said of the 'English' contributors to this volume, all of whom have fascinating – and often amusing – stories to tell. In conclusion, then, it may perhaps be said that whilst this is not a volume 'about' the national/regional literatures of the British Isles *per se*, it most certainly *is* 'about' the significance of such texts in the making/marking of ourselves as 'devolutionary subjects'. The 'readings' of the book's title are thus a promise not of textual *explication*, but of *exploration*: a readerly engagement that has enabled the authors to confront the complex nexus of gender/nation/region (and other aspects of identity-formation) *through* their chosen texts.

To the extent that most of these 'readings' are autobiographically inflected, it is clear that the contributors are also presenting *themselves* (and/or their 'locational identities') as 'texts to be read'. Despite the strong move towards the use of 'the personal' in feminist theorizing in recent years I have, as editor, been constantly aware that this is a practice, or 'method', that will not appeal to all readers; one that – without rigorous monitoring – could easily lead to charges of solipsism and self-indulgence. As I indicate in the ensuing subsection ('Re/locating the Self'), however, a critical evaluation of these 'self-texts' *alongside* the work of others is often anything but 'self-indulgent' for the authors concerned. This is not 'telling one's story' for the sake of it, but for the 'strategic' purpose of enunciating some of the most knotted (and hence 'unspeakable') aspects of identity formation.[13] This methodological point relates, too, to the way in which the feminism of this project as a whole inevitably slips in and out of view, with the 'multi-implicated' author-subject frequently struggling to keep all her political plates spinning at the same time. Once again, I will say more about these silences and 'blind spots' in the enunciation of the 'located self' directly, but to readers of the volume who may occasionally find themselves asking 'what is specifically feminist about this analysis?', I would suggest that feminism (as a 'politics') is not necessarily inherent in *any* text or textual analysis: it is rather what we (as authors, readers and

---

English one has been hotly contested by one or two of my contributors. Ruth McElroy, for example, has pointed out the severe difficulty 'Welsh feminists' experience in getting academic jobs: 'Either Welsh or feminist, but not both for God's sake!'

12 Although it is doubtless iniquitous to name examples, it is striking that many of Britain's best-selling feminist authors of recent years like Jeanette Winterson and Angela Carter have tended toward fiction which, although admirably 'materialist' in some respects, is pointedly non-specific in geographical terms. The superficial 'invisibility' of Englishness may also be compared to similar debates *vis-à-vis* 'whiteness'. See, for example, Richard Dyer, *White* (London and New York: Routledge, 1997).

13 'Strategic use of the personal pronoun': see Elspeth Probyn, *Sexing the Self: Gendered Positions in Cultural Studies* (London and New York: Routledge, 1993), pp. 7–31, and also my own discussion of Probyn's 'method' in *Feminism and the Politics of Reading* (London: Arnold, 1997), p. 26. Further quotations from the latter volume will be given after quotations in the text.

citizens) then elect to *do* with the issues those texts have raised. Thus whilst some of the authors acknowledge the need for this 'second move' in the essays themselves, sometimes the responsibility for converting a 'gender-aware' text into an overtly 'feminist' one lies with the reader/citizen. For a project like this one, with its literary and cultural analyses so explicitly linked to an *immediate* social and political context, the opportunities to initiate change should be clear and urgent. My hope as a feminist editor is, therefore, that taken together, these essays will inspire women throughout Europe to re-think the possibilities of domestic, local and national 'belonging' in ways that are more comfortable to them; to take into their own lives, and communities, new ways of inhabiting the spaces, and places, we call 'home'.

In the remainder of the Introduction I will range through a selection of political, theoretical and methodological issues that I perceive to have informed the volume as a whole. Given the variousness and complexity of its points of intellectual reference – nationalism, regionalism, UK Devolution, discourses of 'home and belonging', feminism – this is no mean feat, but I will do my best to demonstrate the ways in which I see all these interests coming together (and straining apart!). The headings I will be working under are: (1) *The Devolutionary Moment*, which will attempt to map historically the political and cultural impact of devolutionary policy in the British Isles over the past twenty years or so; (2) *The Politics of Location*, which will attempt to theorize, in a little more detail, the crucial and, I believe productive tension between thinking about locational identities in terms of the discourses of 'nationhood' on the one hand, and the more 'homespun' narratives of 'home and belonging' on the other; (3) *Re-locating the Self*, in which I will link the considerable methodological challenges facing the contributors to this volume in terms of 'finding a postion' from which to speak with an epistemological 'defence' of various types of 'personalist criticism' and my own model of 'implicated reading',[14] and (4) *Re-Locating Home* in which I will preview the individual chapters and attempt to draw some general conclusions.

On this last point, it should also be said that the pre-occupations, themes and motifs ranging across the chapters were so ubiquitous – e.g. exile, mobility, 'the border' – that they could not be used to group the contributions in any useful or meaningful way. For that reason, the order in which the chapters appear is more or less arbitrary, and my editorial rationale is simply that readers will make their own connections between the ideas and sentiments expressed. As someone who has had the pleasure of getting quite minutely involved in each of these compelling stories of 'home and belonging', however, I must finally confess to finding the co-incidence of our experiences and our negotiations intellectually and emotionally consolidating.

---

[14] 'Implicated reading': see Pearce, *Feminism and the Politics of Reading*, pp. 13–16.

The devolutionary moment

Needless to say, my own perspective on the 'devolutionary moment' within the UK is necessarily partial and biased. It is the view of someone who grew up in Cornwall during a period when 'Mebyon Kernow', the Cornish Nationalist Party, was enjoying a brief resurgence, but whose calls for 'independence' and the re-opening of the 'Stannary Parliament' (with an historic right to policy-making separate from Westminster) no-one took too seriously. The fact that this was also the period – the 1970s – when Scotland and Wales were launched on their previous devolution campaigns escaped me entirely. I have no personal memories of how that campaign was fought; how it coincided with the demise of the old Labour party and the Tory election victory of 1979; how it marked the end of a decade or more of massively unwieldy (and costly) attempts at local government reform.[15] This amnesia for the first devolutionary moment is mirrored, interestingly, in the 'non-memories' of a Scottish friend. When I asked her about 'the last time' she said that, to be honest, she didn't remember much about it, followed by: 'I don't think we thought it was a good thing – at that time.'

In contrast, the second devolutionary moment – the one heralded by the election of New Labour in May 1997 and followed by the Scottish and Welsh referenda of September 1997, the post Good Friday referendum and elections in the North of Ireland in May/June 1998, and the Scottish and Welsh elections of May 1999 – is something that I have lived through, and will remember. What I will remember most of all is being in Scotland the night of the referendum vote (September 11 1997) and sharing in the excitement of what a resounding 74 per cent of the Scottish population seemed to find *very* exciting: with a few predictable regional variations it was 'Yes Yes' all the way to the polls.[16] The big question two years on, of course, is what was it *exactly* that we were all so excited about? And what was it exactly that the people of Scotland voted 'Yes Yes' for? Although the 'official' answer to the last question is clear enough: the people were voting (1) for an independent Scottish parliament and (2) for that parliament's right to its own

15 Both in *The Break-Up of Britain* (see note 9 above) and in his more recent writing, Nairn draws a depressing connection between devolution and the successive waves of local government reform that have surrounded it. See also Tom Nairn, 'Virtual Liberation or: British Sovereignty Since the Election', *BT Scottish Affairs: Understanding Constitutional Change* (Edinburgh: Unit for the Study of Government in Scotland, 1998), pp. 13–37. Further page references to this essay will be given after quotations in the text where the source is not ambiguous.

16 Taking Scotland as a whole, 74.3 per cent of voters voted for a Scottish parliament and 63.5 per cent for tax-varying powers. There was turnout of 60.4 per cent. Reviewing the press coverage of this referendum vote alongside the Scottish parliamentary elections in 1999, it is striking how this vote, and, indeed, this turnout, was deemed resoundingly positive for the former, but exceedingly 'poor' for the latter when the difference (for the turnout) was less than 5 per cent. It is also striking how such representation distorted my own statistical memory of both polls!

tax-raising powers separate from Westminster, it is clear that 'unofficially' people were voting 'Yes Yes' to a good deal more.

Living through the media 'production' and 'reflection' of the event, I would say that a substantive part of the visual imagery and rhetoric of that long and memorable night had its origins in the discourse of 'rebellion'. It became the moment, right enough, when the spirits of Scotland's long-dead 'Bravehearts' rose and walked again; when the people of a long-oppressed nation made their stand for 'freedom'; when the same people genuinely – if temporarily – believed that they were on the threshold of a new democracy, a better world.[17] On 'the morning after the night before', indeed, those lines from William Wordsworth's *The Prelude* seemed never far away from anyone's lips ('Bliss was it in that dawn to be alive/ But to be young was very heaven').[18] I have distinct memories of Scotland's leading woman (and feminist) writer, Liz Lochhead, saying as much when she was interviewed for BBC Radio Scotland beneath Edinburgh's Salisbury Crags; and, as evidenced in my newspaper archive, it was also picked up on in several newspaper reports, headlines and editorials. My point here, then, is that what 'the people' of Scotland were celebrating that dawn – perhaps even what they had voted for the day before – was 'the moment itself'. Whilst political commentators and theorists are markedly divided on whether this support for devolution and its partial autonomy is based, principally, on social and economic discontent (see Tom Nairn, David McCrone) or a desire for/assertion of 'national identity', it is my tentative belief that that the 'Yes Yes' vote was principally a vote 'for Scotland' in an almost *iconic* sense.[19] I should add that I use this last term advisedly because although, at one level, I am indeed implying that the 'Yes Yes' was for something very abstract, very emotive, and strikingly detached from a grounded political agenda, on another, I am thinking of the research I have done on the press photography associated with the devolution campaigns, and my hypothesis that a good number of 'poetic' images produced by the media were/ have been absolutely central in the making/marking of the voters as 'devolutionary subjects'.[20] Such iconicity can quickly be translated back into

---

[17] A good deal has already been written on the significance of the Hollywood movie, *Braveheart* (1995), in the resurgence of national/nationalist sentiment in Scotland (and amongst the Scottish diaspora), with few disputing the political significance (e.g., a sudden increase in Scots joining the SNP) but many criticizing the *ersatz* version of Scottish history on which the ideological turn was based. See for example Angus Calder, 'By the Water of Leith I Sat Down and Wept: Reflections on Scottish Identity' in Harry Ritchie, ed., *New Scottish Writing* VII (London: Bloomsbury, 1996), pp. 218–38.

[18] William Wordsworth, *The Prelude: A Parallel Text* , Book X (Harmondsworth: Penguin, 1978).

[19] See Nairn, 'Virtual Liberation' (note 15 above) and also David Crone's introduction in the same volume.

[20] Paper presented at the 'Anglo-Saxon Attitudes' conference, sponsored by the ESRI, and held at Salford University July 1999: 'From "Yes Yes" to "No No": Press Photography and the Making/Marking of the Devolutionary Subject'.

nationalism, and/or a desire for independence, admittedly, but I have my doubts about to what extent such connotations were consciously carried forward into the ballot box on 11 September 1997. Beyond that, if I had to attach one word to what the people of Scotland were voting for, it would have to be 'revolution' (and with quite specific echoes the French republican chant of 'Liberty, Equality, Fraternity'): a fantastical dream, way beyond the scope of anything a Westminster-inspired devolution policy could deliver, but a compelling 'vision' all the same. And in creatively 'imagining' this moment, the voters of Scotland were, of course, symbolically joining hands with any number of ex-colonies throughout the world who have celebrated the birth of a 'new nation' *as* the moment of liberation from an old and oppressive one.[21]

This last observation must also remind us, however, that even within the British Isles, devolution has been, is, and will continue to be experienced very differently by the constituent 'home nations'. Despite the fact that the Welsh referenda and elections were seen (by some) to be deliberately rigged towards a 'yes' vote by being staged alongside, or immediately after, the Scottish votes, the results have been far less conclusive. Compared to the 74 per cent endorsement in the Scottish referendum, the Welsh 'yes' vote only just scraped a majority, and also registered continuing stark divisions throughout the country in terms of the historical north/south, rural/urban and language-speaking divides. Most commented on of all, however, was the comparatively low turn-out for both the referendum and the assembly elections in Wales (c.46 per cent), which has caused devolutionary sceptics to argue that there is a distinct lack of interest in constitutional reform. The relative, and surprising, success of Plaid Cymru in the Assembly elections of May 1999 can, however, be used to tell a different story (17 Plaid Cymru seats compared to 28 for Labour), and it has been my impression – reviewing *all* these statistics – that the bias of the press has been absolutely instrumental in both interpreting, and promoting, the 'will' of these two nations throughout this period (see notes 16 and 30).

When we turn to the situation in the North of Ireland, moreover, we are faced with a history and context so specific and 'other' that the government's attempts to link it to the devolution of Scotland and Wales must, in itself, be regarded with suspicion and concern. 'Northern Ireland' is, after all, the British government's

---

21 This distinction between different types of nationalism – between 'nationalisms of oppression' on the one hand and 'nationalisms of liberation' on the other – is defined and problematized by Etienne Balibar and Immanuel Wallerstein in *Race, Nation, Class: Ambiguous Identities*, trans. Chris Turner (London: Verso, 1991): 'There is always a "good" and a "bad" nationalism. There is the one which tends to construct a state or a community and the one which tends to subjugate, or destroy; the one which refers to right and the one which refers to might; the one which tolerates other nationalisms and which may even argue in their defence ... and the one which radically excludes them in an imperialist or racist perspective. There is one which derives from love (even excessive love) and one which derives from hate' (p. 47).

longstanding 'experiment' in devolution (see Chapter 11 by Eilish Rooney), and one that has been spectacularly *unsuccessful* according to the reckoning of most of those who have lived with it (however politically postioned).The attempt to align this war-torn province with the processes happening in Scotland and Wales may thus, at one level, seem almost laughable: an incommensurability rendered graphically, and materially, tragic by the fact that the Northern Ireland Assembly – although voted for by over 70 per cent of voters in the wake of the 1998 'Good Friday' agreement – has yet to meet on a regular basis after the fiasco of the first sitting (see note 2). Because of its very specific history it is clearly impossible for the North of Ireland to enter the devolutionary arena on the same terms as Scotland and Wales, and yet one could argue, once again, that the 'will of the people' (recorded in the emphatic 'Yes' vote) notionally *aspires* towards such a possibility. How we interpret this 'will', when confronted with the apparently intractable problems of the political reality is, of course, a point of serious contention.

Outside the 'home nations', meanwhile, the prospect of devolution continues to mean something rather different again. Although the North-East of England, Yorkshire, Cornwall and several metropolitan centres (most notably London itself) have begun some quite high-profile campaigning for their own 'relative autonomy', their 'devolutionary moment' has yet to come. On this point it will, indeed, be interesting to see if, and when, the government's vague, 'in-the-future' promises to set up regional assemblies throughout the UK materialize. The problem that presents itself here is that all these regions are invested (or not) in devolution for rather different reasons, and represent very different socio-economic and cultural bases. Whilst the North-East is currently arguing strongly that it needs devolution to help it compete with the new economic and other benefits enjoyed by its Scottish neighbour, Cornwall is using its extreme geographical isolation at the other end of the British Isles, together with its acknowledged poverty and cultural distinction (it is seen, historically, as another Celtic country with its own language and culture), to argue for both devolution and massive government investment.[22] Needless to say, both campaigns are predicated on a very different rationale from the case of London whose past experiment with the GLC (Greater London Council) is seen by some as a model of how the capital city would also benefit from a freshly devolved social, cultural and economic autonomy. Such a claim inevitably renews long-standing issues of equality, of course, with the rural regions arguing that further investment in the capital is the

---

22 The economic demise of Cornwall, in particular, came to light with the closure of the last tin mine in 1998. Soon afterwards the region was officially declared the poorest in Britain, and in 1999 won 'Objective One' funding from the European Union. The tin-mine closure also saw the launch of a new quasi-nationalist support movement called 'Cornish Solidarity' which is fighting to keep the economic, social and cultural concerns of Cornwall separate from its wealthier neighbours in what the government is designating the 'South-West' region.

last thing that they (and 'Britain') needs.[23] If, and when, the cake *is* divided up, which regions will be seen as most deserving? Which least? As long as devolution continues to operate as something that the centre 'gifts' to its margins then the tensions must necessarily remain.

To understand a little more about the problems structurally inherent in the present devolutionary model it is useful to delve into recent history, and then work one's way backwards. Here I should also signal, in advance, that most of the analysis and speculation contained in this section is focused on Scotland. This is partly a matter of personal expedience (my part-residence in Scotland over the past few years has enabled me to assess, and enter into, these debates more fully); partly a consequence of that fact, with its devolution most successfully 'advanced', Scotland's case is the one that has been most fully documented and analysed in recent times. However, in as much as most of the complications and contradictions inherent in the devolution process *are* structural, and part of an encompassing centre-margin dynamic, I trust that the other nations and regions of the British Isles will be kept at least implicitly in view at all times.

For many, the obvious way of explaining the success of the present Scottish 'revolution' (and/or drive towards 'independence') is to invoke the spectre of Thatcherism. On this point, commentators like Tom Nairn, whilst entirely sceptical about 'what' is being offered to the constituent nations and regions of the British Isles under the guise of devolution, are clear that it was Thatcherite hegemony – and, in particular, the iniquitous 'experiments' with the poll tax – that ensured that Scotland voted 'yes yes' a second time around.[24] In this context, the 'Yes Yes' vote can be seen both as a vote against the long duration of Tory rule for a nation/region that returned only a tiny number of Scottish conservative MPs for the whole eighteen-year period, and – perhaps more significantly – a vote *against* a national government based in London. Here, again, memories of the poll tax must be seen as absolutely crucial, demonstrating to Scots, in no uncertain terms, that they were not only a 'margin' but a newly-visited 'colony' within the UK.

This concept of 'internal colonialization', first brought to clear consciousness, according to Raphael Samuel, in Michael Hechter's book from 1975, may subsequently be seen as the the most straightforward way in which the Left – feminists included – may support and endorse a policy of either devolution or independence for 'the other nations' currently comprising the United Kingdom.[25]

---

23 The competing claims of the different regions within a devolved United Kingdom were usefully debated in a BBC Scotland documentary, 'Our Friends in the South' (broadcast 23 April 1998). This included those that felt that 'devolution' of metropolitan centres like London (new 'city-states') was not incommensurate with the devolutionary principle: an opinion that has been given further support by the newly elected Mayor of London, Ken Livingstone.

24 See Nairn, 'Virtual Liberation', pp. 14–18.

25 See Raphael Samuel, *Island Stories: Unravelling Britain* (*Theatres of Memory*, Vol 2) (London: Verso, 1998). Further page references to this volume will be given after

Samuel himself links this to the rise of 'four nations theorising' in Britain from the 1970s onwards: a theorizing that (following historians like Hugh Kearney) sees 'British history not in terms of church and state, crown and aristocracy ... but rather in the spatial divisions of core and periphery, metropole and provinces' (p. 24) and where 'we are continually being offered (instead of some spurious notion of constitutional 'union') *worlds within worlds*' (p. 27) (emphasis as in text). Within the discourses of postcolonialism, indeed – and alongside the rhetorical celebration of 'cultural *difference*' – it suddenly becomes important that the erstwhile 'margins' of the UK, like Eire before them, should be allowed a constitutional freedom, independence and autonomy that is *not* still yoked to 'the centre' as it is under the current model of devolution.

Yet the main problem with this vision for the Left, and one to which feminists will be particularly sensitive, is that the 'liberation' of 'the home nations' all too quickly returns us to the principles of ethnic-nationalism: a suspicion that the celebration of 'difference' *vis-à-vis* the 'Celtic fringe' will be at the expense of other kinds of multi-ethnic difference and that this will all too quickly translate into racial intolerance (both for the 'English' and other supposedly 'immigrant' groups) (see especially Ruth McElroy and Charlotte Williams, Chapters 4 and 9).

How various politicians and theorists invested in UK devolution have dealt with this anxiety is, of course, extremely interesting. At the level of party policy, for example, the SNP have made repeated assertions that theirs is/will be '*a civic nationalism only*': claims to Scottish citizenship will be based on residency alone; filiations based on 'blood' and/or ancestry cannot be tolerated because of the attendant dangers of ethnic discrimination. Reasonable as this seems at one level, however, it is equally incontestible that all the national/regional affiliations we find within the UK *are* invested in the notion of an 'ethnic base', and that when it comes to the question of 'claiming' such an identity, these factors are repeatedly brought to the fore. This ethnic nationalism is also linked (perhaps even more problematically for our purposes here) with the *cultures* of the respective nations and regions, which is clearly why the SNP and more materialist commentators like Tom Nairn have been cautious about overplaying this particular card.[26]

Thinking about devolution in *non*-ethnic terms has been a long-term quest for writers like Tom Nairn, clearly committed to the independence of their 'home nations', but ever-striving to historicize and 'justify' that bid for liberation in firmly geographical, social, economic and, above all, *constitutional* terms. What is perhaps most striking (and some would feel most depressing!) about Nairn's work, indeed, is the way in which his analysis of desired/inevitable 'break-up of Britain' has not really changed since the first edition of *The Break-Up of Britain* in 1977. In one of his most recent (re)interventions into the devolution debate, indeed, he

---

quotations in the text. See also Michael Hechter, *Internal Colonialism: the Celtic Fringe in British National Development* (Berkeley: University of California Press, 1975).

26 Nairn, *The Break-Up of Britain*, p. 71.

strongly re-asserts his belief that any delegation of national power to the British 'regions' that leaves the constitutional 'heart' of the United Kingdom unchanged is a very limited reform indeed.[27] His thesis here is that England has exerted its authority over the Union not simply through its elected governments but through its 'sovereignty': a unique congruence of parliament, church and crown that also goes some way to explaining why 'Englishness' has *otherwise* remained such an empty signifier for so long.[28] Whilst governments might 'propose' new legislation (like devolution), it is the sovereign state that 'disposes' it and, in the process, exercises and *performs* an authority that mitigates any real redistribution of power.[29] In both his early and more recent writings, Nairn links this to a long history of impotent legislation which was supposedly designed to devolve centralized power to the regions and to 'the people'. He notes how successive Labour and Conservative governments have all invested wildly in 'local governance mania' (p. 16), culminating, of course, in the scandal of the Tory poll tax. For Nairn, such a hyperbolic attention to 'the margins' can only be interpreted as a long-term, and inherently desperate, political blandishment:

> The notion was always of Britain being thoroughly re-cast – pristinely renewed from its grass-roots upwards. The denouement of this vision in the Poll Tax disorders was the most thoroughly prepared suicide note in modern political history. So there must have been, at least implicitly, some profounder purpose behind the process. Whatever the strategy was, it was clearly continuous and repeated enough to be phrased in terms of the State, or (in my terms today) of 'sovereignty', rather than just as successive government policies. Perhaps one could sum it up by saying that from the 1960s to the 1990s, as the United Kingdom state grew steadily more centralized in operation and unitary in practice, it sought with approximately equal constancy to counter-balance, conceal and legitimate this trend by the reconfiguration of local or 'regional' government. (pp. 17–18)

Even laying aside the faintly conspiratorial edge to Nairn's analysis, this vision of the long-term manipulation and exploitation of the 'margins' by the 'centre' in the

---

27 Nairn, 'Virtual Liberation' (note 13 above).

28 On this point Nairn ('Virtual Liberation') cites Laurence Brockliss and David Eastwood, eds, *A Union of Multiple Identities* (Manchester: MUP, 1997) who write: 'In the United Kingdom ... political discourse was broadly built around the assumption that Parliament, not the people, was sovereign. As long as the inhabitants of the British Isles accepted the very English idea that change could occur legitimately only if sanctioned by the British parliament, there was a limited need to foster unity by State-sponsored acculturation'. In other words, the elusive nature of 'Englishness' (currently being interrogated in publications like Jeremy Paxman's *The English: A Portrait of a People* (London: Michael Joseph, 1998)) can partly be explained by the constitutional strength of the Union and the sovereignty of its parliament. There is no need for anything else.

29 Nairn, 'Virtual Liberation', p. 14.

UK inevitably *does* cast serious doubt on what a centre-led devolution policy can achieve. With the hindsight of another twelve months, we might conclude that Nairn's scepticism is already being all too clearly borne out. Whilst many of us are still enjoying the *symbolic* spectacle of a Scottish parliament up and running, it is true that the more radical visions of its constituent members (the issue of student tuition fees, for instance) are being blocked by forces in Westminster, and the Scottish press has made us all too aware of the extent to which Donald Dewar and the parliament as a whole is in the pocket of Tony Blair.[30]

Yet whilst, on the one hand, Nairn's analysis obliges us to make the rather depressing connection between this pseudo-parliamentary devolution of power (for Wales and the North of Ireland, as well as for Scotland) and the demise of the local government quangos which preceded it, he also offers us the hope that the changes will subsequently initiate a more meaningful 'revolution from below'. Again drawing comparisons with the poll tax 'revolt' he suggests that: 'it may be that the attempt to implement devolutionary policies by a central, sovereign and unitary power, itself essentially unreformed, will once more set up a partly unforeseen dynamic of change' (p. 15).Thinking about this vision and analysis once again in the light of the past twelve months, I would say that there is – as yet – little sign of such 'change'. In simple statistical terms, it was shocking to witness the *lack* of interest in the Scottish and Welsh parliamentary elections (May 1999) compared to the referenda that preceded them.The turnout of voters was amongst the lowest ever recorded, and the media seemed at a loss as how to either report or 'produce' the event.[31] Various theories were invoked to 'explain' this lack of interest, but it would seem to corroborate my earlier speculation that whatever the people of Scotland were voting for in the 1997 referendum it was *not* the political 'reality' of devolution. Whilst statisticians have brought forward powerful evidence (via questionnaire analysis etc.) that the voters *were* more concerned with issues of social and economic policy than with ideological determinants like 'national identity' I, however, remain unconvinced.[32] Comparing the night of 11

---

30 See, for example, Iain Macwhirter, 'Parliament now has full power ... but can it turn the public on?', *Sunday Herald*, Seven Days, 29 August, 1999, p. 7.

31 In the Scottish Parliament Election of 6 May 1999 Labour won 56 seats, the SNP 35, the Liberal Democrats 17, the Conservatives 18, the Scottish Socialist Party 1, the Green Party 1, and Independent Labour (Denis Canavan) 1. The turnout was 58 per cent. In the elections for the National Assembly for Wales (also 6 May) the seats were as follows: Labour 28, Plaid Cymru 17, Liberal Democrats 6, Conservatives 9, with a turnout of 46 per cent. The difficulty of 'imaging' the elections (compared to the referenda) is something I also discuss in the paper I presented to the 'Anglo Saxon Attitudes' conference (see note 20 above).

32 See 'The Scottish Electorate and the Scottish Parliament', Paula Surridge et al. in *BT Scottish Affairs: Understanding Constitutional Change* (see note 15 above), pp. 38–60. These authors conclude: 'Intentions for the referendum were not shaped by social structure or issues of identity, but issues of welfare. The referendum vote was fairly uniform across all social classes, all age groups, and both sexes. It was not strongly influenced by

September 1997 with that of 6 May 1999 it is clear that there has been more than one slip 'twixt cup and lip, and it seems vital that we get the full measure of the spillage. The more hopeful analysis (for aspiring federalists) is that the *disinterest* is but a preface to the revolt to which Nairn still looks forward; the more depressing one, that devolution is, indeed, just another successful manifestation of centrist appeasement.[33] Whilst it would be easy to be convinced of the latter intellectually, my personal experience of the sheer *excess* of 'revolutionary' sentiment released in the 1997 referendum causes me to believe that, for Scotland at least, 'real' change will gradually vie with the cosmetic one. Such reforms might, of course, entail 'full independence', but Nairn's analysis also makes us hope that, somewhere along the line, the 'English centre' will ultimately be obliged to re-constitute itself. For the non-nationally defined 'regions' of the UK, indeed, this will be the *only* way a 'meaningful' devolution can be achieved. So: I have hopes, but I am not holding my breath.

But why hope? As a female and/or feminist reader you might, by this stage, be wondering why any of us should invest political time and energy in a process of insular pseudo-constitutional reform that rarely says anything 'to' women, and shows little evidence of dismantling the traditional patriarchal structures of government. I will therefore conclude this section with a short reflection on what UK devolution could, and should, mean for the female citizens of the British Isles and how it has so far failed them. I will then link this to thoughts expressed and positions held in a selection of the following chapters, speculating on how 'the break-up of Britain' may, or may not, assist a purportedly transnational and transglobal politics like feminism.

The introduction to Christopher Whyte's 1995 collection of essays, *Gendering the Nation*, opens with the citation 'Nationalism is always bad news for women'.[34] It is a hypothesis that most feminists would probably support 'in the abstract', but what Whyte's chapter goes on to do, and what, I hope, this volume will also do, is interrogate its *inevitability* in the context of the constitutional changes presently taking place in Europe and the UK. Whilst it is incontrovertible that the historical 'nationalism' of Great Britain and its empire has been seriously 'bad news' for women and other so-called minority groups, and whilst the liberationist

national identity, probably because the Labour party and Tony Blair had successfully appealed to a sense of modernizing Britishness as one reason for supporting change. Feeling Scottish was certainly one influence on voting in favour, but feeling British was not mainly a reason to vote against' (p. 58). These observations were based on interviews conducted by the 'Scottish Election Survey' in 1997. One of the questions concerned 'identity' (see pp. 50–51 for analysis of this).

33 'Federalism': for commentators like Nairn any effective devolution of the UK would have to change its constitution at the core and replace Unionist 'sovereignity' with a thorough-going federalism of the member nations/regions. See *Break-Up of Britain*, p. 404.

34 Christopher Whyte, *Gendering the Nation: Studies in Modern Scottish Literature* (Edinburgh: Edinburgh University Press, 1995), p. ix. Further page references to this volume will be given after quotations in the text.

'neo-nationalisms' of Irish Repulicanism and earlier versions of Scottish nationalism have exercised a different, but equally problematic, positioning of their female citizens, there remains the hope and prospect of a different order of locational identity.[35] Whyte himself deploys the Queer theorizing of Judith Butler and Eve Sedgwick to suggest how the relationship between nationalism and feminism may be usefully re-thought. By using the dissidence of the perceived 'margins' to expose and unsettle the foundations of the dominant orthodoxies (be that patriarchy, heterosexuality, or an oppressive nationalism), we can perhaps look forward to new 'ways of being' beyond those binaries:

> Eve Kosofsky Sedgwick comments in an illuminating fashion on the parallels between the politics of nation and the politics of gender:
>
> > To suggest that everyone might 'have' a nationality as everyone 'has' a gender presupposes, what may well be true, and may always have been true, that everyone does 'have' a gender. But it needn't presuppose that everyone 'has' a gender in the same way, or that 'having' a gender is the same kind of act, process, or possession for every person or for every gender ...
>
> Just as 'to be a woman' may be a very different kind of activity or experience from 'to be a man,' so '(choosing) to be Scottish' is not necessarily the same kind of process as '(choosing) to be English'. Scottishness may be structured quite differently from Englishness. There may even be a range of possible ways of 'being Scottish'. (pp. xiv)

The radical optimism of Queer theorizing turns, of course, on the hypothesis that, in as much as all dominant orthodoxies *depend* upon the defining presence of 'deviant' others to preserve the *status quo*, so might their foundations ultimately be exposed and toppled. Moving on from Whyte's specific focus on the Scotland–England dyad, we could also use this theory of 'perverse' inter-dependence to support Tom Nairn's prognosis *vis-à-vis* a more widespread UK devolution. As the 'regions' gradually reveal how much the centre depends upon their 'othering', so might the authority and 'authenticity' of that centre be radically undermined. And with the so-called 'crisis of Englishness' well under way, some would say that this is precisely what is already happening.[36]

What we have established so far, then, is that feminist and Queer theorizing can be positively enjoined to help re-think, and ultimately re-formulate, our existence

---

35 For an interesting intervention in the debate on the role and representation of women within the Irish Republicanism see Jayne Steel, 'Vampira: Representations of the Irish Female Terrorist', *Irish Studies Review* 6:3 (1998), pp. 273–84. See also Chapter 11 by Eilish Rooney.

36 'Crisis of Englishness': apart from the Paxman volume cited in note 28 above, other recent titles to engage in this debate include Simon Heffer's *Nor Shall My Sword: The Reinvention of England* (London: Weidenfeld, 1999). See also the TV documentary 'Our Friends in the South' (note 23 above).

as national subjects at a *structural* level. It uses the centre–margin dialectic to look forward to a time when we can, perhaps, inhabit both centres and margins differently; when to 'be' Scottish, or English, or Cornish, or 'from Salford' will not mean the same as it does now. In the meantime, however, and on the proverbial 'ground', it is clear that we still have a way to go. Whilst the Scottish Parliament and Welsh Assembly are not without their visible commitment to women (37 per cent of the new Scottish MSPs are women), issues of gender and women's rights have not been a significant feature of debate and legislation to date. Given the patriarchal history of government, this is hardly surprising, though it is clear that if 'the break-up of Britain' is to herald a meaningful improvement in 'civil rights' in general, and 'women's rights' in particular, then this has to be built into the new constitutions. As Esther Breitenbach and her co-authors declare in their essay 'Understanding Women in Scotland':

> Yet in Britain (and here we refer to the combination of those parts making up the UK) surely the key political issue is the need for the 'reconstitution' of the state (or indeed the need for a written constitution), and how that reconstitution will take place. At the roots of this debate about state and constitution are arguments about democracy, civil rights and the rule of law (that is to say, a system of justice that commands respect).This debate creates a space for talking about women's rights as citizens and their participation in democratic forms of government. For feminists, therefore, a more specific focus on the form of the British state is imperative, both for understanding the past and for developing strategies for the future.[37]

The bottom line of this argument, then, is that – however sceptical (and perhaps weary) – we, as feminists, might feel about the constitutional changes promised by devolution within the UK we cannot afford to ignore them. Nation states around the world might have long been deaf and blind to the emancipatory politics of feminism, but it would be regrettable to see the equation simply reversed without any attempt at intervention. It is this sort of thinking that makes statements like 'nationalism is always bad news for women' ultimately reductive. Notwithstanding Sedgwick's salient point (above), women are 'always already' national subjects of *some kind*, and the challenge must be, first and foremost, to redefine the terms of our affiliation. (See also Chapter 11 by Eilish Rooney.) Whilst to be a national citizen is not, of course, the same thing as being 'a nationalist', it is clearly imperative that the ideological as well as the more material aspects of 'belonging' to a country and/or region be addressed; and it is at this very interface that I believe feminists have the greatest opportunity of helping us formulate an emancipatory 'politics of location' as I hope to argue in the next section.

---

[37] Esther Breitenbach et al., 'Understanding Women in Scotland', *Feminist Review* 58, Spring (1998), p. 58.

In bringing this somewhat polemical overview to a close, I am well aware that a fair number of my fellow-contributors do not share my hope that devolution (or, indeed, *post*-devolution) *will* bring about better conditions of citizenship for the women of Scotland, Wales, the North of Ireland or 'the regions' of England. For many, the potential ethnic 'exclusiveness' of the neo-nationalisms is a serious cause of concern (see in particular, Wren Sidhe), coupled with a sense that the possibilities for change available to women in Scotland, Wales and the North of Ireland may not be available in England. This is especially evident at a cultural level, where the current boom in neo-national/regional literatures, including feminist literatures, does not have an equivalent expression in the rest of the UK. As will be seen, it is striking how many of the contributors struggled to find texts that dealt with the 'regions' to which they 'belong(ed)'. At the same time, it is clearly important not to overstate this point. As Ruth McElroy, Charlotte Williams and Flora Alexander all show, it is not easy to find texts which respond to the complexity/hybridity of our 'lived' identity *anywhere*.

Finally, I feel I should make clear that while the contributors to the volume were invited to consider their changing sense of home and belonging 'in the context of UK devolution', I did not expect (or insist upon) direct political comment. Indeed, as the following section will hopefully make clear, one of the most important things this project has revealed is that it might *not* be the preference of feminist scholars/citizens to rethink the 'politics of location' in these terms. At the same time, other authors – in particular, Ruth McElroy, Eilish Rooney, Flora Alexander, Charlotte Williams and myself – speak quite directly about the urgent need for a feminist intervention in such potentially wide-sweeping constitutional reforms. And whilst the exact nature of that intervention might remain unclear (beyond the fact that it will need more than female seats in the respective parliamentary chambers), there is, at least, the hope that we are not (yet!) too late.

The politics of location

Long excluded from, or negatively positioned within, the traditional nation state, it is hardly surprising that women – and indeed feminists – should be sceptical of, or indifferent to, movements (like UK devolution) which promise constitutional change. It is also entirely appropriate that they should be suspicious of the neo-nationalisms that are one feature of the impending 'break-up of Britain'. Yet what I want to do in this section is turn these purportedly negative constructions on their heads and show that it is women's 'discomfort' and 'marginalization' within our national/neo-national cultures that has put them in the avant-garde of an alternative way of thinking about our locational homes.

It is significant, of course, that feminists are not alone in theorizing, or hypothesizing, such alternative models of 'home and belonging'. I began the

Introduction, it will be remembered, with a quotation from Edward Said who boldly countered all investment in a 'national identity' *per se* with a much more modest commitment 'to think affectionately about home' (see above). Likewise we find Raymond Williams arguing that:

> It is clear that if people are to defend and promote their real interests on the basis of lived and worked and placeable social identities, a large part of the now alienated and centralized powers and resources must be actively regained, by new actual societies which in their own terms, and nobody else's, define themselves.[38]

Such a view, or vision, is, of course, commensurate with a good deal of the devolutionary or regionalist principles presented in the last section. At one level, then, the quotation may be read as simply another plea to remove power from 'the centre' and return it to the 'grass-roots'. But implicit in Williams's wider thinking is, I believe, a perspectival shift that is greater than this: one which requires us to reconceptualize 'place' and 'home' from the point of view of 'being in it'; a shift commensurate with his reconfiguration of 'ideology' in terms of 'structures of feeling'.[39] With respect to this project, it is also a reconceptualization that chimes with the 'experience' of my contributors who repeatedly engage their literary texts to show us their understanding of home 'from the inside'. As I have argued elsewhere it is, however, important to accept that this 'inside' is also, and *necessarily*, a space/place of partial blindness.[40] One of the reasons we find it so difficult to talk about our 'homes', past and present, is that we have invariably experienced them *in medias res* and consequently cannot see, or know, the material and ideological forces that embody them. On the other hand, and more positively, I would contend that when we *do* find a way of speaking from that 'centre' it is often with a fresh, and defamiliarizing, perspective: our partial, changing, and radically provisional sense of 'home' (particularly in the way that it is associated with different people, and different geographical locations) upsets

---

38 Raymond Williams, *Towards 2000* (London: Pantheon Books, 1983), p. 197. Cited in David Crone, *Understanding Scotland: The Sociology of a Stateless Nation* (Routledge, 1992), p. 218.

39 'Structures of feeling': Raymond Williams coined this term as part of his general overhaul of Marxist models of ideology (see, for example, *Politics and Letters* (London: Verso, 1979)). Although difficult to summarize its full import, the term derives partly from Williams's belief that we need to find a way of speaking about how individuals experience ideology 'from the inside', as a 'structure of feeling' common to particular cultural historical moments. Commensurate with this principle is the belief that certain aspects of our social selves can be revealed to us through an 'act of recognition' (e.g., we might recognize the mark of our own regional identity through the behaviour of another).

40 See Lynne Pearce, 'The Place of Literature in the Spaces of Belonging: Gender, Nation and the Case for British Devolution', *Gender, Place and Culture*, special issue on 'Sexing the Nation', forthcoming.

most of the ideological fixity associated with nation-theorizing. For example, the way our experience of 'home' changes as we take up residence in different parts of a given country will necessarily confound the concept of any totalizing 'homeland' (see especially Ruth McElroy and Lynne Pearce); which is why, I believe, the contributions to this volume represent such an important challenge to the more abstract theorizing of what it is to be (or not) a British citizen at the present time.

Having already hinted, then, at some of the major dislocations of 'home' and 'nation' offered in the following chapters, I will now attempt a brief review of some of the ways feminist theorists have most usefully rethought the category 'home'. Although women (at least in modern Western society) have traditionally been seen to be 'tied to the home' as a primarily domestic space associated with family responsibilities and child-rearing, it is striking how feminist theorists have focused on: (1) home as a (variable) geographical location and (2) home as a space/place within a wider community that is *neither the 'family' nor 'the nation'*. Virtually all these commentators, moreover, pay attention to the fact that 'home' is as much a psychological as a material space, and many draw attention to the need to think of it as a space/place of unhappiness and violence as well as one of purported security.[41] Above all, moreover, these theorists are committed to re-thinking a version of 'home' that goes beyond its conservative or negative connotations. Like many of the contributors to this volume, they are invested in trading 'old homes' for new ones.

The first challenge the feminist must face when re-thinking 'home' is how to liberate it from the more oppressive aspects of familial and parental control. On this score, it is, of course, no surprise that the majority of contributors to this volume analyse their (re)locations within the UK through narratives of 'leaving home', several of them engaging texts which also perform this particular 'rite of passage' (see especially Rachel Dyer and Ruth McElroy). A good many of the chapters also make the important connection between family, 'blood', ethnicity, the 'myth of origins'– and how this feeds into the most undesirable formations of nationalism (see Wren Sidhe, Sinead McDermott and Charlotte Williams). As Angelika Bammer notes in the editorial to the 1992 *New Formations* special issue on 'Home': 'Home, nation and family ... operate within the same mythic and metaphorical field', a hypothesis given chilling explication in the 1980s analyses of Etienne Balibar and Immanuel Wallerstein.[42] Take, for example, the following anthropologically-based analysis:

---

41 See Marangoly George, *Politics of Home*, p. 26–9. In problematizing home and drawing attention to the violence often associated with it, George refers readers to Biddy Martin and Chandra Mohanty's germinal essay, 'Feminist Politics: What's Home Got to Do With It?', in Teresa de Lauretis, ed., *Feminist Studies / Critical Studies* (Bloomington: Indiana University Press, 1986), pp. 192–212.

42 Angelika Bammer, *New Formations* (special issue on 'Home'), 17, Summer (1992), pp. vii–xi. Further references to this essay will be given after quotations in the text.

> Thus, as lineal kinship, solidarity between generations and economic functions of the extended family dissolve, what takes their place is neither a natural micro-society nor a purely 'individualistic' contractual relation, but a nationalization of the family, which has as its counterpart the identification of the national community with a symbolic kinship, circumscribed by rules of pseudo-endogamy, and with a tendency not so much to project itself into a sense of having common antecedents as a feeling of having common descendents.[43]

Needless to say, such a focus on communities based on 'common descendents' quickly translates into racist and, indeed, eugenicist thinking, and reminds us why nationalisms linked to 'myths of origins' are so fundamentally dangerous. The link between familial and national/regional 'endogamy' in the context of UK devolution is one that I have myself pursued elsewhere, using Alice Thomas Ellis's depiction of a dysfunctional and endogamous rural Welsh community (*Unexplained Laughter*, 1985) to reflect upon the dangers of the nations and regions of the British Isles defining and, indeed, *defending*, themselves in those terms.[44] Although, in thinking about national and regional identity, there is always a strong temptation to see our 'real homes' in terms of 'roots' or 'origins', it is thus clear that this must be resisted at all costs: we need to find ways of 'belonging' to our nations in ways other than 'the ties of blood'.

At the opposite end of the spectrum to defining and, indeed, problematizing 'home' in terms of 'family' and 'origins' is, of course, the discourse of *nomadism*. Since the early 1980s, this has been perhaps *the* most popular way for feminists to re-define issues of home, belonging and, indeed, self-identity, with the emphasis on the 'provisionality' mirroring the new poststructuralist models of subjectivity.[45] In her *New Formations* editorial, Angelika Bammer reflects eloquently upon this poststructuralist/postmodernist version of home, paying particular attention to the way in which its unfixed, 'indeterminate' quality serves to 'mythify' and 'demythify' the concept simultaneously:

> Semantically, 'home' has always occupied a particularly indeterminate space: it can mean, almost simultaneously, both the place I have left and the place I am going to, the place I have lost and the new place I have taken up, even if only temporarily. 'Home' can refer to to both the place you grew up ... the mythic homeland of your parents and your ancestors that you yourself may never actually have seen, or the hostel where you are spending the night in transit ...
>
> This indeterminate referential quality of the term has two quite different, even (at first glance) contradictory, consequences. On the one hand, it

43 Balibar and Wallerstein, *Race, Nation, Class*, pp. 101–2.

44 See Lynne Pearce, 'Devolutionary Desires' in Richard Phillips, David Shuttleton, Diane Watt, eds, *De-centring Sexualities* (London and New York: Routledge, 2000), pp. 241–57.

45 See Massey, *Space, Place and Gender*, pp. 165–7.

> *demythifies* 'home' as provisional and relative ... On the other hand, its very indeterminacy has lent itself to the continual *mythification* of 'home' as an almost universal site of utopian (be)longing. (p.vii)

This continual relay between mythification and de-mythification of home is, indeed, a feature of many of the chapters which follow here, linked as it is to the powerful psychic forces that identify home as both a space/place of desire and one of fear and loathing.

It is clear, moreover, that it is not only the provisionality and indeterminacy of our homes *per se* that offers (at best) a liberating new perspective on them, but also the fact that they present us with (pseudo) 'fixed points' that we travel between. This sense of 'knowing' home, or re-thinking home, from the 'in-between space' of travel is certainly one of my own major preoccupations, as will be seen in Chapter 8. Yet like Doreen Massey and others, I consider it vital that we do not *overprivilege* the supposed 'knowledge' and 'insight' such travel affords us. Travelling to/from 'home' is, indeed (as my own chapter shows), *one* way of making sense of home and (literally) 'putting it in perspective'; it is also a way of seeing, and knowing, that has been revolutionized by motor transport and which thus belongs to specific cultures at a specific historical moment. But it is important to register that this is not *the only* view of 'home': the only way of seeing it and knowing it. My mother, for example, rarely leaves her house now and, because she gave up driving years ago, has never had much sense of the geography of her location (even within a five miles radius!). 'Home', for her, is a space radically detached from even an immediate contextualizing environment; it is a space to which the outside world comes (ourselves, the media) but which she never leaves: a perspective as opposite to my own as could be imagined, yet no less meaningful.

This, indeed, also relates to the further point which is of huge (yet generally understated) significance for the theorizing of this volume as a whole: that is, the fact that for many millions for women throughout the UK, Ireland and Europe in general, the space/place deemed one's 'home' is not a matter of choice or voluntary relocation (as brought about by moving jobs, for example), but a non-negotiable and material 'given'. Despite the revolution in education over the past thirty years, there are still thousands of women from working-class backgrounds who will never move far from their first and/or 'family' homes (an entrapment brought most starkly to light in Eilish Rooney's chapter on the experiences of women in the North of Ireland). Then there are others who will be involuntarily evicted from the places and communities they have come to know as home, and suffer the trauma of relocation elsewhere.[46] There will be those, too, that are forced to leave their first and/or chosen homes because the lack of work and cost of

---

[46] See Paul Gilroy, *There Ain't No Black in the Union Jack* (London: Routledge, 1987).

housing means they cannot afford to stay there. And there will be those who come to their new homes as immigrants, and whose choice in the matter is merely partial, or wholly absent, and whose welcome and 'integration' may well not be of the 'ideal' kind that I invoke at the end of this section (see Charlotte Williams). In conclusion, I would therefore argue that whilst the postmodern tropes of travel, flux, fluidity, mobility and so on have been extremely useful in helping us re-imagine all aspects of identity (especially ones in which any kind of 'marking' or 'fixity' quickly translates into discrimination), I do not personally subscribe to the more utopian discourses of nomadic existence that cause us to forget, or devalue, the perceptions of all those who inhabit homes and communities they might never leave (from choice, or otherwise). By the same token, I would urge those of us who do enjoy the privileges of quasi-voluntary mobility not to wholly dispense with the idea of home as a 'fixed point'. As Rosemary Marangoly George puts it in her critique of theorists like Caren Kaplan, Chandra Mohanty and bell hooks in her book, *The Politics of Home* (1996), it is important that in our efforts to problematize the notion of 'home' as a 'point of origin' (see my own discussions above), we do not overlook its significance (and reconceptualizing potential) as 'a point of arrival'.[47] And it is to this refiguration of home as a 'point of arrival' that I now turn by way of my conclusion to this section.

As I have already indicated, a good many of the chapters which follow feature narratives in which the author-readers end up trading 'old homes' for new ones. For these contributors, all 'professional' women with the 'benefits' of a higher education, the parental home is invariably presented as something that has to be 'left behind' (though with the proviso that this is often easier said than done). For many of the contributors, moreover, it is problems with these 'first homes' that are most clearly linked with the problems of 'national identity'. Hilary Hinds, for example, presents us with a powerful, and poignant, analysis of the way in which the stultifying domestic order and 'respectability' of her family home in Bournemouth trapped her in a version of 'Englishness' that she profoundly despised. For Hinds, the 'geographical' location of the family home (in a town like Bournemouth) could thus be defined in terms of both 'class' *and* 'nation', with the two becoming virtual synonyms for one another. Extracting oneself from such a heritage, meanwhile, is shown to be extraordinarily difficult, and although Hinds does not make any explicit links with the devolution movement in the UK, it is tempting to read her struggle as symptomatic of what it might mean to be marooned in 'Middle England' 'come the revolution'. Although Tom Nairn has offered us the vision of the 'centre' reforming itself, we have thus to accept that – even were British 'sovereignty' abolished overnight – the cultural 'performance' of the middle-Englishness of which Hinds and her chosen authors write

47 See, for example, Rosi Braidotti's *Nomadic Subjects* (New York: Columbia University Press, 1994) and Caren Kaplan, 'Deterritorializations: The Rewriting of Home and Exile in Western Feminist Discourse', *Cultural Critique* 6, Spring (1987), pp. 187–98.

(E.M. Forster and Barbara Pym) would not yield so easily. There is a sobering suggestion that whereas, for some of us, the *a priori* affiliation of familial and national home can be disrupted or broken through travel and/or relocation, the parasitic nature of 'Middle-Englishness' – the very fact that it clings on to our domestic spaces *wherever* we move them – will ensure its persistence. Yet, notwithstanding her clear acknowledgement of the power of such ideology (she now 'grades' re-useable plastic bags just like her mother!), it is important to recognize that Hinds did escape this 'origin' in part, and has used her *desire* for an 'elsewhere' to keep a critical eye on the space/place from which she came.

For contributors whose first homes were on/in the geographic 'margins' of the UK, the journey from home as a (given) 'point of departure', to one of a (chosen) 'point of arrival', resolves itself via rather different narratives. What the stories of Alison Easton, Ruth McElroy, and myself all suggest is that the imagined coherence of the 'English' centre tends to disintegrate once you actually go and live in it (especially if you take up residence, as we all did, in one of the more marginal 'regions'), and also that one's *own* travelling from place to place, serves to further unsettle the centre/margin binary. In addition, I would suggest that for all of us 'originating' in 'the margins', the sense of cultural/national *entrapment* presented by Hilary Hinds is replaced by a sense of locational *provisionality*. Although, in one sense, all of us, were 'brought up' surrounded by signifiers of the 'alternative', 'more romantic', and (perhaps) 'better defined' locational identity that Hinds conspicuously lacked, it was in the context that we were 'always already' destined to leave (see especially Chapter 4 by Ruth McElroy). Whilst it would be wrong to suggest that we were forcibly *exiled* from our first homes (all of us *chose* to leave), it is nevertheless evident that we have all since been haunted by the difficulty, if not the impossibility, of 'return', if only on economic grounds (i.e., opportunities for academic jobs in 'the margins' are limited). This, in turn, has inevitably impacted on our relationship to our 'destination home', or 'point of arrival', and here it is, I think, important to register the wide range of responses: from my own desire to 'put down roots' in *another* marginal location in the UK (i.e the Scottish Highlands); to Alison Easton's contentment with a 'border location' which keeps her within sight of her 'old home' whilst also signifying a permanent 'elsewhere'; to Ruth McElroy's acceptance of an apparently incontrovertible 'mobility' (locational and identificatory), notwithstanding her current re-location in Wales. Taken together, these margin-to-centre, or margin-to-margin, 'stories', confirm that there is no one way in which subjects are likely to respond to their voluntary/involuntary exile, although I detect in all of them a note of 'home-sickness' (with all the perversity and contradictoriness that the term implies) that is in significant contrast to the sense of entrapment described by Hinds.

Yet the re-negotiation of home as a space/place of 'origins' and one of 'destination' is complicated still further in the case of Charlotte Williams. As will be seen, her attempts to reconcile her mixed-race family origins (she is the daughter of a Guyanese father and a Welsh mother) with her life-long residence in Wales, is one for which Said's 'typical' trajectory from 'filiation' to 'affiliation' no longer applies.[48] For Williams and her family, there never *was* a moment when home was a 'given', and the 'voluntary' commitment of self to a place, or community, *outside* the family was demanded from the start. To even *begin* to be 'accepted', one had to work at it. This is a locational positioning markedly different from those associated with simply 'staying put' (see earlier discussion), and one that clearly complicates the notion of negotiable and non-negotiable sites. Thus, whilst the immigrant status of Williams's family in North Wales bespeaks the trauma of being involuntarily fixed and 'othered', the story she proceeds to tell reveals a host of strategies for re/location from which we might learn.

Indeed, there is a sense in which I believe Williams's negotiation of 'home', for all its complexity and 'hard work', serves us with one of the better models for rethinking our locational politics in terms of both self and nation. For me, the key difference between our originatory homes and those of 'destination' is that the latter require us to re-think our relationship with our geographical, social and cultural space in ways that are *not* 'given'. This is not to say that our habitation of the 'new home' will escape the 'partial blindness' of which I have already written, but the efforts required to achieve any sense of belonging will (ideally) be of service to both the self and the destination-community.

What such a vision translates into in terms of devolutionary politics within the UK *per se*, it is, of course, less easy to fashion. Thinking negatively, the home/family model should continually serve to remind us that home*lands* defined in terms of 'blood', 'origins' and ethnic exclusivity are (and should be!) doomed to failure. Thinking more positively, perhaps the best we can hope for is a vision of the British Isles in which free and easy access between 'the four nations' and their constituent regions is complemented by a 'code of settlement' (unwritten, but 'understood') in which those of us who have re-located within the UK undertake to learn, respect and eventually 'identify with' our chosen 'destination'. A sentiment something along these lines was recently presented by Alistair McIntosh in his address at the Edinburgh Festival (and published as *The Herald Essay*). In this lecture, McIntosh invokes the Gaelic terms *duthchas* and *dualchas* to offer us a vision of how nations, cultures and communities might retain and develop their identities whilst supporting the 'natural flow' of emigrants and 'incomers'. He writes:

---

48 Filiation/affiliation: Marangoly George provides a useful gloss on these concepts (from Edward Said, *The World, the Text and the Critic* (Cambridge, MA: Harvard University Press, 1983)) in *The Politics of Home*, p. 16: 'Said calls "filiation" the ties that an individual has with places and people that are based on his/her natal culture; that is, ties of biology and geography. "Affiliations", which are what come to replace "filiations", are links that are forged with institutions, associations and communities and other social creations. The movement is always from filiations to affiliations'.

> So, as Smout recognises, geography is certainly important in creating identity. In Gaelic culture this is called *duthchas*, a sense of belonging to a particular place. But also important are certain social principles that lie at the core of community – *dualchas* which is *heritage* in the sense of the people of your place who moulded you. It is *duthchas* and *dualchas* together that generate the classical Scottish virtues of *fostership* and *hospitality*. From these can be derived an understanding of belonging that permits the grafting on of new stock. Here is the taproot beneath the grassroots that repudiates 'each one for himself'. Here, indeed, might be a pattern and an example to a troubled world wherever shifting populations conflict with local ethnicity.[49]

The formula for a successful relocation, then, requires this: for our 'new homes' to be happy ones, incomers must develop a 'sense of belonging' based on freshly learned 'sense of place' and the destination community must be willing to 'foster' them. This seems to me a sound principle, for both individuals and for the nations/regions that support them, even if we can all think of instances in which the reciprocity of the exchange would necessarily be more strained.[50] It is also a formula which has interesting echoes with many of the negotiations and initiatives underway in the North of Ireland in the wake of the Good Friday Agreement (see Chapter 11), suggesting that the 'politics of re/location' of which I have been writing here is as relevant, on an epistemological level at least, to those who are 'obliged to stay' as those who are 'free to move'.

(Re)locating the self

The challenge of positively reforming institutions like 'home' and 'nation' is not simply a matter of political intervention or government legislation. Indeed, one of the problems with the analysis of a commentator like Tom Nairn is that it is never absolutely clear who, or what, is to blame for the totalizing grip of 'the centre' on the rest of the British Isles. Whilst particular individuals in history, like Margaret Thatcher, are invoked, the longevity of the situation tends to 'abstract' the hegemonic forces into a kind of constitutional conspiracy. As a firm believer in the power of residual ideology I can, at one level, fully accept this version of events but, at another, I think it obscures some of the profound epistemological problems of thinking about, and speaking about, terms like 'home' and 'nation' and how this (relative) inarticulacy is surely part of the reason 'things go wrong'. Thus, while we can simply accept that the successive waves of local government reform

---

49 Alastair McIntosh, 'The Herald Essay', *The Herald*, Saturday 7 August 1999, 'Comment', p. 15.

50 See my essay, 'The Place of Literature in the Spaces of Belonging' (note 40) for discussion of how the demographic specificity of immigration/emigration from Wales and Cornwall has undoubtedly contributed to their sense of colonization.

in the British Isles are part of the long-term project of the 'centre' to preserve its authority and control, we could also read the long catalogue of impotence and confusion as symptomatic of the failure of both individuals and governments to 'see' and understand 'the local'. The criticism repeatedly aimed at local government organizations, after all, is that – for all their ostensible commitment to their communities – they fail to deliver what the individuals living in those communities desire. That is to say, they cannot seem to 'know' their locations and communities 'from the inside'. Given the extreme difficulty of seeing, or knowing, anything 'from the inside' this, I would contend, is hardly surprising. But it is also why a project such as this one, in which 'located subjects' have struggled hard to articulate what their 'locatedness' means, can prove so valuable. In the ensuing section, I will thus explore some of the strategies my contributors have adopted to 'speak' their sense of 'home', and 'belonging', and 'place', and 'community' in the context of their various relocations within the British Isles.

The problem of how we speak from the 'places we are at' is one that first beset me, in a major way, when I was working on my book *Feminism and the Politics of Reading* (1997).[51] I was impressed, in particular, by the difficulty all subjects clearly have in attending to more than one aspect of their identity-formation at once; a difficulty that came sharply to the fore with my 'ethnographic' survey in which groups of feminist readers from Britain and Canada were asked to use their readings of two literary texts to explore their changing sense of both their gendered and their national/ethnic identities.[52] The (written) responses of my participants indicated that it was often simply impossible to 'think the self' in relation to the two ideological criteria simultaneously, and the most usual 'solution' was for the analysis to attend to first one and then the other. The task the participants had been set was, moreover, complicated even further by the fact that I had invited them to reflect upon the 'emotional' aspect of the reading process *vis-à-vis* these topics; this, unsurprisingly, translated into an invitation to write 'personally', or 'autobiographically', about their 'experiences' as gendered/national subjects, and – in interesting anticipation of this project – involved many of them presenting their complex 'situatedness' in terms of discourses of 'home'. What seemed to me, at first, a reasonably straightforward exercise, therefore ('use your readings of these two texts to explore the sense of your own gendered/national identity') turned into anything but. The participants simply could not respond to or articulate all the implications of my request at once. Yet whilst I was retrospectively sorry for the hard time I had caused them, the results provided me with a fascinating insight into the range of strategies we might draw upon when presented with this sort of challenge. Many of these strategies involve alternative

---

51 'The places we are at': see Paul Gilroy, *There Ain't No Black in the Union Jack*; Pearce, *Feminism and the Politics of Reading*, see note 11 above.

52 See Appendix to *Feminism and the Politics of Reading* for full details of this project and the questions the participants were asked.

modes of self-production and what Elspeth Probyn has dubbed a 'strategic use of the personal pronoun' (see note 13); and many, also, are to do with the processes of narrativization. But before going into these techniques of 'locating the self' in specific relation to *Devolving Identities*, it is first necessary to say something more about the use of literary (and other) texts within this project.

As I signalled in the opening to this Introduction, this is very decidedly *not* a collection of essays 'on' the national and regional literatures of the British Isles. Instead, it was conceived as a project in which a selection of feminist academics, variously located within the UK and Eire, would be invited to 'use' such texts to explore, and reflect upon, their own changing sense of 'home and belonging' within the wider political context of devolution. 'Using' literature in this way is not a new thing, especially within the realm of contemporary feminist scholarship, though its challenge to more traditional textual criticism remains largely untheorized. Whilst it is true that, on the one hand, a significant number of feminist literary critics from around the world *do* continue to perform 'readings' in which the 'text itself' is the 'object' of study and investigation, in the more glamorous orbit of feminist cultural theory, authors like Judith Butler, Donna Haraway, and Elspeth Probyn, have long preferred to make literature – along with a wide range of other cultural and discursive 'products' – simply a *means* to a more general cultural theorizing.[53] Although there are, of course, some troubling political and ethical issues raised by this shift, they should not, I feel, be allowed to obscure the excitement of the attendant epistemological revolution implied. What the writings of authors like Butler, Haraway and Probyn have given us, above all, is a new model of how the text–reader relation can be used to make sense of the world(s) we inhabit: and, in particular, the way in which we can creatively combine the texts of others with the textual productions of 'the self' to gain a new perspective on our complex 'locatedness' within contemporary culture. What such a thorough-going 'exploitation' of the literary forgoes, of course, is any pretence at a disinterested, non-biased, non-instrumental 'evaluation' of the texts concerned. In this respect, it could be argued that Butler and, indeed, Eve Sedgwick's 'school' of Queer theorists have become pastmasters at 'retelling the stories' of their chosen texts in order to support their theorizations.[54] In my own *Feminism and the Politics of*

---

[53] I am thinking here of texts like Butler's *Bodies that Matter* (London and New York: Routledge, 1993) which executes radical rereadings (or, rather, 're-scriptings') of literary texts in order to endorse Butler's own theorizing of gendered and sexual identity, and the less sustained, but equally instrumental, use of an extensive range of literary and cultural texts by Elspeth Probyn (see notes 4 and 13 above) and Donna Haraway (see, for example, *Modest_Witness@Second Millennium* (London and New York: Routledge, 1997)). I am hoping to explore this changing relationship to 'the textual' in a forthcoming volume entitled, provisionally, *Textual Turns: Rhetorical Innovations in Contemporary Feminist Discourse*.

[54] See, in particular, Eve Sedgwick's new edited collection, *Novel Gazing: Queer Readings in Fiction* (Durham and London: Duke University Press, 1997).

Reading, meanwhile, I showed how an 'implicated', as opposed to a 'hermeneutic' engagement of a text necessarily involves all manner of creative 'participation' on the part of the reader (see note 13 above). When uncovering 'the meaning' of a text ceases to be our objective, and we become 'involved' with it and its 'textual others' in a less 'professional' way, the temptations for rewriting, or 'over-writing', are boundless. Indeed, carried to an extreme, and notwithstanding the fact that the text *will* continue to exercise power and control over us too (i.e. meaning production is a two-way process between text and reader), this mode of reading/criticism may be said to result in the creation of what are effectively *parallel texts*: the 'composite' product of text and reader. Whilst more traditional literary critics will, inevitably, view such readerly interventions with (at the very least) suspicion, I feel broadly inclined to welcome it. In the context of my *Feminism and the Politics of Reading* reader-survey, certainly, as in the context of the present project, the more radical, and radically instrumental, reading/writing of texts that I have encouraged has resulted in some stunning eloquence. This is clear evidence, I believe, that such 'textual exploitation' can be profitably used as a springboard for speaking some of the more inarticulable aspects of self and location. Yet, if we are to assess fully the epistemological value of this new 'reading method', it is important that we recognize that such textual engagements are about much more than simply 'identifying with' a text and its characters; they are, I will now go on to demonstrate, rather about the structural repositioning of ourselves in relation to our 'object of enquiry', and, in particular, in finding ways to 'deliver' the self.

As I discovered through my work with the groups of feminist readers in *Feminism and the Politics of Reading*, the most typical – and probably the most effective – way to deal with a complicated reading/analytical task is to separate it out into different layers, or levels, or responses. To some extent, this was, indeed, the strategy I had pioneered and advocated in the central section of the book, in which I had discovered that the only way I could usefully investigate the 'emotional' aspects of reading was to take it in two stages: first, the recording of my readings/re-memories of the texts concerned; and, second, a 'metacritical' analysis. Following this method, my participants in the gender/national identity reading project presented me with readings in which their more personal or 'implicated' engagement of the texts alternated with passages of reflection. This layering was complicated, moreover, by passages of personal anecdote or auto-biographical narrative which had nothing (or very little) to do with the texts themselves, and also (given the political bifurcation of their remit) a tendency to write, alternately, about gendered *or* national/ethnic aspects of self-identity. Even more striking, and especially pertinent for the present project, was the fact that a good many of the more personal reflections – in particular the narratives of 'home' or 'growing up' – did not explicitly allude to issues of gender or national identity *at all*. At these moments, the literary texts which had been the 'basis' for the project all but disappeared, and what I was presented with was a highly personal meditation that was, indeed, showing me 'home' from 'the inside' without ostensibly speaking its political project at all.

Such 'layering', or alternation, of textual engagement and personal reflection is also, and not surprisingly, a key methodological feature of *Devolving Identities*. While the contributors vary considerably in how much of themselves they put into the chapters, a favourite strategy is to alternate passages of anecdote and/or autobiography with more 'standard' readings of the text. It is also striking that almost all of the authors who *do* elect to write themselves into their texts open their chapters with a piece of their own self-writing (see Hilary Hinds, Rachel Dyer, Alison Easton, Wren Sidhe, Charlotte Williams, Flora Alexander and Lynne Pearce), and that many close in a similar fashion. The way in which these 'self-texts' are then connected with the literary texts is, however, much more variable. Whilst some authors (e.g., Hilary Hinds, Charlotte Williams, Alison Easton, Flora Alexander, Eilish Rooney) continue to explore and evaluate their personal involvement with their chosen texts throughout (i.e., the way in which the text resonates with their own 'experiences'; the way in which their 'experiences' 'authenticate' the text), others (e.g., Rachel Dyer, Lynne Pearce, Wren Sidhe, Ruth McElroy) prefer to keep the two 'freestanding' and largely independent of one another, although sometimes in combination with a further level of metacritical reflection.[55] Finally, it should be noted that two of the authors, Helen Boden and Sinead McDermott have actively, and self-consciously, refused the invitation to write themselves into their chapters in any of these ways, preferring to concentrate on textual analyses and theoretical metacommentaries that explore/enact the difficulty of speaking the 'located' self *without* (sustained) recourse to the personal pronoun or its narratives.

As with the *Feminism and Politics of Reading* survey, moreover, there is a clear tendency for the 'self-texts' focusing on 'home and belonging' to lose sight of the political/theoretical rationale informing the whole project. The contributors become so involved in their own stories of their homes, childhoods or other 'places of origin' that they only sporadically think to name, or identify, that space/place as home; they present us with pictures of 'home' seen from the inside (from inside the house, inside the past, inside memory) and it is clearly with effort that they then wrench themself out of that recollection to ask 'how does this relate to my identity as a feminist?' or 'how does this relate to my sense of national identity'? Significant exceptions to this are, of course, the chapters like my own (Chapter 8) and Ruth McElroy's (Chapter 4) where the 'self-text' is not located 'in

[55] Whilst *part* of the 'reading method' enjoined by many of us may be said to include what has been thought of traditionally, and usually disparagingly, as 'authentic realism', this is very much only *one* strand of our engagement. For further discussion of 'authentic realism' within feminist criticism see Sara Mills and Lynne Pearce, eds, *Feminist Readings/Feminists Reading* [1989] (Hemel Hempstead: Harvester-Wheatsheaf, 1996), pp. 56–90.

the home' but in the alternative spatio-temporal site of 'the road'.Yet, it would be wrong to give the impression that these 'self-texts' are entirely untheorized either; within them (see especially Hilary Hinds) we find punctuated attempts to step back and analyse the story being told. The basic methodological principle remains, however: faced with the awesome task of articulating any aspect of our ontological experience of text or world, recourse would seem to be to a synthesizing *narrative* of self-production whose very narrativity significantly obscures, frustrates or otherwise undermines a more 'intellectual' enquiry. When combined with a subsequent or interpolated meta-commentary, however, such narratives may, I believe, bring us closer to the full complexity of 'situated being' (including the necessary 'blindness' of that condition) than any other mode of analysis.

When it comes to the contributors' 'readings' of the literary or other texts, meanwhile, the 'terms of engagement' are rather more various. Apart from the classic 'authentic realist' interventions that I have already mentioned (i.e., the way in which the reader 'tests' and 'authenticates' the text *via* her own experiences), the chapters demonstrate the full range of possible involvements (and degrees of involvement) that I discuss in *Feminism and the Politics of Reading*, and with a broad selection of 'textual others'.[56] These 'others' range from characters in the text which the reader relates to and/or desires; a usurped 'author-function' (i.e., where the reader identifies with the author and/or re-writes their script); through to a readerly connection via more diffuse 'structures of feeling' (see note 39) or (via a more 'hermeneutic' approach) a particular set of theoretical discourses. What is, perhaps, most striking about the contributors' textual engagements in total, however, is: (1) the way in which they move *between* 'textual others' (presumably as the result of my invitation to perform more 'implicated' readings) and (2) the way in which these engagements *interact* with the 'textual selves' produced in the 'autobiographical' sections. What this amounts to methodologically is, I would suggest, no less than a radical revisioning of how literary texts may be used in cultural theorizing, and how, in particular, they can be used *alongside* 'self-texts' to articulate what neither textual readings nor autobiographical readings could achieve on their own.

Stepping back further again, it is my larger hope that this sort of methodological innovation can, and will, yield an epistemological breakthrough *vis-à-vis* those areas of cultural and political 'being' that have remained most obdurately tongue-tied. In other words, it is ultimately to be hoped that the fresh, if still partial, perspectives on configurations like 'home', 'belonging' and 'nationhood'

56 'Textual others': this is the term I coined in *Feminism and the Politics of Reading* (see note 13 above) to specify, and then adumbrate, the wide range of signifying functions the reader may relate to/identify with in a text, ranging from recognizable (if representational!) humanist subjects, through to more abstract signifiers and emotional positionings. See *Feminism and the Politics of Reading*, pp. 17–20.

furnished by such innovative interpretative strategies will result in a better understanding of the complex conditions of citizenship in the historical and political realm.

Re/locating home

As I indicated at the beginning of this Introduction, my initial attempt to group the following chapters conceptually soon proved futile because of the extensive overlap around most of the key preoccupations such as 'exile' or 'mobility'. Furthermore – as I have also already established – there is a pervasive connecting *thesis* running through many of the contributions *vis-à-vis* the 'origins' vs. 'destination' model of 'home'. For ease of readerly-orientation I have, however, attempted to draw out some of the more striking thematic links between each of the chapters, and (incidentally) to indicate their geographical and textual range.

Hilary Hinds's chapter (Chapter 1), which opens the volume, plunges us straight into the geographical 'heartland' of England, and hence straight into the centre of the debates about what it means to have one's 'origins' in a 'Middle England' whose various 'orthodoxies' in terms of class, gender, (hetero)sexuality and 'national identity' have been experienced as deeply oppressive, and yet ideologically and sentimentally inescapable. Hinds's two textual referents are E.M. Forster and Barbara Pym, between whose works the author weaves her own narratives of 'negotiation' and 'relocation', finally concluding: 'I don't mind living with my *stories* of my home town now, but that's as far as it goes. Like Margaret Schlegel, I wouldn't want to live there.'

This sense of being happy to 'revisit' one's 'originary' home on a temporary/textual basis is true for many of the contributors, prompting us to consider the role, and value, of a 'critical' *nostalgia* in the development of our 'locational identities'. Just such an exploration is imaginatively undertaken by our two Scottish authors, Alison Easton (Chapter 2) and Flora Alexander (Chapter 6), whose two chapters both look back to their youth in a country, and culture, that was strikingly *undefined*, and elusive, in terms of any straightforward national or regional identity.[57] Putting the two chapters side by side, what is most striking, indeed, is the way in which various classed, gendered and educational factors kept the authors slightly apart from their Scottish heritage(s) (including their Scottish *literary* heritage) for many years; with Alexander's sense of dis/location coming from her geographical 'isolation' in the Scottish Highlands and educational 'exclusion' from the 'local' Gaelic language and culture, and Easton's coming

[57] Needless to say, one of the things that comes across most strongly in these two chapters, is that – despite growing up in Scotland at a similar time – the authors would not have felt that they belonged to the same 'country' or the same 'culture'. Both emphasize the difference between highland/lowland and rural/urban Scotland.

from a middle-class, lowlander's early perception of there being 'many Scotlands' (not all of them friendly, or desirable, locations for an emancipated woman). Both chapters, however, are testimony to the way in which these 'originary homes' can be profitably revisited from the distance of time and space, and via the 'springboards' of certain 'texts': in this case, Margaret Laurence and Candida McWilliam (Alexander) and Margaret Elphinstone and Ellis Island (museum which tells the 'story' of US immigration) (Easton). For Easton, in particular, this enabling sense of spatio-temporal distance is linked to her interest in *borderlands* as the spaces/places in which we can, perhaps, re-negotiate our gendered/national identities most creatively. This is also possibly the place to register the significance of *generational difference* in these 'stories of home'. Whilst Easton and Alexander are looking back to childhoods and lifestyles some forty years distant, other contributors (namely Dyer, McDermott and McElroy: all still in their twenties) have not long 'left home', and the rest of us (now in our thirties and forties) are negotiating the distance from somewhere in-between.

The possibility of rediscovering/redefining one's 'first home' from a 'safe distance' is given a slightly different spin in the chapters by Ruth McElroy (Chapter 4) and myself, Lynne Pearce (Chapter 8), which are preoccupied with the theme/thesis of *mobility*: a purportedly 'postmodern' (though, I would argue, specifically '1990s') vision of 'homes' being changing, and/or transient, and all aspects of identity (including gendered and national identity) being constantly formed and re-formed in (re)locational space that is somewhere 'in between' the fixed co-ordinates of 'here' and 'there', 'past' and 'present'. Linking their readings of indicative literary texts to their own journeyings backwards and forwards within the UK (McElroy draws upon Freya North and Menna Gallie; Pearce upon Daphne du Maurier and Janice Galloway), the authors nevertheless show that such mobility (and, in Pearce's case, the specific *auto*mobility provided by the motor car) exacts its price as well as affording its privilege. This price is acutely political as well as personal, moreover, since mobility (or *non*-mobility) within the UK is associated with a long history of government legislation that has forced various individuals, or groups of individuals, to either 'get on their bikes' *or* 'stay where they are'. Therefore, whilst both authors recognize the liberating power of postmodern conceits like 'flux', 'mobility' and 'nomadism' in deconstructing national/personal 'homes' and 'identities' in a positive way, both also point to the potential for further inequality and discrimination. It should be said, finally, that these particular 'migratory narratives' also work to reconceptualize the 'centre-margin' mapping of the British Isles, since the authors' own mobility inevitably works to undermine the supposedly 'static' marginality of their regional/national 'homes' (Wales (McElroy) and Cornwall (Pearce)).

Whilst my chapter, in particular, considers these re-locational desires within a generally optimistic reading of what devolution could, or should, offer those of us situated in the 'margins' of the British Isles, the volume does include some dissenting voices. Perhaps the strongest of these is Wren Sidhe (Chapter 3) whose chapter 'I don't want your straight nation', proffers her reading of H.V. Morton's various works as evidence of the hetero/sexist orthodoxies on which all such 'patriotic' discourse is based; observing, too, that the ethnic implications are sometimes 'chilling'. In lieu of *any* locational identity based on nation, region, or even a more unspecified 'sense of place', Sidhe (a Londoner by birth) looks to the City as a more promising site for heterogeneity. She also engages with Sylvia Townsend Warner's *Lolly Willowes* to show how the heterosexist idylls of Morton's 'classic' England may be mischievously deconstructed.

Also positioned starkly outside the more sanguine discourses of devolution is Eilish Rooney, whose intertwining of two stories (almost) 'too painful to be told' (African-American slavery and the twentieth-century history of the North of Ireland), reads the present devolutionary moment through/against the British government's long-term 'experiments' with its Ulster province. Rooney's two texts are Toni Morrison's *Beloved* and the 'Good Friday' Agreement (1998), and she discovers in both the paradoxical, yet insistent, necessity to both 'remember' and 'move on'. Similarly cautious, though this time at a more epistemological level, is Sinead McDermott who actively contests her positioning (for this volume) as an Irish subject (i.e., from Eire) for a number of reasons, not least what she experiences as the relative inarticulacy of that positioning. Through her two chosen texts, however (Nuala O'Faolain's *Are You Somebody?* and Margaret Atwood's *Alias Grace*), McDermott explores, and theorizes, the ways in which, as both writers and readers, we can use the stories of others to 'speak the unspeakable'. Ventriloquizing our own subject/positioning through a (textual) other might be a way of maintaining 'respectability' and strategically keeping ourselves out of the picture, but it might also be the means (the *only* means?) by which that self gets 'told'.

As I indicated in the preceding section, there are methodological as well as thematic similarities linking many of the chapters – not least because this project was consciously conceived to 'exploit' the literary and other texts in a purposefully instrumental way. For this reason, most of the chapters are unconcerned with the 'quality' or 'status' of their chosen texts in any definitive sense: their primary function is as a 'springboard' for the author's own reflections and interrogations. In a few of the chapters, however, the 'texts themselves' – and, in particular, their stylistic and conceptual innovations – are invested in more heavily: literature/art (and its 'performance') *itself* becomes the space/place where questions of 'home' and 'belonging' are best 're-imagined'. This point is made especially clearly in Chapter 10 by Helen Boden and Chapter 7 by Rachel Dyer where special praise is given to contemporary writers and artists that have helped us to rethink our locational identities through innovative textual form(s) and presentations. Both contributors, moreover (although 'English'-born), have discovered these re-imaginings in texts produced in Scotland: in Boden's case, the Elizabeth Ogilvie/Douglas Dunn installation, *Into the Oceanic*; and in Dyer's, Kathleen Jamie's *Autonomous Region*. To invoke the jargon of literary criticism, both these sets of texts effect 'defamiliarizations' that enable us to perceive (and relate) our nations/locations in a fresh way. In Jamie's case, this involves some clever tricks with the Scots language (bizarrely 'relocated' in rural Tibet) and, for Ogilvie/Dunn, an attempt to challenge the traditional post-Enlightenment mode of 'viewing the Highlands' at the level of representation itself. It is interesting that both chapters are also linked by their focus on *travel* and *tourism*, with Boden's reading of Dorothy Wordsworth's *Tour made in Scotland*, and Dyer's narrative of her own sojourn in France, giving further endorsement to the possibility, and pleasures, of 'relocation', and a concomitant investment in the notion of 'home' as not where we come from but 'where we're at' (see note 51). The discourse of 'home as destination' triumphs once again.

What constitutes 'origins' and what 'destination' is, however, complicated in the case of Charlotte Williams (Chapter 9) who (as noted in a preceding section) has been obliged to negotiate her sense of 'home' in a way that makes strikingly visible the humanist assumptions which have accrued about the term. As a 'mixed-race' subject, of Welsh and Guyanese parents, Williams's interrogation of/desire for an 'originary home' has become a major quest in adult life, and one in which literature has played a crucial role. Through her readings of Paula Melville's *Shape-Shifter* collection, and Jen Wilson's 'Zen and the Art of Thelonius Monk', Williams confirms the crucial (though severely problematized) role of literature in 'authenticating' or 'validating' our national/locational identities, and causes us to revise again our notions of 'mobile subjectivity'. As feminist scholars from the early 1980s were wont to point out, the proto-typical poststructuralist model of the subject (i.e., split, fragmented, provisional) is arguably less attractive (and/or empowering) to women who, as a group, never enjoyed the 'illusion' of humanist wholeness and autonomy in the first place.

* * *

This last point is, perhaps, also the one that brings us back to a partial understanding of the somewhat 'perverse' desire for home/homelands that runs through this collection, and which I touched on at a theoretical level in the *Politics of Location* section above. In terms of the chapters themselves, it is a desire that is endorsed by the fact that these narratives of '*re*location' are generally reluctant to yield a sense of 'home' or 'belonging' altogether, even if the site of that location is now configured as 'destination' rather than 'origins'. Meanwhile, rethinking such a difficult, dangerous, but manifestly *abiding* desire in the context of the constitutional changes taking place in the British Isles, as in Europe, at the present time, surely suggests that the nations/regions concerned must seek to redefine themselves in terms of their present, (im)migrant and multi-cultural communities as opposed to their residual, 'ethnic' ones. And similarly we – as migratory, devolving subjects – must learn to use the full complexity of our past dis/locations to commit ourselves to our 'destination-homes' in a creative, and meaningful, way.

Acknowledgements

I should like to thank Hilary Hinds, Ruth McElroy and Tony Pinkney for commenting on this chapter in draft form, and the numerous individuals whose conversations on 'home', 'belonging' and national/regional identity have contributed to my growing understanding of these things, in particular: Rowena Murray, Sara Mills, Jackie Jones. Especial thanks, too, to Rachel Dyer who unofficially performed the role of 'research assistant' for me when I was writing this in my 'Highland home'.

Chapter 1

'The Undeveloped Heart': Forster, Pym and the English South

Hilary Hinds

Beached in Bournemouth

> Nor is suburbia absent. Bournemouth's ignoble coast cowers to the right, heralding the pine trees that mean, for all their beauty, red houses, and the Stock Exchange, and extend to the gates of London itself. So tremendous is the City's trail![1]

For me, now, Bournemouth's pine trees mean sleep. At least, my mother tells me that it is something exuded by those ubiquitous pine trees, edging the broad avenues and lining the chines that lead down to the beaches, that makes visitors yawn till their jaws crack, makes their heads thick, makes them long to sleep early in the evening, and makes them rise late and unrefreshed in the morning. Perhaps she is right. Perhaps the fact that I share this response with others who visit the town should wean me away from my sense that the enervation is psychological or emotional rather than physiological. But, having grown up in Bournemouth, a byword for elderly gentility, I cannot help but think that the lassitude that descends as soon as I get off the train is both residual, the remnant of teenage monotony, and protective, guarding against the insinuations of a town left long ago.

For my parents, as for Forster, Bournemouth was the end-point of the City's trail, but for them it marked a contrast with London rather than a continuation of it, and this was its appeal. For them, in the mid-1950s, London meant smog, frozen pipes, cramped and dark basement flats; it was not a place to raise children. Bournemouth promised the opposite. It meant space, light, air, parks, beaches; it was, I was reminded throughout my childhood, a wonderful place for children. It was a chosen place, somewhere to make a home, somewhere they determined to make their own. Moving there was an act of affirmation.

To their new home they brought stories of their old homes. My mother's stories came from two locations. There were those from Scotland, her father's home: tales

---

1 E.M. Forster, *Howards End* (Harmondsworth: Penguin, 1975), p. 170. All further references to the novel are included in the chapter following the relevant quotation and are from this edition.

of her three aunts who ran a farm, who raised her father, who churned their own butter, who were never seen hatless, even first thing in the morning; these were stories of tough, capable, unmarried, fulfilled, working women, but also stories of self-reliance and self-discipline, of resolution and application and strictness, of conventional Presbyterian virtues. Then there were the stories of Exeter, where she grew up with two brothers and three sisters in middle-class comfort, a world of nannies, housemaids and gardeners, front stairs and back stairs, as compelling, unreal and fantastic as those featured in *Peter Pan* and *Mary Poppins*. My father's stories of home were less sharply defined, but just as impossible as my mother's. Born in Bombay, his father in the Indian Army; aunts and cousins in Belfast, Anglo-Irish Protestants whose forebears had 'gone to Ireland with Cromwell'; boarding schools in England: home for him was elsewhere, nowhere, his nomadic parents alighting finally in North Devon, for no good reason, as far as I could tell. A colonial childhood, the kind I later recognized in the writing of Saki and Kipling, in Forster.

These origin stories ran in parallel with the 'home' that I knew; they both gave me an identity and, at the same time, threw into relief the ways in which Bournemouth seemed to deny me an identity. This was my family, so the stories were, in some senses, about me. 'I'm half Irish, quarter Scottish, and quarter English', I took pride in telling my schoolfriends, but the 'English' part was just a makeweight, something that had nothing to say in itself; lacking the compelling Celtic romance of the other two national elements, it told my friends nothing about who I was. I saw no continuities between my parents' stories of home and the place in which I lived. Bournemouth was not Scotland, nor Ireland, nor was it Devon, 'the West Country'. It was English, southern English, a location that, as far as I could see, was unmarked by any of the things that linked places with distinctive, and desirable, identities – accent, music, food, mythology, extended family, history. Bournemouth was quintessentially suburban, though without the *urbs* that might have mitigated its uniformity and conservatism. It was a parvenu with social aspirations. Bournemouth's thoroughfares were never designated as 'streets' – presumably the town planners found the word too urban, too contrary to their ambitions for the town; only roads, avenues, closes and crescents can be found in its *A to Z*. Beached in Bournemouth, biding my time, I looked for, and looked to, other locations – London, France, Glasgow, Birmingham – to provide me with a grittiness, an authenticity that Bournemouth so heartlessly denied me.

This response to my hometown could be characterized in two ways. First, it was marked by a sense of *dis*location, a feeling that the places to which my sense of self might have been able to anchor itself were elsewhere, and mine only by proxy. Secondly, and at the same time, I had a sense of *un*location, that the place in which I found myself was not a place in which I could find myself, could not offer any of the routes to, hooks for, or narratives of identity that I saw articulated in my parents' stories of home.[2] Bournemouth was the space left when everywhere else had taken what it wanted.

* * *

Such autobiographical accounts are no longer unusual as springboards for excursions into cultural theory. A familiar and conventional tale of a childhood outsider, at odds with her home, her family, of a middle-class romanticization or appropriation of a number of different 'elsewheres', my own account offers possibilities for an extended consideration of the relationship between identity and class, gender, colonialism, nationality, ethnicity, narrative, history. What I want to do in this chapter is to indicate the ways in which some of these different co-ordinates are inflected through, and by means of, the location in which they were articulated – through the specifics of the kind of southern Englishness outlined above. In so doing, I shall also consider the contingency of these analyses and accounts. For, of course, origin stories such as the one produced above have no authority as unmediated reflections of the truth concerning their author's subjectivity. The rehearsal of my discontent with, and my embarrassment at, my middle-England origins, my feeling of being *to one side* of the stories of identity that made most sense to me, is a long-running one, a transmuting one, and one that has its own origin stories. It is clear already that my relationship with Bournemouth, or the English south in general, has since childhood been a thoroughly narrativized one, articulated through and against my parents' stories of home, and in the teeth of Bournemouth as a place, as I saw it, without a history or story of its own. I want to examine in this chapter how this sense of being 'to one side' of my hometown came to be articulated and foregrounded in my account of myself through two encounters with more literary narratives: E. M. Forster's *Howards End* (1910), and Barbara Pym's *A Glass of Blessings* (1958). What part does the 'southern Englishness' of these two novels play in my readings (both first and subsequent) of them and of myself? What aspects of those texts did I recuperate to my own self-narrative? What did those readings ignore – or, rather, how does returning to these texts now whilst in the throes of having to reconceptualize myself as middle-aged prompt me to reread them?

---

2 Or, indeed, that I saw articulated in my friends' origin stories: my best friend at school had a Polish father and had spent her early childhood in Plaistow, East London, and this sense of her being beyond the homogenizing grip of Bournemouth played a significant part in how and why I valued our friendship.

Forster's England: safe as houses

> 'I'll live anywhere except Bournemouth, Torquay and Cheltenham. ... There on no account.' (p. 119)

So says Margaret Schlegel, as she and her brother Tibby discuss where they might live when, their lease expiring, they are obliged to move out of Wickham Place, their childhood London home. Her naming of these towns (together with Ilfracombe, Swanage, Tunbridge Wells, Surbiton and Bedford) as unfit to live in is not incidental to the scheme of the novel. *Howards End* is famous on the one hand for its concern with the question of 'who shall inherit England?', and on the other for its attempt to debate and resolve this question by looking at what there is to be inherited, where it is to be found, and what it is worth, through the condensation, identification and characterization of 'value' (or the undermining of it) with specific places and, in particular, houses – Wickham Place, Ducie Street, the Basts' flat, Oniton Grange and, supremely, Howards End itself.[3] The towns named by Margaret represent, as the quotation with which I open this chapter makes clear, the suburban outposts of the city of London.

But, despite this, these towns are not coterminous with the city: Bournemouth is 'ignoble' (p. 170), whilst London permits the Schlegels' lives to be 'cultured but not ignoble' (p. 115); the litotes here signals the possibility of ignobility in the same move that it is refuted, kept at bay, apparently, by a culture to be found in the city itself but not its suburban outposts. 'Down at Swanage', we are told, 'no one appreciated culture more than Mrs Munt' (p. 29), and the uninformed, bourgeois and rather philistine way that Mrs Munt appreciates 'culture' is one of the butts of humour, and one element in the novel's critique of the effects of culture on different fractions of the middle class, in Chapter V, in which the Schlegels listen to Beethoven's Fifth Symphony. Here, Mrs Munt 'tap[s] surreptitiously when the tunes come', and asserts that 'I do not go in for being musical ... I only care for music – a very different thing. But still I will say this for myself – I do know when I like a thing and when I don't. ... When it comes to music I am as

---

3 'Who shall inherit England?' was named as a question fundamental to *Howards End*, and related to the novelist's liberalism, by Lionel Trilling in 1943, in *E. M. Forster* (Norfolk, CT: New Directions), and provided a focus that has continued to inform much discussion of the novel since then; see, for example, Peter Widdowson, *E. M. Forster's Howards End: Fiction as History* (London: Chatto and Windus for Sussex University Press, 1977); John Carey, *The Intellectuals and the Masses: Pride and Prejudice among the Literary Intelligentsia, 1880–1939* (London: Faber and Faber, 1992); Daniel Born, *The Birth of Liberal Guilt in the English Novel: Charles Dickens to H. G. Wells* (Chapel Hill and London: University of North Carolina Press, 1995), especially Chapter 6, 'Private Gardens, Public Swamps: *Howards End* and the Revaluation of Liberal Guilt'; Robert K. Martin, '"It Must Have Been the Umbrella": Forster's Queer Begetting', in Robert K. Martin and George Piggford, eds, *Queer Forster* (Chicago and London: University of Chicago Press, 1997), pp. 266–273.

safe as houses...' (pp. 44, 51). Mrs Munt's responses, like her hometown of Swanage, are indicative of a small-minded, clumsy, at times self-deluding English parochialism that the novel is concerned to criticize.

Such references to the suburban are a crucial element in the anatomization, diagnosis and critique of 'England' undertaken in *Howards End*. The pleasures of the capital city may be insubstantial, transitory, even illusory ('London only stimulates, it cannot sustain' (p. 155)), the locus of real English value may be in the rural continuities of Howards End and its surrounding farms (p. 264), and the city and the countryside might be the two key elements in the dynamic by which the narrative is played out. However, the suburban is the channel through which the encroachment of the former on the latter is effected. Hilton, the village closest to Howards End, is becoming suburban; suburbia is both symptom and disease, it is the 'red rust' of London, corroding the countryside that constitutes the legacy of the real England (pp. 29–30, 141–2, 329). The rejection of suburbia, its delineation as spiritually impoverished, is a given; it is not a part of the debate between the various manifestations of city and rural values represented by the sparring of Schlegels and Wilcoxes, Basts and Schlegels, Helen and Margaret, Margaret and Henry, and so on. For Henry, suburbia is no good because it is 'neither one thing nor the other', for Helen it is a sign of London creeping, for Margaret it is not to be countenanced as a place to live, for Leonard it is a barrier to the authenticity of the countryside – 'gas lamps for hours' (pp. 142, 126). All except Mrs Munt, and Charles and Dolly – figures who in themselves represent aspects of suburbia's impoverishment – find suburbia undesirable, debilitating, but it is through the voice of the narrator, a voice that gains its authoritativeness through its intimate, confiding, vaguely apologetic yet still self-satisfied tone, that we learn the most about the meanings and dangers of suburbia. In a series of narratorial interventions, short essays or reflections that seek to characterize the meanings of London, the countryside, and thereby England, we are left in no doubt that suburbia has no place in the vision of England that the novel is advocating; indeed, in itself it constitutes the other half of one of the binarisms that help the reader to understand 'England'. As Mrs Munt arrives at the railway station in Hilton for the first time, the narrator asks, 'Into which country will it lead, England or Suburbia?' (pp. 29–30). The two, quite clearly, are not compatible. Suburbia, within the scheme of meaning set up by the narrative, is not 'English'.

This inclusion of suburbia within a scheme of situated values was certainly one reason for the novel's impact on me when, at sixteen years old, I first read it. It offered, quite explicitly, a validation of my own assessment of Bournemouth, and, indeed, of Cheltenham, where my brother had gone to boarding school and where I had endured interminable and much resented weekend visits. Nowhere else in Literature had I ever seen Bournemouth named; here, it was not only named, but done so in such a way that my own sense of being to one side of my town and my family was not just a piece of teenage cussedness, but linked to a wider structure of feeling. The novel gave me a way to insert myself into this structure; it gave me the terms by which to elevate my assessment of my context, that sense of distaste and ennui, into an endorsement of a set of contrary values. The castigation of suburbia is of a piece, the novel suggested, with the ultimate endorsement of the Schlegels' vision, the valuing of the inner life, the unseen, the personal, as set against the profound limitations and fundamental hypocrisies of the outer life of the Wilcoxes, the world of finance, commerce, colonialism, of 'telegrams and anger', 'panic and emptiness'. For me, this legitimated a refusal of the world as seen by *The Daily Telegraph*, with the hypocrisy of its high-toned espousal of family values and Mary Whitehouse's Festival of Light sitting side by side with its relish for the gossip and scandal it grouped on page 3; it rendered comprehensible my incredulity at a town where it was acceptable for a headmistress to pray for a Tory victory in the forthcoming General Election, and to pray that her charges 'might not look down upon the working classes'; and it sanctified my shrinking from a home where the prospect of weekends of Canasta and a small sherry ought to have been enough. Town, school, home, and family melded into a configuration of skewed values, anxious unspontaneity, and finely nuanced shades of tedium. *Howards End* spoke to me so clearly because it offered me a series of linked points of identification. Margaret not only speaks against Bournemouth; she also understands 'the tragedy of preparedness', 'that those who prepare for all the emergencies of life beforehand may equip themselves at the expense of joy' (pp. 115, 71); and it is she who questions conformity and orthodoxy, embracing instead 'the battle against sameness. Differences – eternal differences, planted by God in a single family, so that there may always be colour; sorrow perhaps, but colour in the daily gray' (p. 328). The connections between these elements – Bournemouth, preparedness, difference – made Margaret's the voice of a critical insider: someone with detailed insider knowledge, but a knowledge that was put to work against the values of the inside. It was with recognition and relief that I encountered this voice.

Twenty-five years on from that first reading, the novel's verdict on suburbia, and what went along with it, looks rather less appealing. Fearful of so-called 'mass culture' and its enfeebling effects on genuine culture (however defined), Forster, in common with so many other writers, artists and intellectuals of his day, as John Carey has argued, used the suburbs as shorthand for the narrow-minded and conservative, the trivial, and the inauthentic. Carey notes how the word 'suburban' is 'distinctive in combining topographical with intellectual disdain. It relates human worth to habitat'.[4] This link between human worth and habitat is, as I have suggested, fundamental to *Howards End*'s narrative strategy and argument, and

---

4 Carey, *The Intellectuals and the Masses*, p.53. See too Jon Hegglund, 'Defending the Realm: Domestic Space and Mass Cultural Contamination in *Howards End* and *An Englishman's Home*', *English Literature in Transition 1880–1920* XL:4 (1997), pp. 398–423.

the disdain for all things suburban is just one plank in this. Needless to say, for me now, this disdain for the suburban smacks of a rather crude and embarrassing snobbery and elitism; and, indeed, at the time of first reading the point of identification was not the class politics of this position, but the associated personal politics of those through whom the disdain was articulated. Whilst the novel itself explicitly refuses the dissociation of public and private *moralities*, it does not make a similar case for the connection between public and private *politics* – nor, indeed, between the notions of 'morality' and 'politics' themselves. The novel's imperative to 'only connect' goes only so far.

On returning to the novel, indeed, it seems that a *failure* to connect underpins the project of the novel, and in particular its resolution, and that this failure is as important to the attainment of that resolution as the rhetoric of connection is to the narrative development. On the one hand, the novel asserts – for the most part through the voices of the narrator and of Margaret – the connectedness or interdependence of those things that the liberal middle class like to think of as 'separate spheres' – money and culture, business and the intellect, and so on. On the other hand, however, and at the same time, the narrative actually proceeds by splitting or subdividing what might generally be designated a discrete and homogeneous entity, and then ordering the constituent elements hierarchically. This is the case in particular with the representation of both England and Englishness, and also of 'the middle class' or, in the novel's own terms, 'gentlefolk'. Throughout, the rhetoric of the novel argues for the inclusiveness, the expansiveness, the interdependence of all who fall within these categories. What the novel effects, however, is the stratification of these groups, not along the lines of 'class' or 'wealth' or 'status', but along the lines of 'values', particularly those associated with personal morality. Those characters associated with such values constitute the spiritual elite who shall – or at least should – inherit England. In the end, rather than relying for its vision of regeneration on the grafting, the dialogue, the 'continuous excursions' (p. 196) back and forth between the realms of the seen and the unseen, as advocated by the explicits of Margaret's credo of 'only connect ...', the future of Howards End, the English legacy, is actually finally assured by a policy of 'only divide ...'.

'England', in *Howards End*, is not the geographical entity that that name might seem to designate, that area of land bordered by Scotland, Wales and various tracts of water. The England of *Howards End* is instead only a fraction of that geographical entity: namely, the south of England:

> If one wanted to show a foreigner England, perhaps the wisest course would be to take him to the final section of the Purbeck hills, and stand him on their summit, a few miles to the east of Corfe. Then system after system of our island would roll together under his feet. Beneath him is the valley of the Frome, and all the wild lands that come tossing down from Dorchester, black and gold, to mirror their gorse in the expanses of Poole. ... the

> imagination may leap beyond that onto Salisbury Plain itself, and beyond the Plain to all the glorious downs of central England. Nor is suburbia absent. Bournemouth's ignoble coast cowers to the right ... So tremendous is the City's trail! But the cliffs of Freshwater it shall never touch, and the island will guard the Island's purity till the end of time. Seen from the west, the Wight is beautiful beyond all laws of beauty. It is as if a fragment of England floated forward to greet the foreigner ... How many villages appear in this view! How many castles! How many churches, vanquished or triumphant! How many ships, railways and roads! What incredible variety of men working beneath that lucent sky to what final end! The reason fails, like a wave on the Swanage beach; the imagination swells, spreads and deepens, until it becomes geographic and encircles England. (pp. 170–1)

The reach of this England, with the Purbeck hills of south Dorset at its epicentre, extends from Dorchester in the west, to the 'glorious downs of central England', north of Salisbury Plain, in the north, to London in the east, and to the Isle of Wight in the south. This is a synecdochal England, where selected elements are drawn together to make a polemical point. The vision is not straightforwardly Utopian, for we are shown the threat to England of a craven suburbia. But this threat does not dominate, does not shift the tone from eulogy to elegy; it remains the goblin footfall, 'a hint that all is not for the best in the best of all possible worlds' (p. 57). Predominant in this account are those elements of England that are to be eulogized, in a succession of exclamatory clauses: villages, castles and churches (evidence of England's history), and ships, railways and roads (evidence of England's wealth, industry and empire). Here, men work (we know already that Margaret, the narrator's closest visionary ally, names work as a key virtue in her credo (pp. 117–19)), though to what end is not clear, for, at this point, the narrator's attempt to emblazon the body of England dissolves into vagueness and heightened linguistic whimsy, *asserting* an apparently inclusive geographical Englishness to round off the vision, but unable actually to depict it.

There is no place for the rest of England – the geographical, social or political England of 1910 – in this imaginative vision. It is a masculine England, where 'men work' – a gendering that sits oddly in a novel that so explicitly prioritizes the feminine over the masculine.[5] England here is the countryside of the home counties; the metropolis plays its part, but, in the form of its suburban tentacles, it threatens the rural, that which constitutes the true locus of national worth. The

---

5 The gendering of the nation is effected throughout *Howards End* in a number of ways, but not least through the explicit identification of particular houses as either masculine or feminine. Wickham Place, the Schlegels' house, is feminine (p. 56), Ducie Street, the London house taken by the Wilcoxes, is masculine (p. 167), whilst Howards End itself 'transcended any simile of sex' (p. 206). For a detailed reading of the novel in relation to gender issues, see Elizabeth Langland, 'Gesturing Towards an Open Space: Gender, Form and Language in *Howards End*', in Jeremy Tambling, ed., *E. M. Forster*, New Casebook Series (Basingstoke: Macmillan, 1995).

industrial north figures only in a mention of Manchester as the place from which the Schlegels' mother ('poor Emily') moved when their father first took Wickham Place; the inculcation of culture represented and effected by Mr Schlegel clearly requires the move south (p. 163). The rural north – Yorkshire is its representative here – is quite different from the benign, comradely rural south of Oniton, the Purbecks or Hertfordshire; it is wild, foreign, somewhere to be motored into by the restless, rootless, colonizing Wilcoxes, somewhere where motor smashes happen that send you back to the south (pp. 82–96). The England to be saved, the England whose transmission to future deserving generations is in doubt, is a selective England. The future of the nation is not to be assured by connecting those elements divided and fragmented by a class and social system that the novel acknowledges but does not explore – the strategy of the nineteenth-century 'condition of England' industrial novel such as Gaskell's *North and South* or Disraeli's *Sybil: Or, The Two Nations*. *Howards End*'s rhetoric of personal connectedness does not find a parallel in the public, political world of the nation, the landscape in which the personal connections are played out and to which they either qualify or disqualify the players as legatees.

A similar process of regeneration through division and prioritisation can be seen in the novel's representation of the English people, or, more precisely, the 'middle class' which constitutes its main focus. Daniel Born has recently suggested that the assertion often made by critics, starting with Lionel Trilling, that the novel deals with the middle class alone is unhelpful, since it glosses over the novel's concern with economic oppression and the struggle between rich and poor.[6] Whilst there is no doubt that the term 'middle class' only pertains if it can be made to include those of such diverse class positions as those of the Basts, Schlegels and Wilcoxes, none the less the novel itself argues that we need to think of the connectedness and interdependence of these apparently different social positions, and that might be reason enough to hold on to a broad notion of 'middle class' as those whom sufficient money allows to stay out of the abyss of poverty. The term is, after all, one claimed by Forster in just such a wide-ranging, general sense in his 'Notes on the English Character': 'the character of the English is essentially middle-class ... since the end of the eighteenth century, the middle classes have been the dominant force in our community'.[7] Forster's use of the term here seems to be suggesting something rather broader than the socio-economic sense; indeed, the 'middle' seems to be as important here as the 'class', suggesting both its centrality (positioned at the 'heart') to the nation, and its apparent moderation (eschewing the 'extremes' of the margins). The unifying category deployed by the novel for this 'middle' grouping, however, is that of 'gentlefolk': Chapter VI, in which the narrator fills in the background of Leonard Bast,

---

6 Born, *Liberal Guilt*, pp. 125–30.

7 E.M. Forster, 'Notes on the English Character' [1926], *Abinger Harvest and England's Pleasant Land*, edited by Elizabeth Heine (London: André Deutsch, 1996), p. 3.

introduced in the previous chapter, opens with the words, 'We are not concerned with the very poor. They are unthinkable, and only to be approached by the statistician or the poet. This story deals with gentlefolk, or with those who are obliged to pretend that they are gentlefolk' (p. 58). With regard to their class position, the Basts are, of course, not 'gentlefolk'. Leonard is a clerk; his job allows them to live (at first) just above the poverty line, in a dark and stuffy basement flat. His aspirations to gentility relate above all to his desire for 'culture'. The rationale for grouping together Leonard (a third-generation ploughboy (p. 122)) with the wealthy (though notably landless and rootless (p. 246)) Wilcoxes and the rentier Schlegels as 'gentlefolk' is that it is they who, in the novel, constitute 'the nation' (as defined in 'Notes on the English Character'); it is they who have (or who aspire to have, in Leonard's case) the cultural, social and economic capital to ensure that it is their hands that are 'on all the ropes'.[8] As recent criticism of *Howards End* has emphasized, the novel is concerned to demonstrate the way in which the values espoused by a segment of this class, the segment represented by the Schlegels – cultured, liberal, free-thinking, progressive – depend for their intellectual independence and openness on the activities of those in the business world who manage their inherited wealth for them, and ensure them returns large enough to live on: 'so few of us think clearly about our own private incomes, and admit that independent thoughts are in nine cases out of ten the result of independent means'.[9] In turn, the business world of the Wilcoxes is dependent on the all-too dispensable labour of clerks such as Leonard, who constitute just so much human ballast to be shed when economic conditions demand it. Here, as throughout *Howards End*, it is principally through the figure of Margaret that these connections are articulated; she insists that her family and friends, all of whom, like her, live on the interest from inherited wealth, recognize the economic basis on which their leisured privileges depend. This, then, is one of the principal areas of 'connection' on which the novel insists, and it is this connection that Margaret seeks to consolidate and properly value through her marriage to Henry Wilcox.

However, despite this rhetorical and indeed narrative emphasis on the importance of connection, it is not something that the resolution of the novel underpins; the outcome is not one of mutual recognition, integration or synthesis between these newly 'connected' segments of the middle-class 'gentlefolk'. For, notwithstanding all their faults, notwithstanding the novel's often reiterated imperative to 'only connect' with aspects of middle-class Englishness other than

---

8 The Wilcoxes are said to have their hands on all the ropes on pp. 41, 112, 138 and 165, the Schlegels on pp. 62 and 67.

9 *Howards End*, p. 134; see too pp. 72–3, 132–6. For discussion of the novel's interest in finance and economics, see especially Paul Delany, '"Islands of Money": Rentier Culture in *Howards End*', in Jeremy Tambling, ed., *E. M. Forster*, New Casebook Series (Basingstoke: Macmillan, 1995).

their own, it is the values embodied in the Schlegels, and especially in Margaret, that finally win through. We are reminded of this twice, quite unequivocally, towards the end of the novel. The first is on the occasion of Margaret's meeting with Helen at Howards End after eight months of estrangement, when their reconciliation is confirmed by the understated, perhaps ironic, phrase, 'The inner life had paid' (p. 292). Throughout, 'the inner life' has been identified with the Schlegels, and 'the outer life' – that of telegrams and anger, panic and emptiness, the world of finance, commerce and colonialism – with the Wilcoxes. Now, finally, we are left in no doubt that the Wilcoxes' values are inadequate, bankrupt (the financial metaphors seem unavoidable), stunted. The Wilcoxes might be the backbone of the nation, they might 'keep England going' (p. 268), but their hearts, as Forster famously put it elsewhere, are 'undeveloped'; these middle-class, public-school-educated men 'go forth into [the world] with well-developed bodies, fairly developed minds, and undeveloped hearts. And it is this undeveloped heart that is largely responsible for the difficulties of Englishmen abroad'.[10] They are not up to the business of personal relations, and it is these that, in the end, count.

The second concluding moment in which the Schlegels' values are confirmed as dominant is on the penultimate page, when Henry Wilcox announces his decision to leave Howards End to Margaret in his will: 'There was something uncanny in her triumph. She, who had never expected to conquer anyone, had charged straight through these Wilcoxes and broken up their lives' (p. 331). Such a 'triumph', expressed in the language of militarism, has not been her intention. Her aim had been to connect, and to encourage (or even force) Henry to connect, the seen with the unseen, the inner life with the outer, the prose with the passion, the beast with the monk, the capacity to see life steadily and to see it whole – the novel presents many variations of the polarities that Margaret tries to bring into contact with each other through and during her marriage to Henry Wilcox. Her explicit intention fails, but nonetheless the final outcome is the right one – the one that the first Mrs Wilcox had sought to secure. Howards End's spiritual succession is assured (Margaret, to be followed by Helen and Leonard's son), not because of any success in her attempt to connect with what the Wilcoxes represent, but more because she has made the attempt at all: 'visions do not come when we try, though they may come through trying' (p. 204).

The novel both has its cake and eats it. The rhetoric of connection stands confirmed by its *indirect* results: the (marital) connection between Margaret and Henry brings Howards End to Margaret; the (sexual) connection between Leonard and Helen provides a proper spiritual heir after Margaret. But both experiments in connection also manifestly fail; Henry and Margaret's marriage cannot, because of Henry's refusal to connect, be the force for regeneration that she had hoped;

10 Forster, 'Notes on the English Character', pp. 4–5.

Leonard dies, and Helen cannot help but forget him (p. 327).[11] Ultimately, the divisions between these three segments of the middle class are underscored and reinforced, and the values of the Schlegels, which might have been seen to be compromised or diminished by a more successful connection with the Wilcoxes' (or indeed Leonard's) values, are in fact confirmed as superior, stronger, triumphant. Henry is weak, broken, his 'outer life' unable to sustain him when the crisis comes; Leonard is precipitated into a heart attack by a bookcase falling on him; whereas Margaret and Helen's values carry them through to a point of victory, optimism and plenitude in the final pages. Just as the England to which the novel lays claim is a partial and a covertly divided one, so the class fraction that is to inherit this England has to be, in the end, divided from, and elevated above, those that share their middle-class position; only through them will England be as safe as the houses by means of which the novel debates the meanings and future of the nation.

Howards End offers the southern English middle-class reader a chance to have it both ways: a chance to analyse and acknowledge the material base of their cultural and social privilege, but at the same time to distance themselves from the more detestable aspects of that privilege – for all readers, surely, are Schlegels, not Wilcoxes. The novel thus manages to save the south of England, with all that it comes to represent, both *from* and *for* itself: it offers salvation *from* the genteel brutalities of a particular kind of southern English value system, and the salvation of value *for* a designated subdivision of the middle class, where nothing is to be lost or relinquished, emotionally *or* materially, for those with their hands on the spiritual ropes. For them, the inner life does, quite literally, pay.

Pym and the English south: 'it's the trivial things that matter'

Howards End provided me with a bastion against Bournemouth. It named it, and, with a light touch, refused its blandishments. It elevated the inner life against the outer, asserting that this was where the real value of human society was to be found. And, because this thesis was advanced in a novel written by one of the canonical writers of the early twentieth century, simply to read the novel was to partake of that same inner life. To read, particularly to read 'the classics', was to distance myself from the demands of Bournemouth's 'outer life', and to do so more legitimately, more respectably, and thus more successfully, than I could have done through other forms of teenage rebellion, which inevitably, through argument or recrimination, would have drawn me back into an engagement with the structures and demands of family and home that I was seeking to evade.

The desire for evasion came with the advent of my teenage years. Rosalind Coward has suggested that all children think that their own families are more

11 For instances of Henry's refusal to connect, see *Howards End*, pp. 300, 322.

bizarre than the next one.[12] On the contrary, it was not until I was a teenager, and began to draw comparisons, that I began to think my family bizarre. As a child, I had not realized that the household economy of all families did not run as in mine. I assumed that everyone's mother washed out the plastic bags in which food was stored in the fridge, dried them on the airer or washing line, and then, having graded them by size, stored them in the appropriate kitchen drawer. I thought that all Christmas and birthday wrapping paper, no matter how creased or how scarred by Sellotape, would be returned to the paper box for next time. I took it for granted that no one had more than three inches of water in the bath, and that a lemon meringue pie would last a family of four for three meals. This frugality was accompanied by an adherence to a ritualized routine that, again, I took at first to be normal. The beetroot would go on the table in the round, shallow Tupperware dish. Hospital corners had to be executed during bed-making. Washing should be hung out in a particular way, for maximum wind contact. Vegetable waste went in the compost bucket, paper and tins in the plastic waste bin, and unpleasant, indeterminate rubbish – scraps of meat, the bones from the cats' fish, the contents of my father's ashtray – went, securely wrapped in paper bags, into the special Swedish bin secreted under the sink. Sunday school and, later, church were required on Sundays; the threat of Girl Guides hung over me in case any remaining shortcomings weren't held sufficiently in check by the High Anglican Christianity provided by St Alban's.

Encountering the writing of Barbara Pym in my late twenties, I experienced a shock of recognition. Here, in extraordinarily knowing detail, was the feminine world of domestic ritual and frugality that I had grown up in, a world of small chops, small sherries, plastic doilies, sensible shoes, church bazaars, and even, in one novel, plastic bags sorted by size.[13] Pym's often-noted anthropological gaze – classifying, categorizing, distanced, exploiting 'the potential of a momentary disorientation' to demonstrate the oddness of English cultural rituals – returned this world to me in as strange and fantastic a form as that in which I was coming to see it myself.[14] To find this world narrativized and anatomized, in a form that at once renders it absurd and recuperates, even celebrates, it was at once compelling, reassuring and unsettling. The compulsion lay in the recognition, the reassurance in the humour, and the discomfiture in the recuperation, and I want now to elaborate on each of these three elements in relation to one of Pym's novels, *A Glass of Blessings* (1958). While any of Pym's novels could have been chosen to

---

12 Rosalind Coward, 'The True Story of How I Became My Own Person', in Catherine Belsey and Jane Moore (eds) *The Feminist Reader: Essays in Gender and the Politics of Literary Criticism* (Basingstoke: Macmillan, 1989) p. 41.

13 Barbara Pym, *Quartet in Autumn* (Basingstoke: Macmillan, 1977).

14 Glynn-Ellen Fisichelli, 'The Novelist as Anthropologist – Barbara Pym's Fiction: Fieldwork Done at Home', *Papers on Language and Literature* XXIV: 4 (1988), pp. 436–45 (p. 441). See too Jean E. Kennard, 'Barbara Pym and Romantic Love', *Contemporary Literature* XXXIV:1 (1993), pp. 44–59 (pp. 57–9).

examine this world of well-intentioned parsimony, *A Glass of Blessings* has the advantage of representing this in relation to a degree of suburban affluence, a combination which reinforced for me the points of identification.

At the most straightforward level, this experience of recognition resulted from the novel's depiction of a middle-class southernness that I knew only too well, a world that had something in common with that of *Howards End*. Although the setting is the 1950s rather than the 1910s, it is still a world where people admire the enormous joints of meat at Simpsons, where seaside towns signify the cultural infelicities of suburbia (though in *A Glass of Blessings* Eastbourne takes over this function from Bournemouth (pp. 146, 149)), and where the narrative dynamic is generated by the frictions, misunderstandings and snobberies between different segments of the middle class.[15] In *A Glass of Blessings*, however, the segments of the middle class under scrutiny are not as diverse as those in *Howards End*; indeed, this novel confines its gaze to suburbia. However, in delineating the groupings and the finely differentiated hierarchies that constitute the suburban middle class, the novel shows the social divisions within this section of the middle class to be as pronounced, as clearly defined, as those between Basts, Schlegels and Wilcoxes. Wilmet Forsyth, the first-person narrator and protagonist, is leisured, affluent, buys as many new clothes as she wishes, reads *The Daily Telegraph*, takes a Tio Pepe before lunch and a dry Martini before dinner, and stays at a Trust House hotel with her husband Rodney during their Cornish holiday. Mary Beamish, whilst attending the same High Anglican church as Wilmet, is one of Pym's stalwart 'excellent women'; a doughty worker for church, parish and community, she looks after her aged and demanding mother until her death, gives blood as often as possible, and wears good-quality clothes of unflattering colour that have been marked down in the sale. Miss Prideaux represents yet another gradation of this middle-class congregation: 'she was undoubtedly a gentlewoman, but perhaps reduced circumstances described her position better than any phrase suggesting distress or decay. ... she was wearing a lavender-coloured cardigan which I had sent to St Luke's last jumble sale' (p. 28).

Time after time, the niceties of such social distinctions are drawn for us by Wilmet herself. In the opening pages of Chapter 4, for example, she describes, groups and categorizes the people that she meets at the church social evening, proving herself equal to the finest level of sub-classification: 'The nuns were of two kinds, short and motherly looking, or tall and thin with steel-rimmed spectacles, pale waxy complexions and sweet remote smiles. ...' (p. 54). This taxonomic tendency is underlined by the persistent animal imagery in the novel.

15 For the references to Simpson's, a London restaurant famed for its roast beef and often represented as quintessentially 'English', see *Howards End*, pp. 156–7, and Barbara Pym, *A Glass of Blessings* [1958] (Harmondsworth: Penguin, 1980), p. 87. All further references to this novel are included in the chapter following the relevant quotation and are from this edition.

Men are compared with badgers, sheep, bears, hedgehogs and porcupines, whilst the women are constantly identified by means of the fur coats that they wear. It is not only others that Wilmet classifies in this way; she is capable, too, of turning the same scrutinizing gaze on her own behaviour: noticing a youth skimming through a book with a 'faintly pornographic title', she says 'I turned away with what I suppose was a kind of womanly delicacy' (p. 24). That 'I suppose' suggests a sense of the strangeness (to herself) of her own behaviour, and the same desire to categorize and classify it. Wilmet observes the social rituals of her own kind, and in describing them she denaturalizes them, rendering them bizarre, absurd, and concerned only with the inconsequential.

She also, of course, thereby makes these rituals humorous; it is this distancing of the narrative voice from the object of its discourse (including the speaker herself) that is productive of the comedy of the novel, a comedy of detail and observation, rather than of action. By encountering this world through the eyes and voice of Wilmet, the reader is (to a large degree) aligned with her position, her observations and judgements about those she observes. For those readers who share Wilmet's knowledge and judgement of this milieu, this position of alignment with Wilmet is in many ways a comfortable one; it reassures by confirming that in recognizing the nature of this world, and being able to laugh at it, we are at one remove from it. Recognizing the strangeness of this world as well as its familiarity reassures us that we are not subsumed by that world, and this distance permits readers a sense of sympathy for Wilmet's relationship to it. She is both enmeshed within it and observer/critic of it, making her, like Margaret, a critical insider. Whilst Margaret's critical-insider insights are generative of her guiding credo of 'only connect', Wilmet's, however, are productive only of a sense of disappointment with her life. Romance, which for Wilmet stands for passion, hope, appetite, an unanthropological engagement with 'life', is distanced from her both historically and culturally: it belongs to her time stationed in Italy with the Wrens in the Second World War. Now, her sense is that 'life had been going on around me without my knowing it' (p. 226), and this disappointment – it has not the reach or purchase of despair – permeates the text.

However, sympathy for Wilmet is also undercut by her distancing, anthropological eye, for her version of her world is not only funny, it is also rather unpleasant. She is a snob; many of the acuities of her observations are derived from her sense of social position and etiquette. Father Bode, she says, has a 'slightly common voice', and 'might well be the kind of person who would prefer tinned salmon' to smoked; Keith, Piers's lover, has a 'flat, rather common little voice', comes from Leicester, and uses plastic doilies; Wilmet cannot bear the thought that Mary Beamish might like the same poetry as she does.[16] The laughter occasioned by her observations is in part a laughter of complicity, dependent on sharing Wilmet's snobbery as well as her powers to catalogue and describe what

16 *A Glass*, pp. 7, 189, 213, 193, 83.

she observes – a complicity that might reassure through its assumption of shared values, but also unsettle, owing to the nature of what we find ourselves being complicit with.

The possibility of identification with and sympathy for Wilmet is also undermined precisely by the ways in which she is *not* at a remove from her world. It is her proximity to, her participation in, the world she delineates, and indeed her blindspots regarding herself in it, that complicates the picture and intensifies the discomfiture occasioned by the text. Whilst it is all too easy to understand Wilmet's desire for romance, as evidenced by her fantasies about Piers, it is precisely this longing that makes her into a rather ridiculous figure who, as Piers says, begins talking 'like one of the cheaper women's magazines' (p. 187), and who is the only one who fails to see the signs that Piers is gay. Her attempt to engage with 'life' through romance, then, is in part what makes her a less sympathetic and more pathetic character. At the end of the novel, disabused of her romantic fantasies, chastened by Piers's verdict on her as someone 'less capable of loving their fellow human beings than others' (p. 196), but restored by an indeterminate spiritual vision of confession, reconciliation and plenitude in the garden of the retreat-house where Mary Beamish is working, Wilmet has apparently made peace with her lot, and, in particular, with her marriage to Rodney. Comparing her own situation with Mary Beamish's state of newly married contentment, she concludes that 'there was no reason why my own life should not be a glass of blessings too. Perhaps it always had been without my realizing it' (p. 251). Critics have read this, and the novel's concluding sentence – 'It seemed a happy and suitable ending to a good day' – as unironic, affirmative of what she has learnt through her encounter with Piers, and indicative of the 'recognition that one's own life, even with its deeper longings unfulfilled, is happier than one had thought'.[17] If this is right, then there is a bleakness to her capacity to reconcile herself to a largely unchanged situation, and, by extension, to the novel's recuperation of the situation with which she has been discontented as 'a glass of blessings'. Perhaps she and Rodney are closer than before, and will forge a new beginning in their new flat; however, the linking of happiness with suitability could be seen as dispiriting instance of Wilmet resigning herself more comfortably to the limits of her circumstances. If, however, this ending is ironic (and I think it is ambiguous), and the ending returns to Wilmet's anthropologising commentary on her circumstances ('there was no reason why …'; 'Perhaps it always had been …'; 'it seemed …'), then Wilmet is once again speaking in the

[17] Jan Fergus, '*A Glass of Blessings*, Jane Austen's *Emma*, and Barbara Pym's Art of Illusion', in Janice Rossen, ed., *Independent Women: The function of gender in the novels of Barbara Pym* (Brighton: Harvester, 1988), p. 132; see too Charles Burkhart, 'Glamourous Acolytes: Homosexuality in Pym's World', in Rossen, *Independent Women*, p. 103; Jill Rubenstein, 'Comedy and Consolation in the Novels of Barbara Pym', *Renascence: Essays on Values in Literature* XLII:3 (Spring 1990), p. 182.

voice of disengagement and detachment, at one remove from herself and the world around her, and still ignorant of her own snobbery and selfishness: she does, after all, on this final page and after the reappraisal of her life and values, tell us that Mary's description of her own life as a glass of blessings '*naturally* led me to think about myself' (p. 252; my emphasis). For Wilmet, the return to the self is still conceived as 'natural'. Ironic or not, there is something unsettling about the ending. Either Wilmet is recuperated to a world where, as Mr Bason says, 'it's the trivial things that matter' (p. 86); or she remains unchanged, detached, aimless, marking time, merely observing, albeit amusingly, all that goes on around her. Both seem, if not exactly chilling prospects, at least prospects that make you want to put on a cardigan and turn the gas fire up a notch.

The undeveloped heart of England

Pym and Forster both address the undeveloped heart of England. Both authors are often noted for their concern with Englishness, but it is not insignificant that theirs, in *A Glass of Blessings* and *Howards End*, is a selective, southern Englishness, the region that likes to present itself (despite the West Midlands' attempt to commandeer the term for itself) as the heart of England – its centre, its essence, its life-force. From London, the seat of national government and centre of international money markets, out through the home counties to Oxford, Stratford-upon-Avon and the Cotswolds, and down through the Sussex downs and the Kent countryside ('the garden of England'), that which is claimed as 'quintessentially English' can be contained by and identified in this circumscribed area of the country. Weather forecasts begin here, and work their way outwards; railways and motorways connect 'the regions' to the south with ease, but not to each other; the Channel Tunnel feeds 'the Continent' into the south-east; the majority of the nationally funded theatres and concert halls are clustered here.

For Pym and Forster, despite their exclusive focus on the 'gentlefolk' of this southern region, the heart is an undeveloped one. For Pym, this is owing to the rituals, constrictions and absurdities of the suburban milieu on which she focuses; for Forster, it is because the Englishman has been taught 'that feeling is bad form. He must not express great joy or sorrow, or even open his mouth too wide when he talks – his pipe might fall out if he did. He must bottle up his emotions, or let them out only on a very special occasion'.[18] Both suggest that that most conventional counter to the undeveloped heart, romantic love, is not up to the task. In *Howards End*, the excesses that characterize romantic love lead to trouble, mistakes, misunderstandings and pain; it is the place where men and women lose themselves in sex (as with Helen and Paul, and Helen and Leonard), lose the 'proportion' that is one of the defining virtues of the first Mrs Wilcox. Instead, in *Howards End*, the

18 Forster, 'English Character', p. 5.

English ideal, the noblest kind of love, is a comradeship 'not passionate, ... our highest gift as a nation' (pp. 303, 263). The personal relations that the novel seeks to secure as 'the important thing for ever and ever' (p. 176) are ungendered and asexual.[19] In *A Glass of Blessings*, too, romance dupes those who seek it. Wilmet, Rowena and Harry all recall it wistfully, as a property of their Navy days stationed in Italy, but it has become clear that romance does not travel well; Harry is fatter and balder, emasculated, it seems, by his daily excursions into Mincing Lane, and his sexual advances to Wilmet hold no temptation for her; Rodney is unromantic to the point of giving Wilmet money for her Christmas present; and Wilmet's attempt to recapture romance through her relationship with Piers serves only to confirm its inaccessibility to her, making her look foolish in the process. The 'glass of blessings' to which Wilmet aspires, or rather doubtfully lays claim, at the end of the novel seems a long way from the 'world's riches' to which George Herbert was referring in the poem that gives the novel its title and which forms the epigraph on the title page.

The antiromanticism of these novels was part of their appeal for this romantically challenged southerner, at least. In the case of *Howards End*, the rejection of romantic love as a route to personal salvation was a welcome relief from the exigencies and extremities of the Lawrentian embracing of it that I encountered at much the same time in *Sons and Lovers* and *The Rainbow*. Finding myself 'to one side' not only of home and family, but also of the highly charged heterosexual wheelings and dealings that constituted my friends' weekend activities and weekday conversations, the Forsterian ideal of a noble and ungendered comradeship allowed me to make peace with my position at the margins and my profound disinterest in the possibility (distant though it was) of heterosexual romance; any other kind of romance did not, at this point, enter the frame.

Pym's antiromanticism figured rather differently in the unfolding narrative of my relationship with the English south. With Bournemouth well behind me when I first read her work, there was an undeniable element of *schadenfreude* in seeing *A Glass of Blessings* confirm both the impossibility and the absurdity of romance for one such as Wilmet, who settles for the comforts and trivialities of suburbia. Reading it as I did in the context of the brave new world of women's writing of the mid-1980s, when the extravagances of Angela Carter, the lushness and intensity of Michèle Roberts and the new Lawrentian, if lesbian, romanticism of Jeanette Winterson offered other possibilities for English femininities, such a position as Wilmet's spoke only of compromise, timidity and narrowmindedness. Reading Pym, I felt, reinforced the bulwark between me and Bournemouth.

Now, of course, I know that by then it was already a lost cause. With my own collection of plastic bags in the drawer downstairs, my delight in the wonders of the compost heap, my enthusiastic execution of the rituals of the kitchen, I

---

19 See *Howards End*, pp. 206, 303.

know that it takes more than a couple of novels to keep Bournemouth at bay. Bournemouth makes its presence felt wherever I happen to be, for, as so many recent critics have reminded us, it is impossible finally to separate 'home' from 'self', and impossible to change our selves at will: as Madan Sarup put it, 'identities are not free-floating, they are limited by borders and boundaries'.[20] Those borders and boundaries might be psychic, historical, economic and cultural, but they are also, and at the same time, geographical; in other words, I find myself bumping up against Bournemouth in my reading of the psychic, historical, economic and cultural. However, those borders and boundaries are also, mercifully, permeable, subject to change, and in part this is precisely because of the narrativity of their constitution: the stories that I tell about the borders and boundaries that delimit my self are open to retelling and rereading. This is not to underplay their rootedness, too, in the 'grit and grittiness' of material circumstances: as a careful reader of *Howards End*, I hope I am alert to that particular pitfall. However, I am also increasingly aware of the extent to which my own accounts of the intersection between materiality and identity – those situated stories of home and self – seem to change every time I return to them, whether they are the stories of my childhood or the ways in which I read the texts of Forster and Pym. The Schlegels no longer seem quite so visionary; the oscillation between delight in Pym's observation of the bizarre social mores of the suburban English and castigation of their stultifying narrowness is located in me as much as in the text. Perhaps, like Wilmet, this just means that Bournemouth has recuperated me, by indirect if not direct means. Perhaps, though, rather than seeking to banish Bournemouth, it is now the stories about Bournemouth that attract my attention and which offer the possibilities for analysis and understanding. There are none the less limits to the accommodation I can make with Bournemouth; I don't mind living with my stories of my hometown now, but that's as far as it goes. Like Margaret Schlegel, I wouldn't want to live there.

Acknowledgements

I would like to thank the following for their help with the writing of this chapter: Laura Doan, Lynne Pearce, and, especially, Jackie Stacey. I am grateful too to Alistair Duckworth and J. H. Stape for helping me try to track down the origin of an elusive reference.

---

20 Madan Sarup, 'Home and identity', in George Robertson, Melinda Mash, Lisa Tickner, Jon Bird, Barry Curtis, and Tim Putnam, eds, *Travellers' Tales: Narratives of Home and Displacement* (London: Routledge, 1994); see too Rosemary Marangoly George, *The Politics of Home: Postcolonial Relocations and Twentieth-Century Fiction* (Cambridge: Cambridge University Press, 1996), chapter 1, and Elspeth Probyn, *Outside Belongings* (London: Routledge, 1996).

Chapter 2

The Debateable Land: Ellis Island Immigration Museum, Margaret Elphinstone's *A Sparrow's Flight* and Border Readings

Alison Easton

'All childhood is an emigration'[1]

Three defining memories:

My friends are earnestly debating whether they would marry an Englishman. We are nine years old, middle-class schoolkids in 1950s Edinburgh, and probably none has ever been out of Scotland. The correct answer, they decide, is 'No'. I stand at the edge of the group saying nothing; privately I think this is a 'silly' conversation.

1997, a dreich day, and the Statue of Liberty and neighbouring Ellis Island are grey smudges out in New York Harbor. This will be my first visit to that key site of the unmaking and making of nationality, the immigrant station which processed 12 million people entering the US between 1892 and 1924, and reopened as a museum in 1990. I am following the route of the immigrants, taken directly from the transatlantic steamer by ferry across to Ellis Island to be examined. As my small ferry begins to move, my eyes suddenly fill and, startled, I feel tears run down my cheeks.

Lancaster University, a postgraduate seminar in my 'Fantasy in Contemporary Women's Writing' course. We are discussing Margaret Elphinstone's 1989 *A Sparrow's Flight*, and a student queries my reference to it as a Scottish novel – an understandable bafflement since the novel is set south of the present border and in a distant future when roads, cities and nations have vanished. I hear myself briefly observe, 'Exile is a very Scottish experience' but, while the talk moves on, my head is full of questions about why this has been my instantaneous response and in what senses is it true.

---

[1] Carol Ann Duffy, 'Originally', *The Other Country* (London: Anvil Press Poetry, 1990), p. 7.

'Scotlands'

This book's project has foregrounded for me a particular set of childhood memories about difference – not my customary way of imaging the past, but first steps in understanding how nation, class and gender shape how I read. Marriage to a foreigner now seems a classic site for a gendered experience of nationality, but I remember those nine-year olds' conversation as my first conscious encounter with national difference even though I no longer remember why I so strongly dissented. My first experience of racial difference came around the age of five when an African Christian minister came to tea. His colour fascinated me: he was not 'black' (I knew what black looked like, I had read *Little Black Sambo*), but wonderful shades of brown, and I turned his pinkish palms over in my hands. The first memory of class awareness came around the age of ten – surprisingly late considering I was a minister's daughter in a working-class parish who spoke with a markedly different accent. But, like the rest of the middle-class fifth of Edinburgh's schoolchildren, I was educated in private schools and the church life of my father's congregation went on in a separate sphere – it coloured daily life at home, it shaped the year, its people were liked and respected, but it was a world apart. It was the moment when I started learning French (two years ahead of those who would make it into the state senior secondary schools) which performed our difference. Out of curiosity my fellow Brownies wanted to hear me speak it; I was uncomfortable.

Only my gender identity has no remembered moment of discovery. It was a given and although, of course, sexism was everywhere endemic, I was possibly cushioned from the full shock of inequality by single sex schooling from age five and the school's oddly asexual culture. Sexual difference and homophobia were simply never mentioned, so that when I finally did learn of homosexuality, I did not know why anyone should think it wrong. Only as a 'girl', then, did I have a clear sense of belonging to a larger group though not in any particularly positive sense (I read de Beauvoir's *The Second Sex* at 18 and simply felt doomed). With respect to class and nation I was internally at a tangent to my contemporaries at school.

Part of my explanation for my situation lies in the way that Scotland was then publically defined. Some of it was specific to my generation (it was a relief, researching this essay, to find my earlier dilemmas diagnosed so helpfully by present-day commentators). Certain distinctive, powerful institutions – law, education, church, banking – that had maintained a sense of a separate Scotland after the 1707 Union, were still visibly embodied in buildings, objects and people. But, aside from school, men largely ran these institutions, and even Scotland's cherished image of the 'lad o pairts', representing educational opportunities for any clever child, hadn't been true for women and was only partly true for the working class (my paternal grandfather came from the working class to become a civil engineer, but many did not have such good fortune).[2]

But in mid twentieth-century impoverished Scotland these institutions did not constitute a sufficient identity. From the nineteenth century onwards the tartanry of a romanticized Highlands and the couthie parochialism of the Kailyard world (exemplified in sentimental popular fiction) overlaid other possible self-definitions, while nationhood, despite Union and Empire, continued to be defined in antagonistic opposition to England.[3] The limited Scottish history we were taught (what one Englishman memorably dismissed as 'local history' to my teacher mother) was political and military, that is inherently male. Though the country had been an internecine hybrid for centuries, this history assumed the emergence of a coherent national entity called Scotland. Women hardly entered the picture: as Robert Crawford remarks, 'many Scots might find it hard to name six famous women who didn't have their heads chopped off'.[4] Apart from the Covenanters and Jacobite Risings, Scottish history fizzled out with the unsatisfactory son of Mary, Queen of Scots. Scottish nationalism, in my child's perception, was a matter of stealing the Stone of Destiny and insisting that Queen Elizabeth was the Second of neither Scotland nor Britain. The evident poverty of working-class Edinburgh turned me towards socialism rather than nationalism at the time when Harold Macmillan told the nation that 'They had never had it so good'.

Publicly, Scottishness was celebrated by kilts, drunken Hogmanay and the leering 'Toast to Lassies' on Burns Night (it was years before I discovered the political Burns). The Jock and the Patriarch were dangerously misogynist constructions, and there was no public space to which women could connect. Little even now has been written about women's experience in Scotland. Benedict Anderson rightly sees nations as imagined communities, and, while not much concerned with gender in his analysis, does note their homosocial character.[5] This

2 There was 70 per cent female illiteracy in eighteenth-century Scotland.

3 David McCrone, Stephen Kendrick and Pat Straw, eds, *The Making of Scotland: Nation, Culture and Social Change* (Edinburgh: Edinburgh University Press, 1989).

4 Robert Crawford, 'Redefining Scotland', in Susan Bassnett, ed., *Studying British Cultures: An Introduction* (London: Routledge, 1997), p. 93. See also Joy Hendry, 'Snug in the Asylum of Taciturnity: Women's History in Scotland', in Ian Donnachie and Christopher Whatley, eds, *The Manufacture of Scottish History* (Edinburgh: Polygon, 1992), pp. 125–42.

5 Benedict Anderson, *Imagined Communities: Reflections on the Origin and Spread of Nationalism*, rev. edn (London: Verso, 1991). Dorothy McMillan speaks of the 'overwhelming masculinity of the Scottish cultural tradition at least in the Lowlands': 'Constructed Out of Bewilderment: Stories of Scotland', in Ian A. Bell, ed., *Peripheral Visions: Images of Nationhood in Contemporary British Fiction* (Cardiff: University of Wales Press, 1995), p. 96. See also Esther Breitenbach, Alice Brown and Fiona Myers, 'Understanding Women in Scotland', *Feminist Review* LVIII (1998), pp. 44–65.

Scotland was not how my imagination envisaged a 'community'. This dominant form of nationhood masked uncertainty about Scotland, a stateless nation which had spent 300 years trying to achieve some coherent national identity and in consequence found ideas of plurality threatening.

At home I was surrounded by a different Scottish culture, a different history of Scotland and a kind of internationalism that for centuries was part of Scottish experience, particularly in its political, intellectual and economic ties with Europe, but had been occluded in the last 100 years.[6] If it did not provide me with a self-conscious identity, it was partly because this Scotland was many Scotlands. As Robert Crawford observes, 'The Scots' awareness of centuries of linguistic and cultural pluralism is rarely consciously articulated; but it is deeply felt'.[7] I experienced Scotland as many different places and cultures. For example, instead of the simple Highland/Lowland binary (a binary which tartanry sought further to elide), I also knew the Borders and Orkney as other, highly distinct areas. Moreover, I could see there were several Highlands: Wester Ross crofting communities were different from West Perthshire where my grandfather had farmed, the Islands yet another world, and none of them resembled the Highlandism of tartan and clan. The history of the Clearances was not taught at school; it was not much then in Lowland consciousness and was totally absent from South-British history (though not forgotten by those who suffered directly).[8] But I had some knowledge of it from both parents. This profoundly moving knowledge was made complex by many factors, including an understanding of the Clearances' varied nature historically, and the fact that my mother's family, who took up sheepfarming in Glen Orchy, Glen Falloch and Strath Fillan in the late eighteenth century, was, as she once put it, 'on the wrong side', even though they regarded themselves as Highlanders and indeed could speak Gaelic.[9]

My home (and there were plenty similar middle-class families) provided much more education into Scottish culture and history than school or the public realm: novels (though mostly by men), Border ballads, psalms, hymns and songs, and painting including contemporary artists like Joan Eardley whose Aberdeenshire seascapes enthralled me. I was given a historical sense of how urban and rural landscapes evolved from pre-Roman right through the centuries, and a love and knowledge of buildings and the countryside. Then there was the church with a distinctive liturgy and government, and my family had a relish for the language – a big vocabulary I would not use later in England without explanation. In a

---

6 Kenneth White, 'The Scot Abroad', *On Scottish Ground* (Edinburgh: Polygon, 1998), pp. 95–114.

7 Crawford, 'Redefining Scotland', p. 94.

8 David Craig, *On the Crofters' Trail: In Search of the Clearance Highlanders* (London: Jonathan Cape, 1990).

9 J. M. Bumsted, *The People's Clearance: Highland Emigration to British North America, 1770–1815* (Edinburgh: Edinburgh University Press, 1982); Michael Lynch, *Scotland: A New History* (London: Century, 1991), pp. 367–70.

pre-television world (there was no set in our house until I was 21) it was our parents who unselfconsciously taught us to look and to listen, to understand historically and critically, to know how things were made (medium and context) and to ask, question and find out.

My sister wryly sums up this family world as 'middle-class intelligentsia', but at least it countered the dominant mythic Scotland with one put together by observation and reading. It provided the foundation of what allows me to think of myself as Scottish today. It had, of course, its blindnesses and prejudices, though it did explicitly reject sectarianism. It had no understanding of modernism, there was a complete silence about the sexual, I learnt nothing about working-class radicalism, and patriarchy ruled OK. Still, its rejection of an essentialist 'Scotland' and its espousal of the alternative idea of 'Scotlands' are now important common understandings for Scottish Studies; would that I had learnt that earlier.[10]

This curiosity and exploration characterized our attitude to other nations too. As I said, there is a long tradition of internationalism in Scotland. This version of Scotland might have its anti-English episodes but crucially its foundations did not lie in antagonism to other nations, whose cultures were enjoyed with a sense of connection (in spite of the fact that in the 1950s overseas holidays were uncommon, and Europe still more commonly seen through the lens of World War Two). France was where my father had studied (the Eglise Reformée is sister in history, doctrine, liturgy to the Church of Scotland) and we knew that all Scots had been French citizens by virtue of an unrevoked Auld Alliance law; and from Germany came the silver ashtray inscribed, in the first German which I understood, 'To the Friendly Memory' of a family whom my father had known in Germany 1945–46. The church's connections with Judaism were honoured, English literature hugely read and the European art and music celebrated (sometimes as an adjunct to church worship – it would be wrong to assume that all Scottish churches were dour and philistine). This omnivorous, liberal internationalism made for a relational nationalism; it set up dialogues to add to those other dialogues within Scotland's borders. Cairns Craig argues that from an international perspective the idea of a homogeneous national culture is a false norm; instead, 'bilingualism, biculturalism, and the inheritance of a diversity of fragmented traditions ... [are] the source of creativity rather than its inhibition in the second half of the twentieth century'.[11]

No, I didn't marry an Englishman (though my sister did, I'm pleased to say, and my brother a Frenchwoman), but I did emigrate, physically and mentally, to become an Americanist – not, that is, a citizen of the United States but a specialist in the study of American culture. American Studies' problematization of the

---

10 See Robert Crawford, 'Bakhtin and Scotlands', *Scotlands* I (1994), 57.

11 Cairns Craig, 'Twentieth-Century Scottish Literature: An Introduction', in Cairns Craig, ed., *The History of Scottish Literature*, vol. IV (Aberdeen: Aberdeen University Press, 1987), p. 7.

constructions of nation, culture and identity involved me early in the discussion of immigration, hybrid identities, race, ethnicity, gender and class (this last my main focus these days), though it was a long time before I connected all this with the place and time I had come from. Primarily I was excited by a world that was different, one which I did not know, which was other to myself. I did not know who I was in Scotland, so my first move was to make a stranger my desire – not to identify with, not to incorporate but to get to know in its differences. The other was already not outside but inside the self.

Tränen insel wispa łez île des larmes isola delle lagrime
το νησί των δαχρύων остров слёз טרערן-אינדזל isle of tears.[12]

'Are you a Scottish Easton?' The Indiana bookshop assistant has spotted her maiden name on my cheque; patriarchal name-giving practices momentarily link me with this third generation American.

It is estimated that more than 40 per cent of the US population (100 million citizens) have some forebear who came through Ellis Island. Although African, Hispanic and Asian peoples entered America elsewhere and in different circumstances and Native Americans inhabited Manhattan prior to all immigration, Ellis Island has eventually through a much contested process become a national symbol, consciously linked with other places like Jamestown (where the first African slaves were landed in 1619), Angel Island (the San Francisco immigration station) and Plymouth Rock (the 1620 Puritan landfall); Indian remains found when Ellis Island was restored were blessed with a Delaware ceremony.[13] Its present intended meanings for US citizens are clear; how then did I read this national text?

I went to Ellis Island as a scholar of nineteenth-century America and a 'resident alien' permitted entry into the US to teach American literature. I also came because I had started to wonder about a nation having at its centre such radical dislocations, separations, uprootings, loss and change. I met so many Americans who defined themselves in terms of their immigrant origins and whose grandparents could not or would not speak of that experience. The first time on Ellis Island I was in a nearly deserted museum and attentive to ghosts (including my own). The second time, the place was packed and there was a wonderful roar of

---

12 Georges Perec with Robert Bober, *Ellis Island* (New York: The New York Press, 1995), p. 30. Isle of Tears was the name given to Ellis Island by immigrants from all over Europe.

13 Werner Sollors, 'National Identity and Ethnic Diversity: "Of Plymouth Rock and Jamestown and Ellis Island"; or, Ethnic Literature and Some Redefinitions of America', in Geneviève Fabre and Robert O'Meally, eds, *History and Memory in African-American Culture* (New York: Oxford University Press, 1994), pp. 92–121.

voices in many languages, making me ponder the possibilities of a successful multi-ethnic society.

The museum designers intend visitors to follow the route of the original immigrants: through the huge baggage hall, up the specially rebuilt staircase to the now empty and enormous Registry Room where people had waited in pens and on benches to go through 'inspection', and then through to the two main exhibits.[14] The visitors like the immigrants have sailed past the nearby Statue of Liberty (hackneyed feminine image it may be but as for many of the immigrants it moved me to elation).[15] There, however, the resemblance ends. The visitors are not going to be immediately separated – women and children from the men – by officials in uniforms who scared them, and their precious baggage dumped. Unlike their forebears, they will not be medically inspected (a buttonhook on eyelids to check for disease). They won't be faced with a series of questions posed through an interpreter, where a chalk mark on your coat would single you out for further testing for mental deficiency or illness, followed by detention, appeals and exclusion (over this period, on average about two per cent a year were sent back to Europe).

But in the baggage hall I found myself in tears again (and I was not the only one), standing beside the blown-up photos of arrivals on the pier I myself had just crossed – both eager and confused families humping bags like those now piled up on display (officials could recognize a bundle's country of origin from the way it was knotted, tiny markers of home soon to be untied). Since this was a much photographed event by professional social commentators and local officials, all the exhibits are characterized by enormously enlarged photographs of unsmiling people. The pictures had, of course, been posed for the photographers with agendas, but we know from these photographers that their subjects were more engaged in the overwhelming process they were going through than in the camera.[16] I was more caught up by these mute faces, many of them women, than the recorded memories on audio display or the glass cases full of precious old-world possessions.

Upstairs there are two exhibits, one on the Ellis Island Processing with all its paraphernalia of 'testing', and the other on the Peak Immigration Years (1892–1924), showing the worlds the immigrants came from, how they travelled, what worlds they entered and with what differing receptions. I gazed for hours, totally gripped, reading every caption: the pogrom victims' slashed heads; the Lithuanian mother likening her son's departure to putting him in his coffin; the wall covered with one ship's manifests, recording passengers by age, work, baggage; the

---

14 Mike Wallace, 'Exhibition Review: The Ellis Island Immigration Museum', *Journal of American History* LXXVIII (1991), p. 1024.

15 There are many records of this response to the Statue by immigrants.

16 Lewis Hine, *America and Lewis Hine: Photographs, 1904–1940*, with essay by Alan Trachtenberg (New York: Aperture, 1977), pp. 42 and 120.

woman having her chest examined, with nurses turning towards the presumably male photographer; a group of women denied admission; boys in a coalmine, each snotty nose completely blackened; a life-size photo of 80 members of one Lebanese village, picnicking in America; the unabashed racism of anti-immigration material; and so much more.[17] My profound engagement was simultaneously emotional, intellectual and political, but I did not 'identify' in any obvious way with these people. Instead they seemed to exemplify, in ways my academic and feminist self was now equipped to grasp, the complexities, paradoxes, agonies, transformations and triumphs of diaspora and nation.

I was not a naive visitor. I am aware that museums are institutions of power, that the USA has strong, explicit discourses of nationalism and citizenship and that places defining 'America' will be carefully monitored (this is a federally owned museum opened during the Reagan administration).[18] In addition, immigration continues to be a 'primary site for the policing of political, cultural and economic membership in the US nation-state'.[19] Museums also have unspoken codes of civility which sift out what might cause visitors political or sexual offence (which is why women's bodies don't get properly represented). Memory has a politics; indeed, the business of commemorating America's history really got going for politicians and intellectuals at the end of last century when the influx of immigrants made the definition of the nation's origins an urgent and disturbing matter.[20]

Yet I trusted this museum because of the display, next to the baggage room, with big imaginative models which put this Euro/American migration into historical and present-day global contexts: after all, in the past sixty years 75 million people have been uprooted.[21] The displays address both issues of race and gender within American immigration, and its two-way nature (it came as a surprise to me to

17 Women, unaccompanied by men, faced unique restrictions on grounds of morality and dependence.

18 See Susan Porter Benson, Stephen Brier and Roy Rosenzweig, eds, *Presenting the Past: Essays on History and the Public* (Philadelphia: Temple University Press, 1996); and John Bodnar, *Remaking America: Public Memory, Commemoration, and Patriotism in the Twentieth Century* (Princeton: Princeton University Press, 1992); and Amritjit Singh, Joseph T. Skerrett, Jr, and Robert E. Hogan, *Memory, Narrative, and Identity: New Essays in Ethnic American Literature* (Boston: Northeastern University Press, 1994).

19 Lisa Lowe, *Immigrant Acts: On Asian American Cultural Politics* (Durham: Duke University Press, 1996), p. 174.

20 Barbara Melosh, 'Speaking of Women: Museums' Representations of Women's History', in Warren Leon and Roy Rosenzweig, eds, *History Museums in the United States: A Critical Assessment* (Urbana: University of Illinois Press, 1989), pp. 183–4. Wallace, 'Exhibition Review', notes Ellis Island Museum's omission of gangsters and prostitutes. See also Michael Wallace, 'Visiting the Past: History Museums in the United States', *Mickey Mouse History and Other Essays on American Memory* (Philadelphia: Temple University Press, 1996), pp. 3–32, for the history of the memorializing of America's past.

21 John Vidal, 'The Endless Diaspora', *The Guardian*, 2 April 1999, p. 19.

learn that many immigrants latterly returned to Europe). There is material on slavery and Native Americans in this exhibition, and an emphasis on multi-ethnic culture.[22] This version of US history chimed with my own academic journey from once teaching an almost entirely white male nineteenth-century canon (defining America's project as a complex masculine errand from England into an supposedly empty wilderness) to providing nineteenth-century literature courses which explored this more complex social and cultural vision.

It is significant that in the planning of Ellis Island Museum professional academic historians were involved to an unprecedented degree throughout. Their work was made urgent by the presence of an older immigration museum beside the Statue of Liberty which still pedalled the old myth of escape from old world poverty and oppression into the land of the free and prosperous, and ignored America's long history of anti-immigration legislation. Rightwing interest groups kept this older museum open, while the Ellis Island project got on with presenting its revisionist narrative.[23]

We need now to consider the complexity of what happened during those peak immigration years. Ellis Island has great emotional power because it was a common rite of passage for so many (though second and first class passengers were processed on board ship, so class was a factor). The state had a visible presence here, shaped by Progressive Era reformist and regulatory policies.[24] From the windows of the Registry Room Manhattan seems so close and the Statue of Liberty so large, but after screening the majority went on to desperate poverty.[25] They stuck within their own ethnic groups, adapting old-world ways to new conditions, but seeming 'foreign' to native-born Americans who instituted programmes of 'Americanization' to counter the persistence of 'un-American' ideas of family, home life, economic priorities and political values. Women – especially the daughters of immigrant families – lived at the intersection of these processes of racialization, labour exploitation and patriarchal gender relations; they faced immense changes in both the home and workplace (since they contributed about half of the family income), and were up against old and new constructions of femininity.[26]

---

22 There were 107 different ethnic groups in the US in 1980: see Betty Bergland, 'Reading Photographs and Narratives in Ethnic Autobiographies: Memory and Subjectivity in Mary Antin's *The Promised Land*', in Singh, Skerrett and Hogan, *Memory, Narrative and Identity*, p. 88, n.23.

23 Wallace, 'Boat People: Immigration History at the Statue of Liberty and Ellis Island', *Mickey Mouse History*, pp. 55–73.

24 Virginia Yans-McLaughlin and Marjorie Lightman, *Ellis Island and the People of America: The Official Guide* (New York: The New Press, 1997), pp. 60–3.

25 Even the second generation experienced little upward mobility: John Bodnar, *The Transplanted: A History of Immigrants in Urban America* (Bloomington: Indiana University Press, 1987), pp. 169–75.

26 Doris Weatherford, *Foreign and Female: Immigrant Women in America, 1840–1930*, rev. edn (New York: Facts on File, Inc., 1995); and Elizabeth Ewen, *Immigrant*

Mary Antin begins her immigrant autobiography, 'I am absolutely other than the person whose story I have to tell', yet for most people Ellis Island was not in any simple sense the single moment of change, loss and a new identity.[27] It is not a place of origin, but a *borderland* which marks and then memorializes the enormous changes for those who crossed it, and simultaneously allows one to look both ways, to be in two places seeing the complex connections, continuities and differences. As Homi Bhabha observes, 'Janus-faced' boundaries become '*in-between* spaces through which the meanings of cultural and political authority are negotiated', giving an '*inter*national dimension both within the margins of the nation-space and in the boundaries *in-between* nations and peoples.... The "other" is never outside or beyond us'.[28]

Having passed through Ellis Island, the immigrants continued to live an 'in-between' existence. The long-cherished image of America as a cultural 'melting pot' has now been disproved by immigration historians who have instead debated how quickly, if at all, immigrants Americanized, whether they experienced alienation and isolation, and in what forms were ethnic cultures retained. Immersing myself in the specificities of this complex history was one powerful response to my visit to Ellis Island, as I attempted to understand by example how peoples might negotiate between cultures. Lawrence H. Fuchs argues that a simple opposition between 'American mainstream' and 'ethnic persistence' is false: instead, ethnic pluralism defined American society in everything except civic culture. Moreover, these ethnic cultures and identities were changed by the transition to the New World. They were continually being renegotiated, thus creating, as Werner Sollors argues, multiple codes of 'Americanness', in effect changing America into 'Americas'.[29] This produces, for example in immigrant autobiography, 'a multiplicity of cultural discourses', a Bakhtinian heteroglossia in dialogue.[30] The parallel with my sense of 'Scotlands' is suggestive.

I have found that Stuart Hall's theorizing of cultural identity and diaspora helpful in furthering this understanding of identity formation, both historically for immigration America and for myself. He argues that identity is not an essence; it is not static or coherent. Instead, what he calls the 'unsettled space' of cultural

---

Women in the Land of Dollars: Life and Culture on the Lower East Side, 1890–1925 (New York: Monthly Review Press, 1985).

27 Mary Antin, *The Promised Land* (New York: Penguin Books, 1997), p. 1. Antin had a political agenda in presenting herself this way.

28 Homi K. Bhabha, ed., *Nation and Narration* (London: Routledge, 1990), p. 4.

29 For an overview of immigration historiography, see Gary Gerstle, 'Liberty, Coercion, and the Making of Americans', *Journal of American History* LXXXIV:2 (1997), 524–58.

30 Betty Ann Bergland, 'Representing Ethnicity in Autobiography: Narratives of Opposition', *Year's Work in English Studies* XXIV (1994), 84 and 85. See also Sau-Ling Cynthia Wong, 'Immigrant Autobiography: Some Questions of Definition and Approach', in Paul John Eakin, *American Autobiography: Retrospect and Prospect* (Madison: University of Wisconsin Press, 199 1), pp. 142–70.

identity (like the now empty great hall in Ellis Island or, in certain ways, Bhabha's 'in-between spaces') is reconstituted by him as 'a process of identification. ... [I]t is something that happens over time, that is never absolutely stable, that is subject to the play of history and the play of difference'.[31]

The focus on 'difference' and on 'history' is central to what Hall calls the difficult business of 'trying to think identity *and* difference' (p. 16). First, on difference (my many Scotlands): Hall observes that 'there is no identity that is without the dialogic relationship to the Other. The Other is not outside, but also inside the Self, the identity' (p. 16). This chimes well with my heightened sense of hybridity both in Scotland and the US and in those border spaces between nations. Second, history (the museum we have been exploring and its important presence in my own identity): Hall argues that in order to think the relation between identity and difference or indeed be able 'to say anything at all', you 'have to position yourself *somewhere*' (p. 18). This positioning depends on the complex process of recovering one's history. Hall on this occasion discusses this positionality in terms of ethnicity only, but clearly gender, nation, class and sexuality will all play a part too in constituting both the 'play of history' and the 'play of difference'. These ideas of borders and the role of the past take me now to my next text.

Homecomings

Margaret Elphinstone's *A Sparrow's Flight: A Novel of a Future* also concerns a journey across borders and sites of simultaneous change and continuity. It even begins and ends with an island and visits a kind of museum.[32] This novel, like Ellis Island, has moved me with particular intensity: while I don't identify with characters or situations, I know the novel speaks to me, and its ostensibly nationless world makes it a curious, challenging choice for this essay. Through it I want to develop the idea of living/reading in a borderland. Ellis Island's immigration station both masked and uncovered the 'play of difference' in cultural identity, while as a museum it embodies and facilitates the 'play of history'. Elphinstone's novel opens up both these aspects of identity to further exploration.

The novel is set in the 'Debateable Land', that historically shifting border between Scotland and England.[33] The journey starts at Lindisfarne (once a Celtic

---

31 Stuart Hall, 'Ethnicity: Identity and Difference', *Radical America* XXIII (1991), pp. 10 and 15. See also Hall, 'Cultural Identity and Diaspora', in Jonathan Rutherford, ed., *Identity: Community, Culture, Difference* [1990] (London: Lawrence and Wishart, 1998), pp. 222–37; and Werner Sollors, *The Invention of Ethnicity* (New York: Oxford University Press, 1989).

32 Margaret Elphinstone, *A Sparrow's Flight: A Novel of a Future* (Edinburgh: Polygon, 1989). Further page references to this volume are given after a quotation in the text.

33 'Debateable' is the standard Scottish spelling.

centre), continues over the Cheviot Hills along the line of the present-day border (passing Flodden Field, where an English army destroyed much of Renaissance Scotland), and arrives in the Lake District (once in the kingdom of Strathclyde). But none of these places is named, nor is their history directly recalled. The novel is set in a far distant future when nations exist no longer, all cities have vanished and the land is covered with sparsely settled forest. The country has reverted to a pre-industrial, mostly local economy. Households are matrilineal, each headed by a woman who raises her children with her brothers and male cousins. Meanwhile men's primary commitment is to their female relatives, and sexual partners do not live in the same household. This is a world free of sexism and class distinctions, where gender relations appear to be negotiated without tension.

It is as if the processes of secularization and print-capitalism, which Benedict Anderson identifies for the making of modern nations, have been reversed, though without restoring dynastic rule or religious community.[34] Importantly, unlike many feminist futurist novels, *A Sparrow's Flight* does not operate within a simple Utopia/dystopia binary – indeed elsewhere Elphinstone has shown the interest of refusing all binaries.[35] Like the dance based on the tarot in the novel, it is more a 'progression of opposites' (p. 180); it concerns loss as well as gain.

Through this world, consciously or not, Elphinstone is engaging with two Scottish cultural constructions. Cairns Craig argues that Scotland, excluded from English narratives of progress and therefore suspended in an apparently historyless world, has this century turned in writings to ponder what lies outside 'history', before and beyond it.[36] Nonetheless Elphinstone's novel, political in its awareness but without a political agenda, looks forward in order to look backwards to the past which is the readers' present. For that reason, in spite of its rejection of modernity, the novel also avoids the idealized, but conservative and politically impotent notion of a primitive Highland community that, as Peter Womack shows, emerged in reaction to capitalist change and the effects of Union, and to whose attractions and promise of alternatives few Scots are entirely immune.[37] Instead, the novel seems quite knowing about real life in 'remoter' areas of the British Isles.

Elphinstone's remapping of time and space is exhilarating – what readings of gender and nation are possible, and how does she set up her fictional world? Unlike her previous novel, *The Incomer*, the society of *A Sparrow's Flight* lacks all memory of patriarchy, and can barely conceive of war, capital punishment or

---

34 Anderson, *Imagined Communities*, pp. 9–36.

35 Elphinstone, 'The Quest: Two Contemporary Adventures', in Christopher Whyte, ed., *Gendering the Nation: Studies in Modern Scottish Literature* (Edinburgh: Edinburgh University Press, 1995), pp. 107–36.

36 Cairns Craig, *Out of History: Narrative Paradigms in Scottish and British Culture* (Edinburgh: Polygon, 1996), especially pp. 31–63.

37 Peter Womack, *Improvement and Romance: Constructing the Myth of the Highlands* (Basingstoke: Macmillan, 1989), pp. 115–48 and 166–80.

nuclear power.[38] It never occurs to Naomi, the protagonist, to fear men on her travels, or be surprised to find women in charge. It is the reader, instead, who supplies a political understanding of this. But in one vital respect, gender still disables: to develop her fullest artistic potential Naomi left her infant son for a life travelling.

But what then of the matter of nationhood? Naomi Mitchison in her post-Jacobite novel, *The Bull Calves*, speculates startlingly that a 'new Scotland' might choose to lose the present national markers: 'it might drop everything, the language, the music, the dances, the kilt ... and the kirk session in with the rest'.[39] Elphinstone takes this even further in obliterating nation entirely for reasons I shall presently discuss. Nonetheless, she has inherited some of Mitchison's concerns. Arguably Elphinstone's 'nationless' land is still linked to Scotland's past and present, and the fictional ways in which she approaches questions of belonging, community and land use are influenced by certain elements in Scottish literary traditions: in particular, forms of fantasy writing that are linked with Scotland's history and employ a sense of place; issues of community and the relationship with the land; transnational perspectives; and radical politics.[40] One could trace connections between Elphinstone's several fictions and Mitchison's own feminism, her passionate concern for Scotland's economic/social development, and the ways in which she has explored in both historical and contemporary fictions the tensions between hopes for a fair community and the complexities of living in one.[41]

However, from a modern ecological perspective, nations fade in importance; Elphinstone is deeply aware that nuclear power makes a nonsense of frontiers. The premise of *A Sparrow's Flight* is a nuclear disaster at Sellafield centuries, possibly millennia before, which destroyed Britain as we know it, with parts of the polluted Lake District only recently being resettled. The novel makes the important distinction between a tragic, human-made desert which needs, like the post-Highland Clearances to be restored to productive life, and the true, perennial wilderness which in a different way also transcends the idea of national territory.

But nationless though the novel's world is, it is not an undifferentiated place. Naomi and her fellow traveller, Thomas, both come from specific places ('her family who made her who she was' (p. 5); 'the one spot where he belonged' (p. 90)), and both experience exile. Even in a global universe the local still has meaning, and we all come from somewhere. (As the phrase goes, 'I come from

38 Elphinstone, *The Incomer* [1987] (London: Women's Press, 1997).

39 Naomi Mitchison, *The Bull Calves* (London: Virago, 1997), p. 486.

40 Elphinstone notes the importance of real places and history in Scottish fantasy: see 'Contemporary Feminist Fantasy', pp. 45–59.

41 See Jenni Calder, 'More Than Merely Ourselves', in Douglas Gifford and Dorothy McMillan, eds, *A History of Scottish Women's Writing* (Edinburgh: Edinburgh University Press, 1997), pp. 444–55.

Scotland', however complex my sense of this.) As Thomas says to Naomi, 'you can't tell me you have no people' (p. 194). The recognizable geography of this defamiliarized world stresses this fundamental rootedness.

This being the case, boundaries must exist – the novel is full of images of them, personal, social and geographical boundaries. They mark difference and raise questions of connection, respect and transgression. Puzzled by what the readers know as Hadrian's Wall and told it divides one country from another, Naomi comments, '"But why? The mountains do that. Land makes divisions, the people make the connections between them. A wall like that would be going the wrong way"' (p. 40). The tidal island which begins and ends the novel (the final line is '"We can cross over now"' (p. 257)) figures the necessary mix of separation and linkage between different 'countries' (the word refers to both individuals' private spaces and particular communities). Unlike the historical north/south divide, the novel's east/west journey and entry into the 'Empty Lands' whose ostracized people 'grew apart' (p. 127), 'relate[s] one side of the country to the other' (p. 35), and allows the characters, figuratively speaking, to find the 'border' that separates *and connects* 'two countries' (p. 8). But the novel is not cozy in its conclusions: 'there is a border that should not be crossed' (p. 212) (represented by the ruined cities that are dangerous not so much to body as mind); fear, or at least suspicion of dangerous strangers persists.

The complexity of boundaries lies in their histories: where one comes from is also what one's past is and this may be traumatic. At a personal level one has to find how to live in two countries, the past and the present; at a community level remembering is political, as any museum or memorial demonstrates and fraught with problems. When the rest of the world turns a people into 'strangers' (whether the fictional 'Empty Lands' families or, historically, many US immigrant groups), ritualized memories of 'home' become precious but disturbing legacies for descendants.

'Before the world changed' is how the novel's characters indicate present-day Britain. This marker of radical change also figures the day Naomi left her son, and the day Thomas brought plague (a diseased traveller) into his house that killed his entire family. Shorn of purely disastrous significance, the phrase finds its parallels at Ellis Island – or any day one leaves one's country permanently to live in another. This can be traumatic. One definition of trauma is that it is impossible then to connect 'the world we find ourselves in and the world we hold inside' (p. 163) – as Naomi the musician knows, 'time is not a line' (p. 148). Like the rustless metal in the ancient city ruins which so horrifies Naomi, trauma means a past that is terrifyingly intact.

The novel movingly enacts a healing from such disjunctions through a journey taken over 28 days, crossing borders. It eventually allows both protagonists to tell their story to each other (and in a sense to themselves); the thoughtful dialogues perform a kind of talking cure. The room in Thomas's first home which contains artifacts from the distant past is unsealed so that things will die a natural death, but from it Naomi recovers something precious, though something which she must learn with great effort to read (sheet music of lost Bach partitas). This she takes forward to the future. For each character the past becomes a 'two-edged' gift to be accepted 'whole' (p. 230).

'My beginning matters', remarks Naomi, 'it's who I am, but it's only in my head now' (p. 64). So she crosses the border back to her present life, taking herself with her more easily now. Though Naomi says, 'I never stay' (p. 5), she and Thomas seem now to redefine 'home' – the word is used of the island which they recross the hills to return to, of music and of the mountains. She can be at home on a border between one country and another, between past and present, between self and other, and the friendship finally celebrated between her and Thomas substitutes a different kind of relationship for the previous forms of family.

Debateable Land

The image of the Debateable Land appeals to me, not least because I have lived in the North West of England for a quarter century and feel 'at home' here for all my Scottishness. I don't identify with Elphinstone's Naomi but my profession is like her fiddler's skill in that it takes me travelling beyond my native land to inhabit mental borderlands.

The notion of borderlands as a space/place where one can *permanently* reside distinguishes my position from that other image of the in-between – the threshold, the liminal. The liminal implies movement of a particular kind, the crossing of a line in order to replace one state with another very different one. Ellis Island could be read in those terms, since no-one lived permanently there on land chosen for its off-shore situation. But by becoming a museum, a space one can inhabit if only for an afternoon, Ellis Island gives monumental recognition to the often traumatic experience of transit and limbo, the spatio-temporal border on which many immigrants (and, in certain ways, their descendants) went on to live their whole lives, in spite of physically proceeding on into the USA. This monument pays tribute to all those who commit themselves physically and mentally to new lives in a 'debateable land' with its many voices, many identities, many definitions of nation. Given how strongly the museum affects those still passing through its doors, it has the power to endow its visitors mentally with those border perspectives and encourage participation in its heteroglossia.

And the particular Scots/English image of borderland as the 'Debateable Land' is a productive conceptual/political space for me because of its promise of open, interactive discussion (dispensing, of course, with its original bloodshed). This image also differs from the common trope of margins and centre. I have never thought of Scotland as being on the margins of Britain, let alone England as 'the centre' (though I understand the historical effects of English hegemony) and in an overtly masculine Scottish culture, centre/margins did not map my female position since I had other, more pluralist notions of Scotland.[42] The debate involves not just Scotland with other cultures, but Scotland with its many selves.

Euan Hague explores the geographical, historical and cultural meanings of the border for Scots, 'a space that both unites and divides', which places the nation (he is writing in 1996) between integration and independence. Scotland, he argues, is both friend *and* enemy to England, thus defying categorization and homogenization; 'being a stranger' gives it the option of leaving at any moment.[43] Hague's concerns are national politics and culture, but his exposure of the weakness in the binary 'enemy/friend' distinction leads me to consider instead the attractions of remaining as a Scotswoman on a border.

How then does this affect the way I read? It seems that I don't want to identify with what I read; I am more attracted to what I don't know and can't identify with but must try to understand in relation to my own position. Here I find myself in dialogue with Lynne Pearce's idea of a romance between reader and text, her idea of a 'ravissement' in which the abandonment of self is either associated with the 'impulse towards identification and merger' with a 'textual other' or experienced as an 'exaltation of difference'.[44] I experience a different version of this. Part of my positioning involves, instead, a dialogue with difference – hardly surprisingly, given I study American literature and there are many 'Americas'. Indeed, I agree with Doris Sommer that it is vital politically to recognize that some texts, specially so-called 'minority' literature, are deliberately constructed to resist an outsider reader's 'understanding', let alone the assumption of identification or a transcendence of difference.[45] I am fascinated by what Sommer calls these 'unstable boundaries between the self who writes and the other who reads' (p. 411).

Robert Crawford in exploring the powerful ideas of 'Scotlands' provides me through a quotation from Bakhtin with a compelling description of what I would like to aim for as a reader and as a (non)national subject (it is excerpted here for reasons of space):

> There exists a very strong, but one-sided and thus untrustworthy, idea that in order better to understand a foreign culture, one must enter into it,

[42] Robert Crawford, *Devolving English Literature* (Oxford: Clarendon, 1992) discusses the Scottish literary challenges to the supposed centre.

[43] See Euan Hague, 'North of the Border? – An Examination of Scotland within the United Kingdom', *Scotlands* III: 1(1996), pp. 126–33.

[44] Lynne Pearce, *Feminism and the Politics of Reading* (London: Arnold, 1997), p. 87.

[45] Doris Sommer, 'Resisting the Heat: Menchú, Morrison, and Incompetent Readers', in Amy Kaplan and Donald E. Pease, eds, *Cultures of United States Imperialism* (Durham: Duke University Press, 1993), pp. 407–32.

> forgetting one's own, and view the world through the eyes of this foreign culture. ... [But] *creative understanding* does not renounce itself, its own place in time, its own culture; and it forgets nothing. In order to understand, it is immensely important for the person who understands to be *located outside* the object of his or her creative understanding – in time, in space, in culture. ...
>
> In the realm of culture, outsidedness is a most powerful factor in understanding. It is only in the eyes of *another* culture that foreign culture reveals itself fully and profoundly (but not maximally fully, because there will be cultures that see and understand even more). A meaning only reveals its depths once it has encountered and come into contact with another, foreign meaning: they engage in a kind of dialogue, which surmounts the closedness and one-sidedness of these particular meanings, these cultures. ... Such a dialogic encounter of two cultures does not result in merging or mixing. ('Bakhtins and Scotlands', p. 59, see note 10)

This is the debateable land.

Acknowledgements

My thanks to Ethel Sussman, Patrick Hagopian and Rachel Dyer.

Chapter 3

A Refusal of Belonging: I don't want your Straight Nation

Wren Sidhe

Origins

London in the 1950s was a grey and choking place. The great smogs came down and pushed their way into our body cavities. My tongue lay thick with ash and my ears were as stopped as Pompeii. If I pushed my hand out in front of my face it disappeared into another universe, an uncanny one, where ghosts clamoured for attention. Burning had spread them in the air, and they clogged up our lives in muffled quiet. They fell to earth on our tongues so that we could only call to each other through great caverns of silence, the living and the dead, with mouths that only approximated speech.

It was a time of great pretence in which my mother dispensed words of wisdom to her girl children: 'there is as much creativity in baking a cake as writing a book'. I wasn't convinced because the cakes were all eaten, but the books were still on the shelves. They were the third great universe in a world where the living lied and the truth of the dead haunted.

From this inside-out greyness I was meant to become distinct, identifiable, something with more class and femininity than say, a garden gnome: a mantel-piece ornament perhaps? My identity was meant to prove that my mother's life had valuable purpose and was 'professional'. I was to be my mother's cultural capital.[1] My great talents would be proof of her stay-at-home investment.

I could read at three which was handy because when I was four something happened with soldiers and guns in Hungary. My father told my sister and me that we would be adopting a Hungarian orphan. An illustration from an Enid Blyton book gave me a way to imagine how this orphan would arrive. A big motorized cage would arrive down our street, a bit like the ones that carried animals to the circus, and we would go out and look at the children behind bars and pick the one we liked best. In the event it never happened. Were there not enough orphans to go round for all the 'professional' mothers who needed them? It must have been a

---

1 I have taken the idea of a child as a piece of 'cultural capital' from the work of Pierre Bourdieu. See Pierre Bourdieu, *Distinction: a Social Critique of the Judgement of Taste* (London: Routledge & Kegan Paul, 1986).

great shame for those mothers, because it would have been a much easier way to get a bigger family without all that troublesome business of pregnancy and birth when England was demanding this of them.

I was too little to have babies, but the nuns at the convent educated us into wanting them, and if we couldn't give birth, at least we could name a child in the colonies. I learnt to be white by looking at the chart on the wall where, if I could collect and mark off enough pennies, the fat and laughing, black baby at the top of the chart, the pinnacle of achievement, was mine to name as I wanted. I called her by the prettiest name I could think of, Bernadette: the name of a girl I was half in love with. Really, though, the baby was my object of desire, not Bernadette.

Through 'our' baby we were meant to learn that both racial superiority and 'mothering' (within the context of an orthodox Catholic marriage) was our destiny. If we misbehaved the nuns would call *us* 'Hottentots' as a term of abuse. It was a crude attempt to mitigate any pleasure we might find in the baby, reminding us that we were white and the babies were black. We were to understand that our later mothering was to be of white babies, not black. Our gendering thus had a racial dimension and it was a lesson in white racial superiority: four and five-year old children were given to believe that they had the power to name African babies, whilst the adult African parents, or families, of these children appeared to have little power over them. For something like half-a-crown these babies came cheap, and were useful objects in inculcating mothering 'instincts' in us when white babies were not so publically available for commodification.[2]

The only image we saw of adult Africans was when the man from Cadbury's came to give a slide show on chocolate production and handed out, oh joy of joys – free chocolate! We sat on wooden benches in the dark: a dark that was as silky and smooth as the purple covering of the chocolate bars, and as silky and smooth and clammily gorgeous as the sensation we found down each others' knickers. The heady, ecstatic mixture of chocolate and fannies mingled on the fingers we held to each others' noses and licked with delight. Out of the dark a grey beam of light swung through the hall with something like fairies dancing in it. Far away, up on the stage and in Africa, adult Africans, it seemed, worked picking cocoa beans for us children to have chocolate, and a white man checked that their work was satisfactory. Perhaps they were so busy making chocolate for us that they didn't have time to look after their own children?

I rubbed my eyes to peer out of the grey darkness of the 1950s and found myself in the bright sunlight of the 1960s with a book in my hand, *Hiroshima*.[3] From it I learnt that just as greyness hid ghosts in its silence, sunny days, too, were not all they seemed. There could be a delight in August sunlight, but this was a mistake. People had done these things once in Hiroshima and Nagasaki. They had

2 This was before the money system was decimalized. Currently, half-a-crown represents something between twelve and thirteen pence.

3 John Hersey, *Hiroshima* [1946] (Harmondsworth: Penguin, 1972).

obliviously picnicked by water, played in parks and done quite ordinary things until the sunlight grew bigger, blinding: so bright they were all drawn into it – a light so bright it vaporized some and left others stripped of their skins, wretched and in agony. This world demanded my continual vigilance. It was important to never let my guard slip, and to remember to keep looking over my shoulder for the atomic bomb to fall. I had to try and keep being human, being shocked, in a world that seemed unshockable, inhuman. Later, a naked girl ran crying down a rural road in Vietnam, her skin hanging off, giving me another new word to learn – *napalm* – while the nuns spread their doctrine that 'suffering ennobled'.

Clearly the world was full of lies. There was nothing noble about that image. I had to understand the lies and where they came from, what blackness and whiteness, what Jewishness, Catholicism and Nazism meant. Why was it immoral to be working class, or Irish? Why couldn't I serve as an altar boy like my brothers? I didn't actually want to – it meant getting up early – but I wanted to know why I couldn't. Would my presence as a girl defile sanctity? In a lifetime of reading I searched for answers. James Baldwin wrote that '[w]hite people were, and are, astounded by the holocaust in Germany. They did not know that they could act that way. But I very much doubt whether black people were astounded'.[4] So it seemed that my shock at the European holocaust had a racial and geographical dimension. This was new information for my teenage self to digest. My thinking was informed by my white racial identity and colluded with structures of power I had no desire to protect.

Although I lived in a middle-class London suburb in a house with a swimming pool, I also spent much of my childhood holidays in white working-class Bath on my grandparents' council estate. 'Our London' was racially mixed as well as middle-class: next door lived some Nigerian law students with their baby. There were Irish Catholic and English Jewish families, a Sikh family, a Canadian family with an Austrian Jewish father and an English Catholic mother, a South African poet in exile with his family, a Welsh husband and wife, both doctors, and a religious community from the Belorussian church. The least memorable people were the English Protestants. I grew up thinking that black people in England were all middle class. According to my mother, middle class could be equated with good.

My experience in Bath was different. Class rather than racial difference was the issue there. Some people lived in large houses in elegant crescents and stole evacuees' butter rations. Before my grandparents were bombed out of London's East End, Nana had had to travel from the East End to ensure her daughter, an evacuee in Bath's Royal Crescent with 'titled' people, was given the butter they withheld. The rich thieved off poorer people. Although Irish granddad was a labouring man it was made clear to me that I should think of him as 'one of nature's

---

4 James Baldwin, *The Fire Next Time* (Harmondsworth: Penguin, 1964), p. 50.

gentlemen'. Other working-class people were poor through their own fault. They wasted their money on drink and cigarettes, refused the world of high culture and read dreadful things which could never improve them. At a time when we were too middle-class to have such a vulgar thing as a television, one of my Bath aunts, a cleaner, had a sixpence-in-the-slot television which would bob about in the waters of the Avon which regularly flooded their house. To my mother's disbelief, this aunt wouldn't offer us biscuits with our cups of tea. I suspected she couldn't afford them, but I couldn't understand why it was a moral issue.

Carolyn Steedman defines childhood as 'a time when only the surroundings show and nothing is explained.'[5] A corner niche of my Nana's front room in her Bath council house captured this strange world for me. One of my aunts had died young of diabetes, and a little shrine to her was arranged there. In the middle was a black funeral card with prayers for her soul, a pair of grand candlesticks, a crucifix, and a photo of her, all laid out on on some white lace. It was a pure and holy place honouring a young woman who was so good she had wanted to become a nun. Her presence was tangible through its absence. Underneath this mini-altar, hidden behind a red and yellow curtain were my Nana's books – strange and vile tales of working-class Victorian women who had committed foul murders, usually by gaslight, chopping up their employers with a kitchen knife. Wonderfully gory tales, they made gripping reading, all the more exciting because they were presented as true. Nana's niche helped me to understand that what is on display is not all there is to the world. Display is built on exclusions, but to understand the whole I had to look behind the curtain. Best to keep doubting what seems most obviously true.

H.V. Morton's England: 'a virile and progressive nation'

The historical moment I have turned to for my analysis of gender, sexuality and nation is Britain's interwar period; a particularly formative time for my parents' identities as classed, heterosexualized, raced and gendered national subjects. They seemed to have been able to ground themselves in an authoritative version of what it meant to be English. My childhood identity was affected by their desires to produce a similar subjectivity in their children. So what English child/woman precisely was I meant to become, and why didn't I? What myths of Englishness were they working with? The work of the popular journalist, H.V. Morton, who wrote books suggestively entitled *In Search of England* and *The Call of England* seems to capture the zeitgeist, whereas Sylvia Townsend Warner's *Lolly Willowes or The Loving Huntsman* seems to subvert the particular narrative of Englishness

---

[5] Carolyn Steedman, *Past Tenses: Essays on Writing, Autobiography and History* (London: Rivers Oram Press, 1992), p. 22.

that Morton worked with.[6] It is these works I shall examine in the following section in order to investigate the links between gender, race and nation that have led me to refuse to belong to *any* national collectivity.

Both H.V. Morton and Sylvia Townsend Warner were writing in the 1920s, though in different genres and with different target audiences in mind. Morton's primary designation was as a journalist and travel writer, writing about England, Wales, Scotland, Ireland and his Middle Eastern travels, whereas Townsend Warner committed herself principally to 'literary' writing, in the forms of fiction and poetry. For all Morton's supposed love of England, he actually left to live in white supremacist South Africa, where he died in 1979. Townsend Warner, however, was a politically committed writer, using her writing skills to bring to public attention, for example, the horrors of the Spanish Civil War. Although born and brought up in Harrow she spent a large part of her adult life in a Dorset village with her lover, Valentine Ackland. However, for all Morton's travels, it is striking how his own starting/leaving point continues to be London. When Morton decides to go in search of 'England', his starting/leaving point is London. The problem of locating Englishness in London for Morton is both one of sight and race. London cannot be seen in its entirety, but even if it could, there is the tricky problem of the non-Anglo-Saxon inhabitants from the colonies, and the Jews. To find England, then, one has to leave this degenerate, industrial, and racially impure urban space. Travelling around London inevitably forces an acknowledgement of the presence of 'the other': that is, the colonized subjects of the British Empire present in the metropolis. Morton's visit to Limehouse prompts these musings:

> As I walked on through dark streets, it seemed impossible that the restaurant I had left, with its elegant women, its discreet string orchestra, its air of assured comfort and well-being, could exist in the same world with these gloomy avenues, like a slum in hell, through which shivering lascars shuffled, hugging the shadows, while Chinamen peered with mask faces and sharp eyes from dim doorways.
>
> The squalor of Limehouse is that strange squalor of the East which seems to conceal vicious splendour. There is an air of something unrevealed in those narrow streets of shuttered houses, each one of which appears to be hugging its own dreadful little secret.[7]

Here, Englishness is located in *class*: a visible, white middle class which goes to restaurants. It is open, genteel, ordered, clean and comfortable: everything,

6 H.V. Morton, *In Search of England* [1927] (London: Metheun, 1930), *The Call of England* [1928] (London: Metheun, 1933) and Sylvia Townsend Warner, *Lolly Willowes or The Loving Huntsman* [1926] (London: Virago Press, 1995). All further page references to this last text will be given after quotations in the text.

7 H.V. Morton, *H.V. Morton's London: being The Heart of London, The Spell of London and The Nights of London in one volume* [1925 and 1926] (London: Metheun, 1941), p. 335.

indeed, that the abject, shadowy world of the Lascar and Chinaman is not. However, this Englishness is also emphatically masculine: women are peripheral. As decorative background objects they passively form part of the cultural distinction – the discretion, comfort and elegance of the restaurant.

Unable to use his penetrative vision to reveal the secrets of Limehouse, Morton has to catch a bus back to more 'English' areas of London, just as he does after a visit to Berwick Street where '[i]f all the Jews in Berwick Street would wear long false beards one day, it would be possible to take a photograph which any short-sighted traveller would swear was Jerusalem'.[8] Similarly a trip to Petticoat Lane necessitates catching a 'penny omnibus *back* to England'.[9] His London is built up of pockets of England surrounded by other areas which are made profoundly *un-English* by their inhabitants. In his equation, a Lascar can never be equivalent to an Englishman.

Positioning his readers as sharing a 'common racial heritage',[10] Morton suggests that whilst the 'average city family has disappeared into racial anaemia'[11] racial survival dictates a return to the countryside in order to maintain England as 'a *virile* and progressive nation'.[12] However, the virility of the nation is firmly rooted in a feminized English soil. Arriving in Glastonbury, which Morton identifies as containing the 'roots' of England, he sees 'the pregnant dust of Avalon'.[13] Unlike London, Morton's rural space is visible, ordered, knowable and racially pure, rather like his restaurant. This allows the inscription of a homogeneous Englishness in the face of the problematically disordered and degenerative capital city.

In a rhetoric which valorizes women for the reproduction of more national subjects Morton simultaneously suggests that women cannot ever really be national subjects themselves. On the one hand 'a lone man is transitory and woman is permanent: she means a home and a whole lot more men': her womb guarantees the continuation of Englishness.[14] Women here are the conduit for nationhood, but only via the production of more men. Women are further denied national identity by Morton's view of them as an international commodity that can be sold or traded. Although acknowledging racial differences *between men* of different nationalities, when travelling in Wales Morton concludes that 'Welshwomen are no different from the women of any other nationality'.[15]

The idea of women as commodities can be seen in his view of London, which is populated by markets 'where you could sell an elephant, a werewolf, or your

---

8 H.V. Morton, *H.V. Morton's London*, p. 216.
9 Ibid, p. 12 (my italics).
10 H.V. Morton, *In Search of England*, p. viii.
11 Ibid, p. x.
12 Ibid, p. ix (my italics).
13 Ibid, p. 132.
14 H.V. Morton, *H.V. Morton's London*, p. 50.
15 H.V. Morton, *In Search of Wales* [1932] (London: Metheun, 1947), p. 87.

second best aunt'.[16] The suburbs can be characterized by the way '[e]ach house contains the same lounge hall, the same Jacobean dining-room suite, the same (to all appearances) dear little wife who, now that the weather has changed, goes out shopping in a nutria coat'.[17]

The desire to shop has two main implications for Morton's view of Englishwomen's subjectivity. Firstly,women do not really enjoy rural spaces. In the country 'a woman grows restless and begins to sigh for shops and cinemas and crowds. It's only natural, after all'.[18] This desire to shop, is for Morton, troublingly paradoxical since 'to desire' implies a subjectivity. This desire offends Morton's logic and sensibility so much that women must be both restrained and blamed. Moreover, women's uncontrolled shopping habits can be seen to bring ruin to English*men* since fashions constantly change. Women are thus to blame for the decline of the jet carving industry in Whitby, the Hull whaling industry (because they will no longer wear corsets made from whalebone), and the Birmingham gold industry, which has been '[s]lain by women all over the world'.[19] Morton ascribes enormous power here to women, but it may be a distaste for what he views as women's unregulated desires, and an implicit call to regulate women more thoroughly. If 'authentic' Englishness is to be found in the rural rather than the urban, to position women as 'naturally' wanting the urban in order to be able to shop associates them with degeneracy, un-Englishness, and the possibility of miscegenation. Also women's uncontrolled desires, manifested in their whimsical shopping habits which can destroy men's jobs and the craft industries of Old England, suggest a treacherousness to certain ideals of Englishness based on 'organic communities' organized around craft production. Women's unregulated desires can lead to the destruction of Englishness rather than its production. In the destruction of material products and services that bear the label 'Made-in-England', women are also destroying the immaterial, cultural notion of 'England' that these products signify.

Significantly, it is in Morton's London that women are at their most uncontrollable and abject. Watching a street fight between a woman who has discovered her husband with another woman, instead of censuring the behaviour of the adulterous husband , he is prompted to muse :

> An uncontrolled woman is terrible as the spirit of vengeance. I watched her and wondered how many calm women boil like this yet never spill over, never show it, never allow themselves the luxury of this. How many gentle women have this tiger hidden in them ?[20]

---

16 H.V. Morton, *H.V. Morton's London*, p. 43.
17 Ibid, p. 195.
18 H.V. Morton, *In Search of Scotland* [1929] (London: Metheun, 1984), p. 222.
19 H.V. Morton, *The Call of England*, p. 196.
20 H.V. Morton, *H.V. Morton's London*, p. 169.

His answer seems to be 'probably all women', and that it is only ownership and regulation by men that prevents the terrifying slide into non-feminine grotesqueness and vagrancy.

> Dull, mercifully comatose, Nobody's Women drag themselves about the streets at night looking for a place to rest their unwanted bones. Sometimes you see them creeping like ghouls round the galvanised tins which the restaurants put outside in the streets in the small hours of the morning, digging into the foul rejections of other people's dinners with poor, claw-like fingers which once – who knows? – were lovely and white round the stem of a champagne glass.[21]

By contrast, Morton's men are not in need of control and ownership because when a man is unowned, when '[n]o woman ruffles his smooth life', it is then that English masculine 'Good Form' can be achieved.[22] It is in a state of rural solitude that an Englishman becomes most heroic:'How much of Hamlet, how much of Quixote, how much of Robin Goodfellow is in him never appears until a man finds himself alone in the country'.[23] However, within Morton's rhetoric a man never does find himself alone in the country, because his masculinity is always counterpointed against a feminized, and often pregnant or maternal, natural landscape. This femininity, however, is more easily controllable than that of women's, since it can be landscaped or farmed, for example, without talking back.

Morton organizes his whole world-view around what he sees as the foundational categories of masculine and feminine, and cannot seem to envisage a non-heterosexualized space. His writing on 'cities' or 'cathedrals' thus frequently describes them as 'married' to one another, or bound together in some other heterosexual familial relationship. In a formulation which excludes women except as metaphor, Morton ends *In Search of England* with a description of his heterosexual, masculine love for England as feminine soil, as a summation of his search for England.

> The rich earth had borne its children, and over the fields was that same smile which a man sees only on the face of a woman when she looks down at the child at her breast.
>
> I went out into the churchyard where the green stones nodded together, and I took up a handful of earth and felt it crumble and run through my fingers, thinking that as long as one English field lies against another there is something left in the world for a man to love.[24]

---

21 Ibid, p. 232.
22 Ibid, p. 171.
23 H.V. Morton, *The Call of England*, p. 2.
24 H.V. Morton, *In Search of England*, p. 280.

Just as *In Search of England* ends with a final expression of an Englishman relating to English earth, so too does *The Call of England.*

> And there will come a time in any tour of England when most men from a city will feel that no matter how life disappoints them there can always be one thing worth while at the end of the journey: the sight of the wind moving over their own wheat field; the moon rising over their own home; the knowledge that they have fought their way back to the country and have planted their feet in the splendid sanity of English soil.[25]

The sanity of his feminine soil is in sharp contrast to the *in*sanity of his shopaholic Englishwomen. However, just as man roots himself in soil, so too does soil root itself back into 'the hearts of men',[26] making nationalism a warm thing in the face of *inter*nationalism, because, Morton argues,'[h]ow can we achieve a cold internationalism when to each one of us there is a little piece of the world so dear that we would not exchange the wide earth for it?'.[27] Again, women are excluded from this version of national identity as a bonding of man and soil, because women are international commodities. Most chillingly, though, he presents the nationalist project as:

> Something which no outsider can know: that sense of kinship with the hills, that knowledge of belonging to something infinitely good and enduring, a feeling of possession and being possessed; in other words that irrational emotion which has spilt so much of the earth's best blood – love of home.[28]

It is this notion of 'belonging' that I repudiate: one that is built on exclusions of the 'bad' and inclusions of the 'good' that has led to warfare in the past, and can easily in the future. Morton's particular belonging is based on white racial supremacy in which white women are charged with reproducing both the 'English' race and its cultural values.[29] His discursive construction of Englishness assumes that women must be reproductively controlled by men in order that they can be as fully 'national' as possible. Only through heterosexual relations and heterosexual reproduction can women derive a relationship to the nation, and that is second-hand through their husbands, fathers or grandparents. Outside that control and purpose women are a dangerous, potentially divisive 'excess'.

If women have only a second-hand relationship to the nation through heterosexuality, lesbians are therefore doubly excluded as non-heterosexual women. But

---

25 H.V. Morton, *The Call of England*, p. 205.

26 H.V. Morton, *In Search of Ireland* (London: Metheun, 1930), p. 266.

27 Ibid, p. 266.

28 Ibid, p. 266.

29 See Nira Yuval-Davis, *Gender and Nation* (London: Sage Publications, 1997) for a discussion of the ways women are charged not just with reproducing the nation through childbirth, but also through cultural reproduction.

I am glad there is no place for me in the nation. To paraphrase Virginia Woolf from her 1938 *Three Guineas*, as a lesbian I have no country, as a lesbian I want no country. However as a lesbian I don't want either to colonize the world in the way that Woolf's words might suggest when she says from the standpoint of white western feminism that as 'a woman my country is the whole world'.[30] Why should I want to reproduce the class, gender and race distinctions that the nation relies on for its heterosexual ordering? Carving up national spaces causes terrible outrages. I cannot think of devolution in Britain without reflecting on other parts of Europe or Africa which are similarly 'devolving'. These situations lay bare what nationalist projects entail for women in terms of rape, forced pregnancies and 'ethnic cleansing'. Belgrade 'Women In Black' report that their anti-war demonstrations for peace have led to them being labelled as 'agents provocateurs for the mondialism, recruited for peanuts by our European enemies among the lesbian and similar organisations'. The proof, apparently, 'is in their evident ugliness, the recognizable sign for such sexual pathology'.[31] Although there is no place for the lesbian in a nationalist project, when women break with the nation the charge of lesbianism is thrown at them, revealing the nation's dependence on heterosexuality and its co-option of the womb. Lesbian women are in a double bind in relation to nation: as non-heterosexual women they cannot be controlled by men and thus become 'half-national', and as lesbians they cannot figure as national subjects since nations are heterosexual constructs. Moreover, within the polemic against 'Women in Black' there is a deeply held belief that women cannot act with autonomy. If their actions are anti-national the assumption is that they must be controlled from elsewhere. Women In Black are frequently asked 'Who is behind you?'.[32] So can a woman ever be an autonomous national subject? Can a lesbian ever be part of the nation?

Warner's England: 'a witch made free'

The next text I want to examine is *Lolly Willowes or the Loving Huntsman* because it seems to deal with these questions in relation to England and Englishness. This is a text that attempts to lesbianize Englishness through undoing relations of male homosociality which are sanctioned by a Xtian god, causing the text to turn to Satanic relations in order to inscribe lesbian desire.[33] If women officially derive

---

30 Virginia Woolf, *A Room Of One's Own and Three Guineas* (Oxford: Oxford University Press), p. 313.

31 Women For Peace, 'We Are Still In The Streets' in Stasa Zajovic, ed., *Zene Za Mir/Women For Peace* (Belgrade: Women in Black, 1995), p. 6.

32 Ibid, p. 7.

33 See Terry Castle, *The Apparitional Lesbian: Female Homosexuality and Modern Culture* (New York: Columbia University Press, 1993). The chapter entitled 'Sylvia Townsend Warner and the counterplot of lesbian fiction' has provided a model for

Englishness through heterosexuality, then the English lesbian is an oxymoron. Given Edward Said's claim that 'the corpus formed by works of literature belongs to, gains coherence from, and in a sense emanates out the concepts of nation' how can this nationally incoherent figure of the lesbian be inscribed?[34] How does the text go about disturbing Englishness enough to begin to inscribe lesbian desire? I would like to suggest three main ways in which the text disrupts Englishness. Firstly, in terms of form: the plot configurations and reconfigurations undo the male homosociality of Englishness which supports the construction of the Englishwoman's heterosexual subjectivity. Secondly, in terms of characterization: authentically rural, homogeneous Englishness is disrupted to make the village full of witches, warlocks and gender-bending Satanists! Thirdly, in terms of locational politics: the text refuses to locate Englishness in geographical place, but instead locates it in cultural value and in language.

Terry Castle summarizes Eve Kosofsky Sedgwick's thesis from *Between Men: English Literature and Male Homosocial Desire*[35] thus:

> Just as patriarchal culture has traditionally been organized around a ritualized 'traffic' in women – the legal, economic, religious, and sexual exchange of women between men (as in the cherished institutions of heterosexual love and marriage) – so the fictions produced within patriarchal culture have tended to mimic, or represent, the same triangular structure.[36]

Kinship systems lie in an exchange of women between men, with marriage as the most basic form of gift exchange. Women are the gift, transacted between the men who give and take them, so that women are a channel of a relationship between men, rather than a partner to it. So if women belong to men, this becomes Laura Willowes's problem. How can she dispose of herself within her English kinship system in which, on the death of her father, she is passed between brothers, and in which even her young nephew believes he has the right to occupy the private space she carves out for herself in the village of Great Mop?

Formally the text is split into three parts. The first part is concerned with Laura Willowes's childhood and young adulthood in the Dorset countryside. As her father's housekeeper in their country house, Lady Place, he has no desire to give her away in marriage because her company is convenient to him. When he dies she

---

my reading of *Lolly Willowes* as a lesbian fiction through the example of *Summer Will Show* that Terry Castle uses.

34 Edward Said, cited in Simon During, 'Literature – nationalism's other? The case for revision' in Homi K. Bhabha, ed., *Nation and Narration* (London: Routledge, 1990), p. 138.

35 Eve Kosofsky Sedgwick, *Between Men: English Literature and Male Homosocial Desire* (New York: Columbia University Press, 1992).

36 Terry Castle, *The Apparitional Lesbian*, p. 68.

is disposed of between her brothers, as much a piece of family property as the furniture. Moving to London to live with one brother's family to help with their girl children she resists family attempts to marry her off. At this point she resists marriage, but not the homosocial triangle in which one brother gives her to the other.

The second part of the text is concerned with Laura's attempt to dispose of her own life as an older woman spinster and it is through privacy rather than political power that Laura seeks to escape her oppression as a woman. When her nieces are grown she begins to live a secret life in London and, significantly, through her sense of smell which is sensual yet invisible to any onlooker she experiences an epiphany whilst buying chrysanthemums. At this moment her thoughts and desires turn not to men, but to women as occupying a glorious space where she might find her freedom.

> Laura looked at the bottled fruits, the sliced pears in syrup, the glistening red plums, the greengages. She thought of the woman who had filled those jars and fastened on the bladders. Perhaps the greengrocer's mother lived in the country. A solitary old woman picking fruit in a darkening orchard, rubbing her rough fingertips over the smooth-skinned plums, a lean wiry old woman, standing with upstretched arms among her fruit trees as though she were a tree herself, growing out of the long grass, with arms stretched out like branches. It grew darker and darker; still she worked on, methodically stripping the quivering taut boughs one after the other. (p. 83)

It is at this point that lesbian desire begins to be inscribed. This shift in Laura's imagination in which the woman working on the tree becomes a tree, suggests that the quivering boughs which the old woman strips could be another woman. Against all convention, an older woman is described as beautiful, and a different erotic economy is offered in which one woman views and touches another with pleasure. Out of this imaginary scene, Laura decides to move to the country on her own in order to know, or become, this woman. In this, Laura attempts to reconfigure the triangular relationships in her life by putting herself in central place, and refusing men the power to dispose of her. In Great Mop she makes a relationship with another woman (her landlady, Mrs Leak) of utmost importance. Spending long days wandering through the countryside thinking back over the miserable life she has led, she experiences another great change by smelling cowslips. Through their scent all her misery is released, and she decides that her family is not to blame for the oppressive life she has lived and that :

> If she were to start forgiving she needs must forgive Society, the Law, the Church, the History of Europe, the Old Testament, great-great aunt Salome and her prayer book, the Bank of England, Prostitution, the Architect of Apsley Terrace, and half a dozen other useful props of civilisation. (p. 150)

All these things are implicated in her oppression as an Englishwoman. However, she cannot escape the patriarchal family in Great Mop as the second part ends with the news that her nephew, Titus, sole male heir to Lady Place, has decided to come and live in the village with her.

The third part of the novel is concerned with Laura's attempt to reconfigure her relationships by getting rid of Titus with the help of Satan. Titus has re-made a triangular relationship by inserting himself between Laura and Mrs Leak. This spoils both Laura's relationship with Mrs Leak, who will no longer talk to her, and Laura's relationship with the land, as the 'spirit of the place' withdraws from her. To secure her freedom all social relations have to be shaken up, and the witches' Sabbath to which Mrs Leak finally invites Laura, is central to this. All classes from the village participate in a ritual in which the rules of English polite behaviour are jettisoned; heterosexuality also no longer applies since it does not matter whether one's partner is male or female, or upper or lower class. Laura, who has never enjoyed dancing at County Balls with upper class men, finds it thrilling to dance with a lower class woman. This rejection of heterosexuality also appears to lead to a rejection of class distinctions.

> Laura liked dancing with Emily; the pasty faced and anaemic young slattern whom she had seen dawdling about the village danced with a fervour that annihilated every misgiving. They whirled faster and faster, fused together like two suns that whirl and blaze in a single destruction. A strand of red hair came undone and brushed across Laura's face. The contact made her tingle from head to foot. She shut her eyes and dived into obliviousness – with Emily as a partner she could dance until the gunpowder ran out of the heels of her boots. (pp. 192–3)

Emily and Mrs Leak present Laura to someone whom she believes to be Satan. The two women give her rather as a gift exchange in which they bond as women witches. This represents a reversal of the male homosocial bonding in which Laura is given as a gift between brothers. Moreover, this 'Satan' is neither particularly masculine, nor English. At first glance Laura thinks he looks like a Chinaman in his mask, and his movements suggest a certain effeminacy:

> Mincing like a girl, the masked young man approached her, and as he approached the others drew back and left her alone. With secretive and undulating movements he came to her side. (p. 200)

However his touch is repugnant to her, unlike the touch of Emily, and she leaves the Sabbath. After all the social relations of Englishness have been disturbed, Satan helps Laura to get rid of Titus, and the third part ends with the formation of a new triangular relationship between Mrs Leak, Laura and Satan. All the old male homosocial relations are also destroyed. So the first way in which lesbian desire begins to be inscribed is through this destruction of English relations of male homosociality such that Laura and Emily can whirl and blaze into obliviousness together, and women can bond with one another. The second way that Englishness is disturbed enough to write the figure of the lesbian is through a refusal of dominant ideas of the rural as authentically English. This is central to my third point: that the text refuses to locate Englishness in place, but instead locates it in language.

Although the text does not use experimental language, Laura's language does shift, and the text is wry on the subject of naming and definition. The village named Great Mop, with all its connotations of liquidly messy, feminine, domestic work, is valorized above the genteel country house, Lady Place. In Great Mop, a woman may become god-like: the living-room fire casts shadows such that '[w]hen Mrs Leak smoothed her apron the shadow solemnified the gesture as though she were moulding an universe' (p. 118). In Lady Place, a woman counts for very little, unless she is ensuring patriarchal inheritance through sons. As a non-reproductive spinster, Laura cannot inherit that version of England. But Laura is two people, in that the narrator and Satan call her 'Laura', whereas her family refer to her as 'Lolly'. These two referents are productive of different subjectivities, such that 'when Laura went to London she left Laura behind and entered into a state of Aunt Lolly' (p. 61). However, the text makes clear that simple re-naming will not achieve freedom for women, nor allow the lesbian to be 'written'. Language does not necessarily correspond to woman's reality, and the map and guide book which have led Laura to Great Mop are ultimately useless to her in producing knowledge of the village. She throws them down a well in order to directly apprehend the village without any mediation through language. For Laura, it is not just the naming (or mapping) in language that is wrong, but the values ascribed to these namings. So, the whole system of values in language has to be reorganized in order that the cultural values of Englishness also shift. Laura is clear that English culture is against women and needs reorganizing. 'Custom, public opinion, law, church and state – all would have shaken their massive heads against her plea, and sent her back to bondage' (p. 220). Witchcraft is then offered as the way for women, and Satan does in fact come to her aid, seeing women in a different light than the Xtian god of the Church of England. The devil so loves women he will hunt down a woman's soul. As Laura tells him:

> And think, Satan, what a compliment you pay her, pursuing her soul, lying in wait for it, following it through all its windings, crafty and patient and secret like a gentleman out killing tigers. Her soul – when no one else would give a look at her body even! (pp. 237–8)

Since it is only he that values women, not the Xtian god, Satan has to be revalued in such a way that institutions of church and state lose value, thereby remaking relations of class, gender, and race. Only when this has happened does Laura come to speech, and it is striking how voluble she is when talking to Satan compared to her previous pauciloquence. As a child, and as a woman in the home of her brother's family she is mainly silent, although when she does speak, her speech is often disruptive. However, at the Witches' Sabbath language 'breaks down', and Laura loses understanding: 'voices addressed her, but she did not understand what was said' (p. 199). Only after this breakdown is Laura finally able to clearly describe her oppression as an Englishwoman to Satan in a way that she could not while god was an organizing principle for her Englishness. Her last conversation with Satan reveals that it is not the dichotomy between country and city that she has to escape in order to change the ways in which Englishness constructs her. Although it might appear that Warner's novel links Satanic misrule with rural paganism, later sections of the text make clear that Satan's presence is alive in the city as it is in the country:

> The goods yard at Paddington, for instance – a savage place! as holy and enchanted as it had ever been. Not one of those monuments and tinkerings of all the neat human nest-boxes in rows, Balham and Fulham and the Cromwell Road – he saw through them, they went flop like cardhouses, the bricks were earth again, and the steel girders burrowed shrieking into the veins of the earth, and the dead timber was restored to the ghostly groves. (pp. 230–1)

Englishness is not located in a mythical countryside, but in the cultural relations played out through language and discourse. Laura's salvation, and the possibility of inscribing lesbian desire, thus lies in reconfiguring that which the nation values. In this way, Englishness is destroyed since it depends for its existence on empire, church, state, the architect of Apsley Terrace, and heterosexuality. By the end of the novel the nation is dead for Laura, because it literally has '*no place*', neither geographically nor in the language system. Being older than the nation, Satan is witness to this:

> His memory was too long, too retentive; there was no appeasing its witness, no hoodwinking it with the present; and that was why at one stage of civilisation people said he was the embodiment of all evil, and then a little later on that he didn't exist. (p. 245)

Satan has helped Laura to demolish the tropes of the virile nation that Morton celebrates, by acknowledging her as a human subject with agency. Morton's women are not subjects, but objects. The fact that a non-reproductive older woman is valuable disrupts his grammar of the nation. As the Cromwell Road houses 'go flop' when Satan sees through them, so, too, do the gender, class and race distinctions of Morton's England. There is no locating of the countryside as 'authentically English', and possessed by men because women want the urban for shopping. In fact, when Christmas comes, Laura finds the few things available in the village shop quite adequate as presents. Morton's valorization of the countryside is undermined by Satan's vision which helps Laura to understand the city as correspondingly holy. Unlike Morton, Satan is disinterested in regulating women: he is indifferent to what Laura might do. She is neither obliged to maintain class or race distinctions, nor to act heterosexually to please him. Satan's earth is ungendered, and his relationship to it is non-possessive. This refusal of masculine possession of a feminized earth, such as Morton utilizes, has knock-on effects for women in this Satanic world view. Divorcing national earth from femininity entails a corresponding dissociation of women from conventional national and heterosexual 'femininity'. This Satan thus can be queerly imagined.[37] At the village Sabbath, Satan ritually appears in the form of a masked human man, and the villagers are happy to conceive of him as a mincing Chinaman. But he is not the real Satan, only a performance of him. The real Satan is far behind the mask, appearing to Laura variously in the guise of gamekeeper, gardener and gravekeeper, but still queerly refusing any categorization.

Although by the end of Warner's text the nation is dead for Laura through Satan's help, I would like to suggest that this disruption of Englishness goes only part way toward the inscription of the lesbian, since the text ends with Laura deciding to sleep in a ditch, undisturbed by Satan, but nonetheless in the context of 'his satisfied but profoundly indifferent ownership' (p. 247). This final inscription of woman as 'mastered' suggests the possibility of her co-option back into Englishwomanhood, and because Laura has not yet wrested herself away from all male control she cannot be called lesbian. This highlights the difficulty inherent in private and personal solutions rather than social ones, because although Laura has achieved liberation, her liberation has not touched the lives of other women: her sisters-in-law or nieces, for example, who still act out English middle-class womanhood. So where might she go from here? Should she become a Satanic evangelist, or might that lead women into the cul-de-sac of 'indifferent ownership'? Or should Satan be rejected, if he cannot give up ownership of 'his' people? Perhaps she herself should become a beacon for an alternative community which does not depend on geographical location and cuts across racial and class lines in order that the heterosexual national economy can be more permanently disrupted.

Lesbian Nation?

My chosen texts, written in the 1920s, but seen through the lens of both my 1950s childhood and my changing (and changeable) adult consciousness have helped me explore an identity built on refusal of the discursive connection between 'nation' and 'woman'. Morton's official Englishness is repugnant to me in its woman-

---

[37] Further discussion of how queer theory may be used to dislocate nationhood is to be found in Richard Phillips, David Shuttleton and Diane Watt, eds, *Decentring Sexualities* (London and New York: Routledge, 2000).

hating, arrogance toward the non-English, and its smug middle-class positioning. However, *Lolly Willowes*, which I first read in the late 1970s, seems to offer a more powerful way of being a woman through its repudiation of Xtianity, and its adoption of witchcraft. Like many heterosexual and lesbian feminists of that time, I trained in the Craft and took on the identity of a 'witch' (although not through a relationship to Satan). The lesbian subtext of witchcraft was not apparent to me until I studied it in the 1980s as a lesbian 'academic', when I had hung up my pointy black hat in exchange for a mortar board. *Lolly Willowes* was thus instrumental in my becoming an academic, an identity which seems to me profoundly un-English, since the English are reputed to be so full of common-sense that they do not need to think. I only ever read H.V. Morton as an academic, attempting to understand the discursive relationship between nation and hetero/sexuality. His refusal of national identity to women became a conflict in my own identity about the difference between 'woman' and 'lesbian'. Hidden in his construction of Englishness as a bond between men and soil, *In Search of England* ends with Morton viewing with love a profoundly lesbian moment in which one 'feminine' English field lies against another (see note 24). So were the 1920s and 1930s a period which paradoxically engendered a distinction between 'women' and 'lesbians'? Since his version of Englishness was not available to heterosexual women (save as its source of reproduction), did it inadvertently become productive of lesbian discourse? For me, this relates to the problematic in my own identity. My identity as lesbian is not in doubt, but am I a woman? Monique Wittig has argued that '[l]esbians are not women'[38] since lesbian

> Is the only concept I know of which is beyond the categories of sex (woman and man), because the designated subject (lesbian) is *not* a woman, either economically, or politically, or ideologically. For what makes a woman is a specific social relation to a man ...[39]

Thus, when I see women (and feminists) argue on behalf of nations – however 're-imagined' or 'devolved' – I wonder what they are guarding and whether I, as a lesbian, can have any commonality with them. Why should they argue for structures that will ensure the continuation of the category 'woman'? Are they therefore guarding themselves *from* me? Do women really want to create territories based on shared ethnicities (all be they 'imagined') underpinned by the repressive forces of race, class and heterosexuality? What oppressive structures of power are such women allying themselves to? How can I go along with such desires?

---

38 Monique Wittig, *The Straight Mind and other essays* (New York: Harvester Wheatsheaf, 1992), p. 32.

39 Ibid, p. 20 (italics as original).

If the 1950s were murky, and the 1960s too bright, then I can only picture the late 1990s and beyond through the image of the eclipse of the sun.[40] Heavenly bodies make carnival in the sky: the sun becomes a little crescent moon that performs acrobatic tricks, twisting and turning. Both sun and moon have lost their former identities, locations, and the relation between them that we thought we knew, but neither are lost. Certainties turn indistinct, and in the gloomy night-in-day new spaces and possibilities emerge from the change in perspective viewing an eclipse entails. If identity is a function of desire, understood through difference, then I can only return to the London of my childhood for a model. Although it is a capital city, London never figured as 'representing the nation' in the way that the Home Counties, for example, did (and do). It exemplifies for me how a non-national space might be imagined: queerly multitudinous with more interest in 'difference' than in 'identity'.

Acknowledgements

For their help with the writing of this chapter, I would like to thank Hilary Hinds, Kym Martindale and Lynne Pearce, and most especially, Helen Udo-Affia.

40 Parts of the 'United Kingdom' experienced a total eclipse of the sun on 11 August 1999, and a partial eclipse was visible from many places.

Chapter 4

Traversing Britain: Mobility, Belonging and Home

Ruth McElroy

Introduction

Four corners, four nations, four tales of traversing Britain:

> It had been a long tiring journey to the pink room, traversing England on an intrepid train called the *Cornish Scot*. Knowing both races to be fiercely patriotic, Chloe denounced the name a contradiction in terms. Surely you were either Scottish or Cornish; Land's End or John O'Groat's, one extreme or the other, north or south, top of the land or base of it – and she should know, she was stuck on a train bumbling along its length. As the train moseyed from Lancaster to Crewe, she rued her own lack of identity.
>
> *Could I not be Scottish, with my red hair and passable accent?*
>
> Sorry, Chloe, you've had the misfortune not to be born one.
>
> *Should I search for the place first? And then something to do. Or should I find my metier – and then a suitable location to practise it?*
>
> Can't tell you that.
>
> With the Midlands uninspiringly upon her and the train glued to the track two minutes out of Birmingham New Street, she knew she had no desire to be a Brummy. Cheltenham Spa, however, looked rather promising; she could teach young ladies. By Newton Abbot she was asleep; awake with a cricked neck at Bodmin and feeling quite beastly.[1]

> Rosa Luxembourg Kendrew always loved the moment when she drove across the border from Cardiganshire or Carmarthenshire and was greeted by the county border sign, SIR BENFRO, PEMBROKESHIRE. Rosie saw Sir Benfro as a fat, robustious, moustachioed baronet, Falstaffian, Rabelasian, a 'soldier who was better accommodated': Sir B for beer, E for excess, N for nights, F for effing, R for roistering and O for the shape of his belly. Nor did the facts entirely challenge her loving fantasy. Her part of Pembrokeshire was the Welsh-speaking northern half of the county, beyond the Lansker Line, beyond the 'Little England' of the South, and she often felt that the men of North Pembrokeshire had somehow acquired most of

---

[1] Freya North, *Chloe* (London: Arrow Books, 1998), pp. 290–1. All further references to the novel are included in the text following the relevant quotation and are from this edition.

the attributes of 'that godly knight' almost as an act of defiance, in the teeth of the prissy Englishness of the South of the county, where to be Welsh was to be damned. But, to be honest, the fact of the matter was that North Pembrokeshire had produced the best home-brewers of beer in the whole of a Principality lovingly devoted to drink. A Pembrokeshire beer belly had become almost axiomatic. And there was also in North Pembrokeshire a strange, endearing tolerance of debauchery and sexual licence, which was at violent variance with the rest of officially Non-Conformist Wales. It was Rosie's belief that this kindliness, this forgiveness, sprang from Fishguard, the port for vessels from the Irish Republic, and that North Pembrokeshire attitudes were only an extension of Irish mores, overriding the basic hell-fire intolerance of the traditional Welsh chapels. The uncomfortable adjuncts of this forgiveness – such as penances – had, of course, been dropped into the depths of the Irish Sea en route to Wales.[2]

Some months ago, I turned on the television to find a report on the closure of tin mines in Cornwall. It focused almost entirely on the viewpoint of men in Redruth – hardly a woman appeared in front of the camera. Asked what he thought of government support, or rather neglect, of Redruth, a former miner compared Cornwall as isolated and ignored in comparison with Wales. In particular, he cited not only development grants but roads – 'they have all those motorways', he said. Today, there is fierce competition for inward investment and talk is rife of absurd migrations such as Cornish cream manufacturers lured to South East Wales with the promise of extra grants. A marker of poverty, 'Objective One EU' status, has become, in many parts of the UK, a perverse cause for celebration. It is frightening to see how the global power of multinationals readily exploits 'the local'; how very malleable the devolutionary impulse is to the demands of late capitalism.

Watching this miner speak, I felt an intense sense of being brought home to a place which was genuinely new: a land of roads marked by privileged mobility. Rather than being characterized either by poverty, or by placing persistent demands on an English exchequer, Wales was here being set as a favoured nation, a space comparable to yet unfairly preferenced over Cornwall. The actual absence of 'lots of motorways' was secondary to my sense of regional identification in recognizing South Wales as the site traversed by connecting corridors: the M4 as a direct line from industrial decimation to metropolitan power. The road did not so much produce a concrete connection as it produced a symbolic representation of differential relationships to an economic, political centre distanced from both. A striking absence in this portrait, women's inhabitations of these national and regional homes, was figured only through that most familiar turn: the loss of male employment and an increase in women's paid work. As a potential site for migratory readings across national borders, the gendering of Cornish and Welsh society left me, and implicitly Cornish women, with nowhere to go but back into the home.

---

2 Menna Gallie, *In These Promiscuous Parts* (New York: Saint Martin's Press, 1986), pp. 3–4. All further references to the novel are included in the text following the relevant quotation and are from this edition.

> Since September, I have been teaching at a small college in a predominantly Welsh speaking areas of Wales. During the Easter vacation, I walked into the campus Waterstone's planning to order books but found myself at a loss in this suddenly transformed space. Where previously the tables had displayed an array of texts – literary, critical, historical – they now offered a casebook of Welsh imagery akin to those on display in tourist centres. My initial reaction was to see this as yet another instance of supposed Welsh inauthenticity: putting books on tables as an instance of 'putting it on'; as natural as yet another Welsh plot to fool an English audience susceptible to the vagaries of national performances. But, as I quickly told myself, the effect of this had been to pull a few Welsh texts off the corners of academic shelves: what was always there was now more visible, cushioned between the glossy Celtica which apparently sells well. Popular works on myth, legends and cooking displaced the texts of American, English, Canadian, Caribbean, Irish, Scottish, Welsh and many other authors. It was as if the crossings of international literary texts would break the Celtic spell.
>
> In this hyper-display of Welshness – available for easy browsing – lay the disappearance of the everyday Welsh institution. Who could rely on such an easy grammar of Welshness as Celtica? In a place where English accents summon as much attention as the college chapel's bell, who could believe that it would be possible to be in this place and *not* be aware of its Welsh location, whatever and all that means. Whose eyes are set to see only this difference?

In the matter of belongings there seems to be altogether too much and not enough to say. In approaching the questions which this volume raises, I have found myself constantly turning to a citational structure of thought: to snippets of conversation, extracts of texts and anecdotes exchanged over coffee or dinner. At one stage it seemed as if this entire project would emerge as a series of carefully chosen quotations barely interspersed with a few words of my own. That this is so is indicative of the composite and often clamorous nature of the stories we tell of with whom and to where we belong. My reluctance to produce a single voice, a narrative solely authored by myself, might not suit the conventional demands of academic research, but it does, I think, reflect the impossibility of writing a single story, an authoritative account of one's belongings which are given shape and meaning only through others. Telling stories in the UK-wide context of this volume, I am also concerned to not be cornered by the possible demand to 'represent' Wales, to figure its complexity in my own guise. In too many anthologies and edited collections, Welsh, Northern Irish and Scottish contributors stand as lone figures, denied the clamorous voices which shape our different contexts.

The above quotations stand as episodic exemplars from both literary texts and my own experience. What they share is that they are all contemporary narratives which centre on women's narration of mobility in a cross-cultural 'British' context. Rather than be material for close readings, they are offered as compass points which act both to introduce and to provide evidence of the main themes of this chapter: the ways in which national and regional belongings in Wales and Britain are cited and negotiated through the narration of travel. From the seeming oxymoron of the Cornish Scot chundling its way along the west coast to the sight of books magically migrating to attractive displays, what these episodes demonstrate is the central role of mobility in the stories we tell of our belongings.

This chapter aims to trace some of the migratory narratives which are today one of the main frames through which Britain is fabricated, sustained and resisted. That mobility, travel and journeying constantly re-appear in our discussions of these islands is not a new phenomenon. From early modern narratives of colonial exploration to Romantic travelogues of wild Wales to Matthew Arnold's Celticist imagination (and lectures tours), Britain has emerged as a cross-cultural meeting point shaped by uneven and multi-layered relations of power. In taking mobility as my frame, I seek to traverse the often bounded narrative categories of British and English imperialism, mass migration and the ebb and flow of English, Northern Irish, Scottish and Welsh migrants across one another's borders. I want to insist that the question of UK belongings can only be fully appreciated when we keep in mind how the shifting relationships between the four nations occurs alongside the transformation of the UK from an imperial power to a multi-racial state. Remarkably little detailed attention has been paid to how these two challenges to nineteenth-century notions of imperial Britain intersect and affect one another. Yet the fact that Paul Gilroy's famous claim that 'there ain't no black in the union jack' occurs in the same period as the 'union jack' is being dismantled into its constituent parts, is surely significant.[3]

However, I am equally concerned with an understanding of mobility as the daily movements – physical, cultural and linguistic – of subjects in their everyday lives. All subjects negotiate mobility in Britain, regardless of whether or not they themselves travel great distances or consider themselves migrants. Mobility is not the preserve of the happily mobile, should not be seen purely as the voluntary acts of individuals. Mobility is inscribed in the rhetoric of Tory and Labour government demands to 'get on your bike', in the practices of state benefit offices which shunt the homeless across county and borough borders, in the advertising claims of multinational businesses such as Microsoft and its rhetoric of unlimited travel along the internet highway. The anticipation of movement marks the subjectivities and belongings of the inhabitants of these islands even as the majority live within a close radius of their place of upbringing.

When oppositions are drawn between residency and mobility, between rootedness and migration, the border crossings we undertake within our own square miles are concealed and eradicated. As the second of the tales cited above most clearly demonstrates, journeys within a relatively small geographical area resonate with, and are formed through, their relationship to a whole range of other

3 Paul Gilroy, *There Ain't no Black in the Union Jack: the Cultural Politics of Race and Nation* (London: Hutchinson, 1987).

'crossings', real and imagined. The inter-related nature of our mobilities, their heterogeneity and multiplicity, is then the methodological frame through which I shall explore the question of belongings.

But what do I mean when I title this chapter 'traversing Britain'? According to my dictionary, to traverse is an elastic verb, able to stretch to multiple meanings:

> To pass or go over or back and forth over something, to cross; to go against, oppose, obstruct; to move or cause to move sideways or crosswise; to extend or reach across; to look over or examine carefully; to deny (an allegation of fact).[4]

Traversing Britain signifies the realities and politics of crossing Britain, of passing over across and against it, of examining it, denying its existence as a coherent entity which can demand my/our loyalty, allegiance or engender outright belonging. It signifies the crossed nature of these islands: their sidelong and uneven relations across shifting borders. To traverse Britain is to recognize Britain's instability as constitutive. It is to recognize that Britain, especially as the site of national allegiance, is only the allegation of a fact, the veracity of which many of us doubt even as we experience its force. Britain, as the early modern critic David Baker argues, 'is not an entity but an argument and British citizenship is oxymoronic'.[5] A British passport *both* bears the hallmarks of a privilege denied to many who ally themselves with Britain (as in the case of Hong Kong) *and* testifies to a collective suspension of disbelief: a willingness to adhere to the fiction of Britain as not quite a nation (there are so many) but not merely a state (we are after all subjects not citizens). Supposedly a clear document of one's place in the world, the British passport is a series of hypotheses and possibilities. It is a constant deferral of locations and affiliations which alone are insufficient to the task of locating the British subject:

European Community
United Kingdom of
Great Britain and Northern Ireland
Nationality: British Citizen
Authority: United Kingdom

This chapter is concerned to pose some central and enduring questions. It asks in what ways and for what reasons are British belongings so often expressed and explored through travel? In what ways does gender shape and not merely hamper women's mobilities? To what extent does devolution – as an 'event' as much as a structural change in political government – occasion a reappraisal of British

---

4 Definition taken from *Collins English Dictionary* (4th edition, 1998).

5 David Baker in dialogue with Willy Malley, 'An Uncertain Union' (paper given at Archipelagic Identities conference, 9–10 April 1999, Oxford).

journeys in the 'forging of the nation and the state'? What kind of a journey or narrative of travel is devolution? Can it really be reduced to a narrative of return, of governmental powers 'given back' like stolen gifts of marbles and stones? How does devolution re-centre England in the UK and does it continue the practice of seeing the other three nations in isolation from each other? If the response of many cynical English commentators is 'we're glad we can get rid of them', just where do the English think Britain has gone? Why did Britannia leave her home?

I shall now attempt to tackle some of these questions 'slant' by concentrating on the two literary texts cited above, Freya North's *Chloe* (1998) and Menna Gallie's *In These Promiscuous Parts* (1986). Both novels are based on the journeys of a single female protagonist, Chloe and Rosa (Rosie) respectively, and both aim to amuse and entertain. Where Chloe travels from London to Wales, Northern Ireland, Scotland and then Cornwall, Rosie's journey is between Oxford – her workplace – and her family home in West Wales. Perhaps the most striking contrast between them, is that where Chloe is very much the tale of a single traveller out to 'discover' the UK, *In These Promiscuous Parts* is a more social novel, interwoven as it is with the 'consciousness' of the many characters of the Welsh town. Published more than ten years apart, they are both 'popular' fictions which are shaped by the conventions of heterosexual romance. Whilst both are concerned with women's heterosexual passions, it is the journeys and consciousness of the single women protagonists which are at the centre of the novels. It is questionable whether either text could be described as 'feminist'. Nevertheless, both emerge from the contemporary history of feminist debate: 1990s American 'subject' orientated feminism, in the case of *Chloe*, and the materialist/Marxist tradition in the case of Gallie's novel with its aptly named heroine, Rosa Luxembourg Kendrew.[6] In drawing upon these two texts, I shall concentrate on three key areas: the role of 'mapping' in the narrative traversals of national, regional space; the role of social class in producing mobile subjects' sense of place, and the enduring force of the question of 'origins' within a cross-cultural framework of British belongings.

Unlearning the perspective of England[7]

One of the most enduring memories I have of school, are the frequent, repeated tracings we made of the outlines of Wales. By the end of my school days, I think I

6 The name extends the frame for the novel's concern with region, class and belonging both through reference to the German/Lithuanian socialist heroine but also through the narrator's claim that her father's 'un-Welsh name, Kendrew was a simple agricultural accident', the result of an extended sojourn in Wales which still left him with pride in 'his tincture of Scots ancestry' (p. 33).

7 This is an adaptation of Raymond Williams's reference to 'the learned

could have drawn a pretty accurate Welsh map, coastal and land borders in place, with my eyes shut. I wonder what makes for such knowledge? What are the conditions for its necessity?

In teaching Welsh Studies, I have found that getting England off Welsh eyeballs is harder than getting English minds on Wales. The former is by far the more pressing political demand. With this in mind, and with the aim of dislodging 'England's talismanic power', I recently asked students to draw me three maps of Wales, Britain and England. Two out of three of these were recognizable, barring a few lopped off islands and a rather submerged East Anglia! England, so felt, so often cited, so 'known' was the odd one out. No one (myself included) knew were it began or ended, though its coastal borders – so often figured as susceptible, especially in right-wing Europhobia – were curiously more secure than those with the rest of this island's land mass. What was perhaps even more striking was that this inability to know the limits of England extended to English students; they, it seemed, had not routinely mapped their nation's borders in the schools they had so very recently left behind.

Mapping as a technology of power neither equates to the predilection or ability to map the geographical shape of a place, nor does it often allow for internal differences, the numerous, invisible 'Lansker lines' which frame our relations to a place. In the case of Welsh–English relations, the felt power of England commonly operates by its metonymic obfuscation: the capacity of a very particular England to stand for the mythic, as well as economic and political, power of the whole. When many of us speak of England, it is a very white, upper-class symbolic space to which we refer and if it is to be found on any map, it is likely to exist somewhere around Oxbridge, the ill-named Home Counties and the metropolitan centre. This is a warped view, one whose angle of vision denies far too much, allows itself to be limited and ends up limiting others. But we should be clear not to 'correct' it merely in the service of white, middle-class English quests for 'identity'. As Raymond Williams himself put it:

> [W]e in Wales sometimes *know*, what England is, what the English are. And what was known just happened to exclude both the great majority and most of the diverse minorities of the actual English ... England – we can surely see it now – was this dominant English class, these alien figures who ruled us and disposed of us. England – this class, this system; but there all the time, when we went to visit or live among them, all those other incongruous, incompatible English. Well, that is their problem, though until they solve it there will not be much peace for the rest of us.[8]

It is one thing to appreciate that the challenge facing England in its re-evaluation

---

perspective of England' in his landmark essay, 'Wales and England' reprinted in John Osmond, ed., *The National Question Again* (Llandysul: Gomer, 1985), pp. 18–31.

8 Williams 'Wales and England', p. 20.

of itself is immense and vital for Britain; it is quite another to offer to do this work in the service of a specifically bourgeois English introspection.

As the tone of the four episodes cited above suggests, my own trajectory into the current debate on what it means to inhabit these islands (British, archipelagic, Atlantic?) is informed by my political and cultural commitment to Wales as well as my politics as a feminist critic interested in the literatures of North and South America and the Caribbean.[9] When it comes to the role of literature in debates on belonging and national, regional identifications, what surprises me is my own apparent *lack* of interest in the subject I have studied and teach: 'English literature'. When I compose my academic autobiography in the shape of a c.v., I am struck by my weavings and wanderings around 'English Lit.' and the evidence they provide of how I traverse Britain without bearing either the souvenirs or credibility of an English sojourn. But, for a critic interested in contemporary literature, is this not to be expected? As Robert Crawford points out, 'one should bear in mind that most English-language writing is now produced outside England'.[10] 'To be British', as Herman Ouseley puts it, 'is to be part of a global network that encapsulates and transcends a variety of traditions and cultures'.[11]

As Lynne Pearce argues elsewhere, the role of the literary in the negotiation of our belongings can often be found in places other than books themselves.[12] For myself, my own lack of interest in 'Eng Lit' is one thing as is my recognition that the future 'classics' of 'Eng Lit' are unlikely to be English, yet my own traversals in English metropolitan literary culture are quite another. They make for a more uneven story, at whose heart lies an enduring paradox: that whilst I critique and resist the centrality of 'Eng Lit', the hegemonic power of English literary culture works successfully to make me delighted at the rare sight of Welsh inclusion. In a London women's bookshop, for example, I find a copy of Honno's Allen Raine's *Queen of the Rushes*: such discoveries mark my day as exceptional and memorable.[13] The glee I feel then is an embarrassment to myself, a rather 'uncool' joy at finding Welsh women in the midst of this cosmopolitan feminist literary

---

9 One of the most pressing problems in our discussion of these islands is how to name them. 'British' sounds dreadfully colonial, especially in regard to Eire whilst 'archipelagic' is too much of a mouthful even for the politically committed!

10 Robert Crawford, *Devolving English Literature* (Oxford: Clarendon Press, 1992), p. 15.

11 Herman Ouseley, Foreword to *Roots of the Future: ethnic diversity in the making of Britain* (London: CRE, 1998).

12 Lynne Pearce, 'The Place of Literature in the Spaces of Belonging' in *Sexing the Nation* special issue of *Gender, Place and Culture* (forthcoming).

13 Allen Raine, *Queen of the Rushes* (Dinas Powys: Honno, 1998). Honno is a co-operative Welsh feminist press which prints women's writing – contemporary and historical – in both English and Welsh. It is worth stressing the surprising nature of such discoveries if only as a guard against the current tendency to see Scotland and Wales as 'cool' and culturally omnipresent.

space. But it also embarrasses in the way that Elspeth Probyn argues that 'the very longing to belong embarrasses its taken-for-granted nature': the shock of a Welsh woman's text's presence as testament *both* to the routine exclusion of Welsh writing from British bookshops *and* to the workings of a mind not fully decolonized, eager and grateful to see itself in the other's realm.[14] Crossing London, my visits to this feminist space come as a political relief. Yet for myself at least, it seems that 'unlearning the perspective of England' is rather more difficult a task than unlearning the perspective of 'Eng. Lit.'.

Published in 1998, one year after the devolution referenda, *Chloe* is a novel which is as close to a woman's devolutionary English fiction as we are likely to find. Though explicit discussion of devolutionary debates do not occur in the novel, it is difficult to see how such a well-marketed product could succeed, let alone be produced, without the support of a renewed concern with the relationships between the four nations. As much a woman's *Bildungsroman* as a romance, the novel reads like a metropolitan English quest for an identity which the 'other three' nations proudly possess and which only Cornwall, England's 'Celtic' margin, can fulfil. At the end of the novel, Chloe's search for love, identity and a home, are answered in an idyllic (and not poverty-struck!) Cornwall. Chloe's traversals around the UK, which form the basis of the novel's plot, are enabled by a financial endowment from her dead godmother, and as such, are clearly a sabbatical from the English city life to which she will not return. One of the novel's most striking features is the role the landed gentry of eighteenth-century England play as foils to Chloe's travels: everywhere she carries a rather tattered postcard of an upper-class, English couple (Thomas Gainsborough's *Mr and Mrs Andrews* c. 1748), a copy of which the publishers reproduce on the book's inside cover. The reader, like Chloe, is thus encouraged to keep looking back to these two, to read them as possible commentators upon the UK and romance today. But most notable of all, perhaps, is *Chloe's* reformulation of a practice dating from at least the time of James VI and I: that of seeing the UK itself as a heterosexual union between a masculine England and his three feminized partners. *Chloe* turns this equation on its head and, by way of her own symbolic person, reconfigures the devolving UK as a feminized England in search of the love of the three masculine nations. If this revision succeeds in centring the sexual and emotional agency of our heroine, however, it does precious little to alter the heterosexual and hierarchical frame of the UK's Anglocentric structures. The 'union' of England and 'others' still holds firm.[15]

Chloe opens with a prologue in the form of a letter from the protagonist's deceased godmother, bequeathing her favourite godchild two gifts: a brooch and

14 Elspeth Probyn, *Outside Belongings* (London: Routledge, 1997), p. 8.

15 See Richard Phillips, David Shuttleton and Diane Watt, eds, *Decentring Sexualities* (London: Routledge, 2000).

an adventure – a voyage of discovery around the four nations of the United Kingdom:

> Chloe dearest,
> How very strange to write in life that which will be read on death! [...] For you, dear C, I leave this map. There are four more and you will find them all. Wales first, then Ireland, Scotland and finally England. Trust me [...] I am sending you on a voyage, dearest one, in the hope that, once you are quite travelled out, you might find a small patch that you can at last call Home ...
>
> 'Heavens', Chloe Cadwallader declares for the third time [...] Fingering the Brooch, she looks solemnly from letter to map and back again. Jocelyn's handwriting and the map of the United Kingdom are at once familiar and yet somehow foreign and suddenly illegible. Chloe is aware that she knows the shapes but their meaning is now strangely elusive and forgotten. (pp. 1–2)

Despite the ostensible romantic plot of this 1990s bestseller, we are quite clearly also in the domain of the Gothic. The presence of the dead hand writing its way into the present is the biggest clue to the novel's Gothic undertones and it immediately presents us with a quite startling image of the UK as a scene of suspense and unburied ghosts. For our heroine from Islington, traversing the UK is made possible by the almost supernatural crossings of her dead ancestor whose own ethereal state is compensated for by the gift of that most material representations of space: a map. Quite when this map dates from, or how it would be titled, is unclear, given that the UK's most contentious border between Northern Ireland and the Republic disappears, leaving only 'Ireland'. Richly suggestive though this passage is, I want to concentrate on two key features. The first of these is the centrality of the desire for home as the motivating impulse for travel; the second, is the underlying uncertainty in the novel as to whether 'home', both national and familial, even exists.

Given that it is precisely the dead woman's hand which instigates the quest, the desire for home seems both pre-destined and uncanny. Freud's notion of the *unheimlich*, the uncanny (literally translated as the *unhomely*), is useful here. In particular, it is indicative of how 'home' is figured as a place of security, and yet, simultaneously suggests that 'home' is a place of the most severe uncertainty and undecidability. For the white middle-class Englishwoman, home is something which needs to be searched for: it is not immediately apparent and England – or more precisely its multiracial capital, London – needs to be left behind if it is to be found. It seems that the routes of, and to, this English woman's home lie in a journey through the other three nations, which are almost entirely bleached white. At first reading, it is tempting to interpret this move as a 'rediscovery' of the other three nations as spaces of ethnic homogeneity. The narrative is more complex than 'white flight' however, for there are two moves – distinct but interrelated – which are going on here. First, Chloe leaves the English metropolis for the Celtic countries never to reside in a city again. Second, she becomes a rural dweller whose narrative of belongings centres on rural Celtic spaces. In other words, the specifically *racial* meanings of Chloe's journeys are both distinct from yet mapped on to an enduring fantasy of Ireland, Scotland and Wales as wholly rural in contrast to English urban life. (Needless to say, neither 'fact' is true as the millions of residents in 'Celtic' cities and English rural communities could testify!) Chloe's racial journey imaginatively requires the depopulation of both cities and country in order that she may find her rural English (ultimately Cornish) 'home': it is a vision of a UK whose population is drastically reduced, perhaps to levels closer to those of the Gainsborough painting she adores than to those we know exist today.[16]

Furthermore, *Chloe*'s narrative mapping of these islands relies upon the lexicon of colonial mapping. 'Wales lies unopened' and the Welsh are 'a melancholy, perhaps justifiably bitter nation', for instance. The Northern Irish are 'private, provincial, decidedly mellow' (p. 213), whose landscape is 'unspoilt', 'the Troubles' having 'preserved the landscape against the unpalatable consequences of over-tourism' but which 'no sensitive holiday-maker, let alone traveller, would want to forgo' (p. 134). But it is Scotland, Chloe's godmother's 'favourite country' which comes out on top in Chloe's mapping: 'Chloe felt little waves of excitement; such romantic places were now hers for the exploring, could even be hers for the keeping ... "What a perfect setting," she gasped as she strolled towards the hamlet, "and which one's Braer House?" she wondered. "Which one's mine?"' (pp. 217–18). The gendered frame of Chloe's devolved UK might be woman centred, but it is hardly promising as a national revision: 'You may never want to leave – but go onwards to England, my girl. And then make your choice' (p. 214).

What is particularly striking, especially in the novel's opening, is that home really is little more than a hazy motif, not least because Chloe finds the contours of the four nations through which she must travel to be quite illegible. The presentation of this point is quite tantalisingly ambiguous, as Jocelyn's handwriting and the map of the UK blur: we are never clear which entity is being raised from the dead: the godmother or the UK! It is also difficult not to see this as a literary representation of resurrecting the UK at its very point of feared erosion. Yet, just as reports of the UK's political demise are premature, so the novel's fear that the UK will not be 'readable' are proved unfounded. It is, after all, the aim of this romance novel to make the UK home legible and inhabitable for its newly single and partner-less English woman as well as to rediscover the geographical romance of the British Isles themselves. As the English heroine of a four-nations romance, Chloe thus stands for a newly abandoned England which needs to renew

---

16 The painting's role is important here. It *both* depicts an image of a heterosexual coupling of English landed gentry *and* accompanies Chloe in her imaginative, as well as physical, journeys in re-creating such a landscape for her own romantic home.

its courtings of these nations. And as if the narrative's attempts to make the renewed British home legible are not sufficient guarantee, the publishers kindly provide readers with a copy of the 'British Isles' (all borders absent) sub-imposed beneath the written text of the blurb.

If Chloe's maps and romantic vision aim to provide us with a national panorama of ultimately fulfillable desires, then the two journeys which open Menna Gallie's novel are altogether more ponderous and intimate in their mappings of belonging. In part, this is a consequence of Gallie's quite different narrative structure which seeks to create its fictional world – a village in West Wales – through the interrelated life stories of the residents. Unlike *Chloe* then, no single consciousness is allowed to dominate the meanings of home and belonging. Every bit as important, however, is the novel's insistence on the 'outsiderliness' of all the small town's residents. This goes not only for 'incomers' such as the English commune of 'hippies' keen to 'drop-out' of city life, but is also true of those who were born and brought up in Trenewydd. Where for Chloe, rural Celtic spaces are sites of secure belonging, for those 'on the ground' in Gallie's novel, they are the very places of complexity and ex-centricity. The eccentric characters who people Gallie's fictional town are central to the novel's humour certainly, but they are also the *model* for its politics. This politics centres on the inherently partial and relational nature of all belongings, a fact which the enclosed English 'hippy' commune is especially slow to learn. Only in giving up their dogged adherence to the ethic of 'self-sufficiency' (one which means they won't shop locally even if they'll cadge the odd cigarette from visitors) can they hope to enjoy the sense of place they so desire. Paradoxically, it is this group – adherents of 1960s style 'free-love' – who are the least promiscuous! This is true in terms of how we commonly understand 'promiscuity' to refer to sexual practice. But it is also true in terms of the broader definition of promiscuity which I think the novel, in its title and narrative is every bit as concerned to examine. 'Promiscuous' means to 'mix'; it signifies an indiscriminate mixing of parts or elements of various kinds which are grouped or massed together without any specific order. We should keep in mind here that one of the most enduring sources of English attack upon Wales (as other 'colonies') centred on the supposedly promiscuous nature of Welsh women – a claim which underlay the notorious *Reports of the Commissioners of Inquiry into the State of Education in Wales* (1847), the so-called, treachery of the 'Blue Books'. With this in mind, we can read Gallie's title *In These Promiscuous Parts*, as *itself* a mode of 'unlearning the perspective' of English moralizing.[17]

---

[17] For further discussion of the sexual politics of this report see my 'Cymraes Oddi Cartref? Welsh women writing home and migration' in *Welsh Writing in English* , 3 (1997), pp. 134–56 and Jane Aaron 'Finding a voice in two tongues: gender and colonization' in Jane Aaron, Teresa Rees, Sandra Betts and Moira Vincentelli, eds, *Our Sister's Land: the Changing Identities of Women in Wales* (Cardiff: University of Wales Press, 1994), pp. 183–98.

I want now to turn to the first of the novel's opening journeys, the departure of Lance from Cambridge, both because it is a good example of how Gallie juxtaposes the intimacy of familiar sights with a mobile and ex-centric belonging and because it demonstrates Gallie's insistence that the reader also 'unlearn' a skewed perspective of England:

> Lance walked on his own around Cambridge on the eve of his leaving. Blue-jeaned and ponchoed, long-haired, like most students, he walked slowly down Trumpington Street, passed Peterhouse on his left, and Pembroke, on his right; he paid silent respect to Little Saint Mary's Church and went down Silver Street, to the river ... He crossed the Queen's Bridge, passed Darwin, and turned right at the traffic lights, to look at the spring-flowered Backs. Not to look at them – he had seen and seen them – as much as to salute them before he went his way. He was leaving Cambridge for fresh fields and pastures new; glad to go but reluctant to leave. (p. 1)

The sustained and rather pastiched tone of mastery is undercut by the revelation, some pages on, that Lance does not 'belong' to Cambridge as either a student or a lecturer but as a jobbing porter who is leaving the ivory tower in the hope of finding agricultural work in Pembrokeshire. Gallie's deliberate play on the reader's expectations forces a self-conscious reflection on one's own angle of vision and the supposedly secure cultural and classed place Cambridge holds for many of us, academic and otherwise. Appearances are rendered deceptive and partial because mediated through the consciousness of the subjects' own standpoints. Gallie's narrative method anticipates feminist epistemology's claims for 'situated knowledges', but the multiplicity of Lance's shifting situations and the narrator's later debunking of sociology as the 'promising' but 'undemanding' discipline of a middle-class elite, casts doubt upon the certainties which the work of Nancy Harstock, Sandra Harding, Donna Haraway and others promise.[18]

The second of the two opening journeys is that of the Oxford lecturer, Rosa (Rosie). Having dropped her hitch-hiker, Lance, off at Briwnant, Rosie winds her way back to her familial home and her avowedly Marxist mother. As with Chloe, Rosie is a professional single woman who travels alone and whose 'heroine' status relies in part on her independent spirit. The extended description of her return is interesting here because it provides a distinctively temporal panorama and is the intimate knowledge of a long-standing inhabitant whose vision is renewed upon return. Whilst it serves to place Rosie in the community of Trenewydd, however, it also places her journeying in the context of a history of travels and visitations. 'Rooted return' gives way to a chronicle of 'mobile belongings' – conquests included – though a heavy sense of the past remains:

---

18 For some of the key essays in the development of feminist epistemologies see Sandra Harding and Merill B. Hintikka, eds, *Discovering Reality: Feminist Perspectives on Epistemology, Metaphysics and Philosophy of Science* (Boston: D. Reidel, 1983).

> She came down the hill, passed the ruined Norman castle, perched among its green, sheep-filled pastures, and then the ancient church, squat, Norman-towered, four-square. The end of the thin sun shone, momentarily bright, through the interstices of the gaunt and everlasting Celtic cross, which brooded, oddly human, like a shepherd, over his flock of battered, haphazard tombstones ... She passed the Ancient Briton, fallen upon modern days and boasting neon lighting and a chef [...] The unemployed young of the little town had commandeered the war memorial for their own and they would sit on the ornate Edwardian solidity of its steps [...] as Rosie passed [...] only one long-haired, long-legged girl sat upon the steps, with a plastic shopping bag propped between her widespread knees. *Le Grand Passage*, it read. Someone had evidently been abroad. (p. 23)

From the position of the late 1990s there is something uncomfortably nostalgic and cosy about the feel of Gallie's town, Trenewydd, even if it is set in the early 1960s. Nevertheless, I enjoy the novel because it allows this 'educational migrant' a way in, something which *Chloe*'s Cinderella-style narrative cannot do. My readerly pleasure is no small part the result of my own traversals and belongings. Having been virtually schooled in nationalism in one of the Welsh-medium secondary schools long-campaigned for in the 1970s and 1980s, I left North Wales to become a student in the North West of England. This was not a unique departure; the majority of my friends and room-mates at university were also from Wales (though mostly from the South) and the student-lingo of the day comprised of Welsh words learnt by English-speaking friends; 'Does dim arian o gwbl gen i' (I've no money at all) was one of the most repeated, as I recall. When I left, it was to live (but not work) in Oxford which I left to take up my present post in West Wales in 1998. Whilst I was personally very content with the prospect, many colleagues and friends thought otherwise. I remember quite distinctly, one of the secretaries commiserating with me, as though living in Wales was to be banished to a western colony.

Friends, colleagues and occasionally I myself figure my move to Carmarthen as a return of a native. However, the truth is that the regional differences within Wales make this a distinctly 'new' place to live. From the college receptionist who spoke slowly to me so that I could understand her South-western Welsh to my step-father's and uncle's musings about the character of 'Carmarthenshire people', the realities 'on the ground' challenge the enduring tendency of commentators to figure Wales as a homogeneous entity. For many it seems, Wales is quite 'different enough', thank you, without having to be bothered by internal differences: such differences – regional, classed, linguistic – do not seem to make for a sexy 'product'; too much heterogeneity gets in the way of figuring Wales as 'the next big Celtic thing' as the BBC's Radio 4 programme, *Frontrow*, recently put it. Devolutionary governance also demonstrates this inability and refusal to deal with the realities of internal differences. Whilst much has been made of the relatively favourable gender composition of the Scottish Parliament and Welsh Assembly, for example, neither has any Black or Asian members. Heterogeneity is fine, it seems, so long as it is homogeneously white

In the context of this volume, I have been especially struck by some contributors whose desire for a validated regional identity has been expressed as a 'jealousy' of Welsh, Scottish and Northern Irish contributors who are perceived as enjoying more explicitly secure national identities. I have to confess to being surprised at being read thus, particularly as I am used to thinking of 'Welshness' – or Cymreigtod – as *anything but* secure or definable. In an intriguing analysis of what 'Wales' signifies either side of the border, Fiona Bowie makes the contentious but useful point that:

> Wales presents to the rest of the world a coherent picture of cultural self-sufficiency and a firm sense of identity. What outsiders see, however, is not so much Wales as their own reflection, or stereotypes of Welshness, the Wales of the Celticist imagination. As one begins to penetrate beyond this refracted image of Welshness, not least by learning the language, the unproblematic and monolithic nature of Welsh identity begins to fragment. One is left with [...] a sense of many conflicting and interlocking definitions of identity which actively compete for symbolic space and public recognition.[19]

'Coming home to something new but always known'[20]

A couple of years ago, in the midst of grappling with theories of migration and exile, I returned home to North Wales from the North West of England for a break. Leaving the train station, the first thing I saw was a very dusty, yellow van, a left-over from the days of a nationalized rail service: 'Great Western' exchanged for 'British Rail'. My pathway blocked, I noticed that something had been inscribed in the dust on the rear door and curious, with nowhere else to go except past it, I read the words: 'Nid yw Gymru ar Werth' (that is, 'Wales is not for sale'). In that moment of reading, as a newly-returned subject, I was brought forcefully 'home'. This was a double-voiced slogan which mobilized the image of a house on the market to make a broader national, political point about the destabilising effects of inward migration from England on housing.[21] Implying that this land might also be sold from beneath us, it evoked nationalist concerns that 'Wales' is not fixed, nor

[19] Fiona Bowie, 'Wales from Within' in Sharon Macdonald, ed., *Inside European Identities* (Oxford: Berg, 1997), pp. 168–9.

[20] Gwyneth Lewis, *Parables and Faxes* (Newcastle upon Tyne: Bloodaxe, 1995).

[21] Of course, such concerns are *not* limited to rural Wales. The question of housing regulation often surfaces in the English Lake District, for example. However, the linguistic dimension makes for a quite distinct debate.

stable, but subject always to loss and erasure, as Gwyn Williams' very temporally disorientating question suggests: 'When was Wales?'[22]

The act of reading this political slogan, my surprise encounter with a familiar national politics, marked both my return to this home-land and re-positioned me as an *insider-reader*, one who could swiftly decode the meanings of this concise text. If I could be described as a migrant – as one who had left her abode, together with half a million others who annually cross Offa's Dyke – then it was the act of reading this text which brought home the contradictory nature of migration.[23] I had left this home which was still home, yet in crossing the border, had I become the intended reader, the one being told not to buy up property to fulfil a rural idyll? Was the recognition of home as susceptible and not secure *itself* a mode of claiming identification with that place which both was and was not then home?

Narrating migration is also the effect of a migratory reading of the place(s) one has left, the internally contradictory homes which one re-interprets and re-frames. Contiguously, the act of reading migratory narratives holds the potential to de-stabilize the reader both personally and conceptually, dis-allowing homogeneous notions of a reader who interprets from *one* fixed location. Migration is an experience, and structure, whose meanings are constituted, at least in part, through its own reading and narration; through the interpretative modes employed to make sense of the past and present home. But the meanings of British migrations also involves the ways in which different migrations and traversals are intimately connected and mutually dependent in making sense of 'mobile belongings'.

In Gallie's novel the interconnected nature of British migrations is most obvious when classed belongings are expressed through an explicitly racialized, and sometimes racist, frame. One of the many sub-plots of the novel concerns the theft of a watercolour painting, an incident which the town police constable, Colin, is responsible for investigating. In order to ascertain the provenance of the object, he questions the Anglicized (Welsh) local gentry, a family of spinsters fallen on poorer times and now living in a house called Llwynrhos. What is striking in the way it is narrated, however, is the inseparability of class and colonialism in the servant's reading of one of the spinsters, Miss Olwen:

---

22 Gwyn A.Williams, *When Was Wales?* (London: Penguin, 1991).

23 My tentative naming of myself as a 'migrant' stems partly from a concern to avoid homogenizing migration, thereby collapsing the radically different occasions which give rise to both migration and the migrant subject. The half a million border crossers, I refer to, are figures for outward migration from Wales, a figure which is matched almost precisely by half a million inward-migrants, overwhelmingly from England. See Graham Day 'A Million on the Move?: population change and rural Wales' in Graham Day and Gareth Rees, eds, *Contemporary Wales*, 3 (1989), pp. 137–59. This cross-border traffic is also a gendered and classed phenomenon, occurring often as a departure for ostensibly educational reasons.

> 'Sit with your back to Miss Olwen', she ordered; 'she won't drink with you looking at her. Handsome young chaps in uniform upset her something chronic. She tried to run off with a sergeant in India before the smallpox took her ... Her father was the commanding officer so he put an end to it, of course; it wasn't proper.'
>
> 'Connie, you talk as if you'd been in India yourself, girl.'
>
> 'Well, I've lived so long in Llwynrhos, isn't it ... so I've fallen into their ways ... There was class distinction about the place in their days so they can't help it, fair play. It's a terrible burden, class is. Very frustrating, is class. It scars you for life, like smallpox.' (p. 157)

The burlesque tone of the narration, reminiscent of Southern Welsh writers such as Gwyn Thomas, reveals an incisive view 'from below'. It goes further, however, in suggesting that both 'upper-classness' and 'Rajism' are contagious diseases. Connie's analysis is a self-conscious reversal of the tendency to see working-class and colonial bodies as aberrant and contaminating. Nevertheless, the reliance on such a trope is disturbingly ambiguous and it comes *perilously* close to reproducing that which it critiques. Thus one of the characters describes a friend of the spinsters, 'the colonel's like the Llwynrhos lot, been too involved with India. Can't get out of the habit of coolies. The British Empire is a terrible burden to have to bear, mind, Rosie. We're lucky to have missed it' (p. 136).

The intermingling of class, national, colonial and racial discourses also occurs when the belongings of less august people are the topic of conversation. One such example begins with a conversation between Blodwen, Rosie's mother's housekeeper, and the local Labour party candidate, who disagree on the cross-border traffic of tourism and its consequences (a debate which remains altogether too familiar to many of us). 'Tell the truth, we live off the fat of the tourists, like it or not', argues Rosie. But the candidate sees it differently and pointedly refers to the exceptional privilege of Blodwen's son, Gerald, who is studying at Cambridge: 'Blodwen, there's no work for the young ones, and you know it. Their only hope is to go to England to look for work. ... Gerald, yes, he's all right. He's made it but he's rare ... The English want to keep us poor and picturesque and humble when they come here to retire, and destroy our Welsh way of life'. What starts out as talk of temporary inward migration in the form of tourism, however, rapidly shifts to become a defence of the educational migrant, whose position in both Cambridge and Trenewydd, leaves him open to criticism: 'My boy's in England and nobody's saying 'Go home, Wog' to him, and his Welsh is as good now as it was three years ago when he first went up there' (pp. 58–59). In the first instance, Blodwen is defending her son against what is an explicitly racial slur. Elsewhere, however, she is quite prepared to use such language against the main 'ethnic minority' in the novel, Italians. In the heady mix of class and racial discourses, the novel demonstrates that familiarity with racialized belongings is no barrier to reproducing racism, nor does it engender a critical awareness of race as a structuring principle in a capitalist society.

In the second of her defences, however, Blodwen shows a more astute reading of social belongings. In particular, she is keen to defend Gerald linguistically, for to lose one's language, is a fate worse than class upward mobility. Gerald can move up and out of his class, but to lose his mother tongue is a loss which this mother cannot bear. From such complex understandings, emerge Blodwen's party politics:

> 'Well, Rosie, politics is politics, but local politics is something else. My heart's in the right place ... Gerald wouldn't be where he is but for the Labour government ... And what's more ... I'm Labour because I'm poor, isn't it? But what with your mam and Karl Marx and then my Gerald on about Trotsky, I don't know where I stand, honest. I've gone a bit disenchanted with your lot. Gerald says you're only pigs in the middle and that you're meaningless in the class struggle, so there'. (Ibid.)

Conclusion: where are you (coming) from?

This chapter has been concerned to pose some central and enduring questions regarding the nature of mobile British belongings within the current political context of devolution. Whilst such questions cannot be fully answered here – if only because they are still very much 'under discussion' – I hope that I have succeeded in demonstrating how questions of personal belongings and state politics are intimately connected. Further, I hope to have reminded us, myself included, that when it comes to British traversals and 'mobile belongings', the state and the subject are not as distant as more recent theorizing seems to suggest.

In both my readings of the literary texts and my own autobiographical reflections, I have emphasised that 'on the ground', if not in the theory, questions of travel and belonging constantly engender and make recourse to other questions. So, for instance, my reading of the role of class, colonialism and race in Gallie's novel makes clear the inseparability of these discourses and histories in the question of how one 'belongs' to a class-ridden society which is deeply marked by its colonial and imperial past. The question of devolution engenders not only questions of how do we belong together and what will be our future relationship to one another, but of how did we get here, what modalities of 'union' are available to us and, how can we unpack the meanings of the UK in the international, post-colonial context which radically and intimately shapes our lives. Feminist interventions in this process include active political involvement so that the governmental bodies are not dominated by male representatives. Given the limited power of the Welsh assembly at least, however, we must do more, we must guard against the enduring desire to homogenize the nation, present even in the most self-critical nationalisms, including British nationalism; we must argue for the heterogeneity of so-called 'British' feminism and challenge the Anglocentric narrative it tells; and we need to historicize our own belongings, if only to counter the metropolitan centre's transitory interest in all things Celtic.

This said, I have to admit that for me, a great many of these questions emerge from a more enduring, and apparently more simple, question to answer: 'where are you from?'. Bearing an Irish surname in a sea of Davies', Jones' and Williams', it is perhaps not surprising that I found the question, 'where are you from' to be an awkward moment from an early age. In the context of a stiflingly middle-class nationalist school, I learnt quickly that in the matter of classed belongings, the aim is precisely *not* to tell one's story, is not to readily let the autobiographical subject out of the bag.

Telling the story of 'where are you from' usually involves for me trying to 'tell' what the questioner is like. Llandudno, I say to shopping seaside people, Conwy, for the historically minded, Betws y Coed for the outdoor hiking-boots type, and the nearest town, Llanrwst, is always reserved for those who know Wales. I am at home and outside of all these places – the village and housing estate where I grew up and regularly return, won't fit into any one of these geographical or social centres.

During the day, I feel most out of place in Betws, by night, Llanrwst. In Betws, it seems that there are two classes of people. One are workers – in teashops, hotels, gift shops – the other are walking visitors who, before entering the place, will probably have spent more on their single climbing outfits than most of the inhabitants will earn that week. To wear shoes and a coat – not a waterproof and a fleece – is to stand out. I feel out of place, because what I am doing is not working but walking, not Walking but walking. Usually accompanied by my elderly mother, I naturally pass unnoticed.

In Llanrwst, a market town similar enough to many in Wales and other parts of the UK, the dress code again leaves me standing out. Men dress uniformly in dark jeans and coloured shirts and women in skirts with tights or bare legs. My tailored jacket (even if it was six quid from a charity shop), obviously draws attention to myself, as do my dark jeans, which betray me, a sign of my refusal to 'dress up'. When on a cold night outside the late shop, I meet my cousin dressed for a night in the town's pubs, we cheerfully greet each other across an unbridgeable divide. We are both of us aware of our outside belongings and reasonably content. There is, after all, no need to make a melodrama out of a temporary identity crisis.

Acknowledgements

That there are any references in this chapter to work on Welsh women's writing is due largely to a very small and overworked group of feminists working in Wales today. They include: Jane Aaron, Katie Gramich and Francesca Rhydderch. Thanks go to Lynne Pearce and Sinead McDermott for many anxious and supportive dialogues. Finally, I wish to thank Philip Schwyzer, for generously sharing his own partial belongings which complicate and support my own.

Chapter 5

Putting Myself in Her Place: Identity, Identification and Irishness in Nuala O'Faolain's *Are You Somebody?* and Margaret Atwood's *Alias Grace*

Sinead McDermott

Writing from the wrong place

> Felman suggests that telling the story of the self may be a way of killing aspects of that self or part selves, rather than preserving or maintaining them, while women's alienation from a totalized life-story means that they find the autobiographical in others' stories. The autobiographical is mediated, displaced – 'people tell their stories, which they do not know, or cannot speak, through others' stories'. Autobiography, that is, makes a detour through theory, through fiction, and through literature. And women's autobiography may be marked as much by a resistance to the autobiographical as by an embracing of it.[1]

In this essay I will be using two texts – one fictional, one non-fictional – to reflect upon how I read and write my identity as an Irishwoman. To orient the reader to what follows, I first of all need to present my identification papers: my qualifications, or lack of them, for writing on this topic. I identify as Irish firstly because of biological inheritance (my parents are Irish), and secondly because of upbringing: although I was born in England, I spent most of my childhood in Ireland (and most of my adult life, so far, outside of it). I am also easily identifiable as Irish, in terms of my name, my accent, and so on. My academic research is

---

1 Laura Marcus, 'Theories of Autobiography', in Swindells, Julia, ed., *The Uses of Autobiography: Feminist Perspectives Past and Present* (London: Taylor and Francis, 1995), p. 21. Marcus is citing Shoshana Felman, *What Does a Woman Want?* (New York and London: Routledge, 1994). For other feminist writings on autobiography, see in particular Shari Benstock, ed., *The Private Self: Theory and Practice of Women's Autobiographical Writings* (London and New York: Routledge, 1988).

feminist, but to date has steered clear of engaging with Irish issues. I do not work in Irish studies, and my opinions and emotions on this topic are non-expert and generally non-academic. Perhaps for these reasons, the story of me as Irish has always been one I 'do not know, or cannot speak', and the chance to write this article seemed to me at first like an opportunity to uncover that unspoken story. However, as I began to imagine writing the story of my Irish life, and trawling through my memories for suitable scenes, the emotion I felt was not so much gratitude for the chance I'd been given, as resentment: *What's it to her?* I would think. *It's none of her business*. ('Her' meant the editor of the collection; it was occasionally replaced by 'them', meaning a wider audience, imagined as uniformly English.) At the same time, I also imagined another audience, this time Irish (who would be reading this by accident, I thought, over somebody else's shoulder), and whose response would be unimpressed: *What does she know about it?* or worse, a family audience finding their secrets betrayed: *She shouldn't have said that*. Behind these various voices lurked the ongoing feeling of being in the wrong place: partly in terms of my ability to write this article (living in Britain, not working in Irish studies) and partly in terms of where this article would appear (an article from a southern Irish perspective in a collection primarily concerned with 'UK feminisms'). Thus, what had initially seemed like a positive and creative act (speaking my self), came to feel more like an act of violence both by and against me: in this article, this book collection, I was being called to account, forced to identify myself, positioned in ways and places in which I didn't want to be positioned, and worst of all, my voice and my story were being appropriated for someone else's purposes.[2]

It is these emotions – the resistance to the autobiographical – that I want to address in this article, by asking what kind of difficulty, violence, and misplacement is involved in attempting to account for yourself. While this is clearly a displacement of the requested topic, my argument is that such displacement is precisely what I am interested in. What happens if you write, or speak, from the wrong place and about the wrong things? What does it mean if you attempt to speak through someone else, or tell their story instead of your own? What relations of power and appropriation does this involve? To think about these issues, I will be using two female-authored texts. Nuala O'Faolain's *Are You Somebody?* is there to think about my relationship to texts by other Irish women, and the ways in which I want my story to be told through theirs. Margaret Atwood's *Alias Grace* is there because it raises issues of identity and identification, of possession and appropriation, of speaking in your own voice and speaking through someone else. It is also there because in a sense it represents my home turf: the kind of feminist (but not Irish) novel I would normally use in my academic research.

---

2 As Julia Swindells points out, 'the personal *account* provides both the record of the life, and also the means by which that life can be held to account'. Julia Swindells, *Uses of Autobiography*, p. 9.

Someone else's story: Nuala O'Faolain's *Are You Somebody?*

> I'm fairly well-known in Ireland. I've been on television a lot, and there's a photo of me in the paper, at the top of my column. But I'm no star. People have to look at me twice or three times to put a name on me. Sometimes when I'm drinking in a lounge bar, a group of women, say, across the room, begin to look at me, and send one of their number over to me … 'Are you somebody?' they ask. Well – am I somebody? I'm not anybody in terms of the world, but then, who decides what a somebody is? How is a somebody made? I've never done anything remarkable: neither have most people. Yet most people, like me, feel remarkable.[3]

O'Faolain's text raises a number of issues for this essay. Firstly, I want to think about how O'Faolain's difficulty in writing her memoir reflects back on my own difficulties in writing this article: the fears around speaking out, and the ways in which these are gendered and raced. Secondly, I want to discuss some of the family and nation secrets which emerge in the memoir, in order to examine more specifically what they say about silence and forgetfulness as an Irish phenomenon. Finally, I want to discuss the ways in which other people (somebodies and nobodies) operate in O'Faolain's story: the ways in which her speech depends upon, and acts as a catalyst for, theirs.

First published in 1996, *Are You Somebody?* is an attempt on O'Faolain's part to think about her life and times, from growing up in North Dublin in the 1950s, through to the present day, and her position as a public figure, best known for her opinion columns in *The Irish Times*. It is a self-reflexive piece of work, which constantly comments on the processes of its own production: the conditions which inhibited and produced her speech. Indeed, the story proper begins, ironically, at a moment when O'Faolain finds herself unable to speak at all:

> The psychiatrist was in an office in a hospital. 'Well, now, let's get your name right to begin with,' he said cheerfully. 'What is your name? 'My name is … my name is …' I could not say my name. I cried, as from an ocean of tears, for the rest of the hour. My self was too sorrowful to speak. And I was in the wrong place, in England. My name was a burden to me. (p. 3)

This account of stuttering and inarticulacy suggests immediately the importance of context in speaking the self: O'Faolain cannot identify herself, because she is 'in the wrong place'; and presumably, because she lacks the right audience. More specifically – and this is why I have started with it – the anecdote raises, at least by implication, some of the difficulties of speaking an Irish self to an English

---

3 Nuala O'Faolain, *Are You Somebody? The Life and Times of Nuala O'Faolain* (London: Hodder & Stoughton, 1998), p. xi. All further page references to this volume will be given after quotations in the text.

audience. The psychiatrist's cheerful opening 'let's get your name right to begin with' resonates with all the 'reasonable' English questions which are asked of the Irish ('which part are you from?' / 'what are you, Catholic or Protestant?') and which can prove surprisingly difficult to answer. Similarly, O'Faolain's recognition that 'my name was a burden to me' speaks, I think, for all the labour involved in bearing an Irish name in England – not least in providing information on spelling and pronunciation. The dilemma – and the consequent stuttering – are similar to my own discomfort when asked to write this article: the discomfort of being forced to explain.

While the story of the psychiatrist is a story of the wrong place, a place where her autobiography could not emerge, the story of her eventual writing of the memoir – in Ireland – is equally composed out of desires and fears, this time inflected by an Irish context: the desire to be known and recognized (to 'be remarkable') and the fear of claiming to be somebody in a culture of begrudgery. In the introduction, we learn that the memoir has emerged out of O'Faolain's journalistic writing: she is asked to write a personal introduction to a collection of her columns, and uses the opportunity to turn the introduction into an account of her life and times. The memoir itself explores the tension between that public status (being a 'somebody'), and the reality of her private life: 'to myself I was usually barely hanging on' (p. x). As O'Faolain articulates it, that conflict is between the public and the private voice, which in turn pertain to two versions of female identity:

> [My columns] used a confident, public voice. My readers probably thought that I was as confident as that all the time, but I knew the truth. My private life was solitary. My private voice was apologetic. In terms of national influence I mattered, in Ireland. But I possessed nothing of what has traditionally mattered to women and what had mattered to me during most of my life. I had no lover, no child. It seemed to me that I had nothing to look back on but failure. (p. x)

O'Faolain's conviction that nonetheless her life has meaning ('my life burned inside me', p. x) is held in the face of an anticipated response which would claim the opposite: 'When I called my memoir, *Are You Somebody?* it was largely to pre-empt the hostile people who'd say, at my writing anything about myself at all, "Who does she think she is?"' (p. 217). In the culture O'Faolain writes out of, the fear is of '"making a show" of yourself' (p. 25); a fear which can also be gendered: 'Teachers used to say, "Miss Noticebox! You're nothing but a noticebox!"' (p. 201). This fear is allied, in O'Faolain's account, with a fear of speaking for your nation: of claiming authority for your version of Irishness. The violence and hostility which any such claim may provoke, are suggested by the response O'Faolain remembers to an earlier interview she did on Irish television: 'Eamonn Dunphy reviewed the series, and I've just tracked down his piece.

"Watching Nuala O'Faolain depict herself as poor," he said, "I longed to kick the television set"' (p. 47). The difficulties O'Faolain perceives in telling her story, would suggest that my own resistance to autobiography is perhaps in itself a story of my nation and gender: a fear of calling attention to oneself in a way that implies you think that you are worthy of attention; a fear of breaking taboos and telling secrets; and most importantly, a fear of potentially hostile reactions (of kicks).

The secrets revealed in *Are You Somebody?* are both family secrets and national ones: often emphasizing the connection between the two. While the bulk of the narrative is taken up with O'Faolain's young adulthood through to middle age, the emotional force of the text is situated in the relatively brief description of her childhood and the family relationships associated with it; and indeed, the narrative circles back to the events of her own and her siblings' childhoods (analysing, reconsidering, placing blame and granting forgiveness) throughout the text. The family story is a narrative of carelessness and neglect, allied with secrecy and taboo; and some of the most moving passages describe the conflict between the family's public facade (the father as successful journalist) and its private, occasionally squalid, reality (the mother's alcoholism, the father's absence, and so on). The failures of the family to its children are marked, mainly, by a failure (a forgetting) to take care, which works itself out in gendered ways: the younger brother is allowed to drift off to England; the little sister is sent to school, shamefully, without her knickers. And the ways in which these family failures are exposed at the time is also gendered: 'I remember … the teacher in Miss Ahern's school in Malahide calling me in to her office and fingering my dirty cardigan. "Couldn't your mother find anything better to send you to school in?"' (p. 10). The school works here as a boundary zone between public and private, uncovering the family secrets which do not percolate through to the outside world of the father's social engagements. The disciplinary act ('fingering my dirty cardigan') occurs between women – the female teacher ascribing neglect to the mother ('couldn't your mother find anything better'), while the father, largely, remains exempt. While the evidence of neglect becomes partially public here (it is 'known' by the other children and their families as well as the teacher), it never becomes public enough for anything to change – as the repetition-with-a-difference of these two incidents (the narrator's dirty cardigan as one of her earliest memories, the little sister's story something she has only recently heard) suggests.

The individual woman's failure (the mother sending her daughters to school not properly dressed) is thus revealed, in O'Faolain's account, to have obscured other failures – the shortcomings of a culture in which certain types of forgetfulness, or at least male forgetfulness, are acceptable enough to be overlooked. The personal narrative becomes the story of a society. Through anecdotes about friends, acquaintances, and strangers, O'Faolain charts a culture of secrecy, carelessness and forgetfulness, in which the failure to remember is a political and gendered act:

> I was with a friend of my father's once and he was saying to a girl in the company – this was in the early 1970s – 'I don't know what you women's lib people think you're up to. Can't any woman who's worth her salt get what she wants from a man if she treats him nicely in bed?' He'd forgotten the young woman he was talking to was his own daughter from a long-ago liaison. (p. 89)

The failure of this society to 'take care' – of the past, of its children, of the powerless – is thus at the heart of *Are You Somebody?* It is a carelessness which is catching: O'Faolain documents the moments at which she repeats her parents' behaviour, both by failing to take care of herself ('when I got my scholarship I lost the money – lost the actual banknotes. This was exactly the kind of catastrophe I was used to' (p. 49)), and by refusing to take care of others: 'I mind my self. She can mind herself' (p. 185). Finally, the narrative makes a connection between neglect, forgetfulness, and losing your place:

> I once asked my friend, the broadcaster and writer Sean Mac Reamoinn, who knew my father and mother in the 1950s, what class we belonged to ... [My parents] didn't know their place. Mammy would send me up the field to the big Georgian house where the landlady lived, with the rent. She hated paying the rent. 'Throw it at her!' she'd hiss at me. They were not practising Catholics either ... Whatever the people they came from had lived by just fell away in their generation. But they didn't have other values, to replace what they had lost. They were just careless. (pp. 13–14)

In this sense, the memoir can be read as an attempt by O'Faolain to fix her identity – to figure out her place in Irish society: as the various attempts in the text to decide whether her family were poor or not, might suggest.

What interests me here is not just how this culture of forgetfulness and silencing operates, or indeed how it is gendered; but more importantly, what are the implications of this for O'Faolain telling her story: how is her narrative to avoid replicating the carelessness it describes? If carelessness here is equated with forgetfulness (at one point, we are told, her father forgets her brother's name), then the solution presumably is to take care of the past: to bear witness, not just to your own life, but to other people's. Indeed, if in her introduction O'Faolain had identified her motives in writing the memoir as a desire for a type of self-importance, a wish to claim that her life has value, towards the end of her narrative, a different, equally pressing, reason asserts itself:

> I didn't have to give this account of myself at all. I don't know why this story insisted on being told. Partly, I think something was dislodged in me by the evidence given about his childhood at Brendan O'Donnell's trial for the murder of Father Walsh and Imelda Riney and her little boy. His sister told of the brutality Brendan saw – he saw his father smash his mother's false teeth with a blow, and the mother trying to jump from the car and Brendan screaming at her not to jump. He saw his father's incessant

> beatings. His mother – who was well until her marriage – broke down. Mother and son huddled together so close that she went to school with him: to stand in the corridor, until Brendan could let her go. This evidence wasn't even printed in the *Clare Champion*, the local paper. The waters closed over yet another Irish family. My two brothers in England had their life chances taken away from them in childhood, as surely as Brendan O'Donnell had. Maybe that trial brought me into the presence of my own sorrow and anger.
>
> Or – maybe that's just fanciful. (pp. 197–8)

Here, the need is to bear witness on someone else's behalf, just as O'Donnell's sister is doing at his trial: to counter a culture of forgetfulness (a culture in which families sink under the water and are lost) by committing things to memory. But how do you work between personal memory and cultural testimony? To what extent can this 'somebody's' story be 'anybody's' story? Who have you the right to speak for, and can you take someone else's story as your own?[4] The problems which result from doing so are suggested by O'Faolain's assertion of a link between O'Donnell and her own family in this quotation. She has to assert the similarity ('My two brothers in England had their life chances taken away from them in childhood, as surely as Brendan O'Donnell had'); but her story does not end with murders. It is the difficulty, I think, of holding onto this similarity and this difference which makes O'Faolain assert this moment so strongly, as a physical force ('something was dislodged in me') and then has her, equally quickly, dismiss it ('or maybe that's just fanciful'). There is a difficulty in telling O'Donnell's story; and there is equally a difficulty in telling the unnamed brothers' stories. In the afterword, we read part of a letter, written by one of O'Faolain's brothers to another sister after reading the first edition of *Are You Somebody?* It includes the sentence: 'I shall be writing to thank her for the book but in due course as I haven't figured out at all how to go about writing something that makes me doltish' (p. 233). O'Faolain's desire to testify on her brother's behalf does not mean that she can tell a version of his story which he will recognize. And clearly, as O'Faolain herself realizes, the desire to tell other people's stories (O'Donnell's and her brothers') is in any case also a desire to tell her own: remembering them brings her 'into the presence of my own sorrow and anger' (p. 198). The ways in which self-pity and anger on someone else's behalf interact is suggested again towards the end of her story, when her grief and pity for her siblings and her

---

[4] Laura Marcus writes: 'This shift ... from the self-consciousness of autobiography (which may conceal a cultural demand for confession) and the ethical responsibility to testify, has important implications for conceptions of the status and value of self-writings and for concepts of experience and our relationship to it. It would seem to entail a move away from self-reflection towards a sense that we are all witnesses of history's tragedies and may be summoned to testify to our knowledge of them' (Marcus, *Uses of Autobiography*, p. 20). See also Shoshana Felman and Dori Laub, *Testimony: Crises of Witnessing in Literature, Psychoanalysis and History* (New York and London: Routledge, 1992).

younger self is only made possible by projecting the sense of helplessness on to her pets:

> I took it for granted that they [her parents] had little tenderness towards us. They made me accept that, for myself and my brothers and sisters. But I can stop feeling passive when I think – they would have had no tenderness for Molly! They would have said: 'You're not expecting me to mind that dog, are you?' (p. 208)

Her own sorrow and anger (her self-pity) can only emerge on their behalf; just as, in the quotation above, the anger is on her brothers' behalf, or O'Donnell's, or O'Donnell's mother's.

The justification of this, for O'Faolain, is expressed in the afterword which accompanies the second edition of the book. Here, it turns out that her 'self pity' has itself becomes a motivation, a catalyst, for other stories: the reams of letters which she is sent in the months after the memoir's first publication. She comments:

> This is typical: '... I married and when he was thirty-three he had an affair, while I continued on because I had no money and I wanted the children to have two parents. I nursed him for five years with bone cancer and I am alone now. I passed you once, you wheeled a bike near Trinity, in a fur coat. I whispered "I admire you so much ..."' This is exactly as the woman wrote it: the compressed life-story and the praise of me happen in the same breath. It seemed to me that I was being praised only because, though she recognised her own self-sacrifice, she was unable to praise herself for it. But then I'd think that maybe she'd read my journalism and seen me on television and really did admire me, and that it was I who could not accept praise. (p. 218)

In this example, the anonymous woman's story is made possible – authorized – by O'Faolain's, and in the process retrospectively authorizes what O'Faolain herself has done. Like O'Faolain herself, the woman in the letter can only tell her story through talking about someone else: self-pity or self-praise are only possible if felt, first, on someone else's behalf. This interaction between text and context is something ongoing: O'Faolain's story of her own life is written and rewritten as more fragments of evidence about her family filter through after the book becomes public; and indeed the book itself changes the remaining family relationships. The fears of a hostile response prove groundless ('"Who does she think she is?" I could hear the reviewers saying. But it turned out to be not like that at all' p. xi); the narrative of speechlessness and silence is framed by a narrative of dialogue and response: 'my small voice was answered by a rich chorus of voices!' (p. xii). In O'Faolain's version, then, autobiography works as a process; one story acts as a catalyst for many more, constructing a sort of collective autobiography or a testament: a chorus of voices, bearing witness to their own lives.

I like this idea of autobiography as an opening up of other stories; but I am not sure whether it holds true, for my own use of O'Faolain. When I first thought about using *Are You Somebody?* in this essay, it seemed like a way of killing two birds with one stone. The difficulties O'Faolain articulates in terms of authorizing her account would, I thought, deflect the criticism (the kicks) which might be aimed at me (anticipating, for example, the question *who does she think she is?*). Secondly, my difficulties about writing what it means to be an Irishwoman would be solved if I simply followed O'Faolain's more articulate, knowing account of that topic. My story wouldn't need be told, if her more extreme / more meaningful / more 'Irish' story (of alcoholism and neglect) could be told instead. This is not to deny that O'Faolain's story is meaningful to me (that I recognize myself in it): on the level of emotional experience, mainly, though also, sometimes, on the level of incident. But I don't have an alcoholic mother or an absent father, and I didn't grow up neglected; and it is problematic, I think, for me to appropriate O'Faolain's story as my own; just as it is problematic for O'Faolain to mark the O'Donnell trial as relevant to her own family story (to the story of her brothers). But there is also another level to this. If something is dislodged in me by O'Faolain's story, just as something was dislodged in her by O'Donnell's (heard at second hand), it is also true that something was dislodged in me when I read O'Donnell's story as told by O'Faolain. The structure of that memory (the mother and child, the liminal zone of the school corridor in which family secrets are made temporarily public) reminded me of events, not just in O'Faolain's story (the dirty cardigan and so on), but in my own life. What do you do with that shock of recognition?[5] And does it matter that writing about *Are You Somebody?* has in the end enabled me not so much to tell my story, as to avoid telling it?

I'm not sure, in the end, whether my identification with O'Faolain's story (my desire to inhabit her story) means that I am appropriating her voice, or that she is drowning out mine. It is for this reason that I want in the second half of this article to look at a different text, in which the relationships of voice, place and self – and their inflection in memory – are central.

Letting the other in: Margaret Atwood's Alias Grace

> And then I heard her voice, as clear as anything, right in my ear, saying *Let me in*. I was quite startled, and looked hard at Mary, who by that time was lying on the floor, as we were making up the bed. But she gave no sign of having said anything; and her eyes were still open, and staring up at the ceiling.
>
> Then I thought with a rush of fear, But I did not open the window. And I

---

[5] The term 'shock of recognition' comes from Raymond Williams, but I found it in Elspeth Probyn, *Outside Belongings* (New York and London: Routledge, 1996).

> ran across the room and opened it, because I must have heard wrong and she was saying *Let me out.*[6]

Atwood's 1996 novel, *Alias Grace*, is set in mid nineteenth-century Canada, and is based on the true story of an Irish woman named Grace Marks, who was jailed for her part in the murder of her employer and his housekeeper at Richmond Hill in 1843. There might be obvious reasons for my interest in this narrative: for instance, the fact that two of the main protagonists in this Canadian novel are Irish – Grace herself and her supposed accomplice, my namesake James McDermott. But the apparent possibilities for my identification with Atwood's heroine are undercut in a variety of ways: Grace Marks is distanced from me as a fellow Irishwoman, not just because of historical distance, but because she is Northern Irish, and Protestant, and thus undercuts any unitary notion of Irish female identity. More importantly, the significance of Grace in Atwood's novel lies in the very impossibility of 'identifying' in any transparent way with her. In Atwood's novel, Grace's very identity is open to debate: is she a cunning murderess or naive victim of events? The historical Grace Marks gave at least three different accounts of her involvement in the murders; and while her fellow-defendant, James McDermott, was hanged, enough doubt remained about Grace's role for her sentence to be commuted to life imprisonment; and Atwood's novel also leaves the question of her guilt or innocence unresolved. Secondly, Atwood complicates the issue of identity by introducing a fictional character, Mary Whitney, into Grace's narrative. The historical Grace used the alias Mary Whitney when she fled to America after the murders. In Atwood's version, this name bears a history, as Grace explains: 'Mary Whitney was once a particular friend of mine. She was dead by that time, Sir, and I did not think she would mind if I used her name. She sometimes lent me her clothing, too'.[7] One possibility raised in Atwood's novel is that Grace has been possessed by the ghost of Mary Whitney, whose voice Grace hears crying 'let me in' in the quotation with which I began. My interest in *Alias Grace*, then, lies not so much in the presence of differing versions of Irishness in the text, but rather in the production of identity and identification which occurs

6 Margaret Atwood, *Alias Grace* (London: Virago, 1998), p. 207. Further page references to this volume will be given after quotations in the text.

7 Ibid., p. 117. The swapping of clothes and names (of identities) which occurs between Mary and Grace in the novel is part of a larger set of borrowings and appropriations in the text, which suggests the circulating and unstable nature of identity. Thus, Jeremiah the pedlar becomes Dr Jerome du Pont; the letter J which is supposed to identify the man Grace will marry designates several different characters; and so on. While some of these borrowings seem harmless (Grace inheriting clothes from both her mother and from Mary Whitney as a remembrance; Jeremiah the pedlar bartering goods), the misplacings involved come to signal larger transgressions at the time of the murder, when Mary Whitney's handkerchief is used (by Grace or by McDermott?) to strangle Nancy Kinnear, and when both Grace and McDermott transgress class and other codes by appropriating the victims' clothes for themselves.

in the character of Grace Marks, and in her relationship with Mary Whitney in particular.

From the start, *Alias Grace* foregrounds the problems raised by any attempt to give an account of oneself. The novel is constructed around a set of testimonies: excerpts from historical documents associated with the trial, including fragments of the confessions of Grace Marks and James McDermott, and the accounts of various individuals who visited Grace in prison; fictional letters from some of the main protagonists in the story; and most importantly, the fictional Grace's own story of her life, as told to Dr Simon Jordan, twenty years after the murders. This story (which constitutes the main narrative we get in the text) is problematic for two reasons. Firstly, while Grace remembers much of her life in surprising detail, she has apparently repressed all details of the murders, and much of the suspense of the novel rests on whether Grace will respond to Jordan's techniques for memory recall (the rather farcical use of objects to trigger associations), and in the process prove herself to be guilty or innocent. However, the imagery used for memory in the text (memory as bits of cloth pulled from a ragbag, p. 410) suggests that there is no complete or unitary account of the past to be had: any story which gives the illusion of wholeness will of necessity be the product of an artistic reconstruction (of editing and selecting) akin to Grace's own quiltmaking. As Grace says of her trial lawyer, MacKenzie:

> He wanted me to tell my story in a coherent way ... and at last he said that the right thing was, not to tell the story as I truly remembered it, which nobody could be expected to make any sense of; but to tell a story that would hang together, and that had some chance of being believed. (p. 415)

Secondly, Grace's story is problematic because of the power relationship between her and Simon Jordan. As I suggested earlier, speaking the self is always double-edged; and the fluctuations of power between being forced to account for yourself and giving your version, are suggested in Grace's various comments on the interviews with Jordan: 'he must mean that he has come to test me' (p. 43); 'perhaps I will tell you lies' (p. 46); 'I did not know what he wanted me to say' (p. 77); 'a feeling like being torn open' (p. 79). On the one hand, Grace is reliant on Jordan – his clinical account of her may form the basis of a new appeal which will enable her to be finally released from prison, and thus her story may be an attempt to tell him what he wants to hear (MacKenzie suggests another version of this: that Grace may be in love with Jordan, and weaving a tale like Scheherazade to delay his departure); on the other hand, Jordan's fantasies about Grace and other servant girls suggests that she retains a certain form of power over him, in terms of what salacious details she will or will not reveal.

> Looked at objectively, what's been going on between them ... has been a contest of wills. She hasn't refused to talk – far from it. She's told him

> a great deal; but she's told him only what she's chosen to tell. What he wants is what she refuses to tell; what she chooses perhaps not even to know ... But he'll pry it out of her yet. He's got the hook in her mouth, but can he pull her out? Up, out of the abyss, up to the light. Out of the deep blue sea.[8]

Grace then is someone who claims not to know her own story, and who, by accident or design, tells the wrong story.[9] Instead of the sordid details of the murders which Jordan hopes to hear, the things which Grace 'chooses to tell' her addressee concern her earlier life, prior to working at Kinnear's house: the journey across the Atlantic during which her mother dies, and the daily routines of her life as a servant girl, in particular. Mary Whitney is introduced into this narrative as someone who has worked with Grace in her first post, at the Alderman Parkinson's; and her importance in the narrative seems to lie in the fact that her radical political beliefs and her irreverent attitude to her supposed betters, make her the opposite of the naive and dutiful Grace: 'Mrs. Alderman Parkinson said a lady must never sit in a chair a gentleman has just vacated, though she would not say why; but Mary Whitney said, Because, you silly goose, it's still warm from his bum; which was a coarse thing to say' (p. 23). In Grace's story, Mary Whitney transgresses class boundaries by sleeping with the young master of the house, and the circumstances of her subsequent death (from an illegal abortion) are hushed up, so that only Grace knows the full facts of what happened to her. Mary's story is suppressed, then, but it takes on a sort of afterlife in Grace's narrative: not just because Grace can bear witness to the graphic details of her death, but because Mary's thoughts and ideas continue to haunt Grace's narrative, as the quotation above about Mrs Alderman Parkinson might suggest. However, the possibility is also mooted that Mary is haunting Grace in a more literal sense, given that Grace has heard her ghost crying 'let me in'. In death, as in life, it seems, Mary Whitney does not know her place.

Mary Whitney's story re-emerges in the pivotal scene of the hypnosis organized by Dr Jerome du Pont. Here, ironically, the story Jordan wants to hear (the salacious story) is in the end told, but not in either the place or the voice which he expects. Instead of the intimate dialogue which he had anticipated, the murder story is told in a more public forum, in the presence of five or six other people; and

---

8 Ibid., p. 374. The other story in the novel – which I don't have room to discuss here – is of course that of Simon Jordan himself. His story works as a mirror image of Grace's: Jordan is also displaced (from America to Canada); he also engages in class transgression (his fantasies about servant girls) and in a transgressive affair which almost leads to murder; and most obviously, he also falls victim to amnesia at the end of the novel.

9 Jordan's experiments with object-association prove a dismal failure; and when Grace's narrative finally reaches the day of the murders (the 'breaking day') the effect is in some ways an anti-climax: the murders occur 'off-screen', and much of the action is not accounted for, leaving long gaps in which Grace is apparently unconscious or simply occupied elsewhere.

the voice which emerges is lewd, antagonistic, and happy to recall the murders in gruesome detail:

> 'Ask her,' he says sternly, 'if she was in the cellar of Mr. Kinnear's house, on Saturday, July 23rd, 1843.'
>
> 'The cellar,' says Du Pont. 'You must picture the cellar, Grace. Go back in time, descend in space ...'
>
> 'Yes,' says Grace, in her new, thin voice. 'Along the hallway, lift the trapdoor; go down the cellar stairs. The barrels, the whisky, the vegetables in the boxes full of sand. There on the floor. Yes, I was in the cellar.'
>
> 'Ask her if she saw Nancy there.'
>
> 'Oh yes, I saw her.' A pause ...
>
> 'Was she alive?' asks Simon. 'Was she still alive, when you saw her?'
>
> The voice sniggers. 'She was partly alive. Or partly dead. She needed' – a high twittering – 'to be put out of her misery.' (p. 466)

While initially this voice seems to reveal the true identity of Grace (the side of her which she has kept hidden to date), as the dialogue continues a more sinister possibility emerges:

> 'It was so cold, lying on the floor, and I was all alone; I needed to keep warm. But Grace doesn't know, she's never known!' The voice was no longer teasing. 'They almost hanged her, but that would have been wrong. She knew nothing! I only borrowed her clothing for a time.'
>
> 'Her clothing?' says Simon.
>
> 'Her earthly shell. Her fleshly garment. She forgot to open the window, and so I couldn't get out!' (p. 468)

The murderess, if this voice is to be believed, thus turns out to be Mary Whitney, who has borrowed Grace's body just as Grace previously borrowed her clothes, in order to carry on affairs with both Kinnear and McDermott, and ultimately to murder her rival Nancy. Atwood thus presents us with a way of explaining the discrepancies in Grace's character not by reconciling them, but by dispelling the myth of a unitary identity altogether: Grace 'is' two people; the name Grace Marks itself little more than an alias.

The relationship between Grace's story/voice and Mary's here can be read in a number of ways. Firstly, the possibility is left open that the whole scene could be an elaborate hoax, as Jordan partially suspects: 'Was Grace really in a trance, or was she play-acting, and laughing up her sleeve? He knows what he saw and heard, but he may have been shown an illusion, which he cannot prove to have been one' (p. 472). As the reader (although not Grace's audience) knows, the hypnosis is being carried out by Grace's old friend Jeremiah the pedlar, in his guise as Dr Jerome du Pont; and Grace's subsequent letter to Jeremiah does suggest a conspiracy between them in its reference to 'things we both know of' (p. 496). Indeed, given that we only have Grace's word for the existence of Mary in the first place, then we could also read her entire narrative to Jordan as preparing the way for this 'conjuror's trick'. On the other hand, whether or not the Mary Whitney ghost is an invention of Grace's and Jeremiah's, we can still say that this second voice is necessary in order to 'fill in the gaps' of Grace's story – to say the things which cannot be said in Grace's 'conscious' narrative. In this sense, Grace needs Mary Whitney's voice in order to complete her own story. However, if Grace needs Mary Whitney's voice to speak her self, it is also the case that Mary Whitney needs Grace's body, in order to be heard. Mary is parasitic on Grace, both in the general sense that we only know of her existence through Grace's account of her, and in the specific sense that her ghost needs Grace's body (her 'fleshly garment') in order to exist. The difficulty which remains is to ascertain which voice – which story – takes priority. In a way, Mary's voice is taking over from Grace's here and speaking in her place. On the other hand, the ghost's complaint is precisely that unlike Grace, who has repeated her narrative numerous times, Mary Whitney's story has up to now had no audience: '"I liked it there [at the Asylum] at first, I could talk out loud there. I could laugh. I could tell what happened. But no one listened to me." There is a small, thin sobbing. "I was not heard"' (p. 468). Indeed, even with the ghost's intervention, we could say that Mary's story only gains a small part of the text (the ghost only speaks briefly, from pp. 464–9). The rest of the time, Grace's narrative drowns her out.[10]

In thinking about the relationship between Mary and Grace, Diane Fuss's account of identification may be useful. Briefly, identification can be described as the desire to be the other, to 'put myself in her place'. It exists in a complicated relationship to identity, in that identification both destabilizes identity, placing it under threat, and at the same time is necessary in order to construct identity: 'Identification is the detour through the other that defines a self.'[11] Identification can be understood as a form of haunting, in which aspects of the other are incorporated into the self: 'Identification, in other words, invokes phantoms. By incorporating the spectral remains of the dearly departed love-object, the subject vampiristically comes to life. To be open to an identification is to be open to a death encounter, open to the very possibility of communing with the dead' (p. 1).

---

[10] The relationship between Mary's and Grace's voices, as well as their intimate/antagonistic relationship with their addressee(s), could be analysed through Mikhail Bakhtin's concept of dialogism. See his *Problems of Dostoevsky's Poetics*, ed. and trans. Caryl Emerson (Minneapolis: University of Minnesota Press, 1984).

[11] Diana Fuss, *Identification Papers* (London and New York: Routledge, 1995), p. 2. Fuss offers the following definitions of these two key terms: 'I borrow my working definition of identity from Jean-Luc Nancy. Identity is "the Self that identifies itself." Identification is the psychical mechanism that produces self-recognition. Identification inhabits, organizes, instantiates identity' (p. 2). Fuss's main argument in this text – the problematics of identification versus desire (being versus having the other) – is outside the scope of this essay. Further page references to this volume will be given after quotations in the text.

However, while identification in this sense seems to be giving life to the other, it can also, paradoxically, be seen as an attempt to put the other to death:

> Of course, read psychoanalytically, *every* identification involves a degree of symbolic violence, a measure of temporary mastery and possession … [I]dentification operates on one level as an endless process of violent negation, a process of killing off the other in fantasy in order to usurp the other's place, the place where the subject desires to be. (p. 9)

In terms of Atwood's novel, identification between women can be seen at work in three ways: firstly, in Grace's identification with Mary, which enables Mary to remain alive in Grace's narrative; secondly, in Grace's (Mary's?) identification with Nancy, which results in the latter being killed off; and finally, and most complexly, in Mary's identification with Grace, in which she attempts to usurp Grace's place – literally, her body. In the first example, Grace could be said to identify secretly with Mary's rebelliousness. After Mary's death, Mary's comments and attitudes are incorporated into Grace's narrative (for example, in the Alderman Parkinson quotation above) and into her identity. In this reading, Mary 'vampiristically comes to life' in Grace, because Grace acts in the way Mary would have acted: specifically, in her transgressive behaviour at Kinnear's house. In the second case of identification, Grace (or, if we prefer, Mary) identifies with Nancy, coveting her superior position and her relationship with Kinnear. In this case, the violent aspect of identification comes to the fore: Nancy is killed off so that Grace/Mary can take her place, even to the extent of Grace putting on her clothes after the murder.[12] In the third, and most complex, example, we can argue that Mary identifies with Grace, coveting and in turn attempting to usurp her place also. This is suggested for the first time just before Mary's death, when she wills her belongings to Grace: 'And then she said, Soon I may be dead. But you will still be alive. And she gave me a cold and resentful look, such as I'd seen her give to others behind their backs, but never to me' (p. 202). In this reading, Mary 'borrows' Grace's 'fleshly garment' in an aggressive attempt to take her place, not that different from the subsequent 'borrowing' of the dead Nancy's clothes.

Identification, then, is paradoxical on two levels: firstly, because it is both an act

[12] Grace's story seems particularly apt for a psychoanalytic analysis in this respect, given that, as Fuss points out, 'Freud's later discussions of cross-class identifications between women … tend to focus mainly on a servant's erotic ambitions to kill off the mistress and to take her place with the master' (p. 25). Fuss adds, however: 'we might well ask to what extent this recurrent image of the romantic servant-girl infatuated with her employer operates as a denial and displacement of the sexual and economic exploitation of the servant-girl by the master – by Freud's own admission, an all too common situation in Victorian households.' (p. 53, note 8). Atwood's novel pursues this aspect through the character of Simon Jordan, with his recurring fantasies of servant girls of his childhood; implying that the supposition of Grace being in love with her employer may be as much male fantasy as reality.

of love and an act of violence (giving the other life and putting the other to death); secondly (as the contradiction between my first and third scenarios suggests), because it is not always clear *who* is doing the identifying: is Grace identifying with Mary or vice versa? This second problem can be thought about in a slightly different way: if Mary comes to speak through Grace's body, does this happen because of something which Grace does (does she incorporate Mary), or because of something which is done to her (does Mary inhabit Grace)? If we formulate the problem in these terms (that is, as a problem to do with attributing agency), then we can trace it back to what Fuss sees as a paradox in Freud's original concept of identification:

> These two dominant metaphorics of identification in Freud, ingestion and infection, follow opposite trajectories. While the first (oral ingestion) involves an active subject's conservation of the object of its idealization, the second (contagious infection) entails a passive subject's infilitration by an object not of its choosing. Capturing both the transitive and intransitive registers of identification, the *OED* defines the process as 'the act of identifying or fact of being identified.' We can thus economically summarize the difference between identifications as the difference between an active and a passive relation to the Other: to seize the Other, or to be seized by the Other ... [A] certain confusion in Freud's thinking on the question of identification and agency: does one possess an identification or is one possessed by it? (Fuss, p. 41)

The relationship between Mary and Grace in Atwood's novel is thus relevant to this essay in two ways. Firstly, it suggests the ways in which stories are displaced: both in terms of where they are told, and who tells them. Both Grace and Mary, in different ways, tell their story through the other's story (Grace using Mary's story to express the rebelliousness which otherwise she cannot admit to; Mary telling her story by intervening in Grace's). In other words, identity can only emerge via identification: as Diana Fuss puts it, 'every identity is a private identification come to light' (p. 2). Secondly, the fluctuation between borrowing and incorporation, between admiration and aggression, which characterizes their relationship, suggests that speaking from the place of the other always involves violence: against yourself as well as against someone else.

When I started to write about O'Faolain's text, it occurred to me that my relationship with her novel was similar to Mary Whitney's with Grace's narrative: I wanted to inhabit her story, to speak through it, and it was clear to me that such an identification was also a form of aggression, of wanting to take her place. It occurs to me now, however, that perhaps I have got the protagonists wrong: perhaps the Mary Whitney figure in this story is O'Faolain, and I have incorporated her story into mine as a means of keeping my identity out of the picture. In that case, the model of speaking the self which I am following here is that of Grace Marks herself; who finishes by keeping her own counsel.

Conclusion: making a show of myself – and them

> The truth is that very few understand the truth about forgiveness. It is not the culprits who need to be forgiven; rather it is the victims, because they are the ones who cause all the trouble. If they were only less weak and careless, and more foresightful, and if they would keep from blundering into difficulties, think of all the sorrow in the world that would be spared.
>
> I had a rage in my heart for many years, against Mary Whitney, and especially against Nancy Montgomery; against the two of them both, for letting themselves be done to death in the way that they did, and leaving me behind with the full weight of it. (Atwood, pp. 531–2)

In both *Alias Grace* and *Are You Somebody?*, a female narrator seeks to identify herself to a male interlocutor, with a more or less obvious agenda of his own: the cheerful, anonymous psychiatrist in O'Faolain's text, the rather foolish figure of Dr Jordan in Atwood's. In both cases, the attempt at self-identification goes wrong: Grace's name starts to slip – becomes an alias – while O'Faolain fails to say her name at all. What becomes clear in the process is that displaying your identification papers also means displaying your identifications: the bits of other people's stories which constitute who we are. In this way, confession takes on the burden of testimony; and it is significant, I think, that both texts in a sense take as their point of departure a murder trial, with all its connotations of enforced speech and absent voices. For O'Faolain, speaking for those absent voices is seen as a form of privilege. But as the above quotation from *Alias Grace* suggests, such testifying can also be experienced as a burden, having to carry the 'full weight' of evidence which other people are too weak, or careless, or forgetful, to present for themselves.

In this essay, I have tried to write about how I experience Irishness by telling somebody else's story. On the one hand, I did this so that I would not have to tell my own story (so that I would not have that sensation of squirming in the dock, being held to account); but on the other hand I did it, ironically, so that I would not have to tell other people's stories – family and national secrets which unlike O'Faolain's, are not already in print, and which for whatever reasons I didn't want to have to carry the weight of.[13] In thinking now about this reluctance on my part, I am reminded of one of the anonymous letters included in the afterword of O'Faolain's text. It includes the following sentence: 'on the surface great respectability was kept up – that was the worst of it – keeping up appearances ...' (p. 229). In a sense, both *Alias Grace* and *Are You Somebody?* are stories about keeping up appearances, and what happens when domestic secrets leak out. Grace's narrative, for example, is preoccupied to the point of obsession with female domestic labour, and the work involved in getting rid of stains (an

13 While I can of course claim that I simply do not wish to expose those stories in a voyeuristic fashion, the result is that I am to some extent complicit in a culture of silencing.

obsession which contrasts strikingly with the physical realities of sex and murder which it tries to evade), while the strongest moments of shame in O'Faolain's narrative occur when family respectability breaks down (an outsider sees her dirty house; her mother is found lying drunk on the floor). In both texts, keeping up appearances is woman's work; and society's strongest censure is reserved for women who 'make a show' of themselves.[14] What I am struck by, reading back over this essay, is how much I have bought into this same discourse, which on one level I set out to analyse. Because if this essay succeeds in not telling certain stories (editing out, in effect, the stains on my own life and the lives around me), I did not experience this as an easy omission, but as a form of work: the work of keeping up appearances. In that sense, if this essay testifies to anything, it testifies to the difficult, essential, and ultimately counter-productive labour of maintaining Irish female respectability.

---

14 For further analysis of the work involved in keeping and revealing family secrets, see Annette Kuhn, *Family Secrets: Acts of Memory and Imagination* (London and New York: Verso, 1995). For theoretical accounts of female respectability and 'making a show' of yourself, see Mary Russo, *The Female Grotesque: Risk, Excess and Modernity* (New York and London: Routledge, 1995), and Beverley Skeggs, *Formations of Class and Gender: Becoming Respectable* (London: Sage, 1997). For an analysis of female respectability in an Irish context, see Breda Gray, 'Mixed "White" Blessings / Belongings: Irish Women in London', unpublished conference paper, *Sexing the Nation* conference, Cheltenham and Gloucester Institute of Higher Education, July 1998. While I have in mind in particular O'Faolain's mother and Mary Whitney as women who transgress the bounds of respectability, clearly the two narrators (O'Faolain and Marks) must also 'make a show' of themselves, in order to tell their stories.

Chapter 6

'Lost Voices, and Fresh Perspectives': Margaret Laurence's *The Diviners* and Candia McWilliam's *Debatable Land*

Flora Alexander

The view from the north

I write as a woman from the northern Highlands of Scotland. For over thirty years I have worked in the north-east of Scotland, at the University of Aberdeen. That may not sound like a long distance to move, but the north-east is a quite separate region, with a history and culture completely different from those of my Highland upbringing. Despite having worked here and raised our children here, neither my husband (originally from Northern Ireland) nor myself 'belongs' to this culture, and I am frequently reminded of my difference. It is not just that the north-east has a very specific local Scots dialect that we have learned to follow, but would not presume to speak. As a small city grown suddenly to medium size, Aberdeen still has a well-developed distinction between those who went to school here and have relatives here, and those who did not and have not. And in the north-east there is a culture, which has both good and bad sides, but is certainly different from my own, of steadiness accompanied by understatement, best conveyed through the phrase used for even the highest praise: 'Nae bad'.

I live now in a devolved Scotland, and I am writing in the days immediately following the opening (after an interval of almost 300 years) of the Parliament for which I voted in the 1997 Referendum. On 5 July, the day of the official opening, I walked through the streets of Edinburgh, although I had not gone there to watch the ceremonies, and certainly not to see the Queen and her procession; I was in Edinburgh simply because I was returning home from external examining in the north of England. As I walked past the crowds on my way to Waverley station I was conscious, as I always am in Edinburgh or Glasgow, that Scotland is made up of much more than the Highlands and the north-east. The south of Scotland possesses a network of cultures which interest me, but which I do not know well, although I have learned to understand them better through the experience of my grown-up children. The main polarization that shapes Scottish lives is, of course, that between Scotland and England: much in our day-to-day existence is affected by different legal systems, different relations between Church and State, and different educational systems with, in Scotland, a long-standing emphasis on a broader base and wider access.[1] But within this major oppositional system, Scotland is itself divided by regional differences, and until quite recently I knew several parts of England better than I knew the south of Scotland. My complicated attitude to things Scottish exists within a basic consciousness that I am a Scottish woman, not an English woman. But, in addition, I am a 'northern Scot', which means that in some aspects of behaviour or style, as well as in language, I feel different from people whose background is Ayrshire or Lothian. And this distinction in itself is still too simple, because my mother, whom I remember as having utterly typical Highland speech and outlook and behaviour, was the daughter of an Englishman who emigrated north from Kent to find work. Until I was seventeen I lived 200 miles north of Glasgow and Edinburgh, venturing only very rarely south of Inverness, yet I was aware of first and second cousins in several locations in the south of England, some of them members of my maternal grandfather's family, and others the children of uncles who had moved south seeking employment.

The things that distinguish Highland people from the rest of the people of Scotland are difficult to disentangle. I am concerned here with matters of culture and behaviour, not racial descent. Just as, for the purposes of voting in the Devolution referendum of 1997 and the election of the Scottish Parliament in 1999, the people of Scotland are all the people who live in Scotland, whatever their racial origins, similarly the people of the small town in Ross-shire (now in Highland Region) where I grew up included (alongside the many citizens called Ross, Munro, and Mackenzie, whose heritage was local and stable) others whose English, Welsh or Irish families had migrated there as part of the cosmopolitan workforce of the Invergordon naval base. There were still others whose Italian forebears had come to work in catering, or whose Polish fathers had remained behind in Scotland after the end of the Second World War. All these people appeared to adapt quite quickly to basic elements of the Highland life-style which, in spite of the disruption brought to traditional ways by a second world war following rapidly upon the first, remained slow to change. It was a region conservative, not necessarily in politics, but certainly in religion and in social habits. People were hospitable, and not only willing, but eager, to feed any stranger who came their way. A reticent courtesy was the norm, to the extent that it could obstruct the clear expression of views and wishes. Arrogance and display were frowned on, and this was associated with acceptance of being out of fashion and out of touch; there was almost a satisfaction taken in being a long distance

1 See D.E. Davie, *The Democratic Intellect: Scotland and Her Universities in the Nineteenth Century* (Edinburgh: Edinburgh University Press, 1964).

away from the south and the cities, so that we could do things in our own way. There was also a censorious, fault-finding preoccupation with reputation and respectability. These qualities are no doubt found widely in small towns and I do not claim they were exclusive to us; however, since all of the Scottish cities were at that time a whole day's journey away, and even the bus journey to Inverness took two hours, this life-style persisted unchallenged for a long time.

Scotland has a three-way split in language. In the Lowlands, and in the East, people alternate between the Scots-accented English which is more or less standard, and varieties of Scots. But Highland Scots were in the past speakers not of Scots, but of Gaelic.[2] When I was brought up in Easter Ross, north of Inverness, it was no longer a Gaelic-speaking area, but my parents, and the mainly elderly people they associated with, retained a sprinkling of Gaelic vocabulary. They both remembered (or thought they did) knowing Gaelic speakers in their youth. My father, the older by 18 years, recollected ruefully being compelled in his boyhood (in the last few years of the nineteenth century) to go with his parents to church services conducted in Gaelic, in spite of not having himself been taught the language. Perhaps even more oddly, in his old age he liked to listen to Gaelic services broadcast on radio, still unable to understand the words, but I assume enjoying the very unusual sound of unaccompanied Gaelic choral singing, in which the congregation repeats a line 'put out' by a precentor. Our house contained a number of Gaelic bibles, long unused, inscribed with names from my father's family, and bearing mid-nineteenth century dates. Thus I find myself tantalizingly close to a lost culture, which remains out of reach because I have not found the time or the discipline to learn the language of my grandfathers and grandmothers. My mind is still filled with early memories of Gaelic names for places and people close to me: farms called Achnagarron, Balnaguisach, and Coilemore; acquaintances called Uisdean and Seonaid; houses named Ardnamara and Caberfèidh. Similarly, when I visited Ireland for the first time, I was surprised at how familiar the forms of placenames were. Yet I should not exaggerate the extent of my Gaelic inheritance. While my memories of childhood are scattered with words used between my parents, or between my mother and my aunts (a 'poor *truaghan*' was a pitiful creature; my mittens were *mogans*, and when I was untidy in appearance my mother said I was *ròpach*; instead of darling we might say '*m'eudail*'), these words were for home and not for school. They were part of the language of older people. I was, as academic children tend to be, very much school-identified, and interaction between schoolchildren, especially as we grew into our teens, took place in a cultural climate heavily affected by the Light Programme of the BBC, and Radio Luxembourg. Remnants of Gaelic receded and gave way to national and international culture.

---

2 Tom McArthur, ed., *The Oxford Companion to the English Language* (Oxford: Oxford University Press, 1992), p. 469.

When I think about literary heritage, I realize that – like some other contributors to this book – I was for a considerable time starved of written texts I could relate to personally, in the sense of recognizing them as speaking from the same range of positions I myself could occupy. While making this point, I must also acknowledge that I see truth in A.S. Byatt's assertion that she reads books to transcend the limitations of her own position, not to have them reinforced.[3] Similarly, while I did not grow up as Iain Crichton Smith did in a Gaelic environment, I identify strongly with his remark that, '[t]hough I was brought up on an island where Gaelic was the dominant language, my reading was much the same as if I had been schooled at Eton, rather than at Bayble Public School'.[4] I read books of all kinds, voraciously, following the common pattern of using literature as a means of escape from a life I found tedious and claustrophobic. It has been observed by many of those who went to school anywhere in the British Empire or Commonwealth between the 1930s and the 1950s that we all read the same canonical texts of English literature, and the negative effects of this have become a postcolonial commonplace.[5] It is obvious that great cultural damage was done by creating the impression around the English-speaking world that literature could only be about a society or a landscape belonging to a 'mother-country' and which was far from the direct experience of many readers. From my Highland point of view, I cannot regret the experience of studying those authors, but because the canon conferred on them such prestige, and their presence excluded so much else, I shared with many other postcolonial readers the perception that literature came from 'somewhere else', not from my own territory. In fact, I knew that three novelists were living close to my home town (Eric Linklater at Nigg, Neil Gunn at Evanton, and Jane Duncan almost visibly across the Cromarty Firth at Jemimaville on the Black Isle), but by reason of being alive they would not in those days have qualified for recognition as 'literary' for examination purposes. Meanwhile, such Scottish writers as *were* admitted to the canon, did not mean very much to me. The writers I knew, like Walter Scott, Robert Burns, and William Dunbar, were male and 'southern'. Burns and Dunbar presented problems because they contain Lowland Scots vocabulary never used north of the Highand line. 'Tam o' Shanter' was much harder to read than *The Canterbury Tales*, because the

---

3 Janet Todd, ed., *Women Writers Talking* (New York: Holmes & Meier, 1983), p. 180.

4 Iain Crichton Smith, 'Real People in a Real Place', in *Towards the Human. Selected Essays by Iain Crichton Smith* (Edinburgh: Edinburgh University Press, 1986), p. 27. Crichton Smith's statement plays on the term 'public school', which in Scotland was traditionally used for the local school which provided education for all children free of charge.

5 See, for example, Bill Ashcroft, Gareth Griffiths, and Helen Tiffin, *The Empire Writes Back. Theory and Practice in Post-Colonial Literature,* New Accents Series (London: Routledge, 1989); and Elleke Boehmer, *Colonial & Postcolonial Literature* (Oxford: Oxford University Press, 1995).

strange words in Chaucer were likely to come from French, which we were being taught.

When I explored past literature for myself through the quite wide range of reading that fell into my hands at school, I found, in anthologies, poems by Violet Jacob, Marion Angus, and Rachel Annand Taylor, which were sufficient to let me know that Scots women *could* write poetry.[6] But, again, none of these belonged to the Highlands: they had lived in places that were, for me, a day's journey away, and this made them so remote that they might just as well have been English; not one of them was of my own 'tribe'. With the exception of Jane Duncan, I was not aware of any Highland woman who had been poet, novelist or dramatist, although I later became aware of Naomi Mitchison and Jessie Kesson, and discovered that the novelist and dramatist 'Josephine Tey/Gordon Daviot' (Elizabeth Mackintosh) had belonged to Inverness.[7] More recently – in fact embarrassingly recently – I have learned that there were women composing poetry in Gaelic in the country I saw as mine.[8] Most surprising to me was the fact that an important Gaelic poet, Màiri Mhòr nan Òran (Mary McPherson, or 'Big Mary of the Songs'), lived quite near, in Inverness, in the nineteenth century. I did not know of the existence of these poets because their work was in Gaelic, and now I understand better that because of the transition from Gaelic to English we lost a tradition. So I had an impression of emptiness where in fact there was significant creation. I was familiar with Gaelic singing from radio broadcasts, but in a vague, uninformed way that filled my head only with fragments of melody about 'brown-haired girls' and 'Màiri's wedding'; I lacked the information that might have helped me to connect this with who I was and where I lived.

Margaret Laurence's Highland Women

Thus I was educated very well, but only in part. I had a strongly developed aesthetic sense, and I responded to emotions and rhythms and ideas, but I retained the sense that 'real' literature was beyond the reach of my personal culture. I could not visualize how a Highland woman could develop a voice, or a place from which

6 See Carol Anderson, 'Tales of Her Own Countries: Violet Jacob', pp. 347–59, Christopher Whyte, 'Marion Angus and the Boundaries of Self', pp. 373–88, and Dorothy McMillan, 'Twentieth Century Poetry 1: Rachel Annand Taylor to Veronica Forrest-Thomson', pp. 428–43, in Douglas Gifford and Dorothy McMillan, eds, *A History of Scottish Women's Writing* (Edinburgh: Edinburgh University Press, 1997).

7 See Jenni Calder, 'More Than Merely Ourselves: Naomi Mitchison', pp. 444–55, Isobel Murray, 'Jessie Kesson', pp. 481–93, and Lorena Laing Hart and Francis Russell Hart, 'Jane Duncan: The Homecoming of Imagination', pp. 468–80, in Gifford and McMillan, eds, *A History of Scottish Women's Writing*.

8 Meg Bateman, 'Women's Writing in Scottish Gaelic Since 1750', in Gifford and McMillan, eds, *A History of Scottish Women's Writing*, pp. 659–76.

to speak. My place and people were not validated by being 'in' literature. I was not even capable of recognizing this lack, as long as my approach to literature was dominated by the concept of 'great books'. In this respect the Canadian novelist Margaret Laurence has come to fill an important gap for me, by writing about my heritage in a way that I find meaningful. Laurence writes in four novels, and a collection of short stories, all produced between 1964 and 1974, about the lives of Scottish emigrants to Canada.[9] Although her own family's roots, before they emigrated to Manitoba, were in Fife, and her husband's family came from Shetland, her desire to establish contact with an ancestral culture drew her to things Highland.[10] Her creation in *The Diviners* (1974) of Morag Gunn, brought up in Manitoba by an adoptive father with roots in my family territory of Easter Ross, thus offers me a representation in fiction of things which I had not previously seen written down. Laurence had read Highland history and literature, and was also acquainted with the local writer Jane Duncan, whom she visited at her home on the Black Isle, the deceptively named peninsula of fertile farmland just north of Inverness. *The Diviners* draws on all these sources of knowledge, and Laurence uses the culture of the north Highlands as a key element in her study of the negotiation about identity carried through by her character. Morag grows up in Manawaka, a fictionalized version of the small town in Manitoba where Laurence herself was raised. This was a community where Scottish settlers mixed with others of English, Irish, and Ukrainian origins, and also lived alongside the Métis people (of mixed native and Scots/French descent) of the prairies. An orphaned child, Morag is nourished imaginatively by her guardian, Christie Logan, with tales of her Scottish heritage. Morag's 'Gunn' family have come to the prairies some generations ago from the north Highlands, and in the First World War her father fought alongside Christie, who was brought as a child to Canada from Ross-shire. The Scottish dimension of the novel consists of Christie's stories, which feed Morag's conception of her Scottish identity, together with a visit she makes to the north of Scotland, and a carefully worked out set of connections between the Highland Clearances and the oppression of the Métis people by new immigrants to Canada.

Despite the many differences between myself as reader and the fictional Morag, *The Diviners* has provided me, at a very simple level, with the pleasure of recognition of 'my' country represented in fiction. Much less well known than

---

9 Margaret Laurence, *The Diviners* (London: Virago, 1989). All references to the novel are included in the chapter following the relevant quotation and are from this edition. Laurence's other novels, *The Stone Angel* (1964), *A Jest of God* (1966), and *The Fire-Dwellers* (1969), and her short stories *A Bird in the House* (1970) are also based on the lives of Scottish settlers in Canada.

10 Margaret Laurence, *Dance on the Earth: A Memoir* (Toronto: McClelland & Stewart, 1989), pp. 176–7. Laurence indicates that she regarded her husband's Shetland connections as 'Highland', presumably because Shetland is in the extreme north. Shetland in fact is not Highland, and has its own distinct Norse-influenced dialect and culture.

the more southern territories of Inverness-shire, Perthshire, and Argyll, the north Highlands I come from combines a hinterland of very inhospitable mountain and moorland with a coastal strip of gently rolling, fertile agricultural land. In the setting created for Morag's visit to her lover, Dan MacRaith, in Crombruach, I quickly identify the small fishing town of Cromarty, which I used to look at over the sea from my window as a child; and in Morag's view of Easter Ross and the Black Isle, I see a close representation of a way of life I remember. However, all this is skewed because the representation is seen 'from the outside' through the eyes of a Canadian observer, and it is in this perceptual slippage that perhaps the greatest source of illumination for me lies.

Laurence bases Morag's imagined Highland identity on a mythologised forebear, Piper Gunn. I find in her handling of Morag's reception of this material, to display aspects of her character's growth from childhood to an independent woman, an important set of insights into the available ways of constructing a 'Highland' self. Christie's stories are a version of the history of the Highland Clearances in the nineteenth century, when landlords drove tenants off their land in order to raise large numbers of sheep. There was, at the least, widespread hardship, and in some places atrocities: people were burned out of their houses, and forced on to land which offered them little hope of making a living. Large numbers of Highlanders emigrated, many of them to Canada. Laurence has used a documented journey as the basis for Christie's romanticised 'Tales' of 'Piper Gunn' and 'the Long March' and 'the Rebels' (pp. 40–2, 68–9, 105–7). In the Kildonan emigration of June 1813, a party of Sutherland people left Stromness in Orkney, sailing on the vessel *Prince of Wales* for Canada. The plan was to land them at the Hudson's Bay Company base at York Factory, but as a result of inadequate information and organization they were instead put ashore still further north, at Fort Churchill, without proper provisions for the savage north Manitoba winter. They were led by a man named Archibald Macdonald on the ordeal of a 150 mile walk to their final destination at Red River, and encouraged on their way by the piping of Robert Gunn.[11] Laurence fictionalizes this narrative in Christie's three tales, delivered in a style ornamented with the conventions of Celtic epic, in which Macdonald and Gunn are transformed into a single mythical ancestor for Morag, bearing her own clan name.

The Highlander has been defined in opposition to the Lowlander at least since the fourteenth century. Priscilla Bawcutt, discussing the comic abuse of Highlanders in the work of the southern poet William Dunbar, notes that a century before Dunbar, the chronicler John of Fordun had drawn a distinction between cultured, law-abiding and peaceful Lowlanders and wild, treacherous and thieving

---

[11] J.M. Bumstead, *The People's Clearance. Highland Emigration to British North America, 1770–1815* (Edinburgh: Edinburgh University Press, 1982), pp. 209–13; James Hunter, *A Dance Called America. The Scottish Highlands, the United States, and Canada* (Edinburgh and London: Mainstream Press, 1994), pp. 181–6.

Highlanders.[12] In the early modern period, the Highland area was seen in central Scotland as threateningly unstable, unwilling to conform to Lowland norms in social organization or manners or religion, and, in Tom Devine's words, 'both inferior and dangerous'.[13] After the Battle of Culloden in 1745 we find deep anxiety about Highlanders as barbarous and treacherous, co-existing eventually with a fascination with the romantic loser in the figures of Charles Edward Stuart and Flora Macdonald. Walter Scott's *Rob Roy* employs comic Edinburgh stereotypes of the Highlander, as naive 'country cousin' in Dougal the prison warder, and as devious Celt in the 'urchin' who claims not to understand 'Sassenach' (English) until the offer of a 'bawbee' (coin) reveals his fluency.[14] By the nineteenth century a glamorized Romantic notion of the 'noble savage' had developed into a cult of heroic martial prowess, which was appropriated very effectively by the Highland regiments of the British army.[15] David McCrone draws attention to the conspicuous bias to 'masculine' virtues in this celebration of 'ruggedness and strength'.[16] Laurence, needing a positive model for her example of Scottishness, creates Piper Gunn as a strong, aggressive leader on the basis of her reading about the Scottish clans, but then adds a feminine perspective. Morag as a child welcomes the empowering quality of Christie's stories. But even as a small girl she shows awareness of their gender bias. His 'Piper Gunn' is the father of five sons and five daughters, and while the sons are 'husky', and active in supporting their father in both conflict and cultivation, the daughters are merely 'beautiful' (p. 105) and are not mentioned further. Piper Gunn's woman, appropriately named Morag, shares her husband's spirit, but as Christie presents her she is largely a conventional figure who 'stood there beside her man' (p. 41), and whose virtues are restricted largely to the domestic sphere: she has 'the wisdom and the good eye and the warmth of a home and the determination of quietness ' (p. 69). Morag, the child who is to become a novelist, scribbles her own modifications to this characterization in 'Morag's Tale of Piper Gunn's Woman' (p. 42). Her changes, coming as they do from a character who is a child in the 1930s, cannot be considered radically feminist. They still focus on the domestic, but there is a challenge to patriarchy in Morag's imagining the first child of Piper Gunn and his woman as a daughter. In *her* story, Piper's woman constructs a chariot, so that she and the child can move more easily around the country (rather

12 Priscilla Bawcutt, *Dunbar the Makar* (Oxford: Clarendon Press, 1992), p. 256.

13 T.M. Devine, *Clanship to Crofters' War. The Social Transformation of the Scottish Highlands* (Manchester: Manchester University Press, 1994), p. 85.

14 Walter Scott, *Rob Roy*, ed. Ian Duncan, Oxford World's Classics (Oxford: Oxford University Press, 1998), p. 320.

15 David McCrone, 'Representing Scotland: Culture and Nationalism', in David McCrone, Stephen Kendrick, and Pat Straw, eds, *The Making of Scotland: Nation, Culture and Social Change* (Edinburgh: Edinburgh University Press, 1989), p. 165.

16 David McCrone, Angela Morris, and Richard Kiely, *Scotland – the Brand. The Making of Scottish Heritage* (Edinburgh: Edinburgh University Press, 1995), p. 59.

than remaining at home), and there is an assertion of female capability in the girl's idea that Piper's woman herself cut down the tree and carved the chariot. The ornamentation is feminized: the outline for the description of this chariot is borrowed from the chariot of Cuchulain in James Macpherson's *Ossian*, available to Morag because Christie has an old copy of the book among his battered Scottish relics, but she changes the details of Macpherson's war chariot. Instead of a vehicle delineated in language of weapons and power, she designs one ornamented with carvings of animals and plants, and finished with the comic practical detail of a brass hook on which Piper Gunn can hang his bagpipes (p. 70). Morag's revisions emerge from a traditional view of the feminine, but her attempt to remedy exclusion is a feminist gesture.

As Morag matures, she makes further modifications to the Piper Gunn material. When, in her teens, she asks Christie to tell her some of the stories again, he produces 'Christie's Tale of Piper Gunn and the Rebels' (p. 105–7). In this 'Tale', based on the North-West rebellions of 1869–70 and 1885 in Manitoba and Saskatchewan, Christie celebrates the success of Gunn and his 'Sutherlanders' in defeating the insurrection of the Métis leader, Louis Riel, and his 'gang of half-breeds'. Morag who, as a child, had gently modified stories, now moves on to argue more tenaciously with Christie's Eurocentric view of history. She has a less fanciful version of the Rebellion, gained from school history lessons, and she expands on that and defends Riel, pointing out:

> the book in history said he was nuts, but he didn't seem so nuts to me. The Métis *were* losing the land – it was taken from them. All he wanted was for then to have their rights. The government hanged him for that. (pp. 106–7)

While Christie, lacking formal education, is unable to move beyond his conviction that whatever 'our people ' did must be right, Morag is growing into a woman with an independent mind. There is an uncomfortable truth about the Highlanders evicted from their land in Scotland: some of them went to Canada (and other places as well) and joined in the oppression, and even genocide, of native peoples in the countries where they settled.[17]

The Diviners is constructed very precisely to draw attention to the parallels between one incident of oppression and another, using Morag as a pivotal figure. At the centre of this complex, inter-layered text, a sexual partnership between the adult Morag and the 'half-breed' Skinner Tonnerre has a bearing on all the other representations of different cultural groups. The positive result of the liaison is their daughter Pique, an independent young woman who combines both inheritances, and who at the end of the novel goes away to recover her roots in Métis culture, thus reversing the direction of Morag's journey to Scotland. The juxtaposition of different sites of power and exclusion is reinforced by paralleling

---

[17] See for example Hunter, *A Dance Called America*, pp. 187–93.

the 'Tales' of the displaced Highlanders with matching 'Tales' of the Tonnerre family (ironically once children of thunder), who have been driven from their lands on the prairies and despised by newcomers from the Old World. In *The Diviners* ideas of racial superiority are demolished, and the insight Morag works towards is the need to respect the differences of other people. Laurence's correction of the over-simple view of the Highlanders as *victims* is useful. I relate it to Mary Robinson's reminder, during her Presidency of Ireland, that the people who live in Ireland now are the *survivors* of the famine: similarly, while other people bearing my family names of 'Ross' and 'Munro' were driven out from land near by, my ancestors remained.

Laurence challenges the heroic Highland tradition in her handling of Morag's real experience of the north of Scotland. The glamour of the journey to a remote ancestral homeland is undermined by the practical circumstances of the visit. Morag goes to Crombruach not just to see a place which has been important to her sense of who she is, but also because, by chance, she has begun an adulterous affair with a painter, whose home is there. Comedy is introduced at Morag's expense, by the misgivings she feels about visiting Dan MacRaith at home with his wife and some of his seven children, and her sense that, despite his assurances to the contrary, Bridie does suspect the real nature of Morag's relationship with him. Bridie also represents an alternative version of the Highland woman; she is presented as quiet, practical, reasonably modern, and understandably defensive. This encounter forces Morag to re-assess, once again, the stories of her Highland inheritance, and her own sense of Highland selfhood. Her aspiring 'authenticity' flounders as she confronts yet another version of Scottish regional identity.

Laurence also interrogates Highland identity through the matter of language. Morag's impressions of 'the north' include her awareness of the peculiar quality of Highland speech, which as I know from my own experience tends to puzzle Southerners. Contrary to what might be expected, accents do not become more strongly Scots as one travels north, for a historical reason: most of the Gaelic inhabitants of the Highlands and Islands learned, at some stage from the seventeenth century onwards, a version of *English*, not Lowland Scots.[18] The result of this is the feature that Morag notices about the voice of her lover Dan: it is 'faintly Scots, but with some kind of difference, a low-spoken, almost formal quality'; he has 'perhaps a few words [of Gaelic] here and there, but nothing to speak of, nothing *to speak with*' (my emphasis) (p. 303). In her fiction Laurence develops the parallels between present-day Highland people, and Morag's ancestors who once in Canada lost their Gaelic language, and the experience of the Métis people like Pique's father Jules (Skinner) Tonnerre who are left 'with two languages lost, retaining only broken fragments of both French and Cree, and yet speaking English as though forever it must be a foreign tongue to him' (p. 200).

---

[18] McArthur, ed., *Oxford Companion to the English Language*, pp. 469–70.

This thought has significance in the fictional text, in suggesting something about McRaith's ambivalence about living in the north, and the stresses between his personal life and his work as as artist. It would be romantic nonsense to extend the parallel outside the novel and suggest that present-day Highlanders, after several generations (in most cases) of speaking English, are disadvantaged by functioning in a 'foreign' tongue. But for me Laurence's thought is linked to the effects of a rupture in tradition: the loss of a language is the reason why I did not know of women from my own country who composed poetry. Like Pique, who learned a song by Lous Riel from a book and so does not know what it means (p. 199), I responded to Gaelic songs on radio, but in a very incomplete way. I sometimes feel as if my sister and I are the only people left in the world who remember my mother's 'old words', living, as I do, in Aberdeen which has a quite different, healthy, continuing tradition. Here people refer to children as 'loons' (boys) and 'quines' (girls), and the greeting used in place of 'How are you?', consists of the words 'Fit like?' or 'what (is it) like (with you)'. It is, simply, a different language.

Morag's negotiation of her identity carries important insights about the way in which the dominant heroic stereotype of the Highlander marginalizes women. Laurence also asserts women's need, in constructing an identity, to negotiate sexual and maternal relationships together with ethnic and cultural affinities. This is a text of 1970s feminism in which Laurence expresses things not then widely understood about a woman's need to combine the intellectual, the artistic, and the personal. The novel also stresses the self-indulgence in the idea that Highland people have been only *victims* of the exercise of power, and explores the crucial role of language in the transmission of traditions. Her presentation of Morag (and of her daughter Pique) is alert to the fluidity of identity. Morag in particular understands this with ironic clarity, when, alone and pregnant in a strange city, 'she no longer feels certain of anything. There is no fixed centre. Except of course that there is a fixed centre, and furthermore it is rapidly expanding inside her own flesh' (p. 243). I know as I read that like Morag I am in process. *The Diviners* prompts me to consider how important the Clearances, and fragments of Gaelic, and pipe music are to me *now*. It encourages me to consider wider aspects of living in Scotland that go beyond my Highland beginnings.

Candia McWilliam and the contemporary *Debatable Land*

I have not lived continuously in Ross-shire since the late 1950s, and since the deaths of remaining family members I have not visited it now for more than ten years. I am an Aberdeen resident with various under- and over-layers; certain habits of thought and speech will no doubt remain with me, and there is a spark of recognition when I encounter them in other 'exiles'. But I use the word in quotation marks because I cannot envisage going back, and I know that I left because I wanted things not available in a small northern town. Both work and family life take me regularly from this north-east city to the cities of the central belt, which have much larger and more diversified populations. The whole of Scotland has undergone important development over the last thirty years, and I find it increasingly stimulating. The change is not only political, although devolution and the Parliament are the most conspicuous signs of difference. One effect of long years spent under a right-wing Conservative government has been a growing sense that Scots *enjoy* doing things differently from the way they are done in England (and I write this in awareness that 'England' is far from being homogeneous, but is most often equated with the more populous south-east). Traces of the 'cultural cringe' that used to make many Scots suspect that English institutions and products were better than our own are now hard to find. All forms of cultural expression are a great deal more vigorous in the 1990s than at any time I can remember. Much of the activity is in central Scotland, where most Scottish people (4 out of 5 million) are living, but we have painting, poetry, and fiction which address issues affecting the whole of the country. Nor is it possible any more to think that women don't paint, or don't write. It was legendary, in my youth, that Scottish poets were men who drank in the bars in Rose Street in Edinburgh. Women have gained voices and their work is plentiful, in poetry and in fiction.

Candia McWilliam no longer lives in Scotland, but in her writing she combines a passionate interest in her country with access to external vantage points. She was brought up in Edinburgh, where her father, an architectural historian with Irish origins, devoted much of his life to the preservation of historic buildings in Scotland. In her teens she went to school in England, and has continued to live there, but she is very insistent that her approach to fiction is indelibly marked by awareness of herself as Scottish.[19] Her *Debatable Land* (1994) announces its concern with ways of being Scottish, by drawing on the traditional use of these words for the 'border territory' continuously in dispute between Scots and English.[20] In this novel she re-works conventions and ideas taken from earlier male writers, exploiting them to produce an intelligent exploration at several levels, with a feminine dimension firmly in place, of recent and contemporary Scottish life.

The basic idea of looking back at Scotland, and more particularly at Edinburgh, from the perspective of the South Pacific she has taken from Robert Louis Stevenson, acknowledging her debt in an epigraph from his *Songs of Travel* (1895). The contrast between Scotland and the 'South Seas' that forms a constant

19 McWilliam regularly explains her approach to writing in these terms when she gives readings from her work.

20 Candia McWilliam, *Debatable Land* (London: Bloomsbury, 1994). All references to the novel are included in the chapter following the relevant quotation and are from this edition. See also Chapter 2 'The Debateable Land' by Alison Easton (this volume).

element in the text works to define Scotland, in part, through the absence of the lush, exotic, and at times dangerous sights and experiences of the Society Islands. McWilliam also makes use of the political régimes through which her travellers pass – some French, and some not – to draw attention to colonial issues which have a bearing on Scottish politics, as when one character says of Tahiti, 'It's the French who have done most of the recent harm' (p. 95).

To this retrospect on the 'home country' from a distance, she adds the central narrative device of a tempestuous voyage, during which tangled human relationships are subjected to acute stress and come at the end to some resolution.[21] She adapts the sea-journey, which produces a closed and highly stressed community, by inventing a yacht voyage from Tahiti to New Zealand, in which three of the six people on board are Scots. The interaction between the American-Scottish owner, Logan Urquhart, his Anglo-Scots wife, Elspeth, and Alec Dundas, the working-class Edinburgh man turned artist, who crews for them, is used to produce reflection on, and discussion of, a range of Scottish experience from their contrasting backgrounds. This allows the novelist to manipulate complementary and contradictory views of the country and its history and culture, mostly located within the consciousnesses of her characters, and allows the reader to evaluate their usefulness. The debate that emerges addresses the subject of Scotland and Scottishness with acute social and visual observation, combined with imaginative insight.

Building on the significance of her title, McWilliam initiates the 'debate' with a casual conversation illustrating the way in which Scots are offended by the widespread assumption that England includes Scotland (p. 51); the irritation carries more weight, perhaps, because it is felt by Elspeth, the privileged Anglo-Scot who is at times mistaken for English. The contemplation of the country is developed, and Alec specifically uses the phrase 'debatable lands', in a discussion provoked when he recognizes Elspeth's give-away Scottish pronunciation of 'Post Office' (with stress on the 'o' of 'Office', instead of, as in English pronunciation, on 'Post'): 'Of course, you are one too. I was put off by the carry-on, all so very English' (p. 135). Elspeth mentions her anxieties, as one of the Scots who also has 'an English side', about growing tensions between Scotland and England, and attributes the problem to southern 'stupidity' and 'tactlessness'. Since the novel was published in 1994, we may connect this with the increasing impatience felt in Scotland with a Westminster Parliament imposing policies which the majority of Scots had not voted for (e.g. the 'Poll Tax'), and which sometimes did not commend themselves even to Scots of a conservative inclination. Elspeth fears a separation between Scotland and England which would produce a less plural and less tolerant society; as she says, 'There is less place for Anglo-Scots, whatever the word is, than there was. ... There could be a split' (p. 135–6).

---

21 Elspeth's comment on reading Conrad and Stevenson (p. 171) appears to confirm the debt to Joseph Conrad, *The Nigger of the Narcissus* (1898).

The interplay of ideas is set up through different pairings among the three figures, illustrating the multiplicity of experience afforded by their different Scottish childhoods. Most obviously there is a class division between the prosperous Urquhart couple and Alec, whose mother and father gutted and sold fish. The life lived by the Dundas family is limited and modest, but in retrospect Alec values the 'clarity' and 'simplicity' of their style, and McWilliam's representation of them stresses dignity as well as austerity (p. 18). Elspeth's recollections are of a childhood spent with liberal-minded intellectual parents, and Logan remembers a wealthy but deeply oppressive house in Glasgow. Elspeth and Alec share experience of Edinburgh, and a well-developed capacity for communication about history and visual culture, so that in discussion between them the city comes to exemplify large areas of Scottish life. Since he is socially as well as physically mobile, Alec's experience and thought processes make the point that in Scotland's capital there are 'so many towns in the one' (p. 31). Layers of Scottish history are suggested by his remembered visit to Roslin Chapel, and hers to the battlefield at Culloden. Alec's visual perceptions are particularly acute, and create precise impressions of the shapes and colours of buildings. The language McWilliam creates for her characters and her narrator is finely judged to capture the slight distinctions that characterize Scottish use of English, and emphasizes the contrast between the remembered world of Scotland and the South Pacific environment in which the characters are currently placed.

A major strand of thought in the minds of all three Scottish characters is derived from the conception of the Scots as a nation leaning to extremes. During much of the twentieth century this has become a commonplace in cultural analysis of Scottishness: it has had wide currency ever since in the 1920s Hugh MacDiarmid adopted and exploited G. Gregory Smith's notion that a 'Caledonian anti-syzygy', or fascination with opposites, is a hallmark of Scottish thinking.[22] McWilliam's characters make use of this notion of the 'Caledonian' spirit being driven by extremes. Alec sees himself and his partner Lorna as possessed by two different sorts of excess – his being one of asceticism and hers one of a 'wild dance with the spirits' and the 'feast-or-famine gene that afflicts Celts' (p. 104). It may well be untrue that Celtic Scots are in thrall to such temperament, and such an idea has an essentialist quality that renders it suspect; even the habit of thinking of ourselves as 'Celtic' simply on account of Highland origin is almost certainly unscientific. (Allan Macinnes points out that the racial composition of both the Highland and the Lowland populations of Scotland has been over many centuries altered by successive migrations from across the Irish Sea and the North Sea, as well as from England.)[23] Nevertheless many of us have learned to *think* that we are Celtic,

---

22 G. Gregory Smith, *Scottish Literature: Character and Influence* (London: Macmillan, 1919), p. 23. MacDiarmid develops the idea extensively in his poem *A Drunk Man Looks at the Thistle* (1926)

23 Allan I. Macinnes, 'Scottish Gaeldom from Clanship to Commercial

and construct our selves within the expectations offered by that identity. While we may remain sceptical about any genetic disposition to extremes, there is a certain inclination among Scots to be attracted to the position laid out in MacDiarmid's lines,

> I'll ha'e nae hauf-way hoose, but aye be whaur
> Extremes meet.[24]

The three Scots characters all connect the supposed Celtic fascination with opposites with the other national stereotype expressed in Logan's reflection about Tahiti, that like Scotland it is 'afire with sullen endurance, set with the tinder of unbridled wrath in drink' (p. 87). Indeed Elspeth has chosen the name of the yacht, 'Ardent Spirit', as a reference to the Gaelic for whisky, *uisge beatha*, 'water of life'. To her it is 'the liquid that has shaped Scotland as permanently and destructively as sea-water' (p. 2). McWilliam gives prominence to this set of ideas, but her text is designed to hold them in balance with modifying elements. Both the actions and the inner lives of characters subject the cliché of the whisky-addicted Celt to a degree of interrogation. The personal situations of the characters are treated in a way that emphasizes identity in process, and the capacity of individuals to exercise choice rather than conform to stereotypes. For example, while Alec is eager to offer genetic and deterministic explanations for the difficulties in his relationship with Lorna, he nevertheless thinks in terms that suggest development and possibility of control. His recognition of his coldness, and identification of excess in both himself and Lorna, are prerequisites for progress (p. 104). His capacity for change is confirmed when at the end of the narrative, and at the end of the storm, he sees the need to go back to her and to accept her child as his own (p. 216).

In several different ways the novel asserts the value of the pluralism of modern Scotland. Logan's perception of a similarity between Scotland and Tahiti based on sullenness and drink is immediately undermined when the narrative voice observes that he has failed to see the cultural mix in Moorea, and the process of change associated with it (pp. 87–8). The text suggests a much more productive parallel between Tahiti and Scotland, through McWilliam's representation of a comparable hybridity and change in the Scottish situation. This is vividly realized in the account of Lorna and Alec taking his father on a picnic in Edinburgh with food bought at the Italian food-store, Valvona and Crolla. The old man, despite his protestations, is shown being cajoled into enjoying 'foreign feasts' (p. 120); and

---

Landlordism, c. 1600–c. 1850', in Sally Foster, Allan Macinnes, and Ranald MacInnes, eds, *Scottish Power Centres from the Early Middle Ages to the Twentieth Century* (Glasgow: Cruithne Press, 1998), pp. 162–3.

24 Hugh MacDiarmid, *A Drunk Man Looks at the Thistle*, ed. Kenneth Buthlay, Association for Scottish Literary Studies, No. 17 (Edinburgh: Scottish Academic Press, 1987), ll. 141–2.

the shop is identified as 'part of the city's growing cosmopolitan life' (p. 114), where the proprietor teaches Edinburgh women to appreciate Italian food. The text treats very positively the enrichment of Scottish life with a new dimension, in the shape of Italians who, settling in Scotland after being here as prisoners of war, 'met and blended with the Scots nature as naturally as ice and sauce mixing in a bowl' (p. 118).

Conclusion

I have indicated how enlightening Margaret Laurence's critique of Highland stereotypes has been for me, in drawing attention to the exclusions and over-simplifications they encourage, and in reminding me of the fluidity of identity. I am no longer, except in memory, the daughter of a stable Highland family. I am variously the Highland person in a north-east workplace, or the woman from the north visiting central Scotland for research facilities or entertainment, or the Scottish academic at a largely English conference: wherever I go I do not 'fully' belong, but that is not unusual and not unhealthy. Scotland has become more 'interesting' now that it is, in the commonly used phrase, 'a nation once again', and without being a nationalist I see myself as having a stake in an evolving plural Scottish society. Within the old mix of Highland, Lowland, north-east, and Northern Isles, new ethnic minority groups contribute valuable diversity. Thus I find Candia McWilliam's representation of Scottish hybridity, against a background of tradition, history, and topographic detail, enlightening and deeply satisfying. I write at a point when the Scottish Parliament has sat for only a few weeks, and it is too early to predict its impact on different parts of the country, or on the various aspects of Scottish identities. People in the more remote areas have always suspected that any Parliament will be dominated by Glasgow business people and Edinburgh lawyers. It is only realistic to expect that issues important to the northern parts of the country will receive less attention, because they affect smaller populations, and this situation is exacerbated by the fact that the interests of the north-east, the Highland mainland, the Western Isles, and the Northern Isles, are frequently not the same. But there is bound to be one benefit, even if a negative one: we are no longer able to blame 'the English' for all of Scotland's problems.

I began by tracing my sense of the loss of a Gaelic tradition, especially one that, as a woman, I could relate to my own life. I recognize that that particular Gaelic world has gone and will not be recovered, except as a subject of academic or antiquarian exploration. Yet, in a different form, Gaelic survives. In the last decade there have been major developments in Gaelic broadcasting (including children's programmes and a 'soap opera') and in Gaelic-medium education in Scotland. It is used as a language of instruction at an institution of Higher Education (Sabhal Mor Ostaig in Skye, a college of the University of the Highlands and Islands), and also in around 50 Gaelic-medium primary school units. The fact that education in Gaelic today is not restricted to the Highlands and Islands indicates an intriguing development: as Sharon Macdonald has suggested, the life of the language is now 'being seen as a *Scottish* matter' (rather, perhaps, in the way that in the nineteenth and earlier twentieth centuries tartans and other Highland symbols took on a more national Scottish significance).[25] Currently, consideration is being given to the possibility of its use as an official language of the Parliament. The renewed taste for Celtic folk-music, which has built bridges with Ireland and more distant Celtic communities in Brittany and Canada, also plays a part in making the language more visible.

Margaret Laurence and Candia McWilliam both produce texts that offer a valuable distance in their perspective on Scottish life. Laurence looks through the eyes of a Canadian, and exposes distortion and over-simplification in the stereotype of the Highland character, creating space for the female and the anti-heroic, and also emphasizing the shifting nature of the self. This helps me to make sense of aspects of my past. Now 'uprooted' (in a fairly positive sense), I value McWilliam's refraction, from the other side of the world, of the hybrid nature of Scottishness, and the sense she conveys of future possibilities in a changing country.

Acknowledgements

I should like to thank Lynne Pearce for her constructive suggestions, which greatly assisted the writing of this chapter.

---

[25] Sharon Macdonald, 'The Gaelic Renaissance and Scotland's Identities', *Scottish Affairs* 26 (Winter, 1999), pp. 100–118.

Chapter 7

'We're Coming Home': Accent(uat)ing Nostalgia in Kathleen Jamie's *Autonomous Region* and Shelagh Delaney's *A Taste of Honey*

Rachel Dyer

> The upsurge in regionalism in British poetry in the past thirty years may be a mirror-image of the vernacularisation of Englishes throughout the world but it is a mistake to see the mirror-image of the centre and the periphery as something new: all cultures exist not in themselves – in the autonomy and the autotelic trajectory of their own narratives – but in the relation between themselves and others. Culture is not an organism, nor a totality, nor a unity: it is the site of dialogue, it is a dialectic, a dialect. It is being between. (Cairns Craig, *Out of History: Narrative Paradigms in Scottish and British Culture*)[1]

> To know that writing is neither compensation nor sublimation, that it is situated precisely *in that place where you are not* – is the beginning of writing (Roland Barthes, *Fragments d'un discours amoureux*)[2]

This chapter is about the role of language, and the dis/placement of language in our continuing struggles for a sense of home and belonging: hence the title, *accent*(uat)ing nostalgia. My attention to 'accent' here will thus be both literal and figurative; ethnic and gendered. Can we hear one another across the regional boundaries that connect and separate us? Do women speak in specific accents to other women? To what extent does the separation of time, as well as space, cause us to hear one another differently? I will be exploring these and other, related

---

1 Cairns Craig, *Out of History: Narrative Paradigms in Scottish and British Culture* (Edinburgh: Polygon, 1996), pp. 205–6.

2 Roland Barthes, quoted by Trinh T. Minh-ha in *When the Moon Waxes Red: Representation, Gender and Cultural Politics* (London and New York: Routledge, 1991), p. 218.

questions with reference to two very differently accented texts: the North West playwright Shelagh Delaney's *A Taste of Honey*, and the Scottish poet, Kathleen Jamie's 'For Paola' from *the Autonomous Region: Poems and Photographs from Tibet* (the latter produced collaboratively with photographer Sean Mayne Smith).[3] But first, to locate my own self / history in all this, I begin with an anecdote.

On 15 June 1996 at around 9.00pm (8.00pm 'our time') I was sitting with friends in a French bar, watching a European Championship football match on the TV, complete with French commentary. I was living in France at the time and working for a UK travel company. The only news from 'back home' came from occasional phone calls, letters and, of course, the tourists or 'customers' themselves. Invariably more up-to-date news came from the latter, who seemed, on the whole, incapable of letting ties to the media 'back home' relinquish for even a couple of weeks. It wasn't that I lacked interest in what was going on in the world, but 'news' becomes prioritized in a different way when you are surrounded by different cultural circumstances and a long way from 'home'. Likewise, the way that we 'read' key political events is also affected by the place/position we inhabit at the time, what Paul Gilroy has called 'Where you're at'. Ien Ang, in an article about Chinese 'cultural identity', explains Gilroy's theory thus:

> So long as the question 'where you're from' prevails over 'where you're at' in dominant culture, the compulsion to explain the evident positioning of yourself as deviant *vis-à-vis* the normal, remains – especially for ... migrants marked by visible difference ... It is this very problem which is constitutive of the idea of diaspora, and for which the idea of diaspora attempts to be a solution, where the adversity of 'where you're at' produces the cultivation of a lost 'where you're from'.[4]

Living myself in a 'multi-cultural' community at that time, 'where I was at' tended to remain at the forefront of my day-to-day existence, largely as a result of my desire to temporarily disassociate myself from 'where I was from'.

On the night of the 15 June 1996, however, something happened to temporarily shift my mind back to my place of 'origin'. A young English woman had come into the bar and was telling the people next to me something about Manchester which seemed to be creating quite a stir: 'What's happened?' I asked her; 'A bomb has gone off in the Arndale Centre that's blown away half of Manchester'. My complete amazement and desire for reassurance manifested itself in a bizarre disbelief. Yet why should she have made something like that up? I started to feel

---

3 Shelagh Delaney, *A Taste of Honey* [1956] (London: Methuen Student Edition, repr. 1987); Kathleen Jamie and Sean Mayne Smith, *the Autonomous Region: Poems and Photographs from Tibet* (Newcastle-upon-Tyne: Bloodaxe, 1993). Further page references to these volumes are given after quotations in the text.

4 Ien Ang, 'On not speaking Chinese: Postmodern Ethnicity and the Politics of Diaspora', *New Formations* XXIV:4 (1994), pp. 1–18.

a strong sense of unease for friends 'back home'. I *know* people that work in the centre of Manchester. Were they OK? At that moment, therefore, I felt a devastatingly visceral connection with 'the folks back home', even though I had thought myself content with 'where I was at', and had had no desire, as yet, to return.

Of course when I returned a month or so later, I was belatedly bombarded with media reports concerning the incident, even though 'time lag' led to continually shifting re-readings of the event via the different media.[5] A shopping trip to Manchester renewed this process of 're-reading', when I had the chance to walk right through the aftermath of the bomb; the effect up close was quite astonishing; even M&S, bastion of 'British' consumerism, was completely gutted by the blast. Events at a distance can thus be seen to jolt us back to the local and a desire for a sense of belonging, especially events that involve trauma.

Kathleen Jamie: traumatic homecomings

Kathleen Jamie and Sean Mayne Smith were travelling through Tibet courtesy of an Arts grant from Northern Arts in 1989. Their journey was 'halted at the border of the "Autonomous Region" of Tibet by the events of the time' (Reverse cover). They 'happened' to be in a place being directly affected by events taking place hundreds of miles away. Their poems and photographs interweave the ancient and very current history and traditions of the peoples of Tibet. Jamie also brings herself into the poems through the inclusion of Scottish languages, exploring the 'in-betweeness' of her own identity through that of the cultural 'other'.

One of the last of Jamie's poems in the sequence, 'For Paola', climaxes with the news of the Tiananmen Square massacre: 'they've killed 5000 people in Beijing' (p. 70); in this poem there occurs a literal shifting 'in between' standardized English and what Scots languages expert, Bill Findlay, describes as 'a hybrid, shifting Scots'.[6] The poem begins:

> A boomin echo doon the corridor,
> her door's the only ane open

---

5 Homi Bhabha, *The Location of Culture* (London and New York: Routledge, 1994), pp. 191–2: 'The process of reinscription and negotiation – the insertion or intervention of something that takes on new meaning – happens in the temporal break in-between the sign, deprived of subjectivity in the realm of the intersubjective. Through this time-lag – the temporal break in representation – emerges the process of agency both as historical development and as narrative agency of historical discourse ... When the sign ceases the synchronous flow of the symbol, it also seizes the power to elaborate – through the time-lag – new and hybrid agencies are articulated.'

6 Bill Findlay, private letter to myself, 14 April 1999.

lik a shell, an a wumman sweepin:
saft soun, wings.

A licht-bulb, hingit fi the ceilin
by a short cord.

A slever o gless in the oose
an a black hair. she telt me

they've killed 5000 people in Beijing. (p. 70)

On first reading, I was astonished by the jolt of the last line here: a sudden shift back to Standard English which, for me, heightened the 'shock effect' of the news being purveyed. I wrote to Bill Findlay for his comments on the language of the poem, and he replied:

> The only word I'd identify in the poem, from its spelling, as anachronistic or literary is 'luve'; the other Scots usages occur in contexts that make for gradations of 'thin' Scots (i.e. without the density characteristic of synthetic Scots medium). I say 'gradations' because there is variously, for example: the English-tipped-with-Scots of, e.g., 'A boomin echo doon the corridor', and 'This is a place your friens disappear'; ditto, but with a more evident 'literary' or 'poetic' quality, e.g. 'a wumman sweepin' ... the non-urban or semi urban Scots of, e.g. 'A licht-bulb, hingit fi the ceilin'. The sum effect, I'd say, is of a hybrid, shifting Scots.

Yet whereas I had interpreted the shift from Scots to Standard English as an attempt to reproduce the 'shock effect' of the news being delivered for the first time ('They've killed 5000 people in Beijing'), Findlay pointed out a more subtle accumulation of emotions, one that: '... reflects the narrator's emotional "balancing act" in the face of confronting this place of terror'. Here is further evidence that no matter what 'the language', the tonal 'accent' will always be received differently by different readers.

The confusion around language and accent in Jamie's poem is exacerbated by the fact that it is often difficult to deduce who is saying what. There is a certain sense of overlap between characters, a mixing of tongues and cultures. Apart from the fact that, in 'For Paola', there is a particular sense of ambiguity as to whether the phrase 'they've killed 5000 people in Beijing' is reported speech or not, there is also the fact that the language is regimented; carefully structured words are sandwiched between a mish-mash of other tongues.

In the extremely political context of this poem, moreover, the effects of 'time-lag' on the reporting are clearly linked to censorship. I think that Jamie's poem highlights extremely well the role of language in the 'gap' between the 'actual' events, the 'official report', the media reports, and the key dispute after the event being how *many* people were killed. McKenzie Wark, in an article for *New Formations*, discusses the way that the Western media was manipulated by the

CPC even prior to the Tiananmen Square massacre: the authorities cut satellite links just prior to declaring martial law, creating a gap in the 'information loop to and from the West'.[7]

In Jamie's poem, however, it is the sudden inclusion of Standard English that signals the possibility of an unreliable report: the fact that the narrator speaks in a hybrid Scots serves to foreground her distance from the Western media, and consequently forges a connection between minority cultures who are controlled by events and policies hundreds of miles away. These are situations in which 'being between' in cultural and geographical terms is of crucial significance, as is the practice of 'reading between the lines', and it is possible that Jamie is suggesting that women communicate between the lines through identification *with* other women, and *across* geo-political boundaries. The geographical displacements in this poem are thus very significant *vis-à-vis* accent and dialect; the hybrid Scots out of context seems to suggest a desire for a sense of 'belonging' in a very disturbing national situation, and of belonging to a *particular* nation.

The hybridity of Jamie's Scots language, meanwhile, points to the profound non-homogeneity of the places we call 'home'. John Corbett comments on the use of 'code mixing' in the work of certain Scottish writers. In the Scots translation of Tremblay's *The House among the Stars*, for example, there occur: 'daring examples of code-mixing, that is, the employment of more than one variety of Scots (or English) to dramatic effect'.[8] This 'code mixing' technique has also been attributed to many of the Scottish literary giants. Robert Crawford has described both Scott and Burns as 'bicultural' and as: 'crossing a boundary between the world of the vernacular and the world of the dominant Anglicized culture ... Writing in a culture under pressure, each sought to bind that culture together, to preserve it and to celebrate it through anthology'.[9] For all these writers, including Jamie, regional differences can be foregrounded over national identities through 'local' settings, and identities are re-negotiated upon the literal return to one's 'place of origin'.

In terms of my own negotiations, meanwhile, I now notice that the once familiar settings of childhood, even the streets which I played in as I grew up, are named after battles, many of them from the first Civil War of 1642–46.[10] And upon

7 McKenzie Wark, 'Vectors of Memory ... Seeds of Fire: The Western Media and the Beijing Demonstrations', *New Formations* X:1 (1990), pp. 1–11 (p. 6).

8 John Corbett, *Language and Scottish Literature* (Edinburgh: Edinburgh University Press, 1997), p. 19.

9 Robert Crawford, *Devolving English Literature* (Oxford and New York: Clarendon Press, 1992), p. 113.

10 Stephen Bull and Mike Seed write in *Bloody Preston: The Battle of Preston, 1648* (Lancaster: Carnegie, 1998) that both the Roundheads and the Cavaliers enlisted support from various marginal groups from the British Isles, but that the Scots arguably aligned themselves with the Royalists with a specific agenda in mind: possibly a bargaining chip for a devolved Scotland: 'As early as ... 1644 there were signs of stress within the parliamentarian alliance. There were those who wanted the war prosecuted with the utmost

return from France, I experienced a 're-vision' of what I had previously imagined to be familiar sights and sounds in my home town of Preston, most notably the emergence of a Scottish 'theme' pub commemorating the Battle of Preston of 1648 as a result of which thousands of Scottish men were killed in their struggle to return northwards after defeat by the parliamentarian army.[11] I can't but help find it striking that what was once so familiar to me should now be re-fashioned as a 'battle ground' for identities, although it is also true that childhood places always were, and will remain, sites of struggle. In terms of *linguistic* struggle, moreover, it is clear that it is precisely in these marginal, hybridized localities that some of the most creative and liberating dialogues take place.

Robert Crawford writes about this sort of 'dialogue' in *Devolving English Literature*, by focusing on a provincial set of Modernist writers who began to employ the idioms of everyday speech; at the end of his chapter on these 'barbarians', he calls for a recognition of an alliance of such writers in order to overturn the dominance of traditional 'English Literature':

> Unless we appreciate the subtle and important part played by Scottish culture in the construction and dissemination of English Literature and in the development of post-Enlightenment writing, and unless we examine the way in which Scottish energies interacted and continue to interact with 'provincial' and 'barbarian' writing in English, we cannot finally devolve our reading of English Literature so as to liberate and listen to the full spectrum of suppressed and persistent local accents ...[12]

Similarly, Tony Crowley, in *The Politics of Discourse*, explores the government policy at the beginning of the century designed to eradicate 'barbarians' who were seen as a threat to a unified national, 'British' identity. In ancient Greece, barbarians were those who spoke 'gibberish':

> [who] violate the laws of speech ... a barbarous way of speaking; the use of a foreign tongue, or the use of one's own tongue amiss ... barbarian,

---

vigour, by a new and more professional army; there were those prepared for compromise; and there were those, like the Scots, who had an entirely different agenda' (p. 45). Some of the streets I refer to are called: Lansdown Hill, Marsdon Moor and Roundway Down.

11 David Hunt, in *A History of Preston* (Preston: Carnegie, 1992) writes: '... on hearing of the defeat at Preston, Munro turned north back to Scotland. The locals now took their revenge on the plundering Scots, attacking the parties of stragglers struggling back northwards. As news of Preston spread throughout the country royalist resistance collapsed. The fate of the monarchy – the whole political direction of the country – hinged on the battle of Preston. Following their victory, the parliamentarian army renewed with great enthusiasm their call for the King to be brought to trial for having re-started the Civil Wars. Charles I was executed barely six months later and England became a republic' (pp. 106–7).

12 Crawford, *Devolving English Literature*, p. 305.

> according to at least one etymology, referred to the speakers whose mouths could utter nothing but rough sounds 'Bar-Bar'. This pattern of linguistic difference as a threat, a marker of cultural difference, and an aberration from a central form of the language, is a factor in patterns of cultural exclusion ... the nineteenth-century and early twentieth-century barbarians like their counterparts were geographically and culturally on the wrong side of the barriers.[13]

The way to silence barbarians was to either refuse them an audience, or integrate them into the main group, or 'nation' so that their speech would be rendered 'inarticulate' if they did not conform to a 'standard' group. Crowley goes on to detail a series of early twentieth-century reforms intended to create a 'united utterance' between the wars by creating hard line educational reforms, such as the Newbolt Report, which recommended that regulating speech would regulate the different classes, and that policies should be enforced both in the classroom and in the playground. The Scottish writer, critic and pioneer for Scots languages Billy Kay, writes on his own childhood experiences in *The Mither Tongue*:

> It came as an extreme shock to one's sensibilities to discover that speaking the everyday language of home in the classroom was regarded as giving cheek to the teacher. The dialect was permitted once a year when the Burns Federation was giving out its certificates or the school was organising a Burns Supper. The rest of the time you would be belted for using his language within the school.[14]

He suggests that such attitudes in the classroom caused some children to reject education, and likewise caused divisions in the home. In short, such an attitude can cause distinct social problems by widening class divides and encouraging false value judgements of people. What can be very articulate, 'good' Scots can be considered 'bad' English, and Kay shows the insidiousness of this at every level.

I would now like to argue that there are a number of Scottish women poets who have formed a unique collaboration which has enabled them to return to the playground of language, manipulating both local Scots dialects and Anglicized language in order to appeal to a wider audience. This becomes particularly poignant in Jamie's poems from *the Autonomous Region*, as she negotiates local identities at a distance: a traveller whose memory makes connections with 'home' at a time of national crisis. Trinh Minh-ha writes of the woman writer and traveller: 'Criss-crossing more than one occupied territory at a time, she remains

---

13 Tony Crowley, *The Politics of Discourse: The Standard Language Question in British Cultural Debates* (London: Macmillan, 1989), pp. 217–18. Further references to this volume are given after the quotations in the text.

14 Billy Kay, *Scots: The Mither Tongue*, 2nd edn (Ayrshire, Scotland: Alloway, 1993), p. 19.

perforce inappropriate/d – both inside *and* outside her own social positionings.[15] Linking this back to the 'Paola' poem, I find it significant that Jamie is inviting us into a *domestic* setting: we are voyeurs across the threshold of this woman's world that provides a glimpse of something more sinister, 'swept beneath the carpet'. The day to day fears in her lived experience wave flags, arguably, to the gendered reader.[16] There appears to be an open invitation to the narrator and the reader to collaborate in filling in the censored gaps of the scenario:

> Nou this wumman's haunin her gear
>
> brushes an pens, her worn claes
> for me tae cairry. But she'd a bin waitin
>
> when they cam …
>
> This is a place your friens disappear:
> trust naebody. Luve a.
>
> The smearit wa's o a concrete room,
> a wumman sweepin. (p. 70)

In her poems here, through the multiplicity of voices represented, through 'Chinese whispers', Jamie creates overlap and dialogue with the cultural 'other' by accent(uat)ing the effects of 'time lag'. Perhaps the poem is asking the reader, the cultural 'other' to write down, to record what is happening with her gifts of pens and ink? To engage in dialogue across political and ethnic differences?[17]

In times of political turmoil, the very nature of signification can become unstable, even though the ruling powers do everything in their power to stabilize national signifiers through reported speech. Some feminist critics have suggested that repetition, 'Chinese whispers', and the conversations that go on between women behind closed doors can be *extremely* liberating from this form of national censorship. In her book on women's language communities, *Women Talk*, Jennifer Coates discusses the unique way that women communicate in a collaborative and 'poetic' way:

> By choosing to operate on a collaborative floor, women friends share the construction of text. Repetition – saying the same things as each other and using the same linguistic patterns as our friends – is a powerful symbol of the connection women feel with one another.[18]

---

15 Trinh Minh-ha, *When the Moon Waxes Red*, 1991, p. 4.

16 Lynne Pearce, *Feminism and the Politics of Reading* (London and New York: Edward Arnold, 1997), p. 66.

17 In her introduction to *the Autonomous Region*, Jamie names her key influences in writing the poems, one of which was the mythical character Princess Wen Cheng.

18 Jennifer Coates, *Women Talk* (London and Cambridge, MA: Blackwell, 1996), pp. 230–1.

In *the Autonomous Region*, you can see this kind of collaboration go on too, where repetition and overlap between people, accents and dialogues occurs so that the journey can continue, only halted momentarily, in and through the songs and stories of the people of Tibet and Scotland. I would argue that this *mode* of representation is particularly appropriate for marginal peoples such as the Scots, the Tibetans, and the women as 'cultural carriers' of both nations.[19]

Accent(uat)ing Nostalgia

Nostalgia is about a continuing dialogue with the past, so I'll begin to interweave my dialogue with my own local origins with some of the issues already discussed in Jamie's texts. This dialogue will inevitably invoke a parallel dialogue between the classroom and the playground, the 'civilized' and the 'barbaric', as I attempt to disrupt stable notions of 'origins', 'home' and 'belonging' by accent(uat)ing inter-personal differences. This desire for connections takes me to my childhood, and a place and an accent that I always imagined I would be familiar with: never left to feel 'a stranger'.

I can remember a time when I was sitting in a coffee bar with two friends as an undergraduate. I think it must have been just after a linguistics lecture, because we were talking about 'accents', and all of a sudden I said: 'I don't really think that I have an accent anymore'. My two friends both burst into fits of laughter; 'You do!' they both retorted. I had not, however, realised it was still so pronounced to the outsider's ear. Such an experience serves to remind us that accent and dialect inevitably change with geographical/class (re)locations, especially during childhood, adolescence and young adulthood. We will sometimes consciously, sometimes unconsciously, 'put on' an accent or effect an idiosyncrasy of dialect in order to 'fit in', or as part of a play for power. Ever since I have moved back to Lancashire I have still been conscious of the way I pronounce 'garage', and how not everyone will understand me if I ask them to 'dinner', not 'tea'. Like many others I have developed different accents and dialects for different situations. Dialect can be incredibly empowering: it can help people to fit in, forge a sense of belonging, but it can also put them at a disadvantage, especially in an institutional environment.

---

19 Nira Yuval Davis and Floya Anthias, eds, *Woman-Nation-State* (London: Macmillan, 1989) list a series of ways in which 'women have tended to participate in ethnic and national processes' (p. 7) one of which is: 'The role of women as ideological reproducers [which] is very often related to women being seen as "cultural carriers" of the ethnic group. Women are the main socialisers of small children but in the case of ethnic minorities they are often less assimilated socially and linguistically within the wider society. They may be required to transmit the rich heritage of ethnic symbols and ways of life to the other members of the ethnic group, especially the young' (p. 9).

Meanwhile, our desire for 'origins', for 'home, for 'points of connection' is often mediated through past experience, through nostalgia. But it is important to note that nostalgia is a *process* and not a *chronology*. As Elspeth Probyn writes in her book *Outside Belongings*: 'Nostalgia for beginnings only makes sense within a project that refuses a chronological ground, that refuses the privilege of a personal past as a guarantee of things to come, that explains the present in relation to the past'.[20] Nostalgia is thus *not* about an originary 'site'. Despite the fact that we may desire to return to a 'home' we once knew, we never will: locations and people change over time. Doreen Massey, in *Space, Place and Gender*, also suggests that the idea of nostalgia as 'stasis' and 'enclosed security' has become a popular misconception, and that concepts such as 'home' are *highly* ambiguous; in this respect: 'The identity of a place does not derive from some internalised history. It derives, in large part, precisely from the specificity of its interactions with "the outside"'.[21] Minh-ha, too, concludes that there is a need to reconceptualize 'home' as a place of flux:

> Travellers' tales do not only bring the over-there home, and the over-here abroad. They not only bring the far away within reach, but also contribute, as discussed, to challenging the home and abroad/dwelling and travelling dichotomy within specific actualities. At best, they speak to the problem of the impossibility of packaging a culture, or of defining an authentic cultural identity ... Travelling can thus turn out to be a process whereby the self loses its fixed boundaries – a disturbing yet potentially empowering practice of difference.[22]

The unstable home becomes the place from which she writes, 'finding a home in writing'.[23] Linking my previous observations on 'mobile accents' to the role of nostalgia in our changing perspective of home, it can thus be argued that even those things that seem most 'fixed', and most defined by our 'origins' are not. The very adaptability of speech and language, meanwhile, is what enables us to 'put down new roots' as well as showing solidarity with our old ones.

---

20 Elspeth Probyn, *Outside Belongings* (London and New York: Routledge, 1996), p. 122.

21 Doreen Massey, *Space, Place and Gender* (Cambridge: Blackwell, 1994), p. 169.

22 Trinh T. Minh-ha, 'Other than myself/my other self' in George Robertson et al., *Travellers' Tales: Narratives of Home and Displacement* (London: Routledge, 1994), pp. 9–26 (pp. 22–3).

23 Ibid., p. 16.

Shelagh Delaney: Home, belonging and nostalgic negotiations

Doreen Massey, in another part of her thesis, points out that 'home' has often been constructed around an idealized 'place' and a stable mother figure:

> The occasional idealizations of home by the working-class lads (The Angry Young Men) who came south in the middle decades of this century, and who looked back north with an unforgivable romanticism, often constructed that view around 'Mum', not as herself a living person engaged in the toils and troubles and pleasures of life, not actively engaging in her own and others' history, but a stable symbolic centre – functioning as an anchor for others.[24]

I have a real fondness for a play from this era, which I saw performed several times during my school years in the 1980s: Shelagh Delaney's *A Taste of Honey*. Delaney's constructions of 'home' and 'mother' are, however, far from idealised: far from being 'stable entities'. The play is set in 1950s Salford (Lancashire), and the entire action takes place in a tenement flat in the rough part of town, overlooking the slaughterhouse. The action begins with Helen and her daughter, Jo, moving into the flat. This enclosed domestic space becomes Delaney's forum for challenging idealist constructs; 'Home', from the outset, is a battleground for identities. The play begins with an argument, one of many:

> Helen: Well! This is the place.
> Jo: And I don't like it.
> Helen: When I find somewhere for us to live I have to consider something far more important than your feelings ... the rent. It's all I can afford. (p. 7)

So from the outset, home is set up as something which 'costs', as does motherhood. It is not long before Helen leaves Jo, still a minor, on her own in the flat, in order to go and marry Peter, a lecherous salesman. When Jo asks her why she's marrying him, Helen replies: 'He's got a wallet full of reasons' (p. 34).

When Helen is away, Jo has a love affair with a young coloured man on leave from the Merchant Navy. He eventually leaves Jo pregnant, never to return. Much of the play unfolds around the 'instability' of the 'mother' figure; this is signified by both Helen and Jo, the latter who we see becoming physically larger as well as more disturbed as the play develops. At times she appears to be in denial at the prospect of giving birth: she declares, 'They are revolting. I hate babies' (p. 55) and then: 'I'm not having a little animal nibbling away at me, it's cannibalistic. Like being eaten alive ... I mean it. I hate motherhood' (p. 56). Somewhat ambiguously, however, Jo also declares her disgust at the mistreatment of children in the local area:

---

24 Massey, *Space, Place and Gender*, p. 180.

> It's their parents' fault. There's a little boy over there and his hair, honestly, it's walking away. And his ears. Oh! He's a real mess. He never goes to school. He just sits on that front doorstep all day. I think he's a bit deficient ... His mother ought not to be allowed ... Think of the harm she does, having children ... (p. 54)

Jo seems to believe, on some other level, that mothers are *supposed* to behave in a certain way, even though she has never experienced motherhood as stability. Indeed, she teases Helen about this when Helen is about to disappear with Peter:

> Helen: There's plenty of food in the kitchen
> Jo: You should prepare my meals like a proper mother.
> Helen: Have I ever laid claim to being a proper mother? ... (p. 35)

When Helen returns to a pregnant Jo before leaving again, she decides she's going to tell Jo a few 'home truths', which again involve Jo taking care of herself: 'Well, you fell down, you get up ... nobody else is going to carry you about ...' (p. 63). Helen briefly tries to persuade Jo to move in with her and Peter ('My home is yours', p. 67), but this offers little comfort, or prospect of stability, for Jo.

In many respects the character of Geoffrey, a homosexual arts student who moves in with Jo during her pregnancy, is more of an 'archetypal' figure of feminine respectability and motherly stability than either Jo or Helen. It is Geoffrey who has the 'nesting' instincts, who feeds Jo and prepares the home for the baby's arrival; but it is also Geoffrey who makes the grave error of fetching Helen back into the flat behind Jo's back, believing that she needs a 'mother figure'. He soon realizes Helen is anything but, as she shouts at Jo:

> Helen: You had to throw yourself at the first man you met, didn't you?
> Jo: Yes, I did, that's right.
> Helen: You're man mad.
> Jo: I'm like you.
> Helen: You know what they're calling you round here? A silly little whore!
> Jo: Well, they all know where I get it from too. (p. 62)

Deviant sexuality and lack of pride in cleanliness are the two main insults which the two women in the play level at each other. In her substantive study of working-class women in the North West, Beverley Skeggs suggests that these are two of the core factors that locate women as 'not respectable', not 'moral', not 'English'.[25]

Jo, an expectant mother at the age of 15, has never 'entered a level playing field'.[26] On one level Jo does see herself in Helen, and at times doubts her own

25 Beverley Skeggs, *Formations of Class and Gender: Becoming Respectable* (London: Sage, 1997), p. 3, pp. 98–117.

26 Skeggs writes of the women in her survey that: 'by the age of 16 only limited capital to trade – their feminine cultural capital – and this was only convertible on a

ability to break the mould, to shift the boundaries and become 'other'. Yet she buys into myths of travel and 'elswhere', representing her lover to Geof and her mother as 'an African Prince', when in reality he's from Cardiff; she regurgitates sound bytes she's heard from the news and says he's from the 'Mau Mau' tribe. Here it is important to remember that the potential for travel remained just a dream for many working-class women in the 1950s. My own grandmother rarely travelled further than Blackpool in her 80 years of life (aside from the odd trip to Lourdes!). This was, I understand, partly a fear of what was 'out there'; what was 'different'. What is implicit in this play, however, is the potential for re-thinking boundaries as the audience are invited to engage with some of the moral messages being portrayed, and thus take the characters 'elsewhere'.

In the 1961 film version of the play, contrasts between seriousness and play are accent(uat)ed further through spatial concepts.[27] We observe a sense of claustrophobia 'inside' the flat, the classroom even, where Jo mocks her English teacher's Standard English accent. Outside, however, in the playground, on the netball field, beside the canal where she meets 'the Boy', in open spaces negotiations become potentially more liberating *and* more dangerous for Jo. At one point early on in both the play and film Jo declares: 'I'm not frightened of the darkness outside. It's the darkness inside houses I don't like' (p. 22); this contradiction between the desire for travel and a yearning for stability continues throughout both play and film.

Helen is the character who most often addresses the audience directly in the play; she doesn't 'tell tales'; she offers hard facts, 'home truths', telling Jo that her father was a one-off affair that lasted an afternoon and was a bit 'backwards'. Like Jo, she became pregnant by her first lover. Helen is the character I remember the most clearly from the play, despite the fact that it's now some fourteen years since I've seen it performed. This is partly for reasons such as accent and dialect: the colloquialisms that she uses such as 'Yes, love' which resonate with 'my part of the world'. And it is partly because she is a memorable character 'type'; she is loud and cheeky, and has worked as a barmaid and a pub singer: a pre-figuration, perhaps, of *Coronation Street*'s Bet Lynch. Early on in the play, she sings from a music hall number, reminiscing about one of her first jobs in a pub when she was younger.

Music, indeed, is integral to the play, with characters dancing on to the stage at the beginning of each scene, and it is arguably this invocation of a music hall tradition that creates the greatest sense of nostalgia in the play. The stage

diminishing labour market or as unpaid labour in voluntary caring or family ... "Family" factors which influence all forms of capital also imposed limitations as a substantial proportion of the young women (28 per cent) have had to contend with abusive fathers, children's homes, foster parents, separated or divorced parents, which severely disrupted their ability to accrue capital across various sites. This means that they never enter a level playing field' (Ibid., p. 9).

27 *A Taste of Honey*. Dir. Tony Richardson. Castle Pictures. 1961.

directions in Joan Littlewood's version of the play suggest that a Jazz Trio is present. And the idea of Jazz music, of music hall, invokes the tradition of spontaneous music where everyone joins in the chorus. This is a play, then, which leaves spaces for audiences to participate in at different levels: to literally join in the 'chorus', be it through accent, humour, music, even nursery rhymes, all, of course, regionally specific.[28] Nursery rhymes are first introduced as Geof and Jo engage in playful banter, and exchange such rhymes. Geof has a particular fondness for this game, and introduces the rhyme which Jo remembers at the very end of the play:

> As I was going up Pippin Hill,
> Pippin Hill was dirty.
> And there I met a pretty miss
> And she dropped me a curtsy.
> Little miss, pretty miss,
> Blessings light upon you.
> If I had half a crown a day
> I'd gladly spend it on you. (p. 51)

This rhyme connects Geof to a sense of selflessness that Jo remembers at the end of the play. Geof gives Jo, for the first time, something to yearn for as her labour pains begin, although Geof has left by the time Jo recites the rhyme.

I am reminded of my own childhood by this play: not because I grew up in a Salford slum(!) although I *did* grow up in the North West, and saw this play several times as a student living in that region. And this geographical and class specificity is, I think, important. The play was first performed by the Theatre Workshop at the Theatre Royal in London, and more than one critic has commented on the way that a middle-class audience can be isolated from the set.[29] Performed in the North West, however, this is a play which, I feel, resonates differently, whilst student editions of the text are another framework which potentially widens access across classes.

At the end of the play, Helen reminisces about the 'ideal' point in her own childhood: a fit of nostalgia which is immediately followed by Jo's revelation that her child may be black. Helen's mood shifts – she addresses the audience: 'What would you do?' then exits abruptly for a drink, leaving us uncertain as to whether she'll return (p. 87). Yet there is, I believe, a strong sense that she is looking

---

28 Toni Morrison, in her essay 'Rootedness: The Ancestor as Foundation', in Dennis Walder, ed., *Literature and the Modern World: Critical Essays and Documents* (Oxford: Oxford University Press, 1992), writes: 'To make the story appear oral, meandering, effortless, spoken – to have ... a musician's music is enhanced when there is a response from the audience' (pp. 328–9).

29 Edward J. Esche, 'Shelagh Delaney's *A Taste of Honey* as Serious Text: A Semiotic Reading' in Adrian Page, ed., *The Death of the Playwright? Modern British Drama and Literary Theory* (London: Macmillan, 1992) pp. 67–81.

for the collaborative support of the female members of the audience at this point. In both Jamie's poem and Delaney's play women are called on to collaborate across different regions, nations and classes, in their conflicting desires for travel 'elsewhere' and a return 'home'.

Identities, like nostalgia, are constantly in a state of flux, touching off new responses and new desires in different contexts. The final image in the play is that of Jo, remembering Geof, and yearning; but as an audience, we can perceive yearning not only as an expression of the past, but also as a vision of the future: a yearning to travel to new places and new homes; to new belief systems which open up new spaces for differences to overlap and collide. bell hooks writes:

> Our struggle is also a struggle of memory against forgetting [and there exists] a politicisation of memory that distinguishes nostalgia, that longing for something to be as once it was, a kind of useless act, from that remembering that serves to illuminate and transform the present... home is no longer just one place. It is locations. Home is that place which enables and promotes varied and ever changing perspectives, a place where one discovers new ways of seeing reality, frontiers of difference. One confronts and accepts dispersal and fragmentation as part of the constructions of a new world order that reveals more fully where we are, who we can become ...[30]

Re-reading home and belonging

As I look back over my GCSE copy of Delaney's play, I can't help but notice the overtly simplistic way in which I tried to structure my revision; each of the characters have been allocated a coloured highlighter pen: Jo is pink, so if anyone makes a comment about Jo 'of significance', the text is coloured pink; Helen is blue, Geof yellow and Peter orange. These first, crude attempts at interpretation now fade into my more recent, less naive, markings; the space between, over a decade, makes me look back and laugh a little at some of the words I had once taken so seriously. Somewhere in this 'space between' I also came to realize the full extent of the difference between the text I got to know for the purposes of an exam, and the one I already knew from the experience and authority of my own linguistic 'playground': the space/place where 'non standard' English is allowed, and is, indeed, frequently used as a benchmark for belonging.[31]

30 Massey, *Space, Place and Gender*, pp. 171–2.

31 Elspeth Probyn, in *Sexing the Self: gendered positions in cultural studies* (London and New York: Routledge, 1993) writes: 'Following our move from Germany to Ontario I was treated as a "Hun", only later to be regarded as a strange "Eskimo" by my rural Welsh schoolmates. Both my sister and I became rather adept, in our separate ways, in negotiating the fine line between keeping up difference (the seemingly constant cries of "say something" allowed for the maintenance of a basic vocabulary of "different" words

When Jamie the traveller returned to her native Scotland, she published a collection of poems called *The Queen of Sheba*: the traveller's re-negotiation of 'origins', between then and now, there and here.[32] In one poem called 'School Reunion', voices from the playground overlap with present day identities; the swearing and colloquial playground banter collide with the mother's standardised English, where, once again, being 'ladylike' and being 'respectable' are equated with speaking 'properly':

> a mother's grip
> *can't you be more*
> *ladylike* ...[33]

In another poem from this collection, 'Wee Wifey', Jamie attempts to come to terms with two very different sides of her identity, which she also describes in terms of a battle: of identities 'bleeding into' one another, a conflict between the 'motherly' woman who stays at home and the 'deviant' traveller:

> I think in Scottish Literature the theme of the double often turns up: *Jekyll and Hyde* or *The Justified Sinner*, and it's like I detected two women in myself: one was independent, a traveller, a poet – like the product of the women's movement, and the other half longs for a safe domestic space, and it's this latter one I called Wee Wifey – and like a lot of my poems it makes use of ideas from folklore. In Scotland 'Wifey' has nothing to do with being married; its just an affectionate term for any ordinary unassuming woman ...[34]

Like myself, then, Jamie has clearly had to pay the price for her travels beyond the playgrounds of childhood. She has had to learn to alternate her 'barbarian' tongue with an educated one, and to do 'trade' in different types of femininity. Elsewhere, however, she writes more positively about the experience of living with ambiguous identities, as in this comment on Devolution:

> Perhaps its true, we can evolve now towards new, chosen meanings of nation and culture. Exploring and guiding this choice may be the poet's role ... I voted Yes Yes this year at 35 years old, a mother, a graduate and what they call an 'established poet'. The politics are indistinguishable from my life. There are things I discovered in my journey as a poet and this campaign which I don't want to lose, that's why I favour devolution over

---

depending on the country) and the need to appropriate enough of the local accent in order to avoid total ostracism (swear words being the preferred mode of group identification)' (p. 58).

32 Kathleen Jamie, *The Queen of Sheba* (Newcastle-upon-Tyne: Bloodaxe, 1994)

33 Ibid., p. 21.

34 Kathleen Jamie, in her introduction to her recording of *The Poetry Quartets:1* (Newcastle-upon-Tyne: Bloodaxe, 1998).

> independence (so far; don't push me). 'Difference' is what I have grown up with as a poet, and frankly, I like it. 'British', but not English. Scottish in a British context. That sense of being a slight outsider is one that I am now comfortable with and would be loath to relinquish. I like juggling contexts, and watching how things shift accordingly. It has been the source of great creative energy and fun.[35]

Juggling any aspects of identity can be difficult, even dangerous; like poetry, it is a skill which combines both discipline and frivolity at times. And for this reason I would argue that poetry is the medium *par excellence* for allowing us to juggle contexts: to combine different voices, and to enable the 'respectable' and the 'barbaric' to collide.

So let us return now to the beginning: Euro 96, a bar in France; the match that's on TV is England vs Germany. The Dutch members of the bar are now supporting the English, even though they were adversaries in the previous match; certain proof of how easy it is for this level of national allegiance to shift over time. 'Home', in this respect, depends upon which 'team' you are currently backing: where your 'belief systems' (ethnic, national, gendered) currently reside.[36] And although it is important to recognize that not *all* re/locations are as simple, cynical or voluntaristic as this, there is no doubt that human beings are often as pragmatic as they are nostalgic when negotiating feelings of home and belonging. To return to Paul Gilroy's formulation ('It's not where you're from, it's where you're at'), it is clearly liberating *not* having to think of home in terms of one's 'origins' all of the time.

Acknowledgements

I would like to thank Bill Findlay, from Queen Margaret College, Edinburgh, for taking the time out to comment on the Scottish languages used in Jamie's poem, and to Lynne Pearce, for encouraging me at every step along the way.

---

35 Kathleen Jamie, 'Dream State: Kathleen Jamie on the New Scottish Parliament', *Poetry Review* LXXXVII:4 (1997/98), pp. 35–7 (p. 36).

36 Jonathan Rutherford, 'A Place Called Home: Identity and the Cultural Politics of Difference' in Jonathan Rutherford, ed., *Identity: Community, Culture, Difference* (London: Lawrence & Wishart, 1990), pp. 9–27 (p. 27).

Chapter 8

Driving North / Driving South: Reflections upon the Spatial/ Temporal Co-ordinates of 'Home'

Lynne Pearce

Driving South

Driving South this time – late July, 1999 – I am struck by how arid it is, how yellow the wayside grass. It is not an especially dry year – we are still way off any talk of 'drought' – and yet, coming from the 'total' green of Scotland, it is one of the markers that tells me I have passed into a different country: a land whose very seasons bespeak a different time, a different space.

This journey south, to Cornwall, is but the latest of many. During the past year – since coming to live in Scotland on a part-time basis – I have covered more thousands of miles than I care to imagine, especially since I continue to visit my parents down here on a regular basis. The journey from Taynuilt to Lancaster takes from five to six hours; the journey from Lancaster to Cornwall, from seven to eight. Placed back to back it is thus a distance that cannot be driven (safely) in a single day. It is also a distance that almost measures the entire length of the British Isles, and takes me through fifteen counties or 'regions' *en route*.

Travelling 'back home' is always, of necessity, a jouney through time as well as space. Although my life elsewhere might move on, my parents' home in Cornwall – a small-holding on the fringes of the Redruth-Camborne mining area – retains the illusion of a fixed point. Look closely, of course, and you see the illusion for what it is: things *are* changing – in the house, in the surrounding villages – even if it is just the sad and simple process of decay. Similarly, my parents are ageing. But the fact that the location itself remains fixed, combined with the fact that my returns are consistently, and frequently, repeated, blinds me to a good deal of this. My apprehension of this home, indeed, has all the quality of a dream where past and present mix and coalesce. Sometimes my parents are seen and remembered as they were ten, twenty, thirty years ago; sometimes as they are now. My own ghost, meanwhile, flits around the place in a state of intermittent erasure. My 'going away' to a life, and land(s) so far from these origins in every respect means that the person I have 'become' is almost totally unseen. So home – this home – is a space and place in which my family and myself can only 'see each other darkly'.[1] But it is perhaps good to have a fixed point to return to, nonetheless.

With a destination so fixed in place, but so floating in time, it is inevitable that my journeys south challenge my perception of the 'here and now'. Part of the function of the fixed point (however illusory) is that of the measuring post. How far have things (relationships, career, fitness; attendant projects) progressed, or not, since I was here last? How is this latest passage of time requiring things to be re-read? And with such an impassive, such an indifferent, benchmark waiting there is no point at all in 'pretending': home is there to pull any number of carpets from under our feet; it returns us to a childhood where we were permanently partial, contingent, undefined ... spectral.

Whilst I am driving, I am nearly always happy. Driving *towards* virtually anywhere makes me excited, expectant: full of hope. This includes the journey home to Cornwall, despite the fact that my repeated experience is to have that euphoria laughed to scorn almost as soon as I arrive. For many years I blamed my family for this: focused on their apparent lack of interest in my arrival for my feelings of erasure, but now I accept the disappointment is more psychically fundamental: the consequence of the ego passing from the fantasy of integration to the 'reality' of *dis*-integration; the blighted hope of *this* being the journey where the person I have become meets and recognizes the child I was. But, of course, it never *is* that journey. Instead the different times slide by one another, and – as soon as the car door opens – my adult persona is rendered almost totally unseen.

When I drive, I listen to music. Hours and hours of it. Some of it from 'today', some of it distinctly 'retro': albums that span, recuperate, and rewrite the two decades since I first left home. A long journey, then – such as the one down here – becomes an emotional palimpsest of past and future, in which events and feelings are recovered and, most importantly, rescripted from the present moment in time. Listening to the music, re-telling my stories and re-writing their endings, thus grants me unique, if temporary, imaginative empowerment.[2] Between there and here, between then and now, I feel suddenly – impossibly – in control of my destiny. By the time I arrive at the fixed point of 'home' (that is, the home of my imagination), past, present and future have been rendered coherent by the narratives I have forged. The causal threads so wildly flapping in our day-to-day experience of being in the world are now securely knotted. Everything makes

1 'Space and place': as one of my readers has pointed out, it is important to highlight the specificity/difference of these two terms *vis-à-vis* the 'politics of location'. In my own mind, 'space' is the more geographically neutral term, whilst 'place' is social/historical nexus that links directly to the discourses of 'home' and 'belonging' with which this volume is concerned. For further discussion of these terms see Doreen Massey, *Space, Place and Gender* (Oxford: Polity, 1994).

2 The extent to which we, as readers and viewers, usurp and re-script the narratives of the texts with which we engage is explored in some detail in my book, *Feminism and the Politics of Reading* (London: Arnold, 1997). See especially pp. 119–37.

sense of everything else, no matter how painful. From this seeming passage between times, then, so is 'time conquered'.[3] It has become a manageable continuum ... Until, that is, the moment the car stops, the doors open, and I am swept back into the darkness of my 'real' home: the space and place where there is no narrative, no sequence, no necessity – and the proverbial smile is smartly wiped off my face.

But driving into Cornwall, in high summer, with the sun blazing, and the fringing oceans meeting the cloudless skies in a fine strip of prussian blue will always be a special thing. This is a uniquely defined land – and landscape – at the very tip of the British Isles, and it also happens to be 'my own'. The place I 'belong' (i.e. 'come from'), as the Scots would say.

At this point in the journey I am near to the dream's ending, perhaps (soon I will turn off the music and psychologically prepare for 'descent'), but for a short time I can still imagine it all coming together: the child I was and the woman I now am; the place/s I inhabit today brought, literally, to the door of the one from whence I came. Apart from some new stretches of dual-carriageway and the wind-farm at Four Burrows, this road, for one thing, never seems to change. It will always be here to take me home. It will always be here to provide me with my *dream* of home: the last breath, the suspended moment, before arrival. Cornwall as seen from the A30: no longer a country in which I live, perhaps, but one to which I am obliged to return again and again.

Driving, dreaming, and the devolutionary moment

True to the discourse of postmodern dis/location, it is striking how the preceding reflection is overlaid – at least to my own ear – with the nostalgic whine of loss and deprivation. The effect of being constantly on the move – of never being fixed, or grounded, or belonging to one place – is widely recognized to be one of the problematic consequences of contemporary living. Not only has the millennial subject lost touch with his/her 'roots', but s/he is rarely ever in any position to set down new ones.

But this, I would argue, is to mask the extreme *privilege* of such mobility: a privilege that, as my own reflection suggests, offsets physiological discomfort with substantial psychological gain. How many 'national' subjects – allowing for different cultures, different historical moments – have been able to play *fort/da* with the places they call home in quite this way? Only those of us living in the 'first' world, in the last twenty or thirty years of the twentieth century, that's for sure; only those of us living, and working, in countries whose distances are small enough to be travelled in this way; only those whose country's geography and

3 The source of this phrase, i.e. T.S.Eliot's *Four Quartets* (1943), compounds its problematic mysticism.

communications network permits it ... only, perhaps, those of us living in a handful of European nations at the present time.[4]

Meanwhile, the primary source, and means, of this unique form of transnational migrancy is incontrovertibly the motor car itself. The rail network, it is true, offers something similar in terms of accessibility: most of us in the British Isles can travel backwards and forwards between past and present 'homes' whether we have a car or not. But nothing except the car provides us with quite the same uniquely *privatized* (or, indeed, 'customized') psychological spatio-temporal vacuum in which to explore, and measure, the distance between those 'fixed points'.[5] Whilst friends who do not find the same euphoria in car driving as myself have argued that the train offers them similar 'day-dreaming' opportunities, I would respond that, for me, this is mitigated by the 'public' context of the transportation, together with the fact of that mental/material time-space continuum no longer being under one's direct and autonomous control. And yet this 'privilege', enjoyed by thousands, every weekend, every holiday, is – in terms of our long-term history – as ephemeral as a dragonfly. In thirty years time (maximum?) car travel between homes, partners, and the various towns, cities, and regions of these islands will be as economically and logistically impossible as it was forty years hitherto. The way we know 'home' now is not the way we will know it then.[6] Time and space will be differently experienced, differently calibrated. My vision of Cornwall from the A30 – with the music from my car stereo carelessly bleeding the 1970s into the 1990s – will simply not be available any more. The days of 'home' being, and remaining, a space/place that we can permanently travel towards (or leave behind) will be over. This, I contend, *is* a thought worthy of some anticipatory nostalgia. And yet, because the social theorists that have begun to take this environmental crisis seriously are, by and large, writing from the position of a 'green politics', the psychological and emotional aspects of what drivers are being asked to 'give up' seem to be being significantly underplayed.

The next question, of course, is how all this of this links to what this volume has conceptualized as the 'devolutionary moment': the two years or so since the

---

4 See especially Massey, *Space, Place and Gender* (1994).

5 See Mimi Sheller and John Urry, 'Towards a Sociology of Automobility' (Lancaster Department of Sociology, *Mimeo*) and 'The City and the Car' (International Journal of Urban and Regional Research, forthcoming). In these extremely useful essays which attempt to grapple with 'automobility' in terms other than straightforward lifestyle/ consumption, Sheller and Urry comment on sociology's failure to 'consider the overwhelming impact of the automobile in transforming the time–space "scapes" of the modern urban/suburban dweller'. The authors also draw attention to the particular way in which cars represent a unique 'quasi-private mobility': 'a mobile capsule that involves punctuated movement "on the road" from home-away-home'.

6 This sentence is a self-conscious echo of one of Jeanette Winterson's: 'The way you see it now is no more real than the way you'll see it then'. Jeanette Winterson, *The Passion* (Harmondsworth: Penguin, 1987), p. 28.

general election of 1997 in which New Labour's promise to devolve 'limited' economic and political power to selected regions of the British Isles has been partially fulfilled.[7] During that time, the peoples of Scotland, Wales and the North of Ireland have all voted in favour of some measure of regional autonomy (they have expressed their 'will'), and legislation has been passed to initiate the change (the Scottish Parliament and Welsh Assembly are now 'open for business'). Yet whilst all those presently engaged in converting the dream of devolution into its political reality are doubtless acutely aware that, in so doing, they have already moved from one historical moment to another, it is, I feel, worth reflecting on what *other* social and economic factors are destined to set their limit upon this period of constitutional change.

Foremost among such limits is, I would suggest, the impending crisis in transport which is now destined to drastically reverse the accessibility of the devolved 'margins' of the British Isles. In the same way that we appear to have forgotten that it was the dramatic expansion of road transport in recent times that has made the 'relative autonomy' of such regions a social and economic possibility (albeit often through a further aggrandization of the south-eastern 'centre'), so, too, do we appear to be blind to the fact that this must necessarily be for a short time only. The intricate network of roads that presently serves to connect even the furthest extremities of these islands together in a matter of hours, will soon (and no-one knows how soon) grind to an economic and environmental standstill. The fact that I can, today, drive from the north of Scotland to the south of Cornwall in a matter of two days should thus be regarded as the extraordinary, but ephemeral, perversion of space and time it surely is. Very soon the shrinking of the time–space continuum that we have come to take for granted is likely (for road transportation at least) to be set in reverse, and even the relatively small distances that separate one region of these islands from another will become prohibitive once more ... All speculation, I know, but should it prove 'the truth', the relation of the erstwhile devolved regions to the geographical centre (and *to one another*) will have changed yet again: will be enforcing a renewed economic and social 'separatism' that may, or may not, be to the advantage of the communities concerned. And with the prospect of history coming full cycle and returning the 'devolved' regions to the conditions of marginalization that made them 'what they

---

7 At the European Studies Research Institute [ESRI] sponsored 'Anglo-Saxon Attitudes' conference held at Salford University in July 1999 I presented a paper on the role of press photography in the making/marking of the 'devolutionary subject' in which I compared and contrasted images associated with the Scottish Referendum of September 1997 with those marking the official opening of the Scottish Parliament in July 1999. Needless to say, the romantic imagery and symbolism associated with the former – e.g., the saltire raised on Salisbury Crags in Edinburgh at dawn – was replaced in the latter with far less inspiring images of the key political figures ('men in suits'), confirming the impression that Scotland has moved from the 'moment of devolution' to the 'moment of government'. (See also Introduction to this volume.)

are', we can only be reminded of the extreme difficulty of an effective regional policy (see Introduction); one that somehow preserves and promotes (socio-economic) autonomy and (cultural) difference at the same time as working *against* geographical isolation.

The Road to Manderley

Like myself, the central characters of Daphne du Maurier's 1938 text, *Rebecca*, see and 'know' Cornwall from the wheel of a car.[8] For them, as for me, a 'home in Cornwall' exists as something that one travels towards or leaves behind: it is a time/space at the end of what was, even then, the A30 or the A38.

When, as readers, we return to the oft-quoted, and famously memorable, opening of the novel it is thus to become fellow-passengers on a journey that takes us from the busy streets of central London (left in a 'heavy shower of rain', p. 66), along the long, white road south through Salisbury, Wiltshire, Exeter, Plymouth and, finally, across the border into Cornwall, where (as Maxim promised) the sky is blue and the sun is shining. What was especially striking to me on this re-reading, however, was the way in which the different stages of this motor journey may be seen to constitute four, distinct, 'chronotopic' thresholds, in as much as the rain-filled London streets (1) and the 'long white road' (p. 66) (2) subsequently give way to the interminable passage down Manderley's own, rhododendron-banked driveway (3), until the car finally comes to a halt (4) at the front of the house as the heroine fumbles to open the door. The 'road' which the protagonists travel is not, therefore, an entirely seamless time-space continuum, with the contrast between the 'open road' and the 'closed driveway' being very marked indeed.

Although I did not re-read these opening pages until I had completed the 'reflection' (above) on my own most recent journey 'home', it is also clear that – for these fictive characters, as for myself – it is far, far easier to travel hopefully than to arrive. Although she might not have had a loud blast of music to assist her anticipatory euphoria, the heroine is certainly elated and liberated by the sense of freedom and adventure associated with the open highway. This is reflected in the adjectives used to describe the road itself and the 'gay west wind' blowing in the heroine's face 'making the grass on the hedges dance in unison' (p. 69). Despite some brooding anxiety, the Cornwall imagined and, at last, seen from the road remains a benign prospect: the beautiful and fantastical 'garden paradise' described by Maxim; the perpetually sunny 'Cornish Riviera' featured in the 1930s posters for the Great Western Railway. The fact that the precise destination of these travellers is not Cornwall *per se*, but a country house estate 'hidden' in the

8 Daphne du Maurier, *Rebecca* [1938] (London: Arrow Books, 1992). Further page references to this volume are given after quotations in the text.

creek of one its most secluded estuaries inevitably adds to its utopian prospect. Manderley is most certainly not the Cornwall of my own rural, working-class childhood although, to the extent it impacted upon my adolescent imagination, it may doubtless be seen as part of the total fictional 'reality' of my 'home/land'. Historically, the rural economy of Cornwall was manorial, and a good many of the young women growing up in the shadow of estates like Manderley have probably dreamt of crossing their thresholds in the manner of du Maurier's heroine. And although the semi-wild, semi-cultivated, demi-aristocratic enclave of Manderley may also bear only a tenuous, metonymic connection to Cornwall 'the county', it doubtless rides high in the imaginations of many middle-class tourists as they begin their drive South. For these travellers, 'the road to Manderley' *is* 'the road to Cornwall'.

Returning to the du Maurier text itself, however, we are obliged to consider the symbolic significance of the the 'road-end': the moment Maxim and his young bride leave the 'white' and 'open' highway, pass through the iron gates of the estate, and begin their passage through the dark and gothic vaults of 'the drive'. Although notionally still part of the 'journey south', it is clear that the drive is its own, autonomous chronotope: a time-space in which (for the protagonist) dread replaces anticipation, and the Cornwall/Manderley of her brighter dreams is replaced by an empty void in which she, and everything about her, threatens to implode. Her worst fear, then – given striking expression in the sentence '*this drive that was no drive* twisted and turned like an enchanted ribbon through the dark and silent woods' (my italics) (p. 70) – is similar to the one expressed in my own 'reflection': the fear that there is nothing at the end of the tunnel: no ending, no closure, no 'home'.

Although the heroine is thus still ostensibly 'contained' within the time–space continuum represented by the car ('I gripped the leather seat of the car with my two hands', p. 66), her imagination is in the process of being catapulted into a new and hostile environment. So overwhelming is this experience, moreover, that the text affords it as much narrative time as the whole of the preceding journey: 'home' seen from the drive bears no resemblance to 'home' seen from the open road; indeed, it is something that cannot be seen at all. This is a a psychological respresentation that – in terms of the thesis I am pursuing here – dramatically highlights the distinction I wish to draw between 'home' as a 'journeying towards' and 'home' as a 'point of arrival'.

Before her own final arrival at Manderley, however, du Maurier's heroine has her anticipatory dread reversed. As the car rounds the final bend and Manderley comes into view, the void is temporarily, phantasmagorically, filled with a vision of the 'home of her dreams'. Virtually identical with its postcard representation, the Manderley she then glimpses is 'identical with her desire'.[9] Yet the language

9 'Identical with her desire': see Roland Barthes, *A Lover's Discourse: Fragments*, trans. Richard Howard (Harmondsworth: Penguin, 1978), p. 20. For Barthes, one of

used to describe it, 'faultless and perfect', 'lovelier even than I had ever dreamed' (p. 71) propels the house into the realm of what, in postmodern discourse, we think of as 'hyperreality'. It the apotheosis of her 'journey towards', right enough, but – as such – is destined to evaporate the moment she steps out of the car. And this is exactly what happens. The heroine's jarring transition from 'journey' to 'arrival' as she fumbles, repeatedly, to open the door is something I myself recognise only too well. This is the moment 'home' ceases to be a fixed point of desire, and becomes, instead, a fixed point of (at worst) entrapment, isolation, entropy. The space/place that, suddenly, we wish to escape.

But let me take you now to the novel's ending and a repeat finale of the journey south I have just described. Many readers, I'm sure, will be quite familiar with how *Rebecca* ends, but *vis-à-vis* the figuration of time/space in terms of motorized transport that I am exploring here, it is worth looking at again:

> He got in front and switched on the engine. I shut my eyes. The car drew away and I felt the slight jolting of the springs under my body. I pressed my face against the cushion. The motion of the car was rhythmic, steady, and the pulse of my mind beat with it. A hundred images came to me when I closed my eyes, things seen, things known, and things forgotten. They were jumbled together in a senseless pattern …
>
> I fell into a strange broken sleep, waking now and again to the reality of my narrow cramped position and the sight of Maxim's back in front of me. The dusk had turned to darkness. There were the lights of passing cars upon the road. There were villages with drawn curtains and little lights behind them. And I would move, and turn upon my back, and sleep again …
>
> * * *
>
> 'What's the time?' I called. 'What's the time?'
>
> Maxim turned round to me, his face pale and ghostly in the darkness of the car. 'It's half past eleven,' he said. 'We're over half way already. Try and sleep again.'
>
> 'I'm thirsty,' I said.
>
> He stopped at the next town. The man at the garage said his wife had not gone to bed and she would make us some tea. We got out of the car and stood inside the garage. I stamped up and down to bring the blood back to my hands and feet. Maxim smoked a cigarette. It was cold. A bitter wind blew through the open garage door, and rattled the corrugated roof. I shivered, and buttoned up my coat.
>
> 'Yes, it's nippy tonight,' said the garage man, as he wound the petrol pump. 'The weather seemed to break this afternoon. It's the last of the heatwaves for the summer. We shall be thinking of fires soon.'
>
> 'It was hot in London,' I said.

---

the primary conditions of romantic love is the sense that the loved one perfectly matches/ fulfils one's 'abstract' ideal.

> 'Was it?' he said. 'Well, they always have the extremes up there, don't they? We get the first of the bad weather down here. It will blow hard on the coast before morning.' ...
>
> 'We ought to be going', he [Maxim] said. 'It's ten minutes to twelve.' I left the shelter of the garage reluctantly. The cold wind blew in my face. The stars raced across the sky. There were threads of cloud too. 'Yes, said the garage man. 'Summer's over for this year.' (pp. 394–7)

The first point to make is that this (re)presentation of the text is, in many respects, manifestly distorting of the reading experience solicited by the novel itself. This is because, instead of reproducing the the narrative thrust towards closure, I have focused on the the interstices: the apparently incidental details of the heroine's experience of the journey from the inside of the car; the houses and villages passed along the way; the midnight stop at the garage to get tea and petrol; the denaturalized use of direct speech throughout (a rhythmical litany that both slows down the action, and renders the last few pages the 'elegy' they effectively are). What these devices add up to, then, is not only a typically protracted *denouement* of the plot, but also a significant re-figuring of the 'chronotope of the road' with which this chapter is preoccupied.

Whilst on the one hand it can, of course, be argued that having the protagonists make their final drive to Cornwall at night is simply a device that enables us to explore/revisit the heroine's dreams, it nevertheless also supports my hypothesis that car journeys are peculiarly conducive of such fantasy. Whereas here the 'time-out-of-time' induces 'sleep-dreams', on the first drive down the heroine (as we have seen) is subject to hardly less vivid 'day-dreams'. Moreover, the intermittent – but very precise – recording of 'real-time' throughout the night causes us to reflect upon the profound disassociation between this 'subjective time' and that of the 'external' time of the clock. Measured in these paradoxical terms, a car journey is thus rendered simultaneously finite and infinite.

This philosophical point ensured, there is still the question of why – and to what extent – the text should spend such an extraordinarily long amount of narrative time on the garage stop. Whilst it could be argued that this is simply a device to slow down the action, it has become, for me, a fascinatingly sensuous evocation of what it must have been like to make the journey to and from London by car back in the 1930s (something that my own parents did on many occasions in the 1940s and 1950s). For me, then, the account of the garage stop is an end-in-itself: an exciting, even glamorous, depiction of what the 'chronotope of the road' must have meant at that time. The comments of the 'garage-man' also work to refix the co-ordinates of London and Cornwall, of course: to establish the distance, and also the difference, between them (the fact that London is a place of 'extremes', and that the West Country always gets the 'bad weather' first). Perhaps most of all, however, the garage stop confirms for me the sense that the time-space continuum of the road really is, in Bakhtin's terms, an 'empty-time', where our relation to 'home' (amongst other things) is temporarily frozen, suspended, yet held up to emotional account.[10]

The symbolic conclusions to be drawn from all of this, *vis-à-vis* the novel itself, are perhaps rather less surprising and interesting. Having established already the way in which this final journey south both repeats, and confirms, a notion of 'home' as a 'travelling towards' rather than something realized 'upon arrival', the conflagration of Manderley (p. 397) simply re-states what we already know: 'home' is (and always was) *nothing but* a dream.

In conclusion, then, I would like to suggest that du Maurier's classic romance is an historically evocative representation of how motor-travel has transformed our perception of 'home' within the British Isles: how it has enabled us to to explore, and fantasize, its seductions and traumas from the relative 'safety' of the open road. As we know from the novel's retrospective beginning, it is clear the heroine is ultimately relieved to have escaped domestic imprisonment at the 'fixed point' that was Manderley.

Driving North

My drive north, from Cornwall, to Scotland takes three days. This is because I stop at Lancaster to put in a couple of days work in my Department. The sojourn makes me think of the old stage coaches in the days when it took a week to travel from London to Edinburgh. Lancaster is a staging post. It is also, for me, the place/time where I leave my first 'home' behind. When I pull up at the University in the hot and humid August afternoon and quietly close the car door behind me, Cornwall disappears and my adult self, with its semblance of autonomy, is reconstituted. On this particular afternoon, the campus is very still and quiet, and my sense of relief is overlaid with something approaching grace. For all that we remain bound up with our 'home of homes', most of us who have 'moved away' will know this feeling: the new-born wonder of having come through, and arrived on 'the other side'.[11]

The journey north itself, however – at least, this section from Cornwall to Lancaster – constitutes a limbo that is qualitatively different from the 'travelling towards' home that I previously described. When I leave home at eight-thirty in the morning it is, as ever, in a state of numb semi-consciousness. My time 'at

10 'Empty-time': Bakhtin writes of 'empty-time' and 'time standing still' with respect to the literary-historical genre of the 'adventure chronotope'. See Mikhail Bakhtin, *The Dialogic Imagination*, ed. Caryl Emerson and Michael Holquist (Austin, TX: University of Texas Press, 1981), p. 91.

11 'Home of homes': see John Clare's poem 'The Flitting', in *Selected Poems and Prose of John Clare*, ed. Eric Robinson and Geoffrey Summerfield (Oxford: OUP, 1978), p. 176.

home' has robbed me of any clear sense of who I am, what I am doing, where I am going. Often I find myself driving along the (wrong) road to Truro before I know it. This is no longer the best route onto the A30 Northbound, but old habits die hard. This is the road I would have travelled twenty years ago, when I first left home, and instinct takes me there. But for the first hundred miles or so – to Exeter Services, or more frequently these days, Taunton – I am more asleep than awake. The persona that sped down these roads with such hopes of 'integration' is now the loosest collection of signifiers. And the landscape framed by my car window this time means little to me. Even when I cross 'the Border' back into England (with its 'Kernow ys ny England' graffiti recently whitewashed out) I am unstirred, although soon afterwards I begin to think of coffee and the fact that it will soon be time to wake up.[12]

Taunton Deane service station is blisteringly hot, even at this relatively early hour. The embankment grass is burnt to orange, and the buzzing insects remind me of the summer I spent in Indiana three years ago. With the coffee some of my powers of observation begin to reconstitute myself, and when I eventually get back in the car again I mentally shake myself awake. The forecast for the middle of the country mentioned temperatures near thirty-degrees Celsius, so the next stage (to Wolverhampton) is going to be hard. I wind down all the windows, open the roof, and put on some music. My dog is already hyperventilating, and if we get stuck in a jam it is going to be hell.

At the M5/M6 intersection (Birmingham) the traffic grinds almost to a halt, but mercifully we are through it in about half an hour. The slow-moving traffic gives me time to reflect, as ever, on what I now perceive to be the claustrophobic hell-hole of England's epicentre.[13] This is despite the fact that I myself lived in Birmingham for eight years, and have friends who are still happy to stay there. I register the the prejudiced and chauvinistic nature of my response but am too hot to correct it. Instead I begin to dream of the motorway beyond Manchester, beyond Preston, when the traffic will suddenly, magically, fall away. I turn the music up a little louder and feel a familiar excitement stir within me. Three hundred miles on, the sense of escape finally takes hold. I have crossed another chronotopic threshold, and am on my way out of limbo.

Once north of Manchester, the magnetic pull of the north takes over. I realize that, as always, I am driving faster and faster: from seventy, to eighty, to eighty-five mph. With the increased speed comes, too, an ever-sharpening consciousness. My mind begins to dart and play and formulate ... but in a way that is very different from that experienced on my journey south. If there, and then, all my imagination was focused on bringing me, my journeys, my past and future

---

12 'Kernow ys ny England': 'Cornwall is not England'.

13 In terms of geographical/political accuracy it is, however, worth pointing out that the epicentre of the British Isles as a whole is much further North: at Dunsop Bridge, in Lancashire!

together into one fixed point, now my vision is driven and directed by something powerfully outwith myself. This time I am finding myself by losing myself; here are thoughts of another landscape, another person, another home so powerful that they leave the still-floundering ego blessedly behind. Who I am 'now' is no longer *how* I was born, raised, interpellated, but *who/what/where* I desire: home defined by destination, not by origins.

Forty-eight hours later, I leave Lancaster and begin the final stage of my journey north. It is six o'clock in the evening, and already the August sun is getting low, the traffic thinning, and by the time I get to Shap summit, the sunset has officially begun. This, then, accompanies me all the way to Loch Lomond where I make my final stop for coffee. By this time I am euphoric, and almost as witless as I was two mornings ago. My throat aching with exhaustion and emotion, I take ten minutes to walk on the beach, and look up at the Ben. This is not my 'home' in the first, final, and absolute sense of 'origins', and never can be; but that does not mean it is not a 'home' of sorts. In many ways, indeed, my relationship to this space/place – provisional and unrealizable as it is – is the finer. How we relate to things – places and people – by not 'owning' them or knowing them 'too well', is something to be valued. It allows, perhaps, a more desirable form of subjectivity. Certainly when I finally arrive at Taynuilt and get out of the car this time, there is none of the traumatic dis-integration that accompanies my arrival 'home' in Cornwall. This is a chronotopic space/place where the 'travelling towards' is not undermined by a sudden, violent appropriation by 'the past'. It is a space/place where, even as I arrive, I am still 'travelling towards'.

Nightdriving

> The city road is a narrow stretch with hills that rise on either side, steep like the sides of a coffin: a lining of grass like green silk and the lid open to the sky but it is a coffin all the same. The verges hang with ripped-back cars from the breaker's yard, splitting the earth on either side, but you keep on going, over the dips and bends between the rust and heather till the last blind bend and it appears. Between the green and brown, the husks of broken cars: a v-shaped glimpse of somewhere else so far away it seems to float. It's distant and beautiful and no part of the rest: no part of the road I am travelling through, not Ayrshire, not Glasgow. It comes and goes behind a screen as I drive towards it, a piece of city waiting in the v-shaped sky if this is my day to make a split-second mistake. It's always there. And I know too it's simply the way home. I accelerate because it is not today. I am still here.
>
> Driving.[14]

[14] Janice Galloway, 'Nightdriving', *Blood* (London: Minerva, 1991), pp. 124–7.

This extract is taken from a short-story called 'Nightdriving' by the contemporary Scottish novelist, Janice Galloway. The short story comprises a trilogy of brief sketches all featuring 'drives by night' of which this is the last. None of these sketches is particularly 'Scottish' in the sense that it names and explores its location; indeed, the fleeting, negative invocation here – 'not Ayrshire, not Glasgow' – is the closest the text comes to identifying a geographical context. For myself as reader, however, the locations are very specifically Scottish in as much as I have chosen to imagine them that way. The metaphysical disclaimer, 'not Ayrshire, not Glasgow', in this sketch, for example, serves only to make me speculate which route into Glasgow Galloway is describing. Is it the A737 to Irvine perhaps, with the 'steep hills' on either side referring to the embankments of the dual carriageway which line this route, or is it one of the more minor roads through the countryside where the hills are more literally hills? All this matters because, for me, a major part of the appeal of Galloway's stories is their Scottishness, their location (albeit incidental) in the country that has become my adopted home. And for this reason, my reception of the text must be seen to be seriously at odds with the positioning of the narrator's. The 'home' to which the latter ironically refers at the end of the extract bears different connotations for me for whom this journey, on the crater-edge of death, is not about 'return', but about driving towards the new, the 'other': the space/place of desire, distance, destiny. In other words, what seems to feature as a typical 'road to Manderley' for Galloway's protagonist is read (and 'remembered') by me as a figuration of some of my first 'nightdrives' to and from Glasgow: a city so bright, so beautiful and so *distant* from my home in Cornwall that it possesses, in 'reality', all the mythical glamour that this narrator equates with the 'afterlife'.[15]

Notwithstanding the extent to which I have permitted myself to over-ride and, indeed, reverse, the subject-positioning of Galloway's narrator, there is also a good deal that resonates with my thoughts on the spatio-temporal co-ordinates of 'home' that I have been exploring here. In all three parts of the story, for example, the motor car is presented as as a kind of hermetically-sealed capsule that 'suspends' the driver from on-going, chronological time.[16] This, indeed, is presented by Galloway, as by me, as what is most desirable, most liberating about motor transport; and in the second section this is given a specifically sexual twist:

> Then we'd snake out into the open lanes and uphill, the whole frame lifting while he reached to turn the music loud with one hand on the wheel. And the rising and the music would fill up inside the car; pressing my spine, bowling back against the falling leather so I could hardly bear it. Sometimes he would smile from the corner of his mouth, feeling for the

---

[15] For further discussion of 'reading and/as remembering' see my *Feminism and the Politics of Reading* (note 2), pp. 24–8.

[16] 'Hermetically-sealed capsule': for more on the psychology of the car interior see Sheller and Urry, 'Automobility' (note 5 above).

> overdrive with one hand on the wheel as we were tearing down the white lanes, their patterns in the mirror streaming behind like ribbons on the wind. (pp. 125–6)

I would argue, however, that it is important to read this sexualization of the driving experience as metaphor for something *more* – i.e. the 'desires' associated with driving as not simply reducible to sex. The most obvious 'more', in this short story at least, is, of course 'death', but here we hit what I perceive to be another 'false limit'. Despite the fact that a good deal of 1990s theory and popular culture has invested heavily in the driving/sex/death nexus (all the debates around the novel and the movie *Crash*, for example), I personally prefer to read such texts as 'elegies' to the precise, ephemeral, un-repeatable historical moment in which we are poised *vis-à-vis* time/space/distance/travel.[17] And in as much as du Maurier's text represented the beginning of the fantastical and sublime possibilities offered by this form of travel, so might we see Galloway's representing (or anticipating) 'the end'. How else explain, for example, the incongruous, almost 'sci-fi' references to the 'ripped-back' and 'rusted' cars in the passage quoted above? As far as I am aware, no Scottish or English waysides are as yet 'littered' with the hulks of rusting, abandoned, cars ... and yet, in the near-future, in ten or twenty years time, might this not conceivably be the case?

Although this sketch thus appears to deal with driving/home at a metaphysical level, there is, I would argue, good reason for us to read it as anything but. What this story spells out, for me, indeed, is the economic/environmental limits to our driving, by day as well as by night. Whilst in Galloway's second sketch this 'escape' is linked very solidly to the protagonist's occasional trips out of the mental hospital, in all three parts the car is the space/place which offers the driver a critical perspective on the confines of their present 'home': be that 'home' in the sense of a 'place of origins', a 'temporary incarceration', or a 'chosen destination'.

As a reader, then, I have found that Galloway's text, like du Maurier's, offers a sensuous evocation of the role of the car and motor travel during the twentieth century. And whilst it is doubtful that the authors were intent on using this focus for quite the kind of philosophising I have been engaged in here, it is clear that for many of us, the 'time out' represented by such transportation is redolent of excitement, liberation, and unconscious privilege. Such an observation also brings me to a consideration of the significance of gender in all these spatio-temporal calculations: a factor noticeably absent in my reflections thus far, but one which I will now deploy in the short drive towards my conclusion.

---

17 See M. Selzer, *Serial Killers: Death and Life in America's Wound Culture* (London and New York: Routledge, 1998); Ian Sinclair, 'Crash: David Cronenberg's Post-mortem on J.G. Ballard's "Trajectory of Fate"' (London: BFI Publishing, 1999); Barbara Creed, 'Anal Wounds, Metallic Kisses', *Screen*, 39, 2, Summer (1998), pp. 60–72.

Conclusion

Women and cars do not, historically, go together – although there has now been some interesting feminist research which has sought out information about early twentieth-century woman motorists and the discourses surrounding their 'adventures'.[18] Yet from these beginnings, when only a tiny minority of (wealthy) women were motorists themselves, to today there has been a revolution in motor access. True, there are still significantly fewer women drivers than men throughout the world, and car advertising is still focused primarily on men, but significant numbers of woman across the social spectrum now *do* have access to motor transport. For us, the co-ordinates of time and space have been gendered anew. Likewise, our relationship to 'home'.

With respect to the two literary texts I have looked at here, for example, there is a stark contrast between *Rebecca*, where the heroine is a passive and powerless 'passenger', and the Galloway sketch where the female driver is acutely aware of her own agency ('You see your own grey hands wrapping the wheel', p. 126). Whilst the car journeys between London and Cornwall provide du Maurier's heroine with a new spatio-temporal perspective on 'home', she is not granted the further freedom of the car owner and driver: that of autonomous travel to/from her destination or the abiding possibility of 'escape'. Galloway's protagonist, by comparison, is free to explore the 'freedom' between 'fixed points' whenever she wishes, and with a degree of agency and responsibility that might, one day, include responsibility for her own death. This is, I feel, a significant 'freedom', no matter how darkly painted; and it finds its own significant point of contrast in the two other 'Nightdriving' sketches where the woman is the powerless 'passenger' again.

Superficially, then, the implications of improved access for women motorists throughout the twentieth century are not difficult to see. Within the UK, the increasing trend of women of my generation and younger to 'leave home' and go to a University or College elsewhere in the British Isles was – at least in the 1980s – directly tied to such access. Not all students had cars, but many did, and so the 'rite of passage' involved in this late-teenage weaning took on the specific profile of 'periods away' interspersed with 'journeys home'.[19] It was during these student years that I, at least, developed the historically and culturally specific 'sense of home' with which this chapter has been concerned. An 'old home' that is seen

---

18 See for example the work of Georgine Clarson whose publications include 'Women, Modernity and Cars in Inter-War Victoria [Australia]' in Martin Crotty and Doug Scobie, eds, *Raiding Clio's Closet: Postgraduate Presentations in History*, The History of Melbourne Conference Series, No.5, 1997, and her forthcoming 'Tracing the Outline of a Nation: Driving Around Australia in the 1920s' for *The Journal of Australian Studies*.

19 This dating is very historically precise. The changes in student grants and travel expenses in the UK which began the late 1980s means that today's student is likely to elect to stay much closer to the parental home and to return there at weekends.

repeatedly from the chronotopic horizon of the motorway, and a 'new home' that retains the illusion of being linked to the old one more seamlessly than it actually is. Like many of my generation, however, I have only recently become fully aware that *until* the late 1970s or early 1980s very few young women from rural working-class backgrounds would have had access to either Universities or cars. Born even ten years earlier, 'home' for me, as for my sister, would have undoubtedly remained a 'fixed point'.

My closing hypothesis, then, is that access to motor transportation has been instrumental in enabling a significant number of British women (yet still the minority, of course) to gain a new perspective on both their parental homes and the different geographical regions of the UK in which they come to reside. More important still, the repeated travel *between* these homes, old and new, affords those of us granted this privilege the opportunity of 'measuring' the differences and similarities between locations and communities. It enables someone like myself, who has lived in Cornwall, Hull, Lampeter (Wales), Birmingham, Durham, Lancaster, and Argyll (Scotland) to approach regionalist and devolutionary politics with, at least, some measure of insight: an insight, I would suggest, that is less about knowing what is historically, culturally and geographically specific to those regions *per se*, than what it means to inhabit their communities both as a 'native' and as an 'incomer'.[20]

This brings me back, finally, to my earlier quasi-philosophical gambit that the model of a devolved British Isles with which our politicians are currently working has been born out of a very singular historical moment; one linked specifically to the revolution in motor transport, and one, consequently, that *cannot last*.[21] This, as the preceding reflections will surely have indicated, gives me some cause for concern. What has often seemed most politically encouraging about this most recent devolutionary moment, after all, is the fact that the constituent nations and regions have been defined not through their isolation from, but their relation to, one another.[22] Similarly, the national parties of Scotland and Wales have

---

20 'Local knowledge': as one of my readers pointed out to me it is often very difficult to distinguish between 'incomer' and 'native' 'knowledge' of a region in any absolute sense, in as much as an 'incomer' may become *rapidly* familiar with the geographical/cultural specificities of that place. In as much as their epistemological 'situation' *vis-à-vis* that place/knowledge will be necessarily different, my point nevertheless stands.

21 For a prognosis of traffic growth and road congestion in the UK see the government white paper 'New Deal for Transport, Better for Everyone' [CM/3950] (1998). One of the studies referred to in this document predicts that over the next twenty years car traffic could grow by more than a third, with van and lorry traffic expected to grow even faster.

22 My comment on the way in which the devolved nations/regions should ideally relate to one another should not be seen as part of an appeasing 'centrist' doctrine but as a (hopefully) more radical vision of how the 'margins' can learn fom each other in their dealings with the 'centre'. For a *less* ideal vision of how the regions may, in the meantime,

taken particular pains to emphasise that 'citizenship' of their countries can *only* be defined in terms of residency and not 'origins' if ethnic intolerance is to be avoided.[23] The question thus raised is whether or not such a progressive vision can, and will, be maintained should the co-ordinates of our various regional homes become more fixed again.

Meanwhile, what all this all translates into on a more personal note is that an erstwhile regionally-bound subject like myself has been given the opportunity of making a new home in another, far distant, part of the British Isles whilst retaining contact with the old. The unique privileges of motor travel have thus enabled me to gain a rare perspective on *both* spaces/places from 'the chronotope of the road', the spatio-temporal continuum of 'in between'. Yet it has also become manifestly clear that the latter is as psychological as it is material, and in as much as it promotes exploration of our various *fantasies* of home it should not be seen as in any way an 'objective' perspective. Far from it. As all the preceding readings will hopefully have made clear, the view of 'home' from behind the wheel of a car is a privilege primarily because it *is* a fantasy space. And no matter how often our moments of arrival serve to remind us of the utopian nature of 'home' seen from the open road, it is, I would contend, a dream, and a desire, worth having. It has, at very least, enabled me to conceive of home in terms other than 'origins' and 'family' and 'staying put'; indeed, it has enabled me to imagine home as something which I shall *always* be 'travelling towards'.

Acknowledgements

Many thanks to Hilary Hinds, Alison Easton, Beverley Skeggs and John Urry for their helpful contributions to this chapter.

Beverley Skegg's comments have alerted me to the fact that this essay deals less with the 'colonialist' dimension to middle-class 're-locations' than my other work, and lest readers should think I am unconcerned by these issues I would refer them both to the Introduction of this volume and to my essay. 'The Place of Literature in the Spaces of Belonging', *Gender, Place and Culture* (forthcoming).

---

be set in competition with one another *vis-à-vis* transport and communication see the introduction to Chapter 4 by Ruth McElroy (this volume).

23 For an inspiring 'vision' of how national and regional identities can be newly conceived to unite 'natives' and 'incomers' in a positive way see 'The Herald Essay' by Alastair McIntosh cited in the Introduction, p. 26.

Chapter 9

'I Going away, I Going home': Mixed-'Race', Movement and Identity

Charlotte Williams

I present myself on these pages within the context of journeying, both literal and spiritual towards what Wilfred Cartney has called '*presence*'.[1] My self-script has become of late best communicated through the movement suggested within Cartney's expression 'I going away, I going home' . I say of late, because this is how I have come more latterly to understand how the facets of my identity are located within a process of becoming as a perpetual movement rather than any singular or static statement of being. My selection of readings and my writing of self here reflects something of this Cartney idiom on the Caribbean experience of 'movement from personality to the attainment of presence'(p. xiv). Cartney's analysis of the Caribbean condition provides an explanatory frame in which to consider self on both an individual and personal level and yet as fully social, collective and historically located. He says:

> *Personality* as used here is an historical term; it evokes the person as affected by the forces of colonialism, of economics, of historical imperialism and Great Power rivalry. *Presence* is a cultural or spiritual term; it suggests the person in his own spiritual interiority, his selfhood as bestowed on him by his own people, their values, their worldview, their mores. Both personality and presence are in a constant state of tension and interaction.[2]

Cartney's proposition, whilst clearly gendered, offers some parameters for my thinking about my own experience of 'going away' or more exactly, of breaking

---

1 Wilfred Cartney, *Whispers from the Caribbean – 'I Going Away, I Going Home'* (Centre for Afro-American Studies, University of California, Los Angeles, 1991), p. xiii. All further references to this text included in the chapter are from this edition. I acknowledge the use of Cartney's sub-title as the stimulus for this piece.

2 The gendering in this quotation is quite striking. I have to consider if this is Cartney's own tendency or a reflection of an historical focus on male writing and male perspectives in the Caribbean literature. See Alison Donnel and Sarah Lawson Welsh, eds, *The Routledge Reader in Caribbean Literature* (London: Routledge, 1996), p. 17 for a discussion of this.

away from dysfunctional and negating forces and conditions towards my own journey of 'going home' or self realization, integrity and the process of indigenizing my identity. Maybe the possibilities of presence are always there but for a long while my immediate environment, my home place and the reach of my thinking offered no stimulus for its realization. I had no consciousness of how to journey. I see myself in those moments, standing alone on the sea's edge in the north of Wales looking outwards across the waters pondering vague horizons, my hair tied tightly against the push of a huge wind blowing down on my back from across the Welsh mountains. Those catalytic questions would come later. *Was I Welsh? Was I Guyanese? Is there such a thing as black Welsh? Where is it I belong?*

My usurping of this idea of moving away and moving back as continual processes of border crossing allows for a recognition of multiple points of identification. It is within this rhythm of to-ing and fro-ing, of criss-crossing of the Atlantic in both a physical and spiritual sense against an historical backdrop of such crossings that helps me to explain and locate myself. In some ways this is a trajectory from the traditional Caribbean formulation of stories of exile and return in that the return is never absolute but an ongoing interaction with all the tensions, contradictions and rewards that it involves. This positioning also acts as a counter-discourse to depictions of home and belonging that posit rootedness in specific locations and places and times.[3] So the art of negotiating self lies in managing this dynamic where there is a constant mixing of heritage and traditions and a constant movement towards their identification and reformulation. It is within the remix that the spaces open up for the claiming and negotiation of multiple identities.

I have chosen to bring together two short stories that illustrate my 'border crossings'; crossings that must straddle 'race', gender, nation and territory as categories.[4] I have selected these pieces of texts in as much as they both, albeit in different ways, raise the idea of criss-crossing of the Atlantic in journeys literal and psychic and in doing so raise themes of home and exile, local and global consciousness, dispossession and belonging, hybridity and mixing and question notions of 'pure' and 'authentic' identities.

I begin with the sense of deep anxiety that clouded my search for texts that might offer such a springboard or some scenery on which I could impose these reflections on self. As my search went on over months of reading I began to

---

3 See B. Hesse, 'Black to Front and Black Again: Racialisation Through Contested Spaces' in Michael Keith and Steve Pile, eds, *Place & the Politics of Identity* (London: Routledge, 1993). Hesse challenges the dominant and indeed masculinist narratives of home that posit the idea of an authentic self rootedness located in a specific time, place and culture. These interpretations of home leave for the diaspora peoples only a sense of 'lack of' home, nation and identity. For other counter discourses on 'home' and nation see Homi Bhabha, *Nation and Narration* (London: Routledge, 1990).

4 Maggie Humm, *Border Traffic: Strategies of Contemporary Women Writers* (Manchester: Manchester University Press, 1991), p. 2.

understand some of the elements of this profound anxiety. Initially I had put it down to the fact that I am not trained in literary criticism and that my choice might somehow not be acceptable to or would indeed disappoint a wider 'interpretive community'.[5] I was concerned that those ready-made 'grids of interpretation and evaluation' so accessible to so many might elude me or worse still prevent me from engaging in any authentic way with the texts.[6] So whilst I felt I ought perhaps to choose Jean Rhys's *Wide Sargasso Sea* or a piece by Grace Nichols and seek out some reflection of my Welsh heritage through writers like Kate Roberts and Marion Eames, I could not. I teetered between being attracted by the credibility of the established voice of these writers within the reading community and a deep fear of this very public territory.

However, as my reading search progressed, I understood my anxiety to hinge more on issues of representation, identification and authenticity. I was looking for texts that might provide an emotional resonance with my own biography; texts within which I could locate myself but more accurately see myself not as alienated, oppositional and other, but as central to the themes, characters and images and in some ways associated with the author herself. This was not easy. My origins are Welsh/Guyanese but I had grown up in small-town Wales completely divorced from any wider Caribbean experience or even from any sense of black community life and association. This appeared to be no credible basis on which to claim anything of a 'Caribbean identity' and although the literature was replete with issues of black and mixed race women and marked out an historical landscape that I recognized intellectually, I wanted to *demonstrate* the gulf between these texts and my 'lived' identity. I began to see myself as a fraud to this writing exercise. Was my rejection of some very obvious literature as 'unsatisfactory' somehow a rejection of the label 'black'?

My troubles with the literature of Wales were even more profound and threatening. I had read 'white' for so long in the available texts of my mother country and I wanted to somehow reinscribe a black presence in Wales through my choice of text, both as a political gesture and as a message of 'belonging' to myself. The more I read the more it appeared that my *dis*-identifications with the central themes of Welsh women writers were multiplied. I discarded book after book in my efforts to touch down on some version of Welshness, of home and belonging, that could give me voice. I sought a positive expression of self in this context, not an oppositional one.[7]

---

5 Lynne Pearce, *Feminism and the Politics of Reading* (London: Arnold, 1997), p. 211.

6 Lynne Pearce, *Politics of Reading*, p. 212.

7 For discussions of Welsh women and alienation within their homeland see Ruth McElroy's essay on the work of Marian Eames in 'Cymraes Oddi Cartref': Welsh Women Writing Home and Migration', *Welsh Writing in English* VIII (1997), pp. 134–56. Also Francesca Rhydderch 'Dual Nationality, Divided Identity: Ambivalent Narratives of

In addition to this anxious induction to my selection of texts, I had issues to resolve with the 'writing of self' more generally. Within black feminism, autobiography has been a key mechanism of restating collective experience and of challenging the very category 'woman'. I was reminded of Sara Ahmed's deliberation on the dilemmas of 'individuation' and autobiography.[8] She asks of herself 'under what conditions does the autobiographical gesture become possible and desirable?' and 'how to perform that gesture without being implicated in a discourse of authenticity, whereby the remembering of my gendered and racialized encounters would become readable as representative?' (p. 153). It concerned me that my writing of self would inevitably become an exercise in individuation and serve only to further disconnect me from the context of wider social and political forces. I wondered if in the demonstration of my individual difference and (dis)identifications I would implicate myself so wholly as to deny the possibilities of any collective address and, indeed, the possibilities of broader systems of identification.

For black feminists autobiography has served to demonstrate the subject as an embodied and located entity; that is, through the writing of self comes a partial negotiation of the individual in the processes of wider contextual immersion. Yet within this process of wider immersion there exists a dynamic that is fraught with contradiction as the potential points of identification – gender, race, territory, national allegiance and so on – collide, sometimes conflictually. How could I name myself simply when weighted with the contradictions in the identifications of 'woman', 'black', 'mixed race', 'Welsh', 'Guyanese' and of course, 'class allegiance'? I needed to tackle that impossibility of demarcating myself with any stable and secure 'name'. The more I searched the more I experienced the anxiety produced by the different and often divisive and contradictory identifications. The more I searched the more I experienced a sense of loss at the lack of available and convenient signifiers. I felt inadequate to the predominant representations of Welsh cultural identity and inadequate against some notion of 'Caribbean-ness'. However, it was within this quest that I came to a profound rejection of the 'half-half' binary as it had been presented to me. I grew up half-Welsh, half-black, half-caste, half-white, never whole. It took me a long time to puzzle this half-half alternative and to understand that to be mixed race was not to be half of anything. There could be no singular mode, or even binary mode, of identifying across these potential positionings; only instability, shifts, repositionings, loss, ambivalence and movement. Along with this might always exist this sense of anxiety, of masquerade, and sham.

Britishness in the Welsh novels of Anna Maria Bennett', *Welsh Writing in English* VIII (1997), pp. 1–17.

8 Sara Ahmed, 'It's a sun tan isn't it? Autobiography and Identificatory Practice' in Heidi-Safia Mirza, ed., *Black British Feminism* (London: Routledge, 1997), p. 153.

So it is this sense of movement and 'becoming', rather than 'being' (as in fixed and stable) that attracts me and that guided my selection of reading: the idea of negotiating multiple regimes of (dis)identification. This sense, Ahmed has argued, represents a shift from a focus on *identity* to a focus on the processes of *identification*: 'What is required is an analysis of the processes and structures of identification – both psychic and social – whereby identities come to be seen as places of belonging' (p. 155).

My movement towards presence is thus characterized by constantly revised articulations of self and belonging and the very seeking out and searching for points of (dis)identification within my given contexts. My journey is about how I re-appropriate and reinvent those spaces.

Shape shifting with Pauline Melville

It is this notion of transformation, of shifting frames, of the multi-layering of identity that ties together the collection of short stories in Pauline Melville's *Shape-Shifter*.[9] Melville constantly challenges conventional assumptions about identity, about time and about place. She presents moving pictures of identities as fluid, flexible and fragmented and this notion echoes both in the construction and content of the stories. It is possible in Melville's work to fall 'Alice-like' into other worlds, to cut the boundary between reality and myth, rationality and irrationality as a representation of the experience of dislocation.

I am remembering being enchanted by the transformations of the 'Girl with the Celestial Limb' who develops a terror of infinity. The protagonist in 'The Truth is in the Clothes' encounters a man in Club Sozo wearing a suit 'the shape of Africa ... the left sleeve cut away sharply, following the outline of the coast of Ethiopia, dipping up to Somaliland and the Horn of Africa'(p. 103). Later the subject of the same story, offered the possibility of new adornment, slips through the plaster of the wall of her London flat. She tells us: 'I couldn't believe that I had lived in my ground floor London flat for five years without ever realising that Jamaica was just on the other side of my back wall. Relief flooded me. Now I would be able to return whenever I wanted by going through a hole in the wall' (p. 111). I was immersed in that same relief of making connections and connectedness. Every story held its own wonderful confluence of connections with other worlds, dense with recognizable and endearing characters negotiating in their particular ways very ordinary lives through disguise, disappearance and transformation. I felt rich and legitimated from my first reading to my most recent.

I am remembering the exhilaration I experienced in the induction to this text. I think it was the contemporary connections between Britain and the Caribbean that

9 Pauline Melville, *Shape-Shifter* (London: The Women's Press, 1990). All further references to this text will be given after quotations in the text.

grasped me so powerfully at first. Later I was struck by Melville's ability to fracture racial boundaries and make connections so natural and ordinary. She removes geographical and territorial boundaries in many witty ways (as in 'The Truth is in the Clothes') and also those more subtle boundaries that exist within the realm of the cultural and social. In this sense, her work, like that of Jean Rhys, utilizes images and languages of the border in order to undermine them radically and substitute realized unities and points of connection between people of different races and between places.[10]

Yet it was more than this political challenge that pulled me into the book. I recall now my clear surprise as I encountered not so much the stories where the central figure was black and negotiating British culture (such as Winsome in 'A Disguised Land', or the inept young Jamaican burglar in 'Tuxedo'), but the fact that so many of these stories were peopled almost *incidentally*, with black and mixed-race individuals alongside white people in everyday situations. This was true multiculturalism invading the privet-hedged-small-garden-world of 'little England'. The realization of this surprise has since re-opened in me the sense of deep and ongoing isolation, both physical and mental: isolation from the ordinariness of multicultural life and recognition of my sense of estrangement from any community of black people. I was confronted with the spread of colonialism into my own mind, my thinking and my dreams; that is, the 'whiteness' of my own reading assumptions. Would this be demonstrated in my interpretive tools and thus be exposed to my reader? Melville permits me to give expression to a painful search for belonging, connection and home with all the ambivalence these notions provoke in me, but also to consider how I am implicated in a wider writer–reader relationship given my positioning in 'white Wales'.

In the re-reading of just one of these stories 'Eat Labba and Drink Creek Water' I am able to view and to voice something of my own story. In this story Melville explores the idea of 'return' by tackling the mismatch between the 'imagined' and 'reality'. The Guyanese saying goes 'eat Labba and drink creek water and you will always return'. The protagonist opens the piece with a vague and nostalgic pining which she cannot wholly locate which speaks to the tenacity and yet the fallibility of this strange little myth. 'Can there be a return?' is the implied question and this becomes my own meditation.

Why do I find myself perpetuating this idea with my own daughters for whom it may have no direct relevance? I muse on my own relationship to the notion of 'return' given that I was brought up in Wales and, in reality, had no *literal* place of

---

10 See Jean Rhys, *Wide Sargasso Sea* [1966] (London: Penguin Books, 1968) for her most significant statements of 'border crossing'. See also *Voyage in the Dark* (Harmondsworth: Penguin, 1969) where Rhys explores the identifications of Anna with the 'mother' world of her childhood and the black mother/nurse. For an interesting discussion of Rhys's use of border crossing see Maggie Humm (note 4 above), p. 62.

return. I consider the outsider status implied or embraced by this idea. The idea of return is imposed upon us by those thousand and constant little assumptions buried in the phrases: 'Where do you come from then?' and 'What's it like in your country?' that marked my childhood. I have a clear recollection of the many ways in which I learned to negotiate such questions in order to satisfy the curiosity of the speaker and yet salvage something of myself. This *imposed* idea of return is part of the negating influences in my struggle for black Welsh identity and 'belonging'. Its assumptions are part of the very denial and rendering invisible of my experiences as Welsh. The equation-of-nation here is: to be Welsh is to be white and belong, to be black is to be outsider, temporary visitor, stranger. At the same time, to evoke this magical idea of return opens the possibility of escape from all the cynicism of 'home' for many black people.[11] For some, 'return' represents nostalgic recollections of a lost past, for others perhaps a release from oppressive sets of circumstances. For me it represents a reaching out to a global consciousness beyond the boundary of nation and a reconnection with a wider diaspora experience. My own passages of 'return', like the protagonist of Melville's story, are characterized by ambivalence and contradiction, but also inevitability. The protagonist dreams that she walks a tightrope that links Big Ben to St George's Cathedral in Demerara. She postulates: 'we do return and leave and return again, criss-crossing the Atlantic but whichever side of the Atlantic we are on, the dream is always on the other side' (p. 149).

I made my first literal journey to Guyana in my late thirties. I knew nothing of the country. I had been brought up in a very white patch of Wales, stranded with my ma and my four sisters as a Maroon community in a seaside town in the North.[12] It was good for us to live by the sea, a sea that brimmed over with beginnings and endings, reminding us of passages of the past, of our present and our future. We would always be able to look outwards. I never felt hemmed in by boundary or border, though at that time I had no dreams of another homeland. Yet we can never be indifferent to the sea. It is the focus of a powerful collective memory for all the diaspora peoples.

My father made his own journey of return when I was twelve. He left us adrift on a shore of white faces: an all-woman family with no compass point to reference our black selves. I was brought up womanist, not really black and not really Welsh it seemed – those conspicuous identifications would come later.[13] Access to my

---

11 Wendy Webster, *Imagining Home: Gender, 'Race' and National Identity 1945–1964* (London: UCL Press, 1998), p. x. Webster illustrates the ways in which colonialism and racism have shaped the meanings of home for black women in Britain. A main theme of this book is the tracing of constructions of home as white and the raced answers given to the question – Who belongs in Britain?

12 'Maroon communities' is the name given to the original communities established by runaway slaves.

13 'Womanist' is a term used by Alice Walker (1984) as a challenge to the homogenizing assumptions of much of early feminism. She coined the term in *In Search of*

black identification was denied through this isolation and denial; access to any sense of Welshness denied by nationalist racism. No community claimed us. But the idea of return lived with us. Just as my father's presence grew by his absence, so did the spiritual attachment to some vague notion of 'elsewhere' exist, some link to ancestry and second homeland. It was largely an invention. I knew on my first encounter with Guyana that I could never swim in the creeks with any recollection, or jump a trench and feel the flood of memories wash back into my consciousness. I would never walk in Bourda Market and know the smells of my childhood. Guyana was a stranger in this respect. I had to learn it and invent myself within it.

What I see now in Melville's story is both the hopelessness and the ambition of return. As the story unfolds so it opens my consciousness and widens my sense of place. I can experience return through Melville's story. I feel refreshed by the possibilities of spiritual regeneration that the idea embodies, but also by the potential for escape. The desire for the freedom to escape to some kind of sanctuary is always present because my connection to Wales has to be constantly claimed; it is not spontaneously granted to me. I recall the desire to name a specific place as 'home' and my ambition that Guyana would provide this. But Melville's 'return' theme is deployed beyond the realm of individual interpretation. Its subtext is inscribed with the sense of a thousand criss-crossing journeys, and criss-crossing stories, against a backdrop of imperialism and colonialism. She symbolizes the intertwining of these historical patterns of relationships by cutting her storytelling into sections, each a discrete story of movement and coming or going but each ultimately and intimately connected. In this way she peeps into different epochs of imperial and colonial relationships between Britain and the Caribbean and litters the story with the commodities of exploitation and exchange: gold, sugar, the US dollar. We see the era of explorers trekking the massive interior terrain of the Guyanas for the 'El Dorado' and when the white boy, Watt, dies in the brown waters he leaves an ancestral trace. His father returns without him. We see a young man leaving British Guyana to fight for the 'mother country' in the Great War, and his return. A forgotten history. We see the generation of my father represented by a young man wishing and hoping for exile to the mother country to work and to study. We hear the echoes of the stories of exile, of others, and then of the contemporary comings and goings of the protagonist and her friends: all very modern women.

I note that the focalization of these stories of 'the past' is male, portrayed in the experiences of explorers and the migrants, but that the more contemporary stories show us the world through the eyes of women. The main protagonist, for example, articulates her return by reference to her 'aunties' and a visit to see her friend Evelyn. It is through the aunties that we see the lost opportunities of women and hear their left-behind stories and struggles; and it is Evelyn who voices a

---

our Mother's Garden (London: The Women's Press 1984) to signify identity shaped by issues of both sexism and racism.

commentary on the state of the country. The interactions of the foreground are female. My points of identification are multiple here, with the themes of imperialism and colonialism interwoven with my 'feminist' reading. I am thinking that these intersections carry all the tensions between the concerns of post-colonial writing and of feminism.[14] I am thinking about the strength of my connections to the issues of race, to the concerns of black peoples which cut across the boundaries of sisterhood and of nation.

I experience a strong emotional resonance with these historical markers. As I read, I am reading my personal history and recovering a shared history that has been hidden from me. As with the story of my own father's exile, I encounter a young man desperate to escape from his claustrophobic and stifling home town for the promises of the 'mother country'. The young man despises the impotence of his country: 'it is impossible to be a real man until you have been to London' (p. 153), he says. I know this exile to be part of a collective memory to which I have access, and through Melville's young man I hear verbalized the expression of feelings, wishes and hopes that underscored this exile. And so it is that my father's generation speaks to me. The boy dreams of an England where there is a library 'that contains all the books in the world, a cathedral of knowledge' (p 151); he dreams of theatres and galleries and women with 'skins like cream of coconut'; of Westminster Abbey which he has seen on a postcard, and of a place 'where white men work with their hands' (p. 151). And so I hear the echo of my father's experience, but also understand how colonialism shapes our minds, our mental structures, our horizons and our dreams.

These historical and rhetorical reference points provide important identificatory locations for me. As Stuart Hall has said:

> Far from being grounded in a mere 'recovery' of the past, which is waiting to be found and which, when found, will secure our sense of ourselves into eternity, identities are the names we give to the different ways we are positioned by and position ourselves within the narratives of the past.[15]

My return is about just such a positioning of myself within Melville's 'narratives of the past'. As such, this is a clear testament of the role literature has to play in helping us to actualize our ever-changing identities and identifications.

---

[14] For feminist post colonial work, see Gayatri Spivak 'Can the Sub-Altern speak' in Patrick Williams and Laura Chrisman, eds, *Colonial Discourse & Post Colonial Theory* (Harvester Wheatsheaf: Hemel Hempstead, 1993), pp. 66–111, and 'Three Women's Texts and a Critique of Imperialism' in Bill Ashcroft, Gareth Griffiths and Helen Tiffin, eds, *The Post Colonial Studies Reader* (London: Routledge, 1995), pp. 269–73. See also Sara Mills, 'Post Colonial Feminist Theory' in Sara Mills and Lynne Pearce, *Feminist Readings/ Feminist Reading*; Second Edition (London: Prentice Hall, Harvester Wheatsheaf, 1996), pp. 257–79.

[15] Stuart Hall, 'Cultural Identity and Diaspora' in Jonathan Rutherford (ed.) *Identity, Community, Culture and Difference* (London: Lawrence & Wishart, 1990), p. 225.

It is also interesting that in many ways, I establish a relationship with Melville herself and what I hear of her in these texts. I remember, on my first reading, being envious of the luxury of attachment she had to Guyana. I know her to be born and brought up there as a small child, and even though she is white, she appeared to be able to make a stronger claim to the country than I would ever have. I envied her claim, although initially I challenged its authenticity: she had left the country as a child and had a British upbringing; moreover, she was 'fully white'. 'On what basis is her claim more authentic than mine?' was my question then. My question *now* is 'Why did I experience this envy so powerfully?' I see today, that challenge was essentially misplaced as it was directed to constructions of 'authentic' and 'pure' identity, and ideas of nation that cling to these constructions. But it also revealed my ongoing sense of loss and displacement and my consequent feelings of 'sham'. However, my own literal voyaging to Guyana has since provided me with the vocabulary to speak of Guyana with some sense of authority: now I also have the credibility to read and to recognize the Guyana of Melville's story. Now I too possess the luxury of identifying the cultural codes that lace the text: that specialized cultural knowledge that allows me to touch down on phrases like 'the bottom house' ... and cultural signifiers such as names and places, and all those linguistic shifts that are so Guyanese. So now, at last, I feel included as I conjure up those unique 'adjectives of nation' and mark out the cultural landscape that is Guyana.

A sense of inclusion is also won through my recognition of the physical landscapes of the story. The aesthetic pleasure of the pictures Melville paints absorbs me at every reading. Her protagonist dismisses the British stereotypical view of the Caribbean: 'all those white beaches and palm trees' and in doing so dismisses the outsider gaze (p. 149). We are insiders: we know a Guyana with its 'crab infested mud flats and trees dipping into the water' (p. 149). In this Guyana there is 'mud, green bush, river and more bush' (p. 150) there is the mighty Kaeteur; 'a waterfall so enormous that it makes a sound of a thousand bells as the column of water falls thousands of feet to the river Potaro' (p. 152). Watt is lost in a 'labyrinth of rivers, a confluence of streams that branch into rapids and then into more billowing waters all crossing the other ebbing and flowing' (p. 158). And there are the creeks, sometimes glittering in the moonlight, some the colour of Pepsi Cola, some sweet brown ... and I feel submerged in this land of many waters. I visit and revisit the adjectives that conjure the sugar, the rum, the molasses of the country with all the smells and the tastes of a place discovered for myself as an adult. I am transported to Georgetown: a 'city of wooden dreams, a city built on stilts belonging neither to land nor the sea but to land reclaimed by the sea' (p. 152) and I too am reclaimed. Through this knowing, this familiarity with place, I experience the idea of shared territory and I claim it for myself. This is more than memory and remembering. It is more even than the evocation of my ancestral record, both personal and collective. I see myself, creek-brown, swimming in sugar-brown waters and inconspicuous in a field of black faces, and I feel a personal symmetry. I am called back, pulled towards the idea of return and its multiple sites of identification.

Yet return in Melville's story is also futile and empty. Through one seam of the multi-layered story we see the frustrations and the futility of the protagonist's return to Georgetown. The notion of the 'Great House' of Caribbean literature is echoed but displaced by the crumbling and decayed realities of the aunties' house where she grew up. The aunties have gone mad and the protagonist finds them ruminating on hierarchies of colour and race and rejecting of her. The family is 'all busted up' (p. 161) and so is the country of her dreams: 'a pin ball economy', bankrupt, 'past caring about crime and corruption', where there is no milk and no flour and 'money is dancin' around the streets' as the black market rules (p. 164). So, notwithstanding the identificatory pleasures, the story also opens up for me feelings of deep rejection and 'othering', epitomized through the disappointments of this 'decayed reality'. I, too, suffer the immense power of the landscape that overwhelms Watt and his father, and feel painfully the unresolved disputes over race that cut across the intertwining stories. The 'central tension' of the stories is, indeed, between notions of multiculturalism/mixing/mixed-heritage on the one hand, and racial antagonisms on the other. Melville's story thus provides a springboard in which I revisit all the discomforts of my mulatto positioning. The ugliness of race lies in the intertext of this story. Melville deploys 'thick' description to demonstrate the pigmentocracy of the Caribbean and the preoccupation with 'type' that is embedded in the culture. Lorna is a 'white looking creole girl' (p. 148), Watt is a pale boy, and more and more we are invited to consider the infinite gradations of colour and their meaning and social nuance. Frank's daughter is fair skinned and 'no one would ever know' (p. 156); Melville inscribes herself as 'ice cream face', there is a young man 'with not much African left in his appearance' (p. 151). The issue of pigment is most forcefully played out in the fourteen lines on Gail's family. The fact that we hear Gail's surname, Fraser, marks her out in the Guyanese repertoire of colour and race. Her great aunt Bertha is 'yellow skinned'; Gail's mother is square jawed with iron grey crinkly hair'. Gail is honey coloured and Edmund has 'a creme de cacao complexion, tight black curls and full lips' (p. 158). 'White' as a passport to privileged and social elevation forms the backdrop of the black lines on the pages, culminating in the old aunties' rounded diatribe on race in which the protagonist is accused of trying to 'pass' for white. The aunties spit out accusations. 'Just because you've got white skin and blue eyes you think you haven't got coloured blood in you? But you have. Just like me. It's in your veins. You can't escape from it. There's mental illness in the family too' (p. 162). Her presence to them has become like a bad smell. It is incontrovertible that it is race that busts up this family. The aunties tell us they were left behind because they were too dark and the men have long left and married 'white street-walking bitches' (p 161).

Within these juxtapositions I find many points of identification, some of which evoke pride and attachment, others dispossession, shame and the burden of betrayal. I am mulatto. I feel the comforts of white advantage that have protected me: my mother's white skin, my place secured in her white country, the advantages of class and status, and I know that I too have betrayed 'the aunties', that I too must listen to their accusations. These lines arrest me in guilt, white guilt and shame, yet I am not white. I am reminded of my Guyana days when I longed to 'belong' and of my naive attempts to fit in. I walked the market streets and rode the minibuses rejecting the privileges of the available large, white Landrover; I took a job downtown for local money; I bypassed the white parties and made friends of black women; I tried to disguise my accent, appear knowledgeable about the country; I read and I re-read its history and its literature, looking and searching for myself. And still the aunties' words punish me, cut me now and remind me of the discomfort of my historical positioning. I am the product of the relationships between colonizer and colonized. Will I always be outsider? I long for Evelyn's authentic and untroubled identity. She is black. My insecurities are a shadow to her confidence. I am, again, simply masquerading.

It is, at the same time, possible to locate myself amongst the 'black skinned', the 'yellow skinned' and the 'creme de cacao' peoples of the piece and to seek comfort in all the mixing and intermixing that is Guyanese society. Melville constantly cuts across the rigidities of racial boundary. She mimics and ridicules them. The aunties are, after all, going mad. She points to the inevitability of connections between these women, connections of blood, of friendship, of territory and soil, of ancestry and of political sisterhood. Just as race divides us so also it ties us together: explains us and gives us a collective voice. We are bothered by race *and* accepting of it. We are both called back and rejected within this parameter.

Through reading Melville I connect at a personal level, but also with a collective and global consciousness, as I place my experience along these encoded registers. In this way I reaffirm both personal and political attachment and belonging and thus find some sense of 'authenticity'. I move towards *presence*. However, like the protagonist I am also rejected by this country and alienated from it and must manage that tightrope; that 'frail spider's thread suspended sixty feet above the Atlantic attached to Big Ben at one end and St George's Cathedral, Demerara, at the other' (p. 149).

Remix with Jen Wilson's 'Zen and the Art of Thelonius Monk'

'Hiraeth' (yearning), as the Welsh say, always calls me back to Wales. I know a Wales. I can read the cultural scripts more easily. My brown skin does not blend with the landscape in the way that it melts in the Guyana waters yet there are many many points of identification that will allow me to use the word 'home' albeit tentatively. I choose Jen Wilson's short autobiographical piece as my home story, my 'going home' story.[16] Returning to Welshness is a prevalent theme in the work of some of the best known Welsh women writers and poets, for example Gillian Clark and Christine Evans.[17] The idea of 'hiraeth' probably compares quite well with the Caribbean myth of 'return'. It is an echo that resonates across the Welsh landscape most usually conjuring up a nostalgia for the lost landscapes and moodscapes of Wales, or a loss of language and culture and traditions; or for the 'community idyll', whether the rural village, or the urban mining communities. Stereotypical images of Wales abound in our literature; the evocation of domestic space (hearth and home), themes of chapel and Bible reading;[18] 'mam'; Welsh dressers; names and other potential ethnic markers that, to me, are both elusive and exclusionary. Indeed this world of words and pictures, of icon and images for a long time seemed wholly closed off to me. Moreover, the Welsh literary tradition appeared to provide no obvious access point for me either, except in positioning me as 'different' and 'other'.[19] Where were all the grimy seaside towns flooded with tourists? Where were the Italian ice cream sellers, the Polish emigrés, the Irish, the factory workers, the Chinese restauranteurs, the black Welsh? Indeed feminism itself appeared alien to the Welsh culture we were fashioning.[20] The political focus for Welsh women was/is the language and nationalism and my positioning in relation to these issues is contradictory and complex. I have a Welsh-speaking mother, but I am not Welsh speaking myself. It is the language of my home but, like many in Wales, I feel disenfranchised by formulations of national identity that are coupled exclusively to language. I have little direct access to the politics of language or the Welsh language literature or to what is so often constructed as 'proper Welshness'.[21]

---

16 Jen Wilson, 'Zen and the Art of Thelonius Monk' in Leigh Verrill-Rhys (ed.), *On My Life: Women's Writing from Wales* (Dinas Powys: Honno Press, 1989).

17 See for example Gillian Clark, *Selected Poems* (Manchester: Carcanet, 1996) and Christine Evans, *Looking Inland* (Bridgend, Mid Glamorgan: Poetry Wales Press, 1983).

18 See Noragh Jones, 'The Comforts and Discomforts of Home', *Planet*, 107, Oct–Nov (1994), pp. 75–83. Jones discusses the domestic themes in the literature of Kate Roberts and the place of feminism in Welsh women's writing.

19 See note 7 above.

20 Jane Aaron discusses this point in 'Finding a Voice in Two Tongues: Gender and Colonisation' in Jane Aaron, Teresa Rees, Sandra Betts and Moira Vincentelli, *Our Sister's Land* (Cardiff: University of Wales Press, 1994), pp. 183–98.

21 For a discussion of language and Welsh identity see Jane Aaron cited in note 18 and Charlotte Aull-Davies 'Women, Nationalism and Feminism' in Jane Aaron, Teresa Rees, Sandra Betts and Moira Vincentelli, *Our Sister's Land* (Cardiff: University of Wales Press, 1994), pp. 242–59. Also Bre'ched Piette 'Identity and Language: An Example of Welsh Women,' *Feminism and Psychology*, VII (1) (1997), pp. 129–37.

This aside, I have found too much of the women's writing in Wales nostalgic, ritualized, escapist and, at times, no less than frightening because of its exclusiveness. I seemed to hold none of the authentic markers of the publically proposed constructions of 'proper Welsh identity'. My identity/identities appeared 'wrong' or 'spoiled' by comparison. Indeed the Welsh national space seemed very small and its access points increasingly narrowing. My coming home would be about challenging that space for myself, fracturing the Welsh imagining of itself and finding a way to indigenize what I was. I wanted to interrogate the question: Who is of this place? and establish *presence* for myself.

When I stumbled across Jen Wilson's piece I can remember feeling a sense of profound joy. The opening lines pulled me in with their alliteration of the word 'wrong' representing the idea of multiple dislocations and spoiled identity:

> I was born the wrong time, wrong place, wrong era and, if I was honest with myself, the wrong colour! (p. 132)

By implication she constructs a notion of 'proper Welsh' which she challenges and, by implication, her desire to be black woos me and meets my own desire for permission to be black within a Welsh context. Her wish, presenting as it does a positive image of the black woman and of black culture within the context of writing in Wales, touches the deep feelings of marginalization and isolation that characterize my pictures of Wales. Her subject opens up a space for a black identity in Wales, and for my reinvention.

Wilson's narrative is located solidly within the genre of Welsh women's writing in that she chooses the domestic space of the front room and its echoing themes of hearth and home, mother's knee, tradition and culture, religion and so on. However, within the confines of this tradition she fractures the space with rhythms and spirits of black women jazz players. She claims them as an ancestral inspirational heritage together with her Welsh genealogy and stages the cultural remix in the heart of Welsh national space epitomized by grandmother's parlour. Wilson uses the metaphor of music and improvisation to illustrate cultural heritage and processes of cultural change. Her narrative is punctuated by the rhythmic tones of the two lines:

> Boom chicka boom chicka boom chicka boom
> We always had music in our front room. (p. 131)

In this way she creates a type of 'dub', scratching a new trajectory across the Welsh hymnal sheet, infilling a new range of tones to the chorus of the Welsh choir or, in other words, improvising on the traditional Welsh cultural and literary repertoire.

I touch home with several chords in this piece. I feel the sense of being marooned that Wilson experiences through her identifications with black jazz culture. Wilson is as out-of-synch with her immediate world because of this element in her identity as I am because of the colour of my skin and my mixed heritage. I recognize her use of a domestic space as alive and 'real' compared to the negating influences and dysfunctional experiences in the public sphere; I recognize my experiences as a child. Being a lone black family, our 'real' world and our 'real' life could only ever be experienced in our front room out of the distortions of the public gaze and away from all the corrupting assumptions. Our parlour was a locus of reaffirmation and pride, a sanctuary in a benignly hostile environment. As I read I can reflect on my profound isolation within this white Welsh community and yet know the inevitability of my deep attachment to it won through time, local connectedness, blood and ancestry. I had grown up trading bits of myself for recognition within this white community; denying aspects of myself in the search for the acceptance and 'belonging' that could only be achieved by being white. This split between the freedoms of the private space and the public domain is a dominant theme of black writing from slavery to the current day. The oppressions of the public space can only be mediated within the inner spaces of 'home', which becomes both the metaphorical and literal location of resistance. Yet in its symbolic reaches, 'home' has the potential to transcend any literal space.

Wilson's 'play' on the front room theme as a place of invention, resistance, improvisation, education and freedom resonates with my construction of a global consciousness of private space in black diaspora culture. More than this, she imbues this space with a life and activity and colour that disrupts the powerful Welsh overtones of chapel, Bible-black claustrophobia, religiosity, tradition and constraint. She frees up the historical legacy to melodious, syncretic and improvised tunes: hybrid tunes, mongrel tunes that sing of cultural change. Like the Melville story she too is 'border crossing'. From the confines of the dark and intact parlour of her grandmother the 'drums and the piano are free to escape' (p. 136) as the young 'let fly' ... and 'let rip' ... while grandmother is out and 'boom chicka, boom chicka boom chicka boom' ... In this way Wilson demonstrates an ambivalence about Welsh culture that resonates with my own experiences: she evokes this through a series of images: miners and the colliery; the Bible; chapel; Sabbath; grandpa dying at home; 'abide with me', 'and her reference to 'yards of Welsh verses' (p. 132). Wilson seizes ownership of these images but inscribes them new meaning and import. I remember our own front room in Wales and the easy intermingling of cultures within it: my mother and her sisters speaking Welsh and their bible philosophising; my father's paintings of Africa, the masks, the talking drum, the African rugs from our childhood journeys and the vague trace of his Caribbean heritage. These were the only available cues to our black selves, nothing real: no real life points of reference, no literature, no role models. There were no representations in our mirrored world to 'who' or 'what' we were: only caricatures. Was I doomed only to view myself on the labels of Robinson's jam jars? Our history was still hidden: just small fragments seeped through, so our art became invention, improvisation; we made our own 'dub', drawing elements from some largely imagined 'master tape'.

Wilson's willingness to draw parallels between black culture and Welsh culture allows me to reflect on the points of connection and disconnection in my dual heritage.[22] She compares the Welsh valleys with the southern United States: two oppressed nations with their Baptist churches ringing with soul and with 'hwyl'. She bemoans the loss of language through English oppression, and points to the oppressions of race. I consider how these factors were demonstrated in my childhood, sometimes conflictually. I recall how my mother joined with her people to fight for her Welsh self and fought against them to protect our black selves. I remember on my return from Guyana to Wales how I rejected these parallels that allowed the Welsh to hide away from any recognition of themselves as part of the Colonial and Imperial forces that oppress black people. My dis-identification with Welshness (white Welsh) was important to my restatement of myself as a black person in the Welsh context, to my becoming visible. How could this nation so wholly have submerged that memory of religious domination of 'the natives' and its part in missionary colonialism? How could it have forgotten walking the lands that the English soldier had so ruthlessly plundered? I am remembering my protest at this national amnesia. Just as the assumptions of 'sisterhood' have been challenged, so I interrogate those versions of nation that assume homogeneity and fail to acknowledge their role in the historical cast of racialized relations. I challenge Wales imagining of itself as a tolerant nation of oppressed peoples. This questioning of Welsh national imagining is part of my journey towards *presence*.

And so 'I going home' and, in my journey I nudge against the closures of this national space. I consider small ways in which I have mobilized my sense of *presence*. On my return to Wales, I changed my name back to my maiden name 'Williams' with tongue in cheek at the 'passport' this would afford me to Welsh cultural and social life. Williams is a plantation name, a name of conquest, and yet in Wales a signature of authentic identity. I think about the fragility of many of the exclusionary markers of Welsh ethnicity – language, accent, locality, name – and the ways in which these categories are constructed to create smaller and smaller sites of authentic identity. I think about my ambivalence to this type of national 'bordering', how I seek both to evoke and deny it. By definition minority communities will fracture the dominant national imagining of Welshness. Yet all the while I know the depth of my connection to this place.

Wilson's theme of 'mis-education' is also obliquely focused on Welsh cultural life. She implies omissions in the nation's education through challenging the content of her own learning and the historical blackouts. Wilson's jazz women are uncovered and celebrated one by one. She calls down the jazz greats – the women of jazz history – and restates their contributions that have become lost through

22 See Francesca Rhydderch's reference to the 'nabob' figure in Welsh literature – in the article cited in note 7.

time, through neglect, and through patriarchy. She gives these marginalized women the foreground in this deliberately feminist statement of self and in doing so gives me voice, and place, and attachment.

More than this, the women in her passage are identified as key communicators of culture. The theme of culture passed down from women's knees is a feminist theme that unites us. These women are the 'cultural carriers' pivotal to transmitting the rich heritage of ethnic symbols and ways of life and ideas of nation.[23] Wilson usurps this idea for its transformative potential. She will not be charged with a preservation of culture as intact, unspoiled and consensual but sees herself as a transmitter of interpreted narratives and renegotiated frames of reference, valorizing the traditional but allowing for it to be reinterpreted and reshaped. As 'mother', she embraces hybridity, loss, change and transitions as creative forces, as processes of 'becoming' rather than as fixed and static transferable identities. She holds the remix as progressive and authentic and confronts the way in which our national space is imagined and claimed. I share in her imagining and project my desire onto our newly devolved nation. In this political remapping of Wales I know that a shared nation may be no guarantee of inclusivity.[24]

Now I think about my own white Welsh speaking mother: I see her blue eyes and her soft peachy skin and hear her language of care and protection, 'Cariad bach', shielding us from the hostilities of her own nation whilst nurturing us with its richness. And I see myself wearing my Welsh tapestry coat, my black hair wild and free in the wind, talking of journeys and passages. And I see my brown-skin daughters claiming a new sense of Welshness with no echo of 'return' in their ears. And I see my grand-daughter with her eyes shining like the blue of the Atlantic and I feel a great sense of the '*presence*' connecting us all.

Acknowledgements

My thanks to Lynne Pearce for her inspiration and encouragement to venture into some unchartered territory.

---

23 'Cultural carriers' is the term used by Nira Yuval-Davis and Flora Anthias, *Women–Nation–State* (London: Macmillan, 1989) to denote the role of women as ideological reproducers of culture, tradition and ethnicity.

24 Nations often imagine themselves as homogeneous entities and powerful groups police incursions into dominant constructions of authentic identities. Wales as a nation is internally fragmented by divisions and borders: between Welsh speaking/non Welsh speaking, rural/urban, north/south, black/white and so on. My ambition is that our newly emerging vision of nation will engage with this rich diversity and allow for multiple constructions of Welshness that are open and inclusive.

Chapter 10

Highland Lines: The Production and Imagining of Highland Scotland 1803–1999

Helen Boden

Towards the end of his study of the 'production' of the Scottish Highlands since the mid-eighteenth century, *Improvement and Romance*, Peter Womack claims that 'the Highlands are imaginary'[1]. Peripheralized, defeated, but morally superior, 'the region was committed to the privileges, and condemned to the marginality, of fiction' (pp. 179–80). Using Womack's theorization of the Highland dilemma as a springboard, I want to unpick some of his remarks, to test them against texts from the beginning of the nineteenth century, when the respective claims of 'improvement' and 'romance' were most vigorously contested; and from the late twentieth century, when the very different circumstances, of mass tourism and commodification of travel, can nonetheless be traced back directly to those established during the Enlightenment and exploited in its aftermath. If the mutually sustaining discourses of improvement and romance have not conclusively been superseded as the foremost means of representing matters pertinent to the Highlands, a definite presence of some promising new interventions is however being felt.

As the selection of *two* texts risks manipulating the argument into a narrative (for me) limitingly constructed around the binary oppositions of, for example, a personal past and present, or here and there, I have chosen both my 'texts' – Dorothy Wordsworth's journals of her Scottish tours in 1803 and 1822, and Douglas Dunn and Elizabeth Ogilvie's *Into the Oceanic* (1999), because of ways they respond, in different time periods, to the same 'region': the Scottish Highlands. Even though I am 'from' the north of England, and live in Lowland Scotland, in the spirit of Nicole Ward Jouve's statement 'it is because subjecthood has become so difficult, has been so deconstructed, that we need to work towards

[1] Peter Womack, *Improvement and Romance* (Basingstoke: Macmillan, 1989), p. 166. Womack uses the term 'imaginary' partly in its Lacanian sense (especially in Chapter 6, when he refers to Gaelic as 'the native tongue of the Imaginary' (p. 133), in contrast to the 'Symbolic' of English), and partly in its conventional sense, as a production of the imagination, or of fiction.

it', I want here to 'work towards' subjecthood (and my chosen texts) by taking as my locus/focus Highland Scotland.[2] My familiarity with parts of this region (I use the term 'region' warily, with full awareness of its limitations and contradictions) are now greater than that with my home county. Nonetheless, as an 'implicated reader' this leaves me rather exposed, as it could be argued that I am less qualified to write about the Highlands than many other parts of the British Isles, and that, as an outsider with very little Gaelic, it is impossible for me to do so in a way that is not itself a form of cultural imperialism.

This choice, however, allows me to consider new possibilities for subjectivity, predicated on 'the idea of identity as fluid and transitional, based on fragments of place memories, on desires and experience', rather than a selfhood articulated through difference and locked in binary oppositions.[3] I grew up between working and middle classes, and between urban and rural societies, and am of course the product of these intersections, but what most interests me now is a number of interrelated questions, including why and how the outsider finds points of identification in new spaces and what demarcates the human subject's point of identification with a region or place. In asking questions rather than supplying answers or anecdotes, I am not deflecting attention away from the personal, but am engaging in the process of responding critically to my emotional preferences and identifications.[4] So, how is the difference between tourist/visitor and native represented; how does the outsider function as interpreter, and is it possible for her/him to avoid the subject-position of re-colonizer? To what extent is power devolved to the represented region in writings about it, and in different genres? What purpose do national and regional stereotypes, and stock responses, to places that seem always subject to some prior representation and interpretation serve, and how can they be reinterpreted and reappropriated?

What effect does the additional consideration of sexual difference have on answers to the above questions? It might well appear that using Highland Scotland as a site in a book of feminist readings is a non-starter: the region is traditionally gendered, along with its language, Gaelic, as feminine (therefore 'imaginary'), whilst its female inhabitants have been oppressed, marginalized and silenced by an overwhelmingly patriarchal culture legitimated and manifested through institutionalized religion.[5] Women are therefore consigned either to mythic status or to the silence of domestic servility. Without denying either the gendered

---

2 Nicole Ward Jouve, *White Woman Speaks with Forked Tongue: Criticism as Autobiography* (London: Routledge, 1991), p. 11. Jouve's was one of the first studies to use 'personal criticism' as the basis of its methodology.

3 Linda McDowell, *Gender, Identity and Place* (Cambridge: Polity, 1999), p. 220.

4 Compare Jouve, *White Woman*, p. 4.

5 Womack, *Improvement and Romance*, pp. 131–40.

symbolic image or the real experience of women in the aesthetically feminine/materially patriarchal Highlands, I want here to look at some sites for textual resistance in work that undertakes to represent their topography and/or culture. I shall implicitly suggest how to move beyond the simplistic formulation, which sometimes still structures the criticism of travel writing, that women are community-based, defining themselves in relation to other human, especially female, subjects, while men define themselves in relation to, and mastery over, a non-human landscape.

I have therefore selected a female-authored text written at a time when response to the landscape (usually experienced and appreciated through feminine-inflected sentiment) was heavily prescribed, and when the stereotypes associated with Highland, rural Scotland first began to be (as Homi Bhabha would put it) 'fixed' (this is also the time-period in which the bulk of my academic research is focused);[6] and a collaborative work produced at the end of the twentieth century which exemplifies the enabling possibilities afforded by the most recent developments. Such new images are often produced by outsiders, people not steeped in the religious and linguistic traditions of the region, and I am not happy to claim that this doesn't matter.[7] Nor do I wish to deny the significance of new work by 'local' writers and artists, and native Gaelic speakers, such as Ian Stephen and Kevin MacNeil, or of recent initiatives in Gaelic medium education and broadcasting. But because of where I am 'coming from', intellectually as well as personally, my focus is on the image of the Highlands provided by those who have travelled there to produce their work (or who have produced their work because they have travelled there).

Perhaps more than any other region of the UK, the Highlands, or at least knowledge of them, have been produced through literary texts. And precisely because of the region's consignment by the intelligentsia to the status of the 'imaginary', and the ways in which its peripheralization is managed, it presents a crucial site for analysis in the early days of devolved power in Scotland, especially if the ways in which its representation has changed, evolved (or remained static) over a 200-year time period are considered. For example, the (plural) Highland*s* have long been considered as a homogeneous unit, resulting in the disallowance of cultural and topographical differences within their physically vast area. Remoter parts receive funding for improvement to the infrastructure from the European Regional Development Fund, rather than the UK government. One of first things to impact upon me on my first visit to the Uists, in 1991, was the large EEC symbol on notices by the causeways connecting the islands (as the SNP slogan goes,

6 'The stereotype ... is an arrested, fixated form of representation', Homi K. Bhabha, *The Location of Culture* (London: Routledge, 1994), p. 75.

7 For a native Gaelic speaker's perspective on this problem, see Donald MacAulay, 'Canons, Myths and Canon Fodder', *Scotlands* 1 (1994), pp. 35–54 (pp. 53–4).

'Scotland in Europe'). The Western Isles are effectively erased from the political and economic maps of Britain. Such practices may seem unjust, but they are entirely consistent with those developed since the mid-eighteenth century; and are analogous to the way the Highland Scotland is represented in writing.

I am particularly interested in the way the modern visitor renegotiates the legacy of Romantic Scotland – for this to a large extent continued to influence and determine its reception for most of the twentieth century. I wish therefore to look especially at possibilities for dialogue between sentimental/emotional responses, and intellectual engagement or interpretation: to consider alternatives to this 'Caledonian antisyzygy' of head and heart; and how the non-urban can be recovered from its ostensible position as terminally outmoded by/in the intellectual avant-garde, remaining, literally, the 'preserve' of the conservative middle-brow consumer. In other words, to ask more questions, about how 'I' articulate my subjectivity, or identity, in relation both to cultural texts and topographic locations: how far are my responses derived from/limited by/departing from those of eighteenth-century aesthetics informed and supplemented by my reading of critical theory and of fictional interventions? What is assisting me in, and blocking me from, seeing things in new ways, and (how far) is this a gendered problem? How far has my academic research affected or distorted my reading of the Highlands today?

The identity of the Highlands was fixed (as morally superior, materially inferior, politically impotent, therefore 'imaginary', therefore feminine) by their post-Enlightenment romanticization, and until very recently, little has been done to resist that fixity – certainly from within; and any attempts at change from without have been regarded as doomed to failure due to a collective refusal of externally-imposed schemes for 'improvement'. This response is entirely understandable given the region's political history, but unfortunately it also serves only to consolidate the prejudices of those who are of the opinion that the Highlanders constitute a single ethnic group who are less advanced/developed than other UK citizens, and who hold common (read 'quaint', 'anachronistic') aims and beliefs. What happens, though, if we *do* resist these old categorizations, and consider the Highlands instead as being themselves in a state of becoming? By this I do not mean that they should be reinvented purely as a metaphysical, abstract idea(l), because while this may resonate comfortably with postmodern notions of the constructedness of the nation, this approach may well ultimately serve only to reinscribe the 'Highlands as imaginary' dogma; and irresponsibly to ignore the possibility of their continued political peripheralization by Holyrood, as by Westminster. However, we can instead regard them as a place which itself comprises many regional variations, and which affords a site for challenging new creative responses. It can, for example, no longer be claimed that the Western Isles are impossible to (re)theorize in terms other than Womack's, or that they have failed to participate in modernity and to produce new symbolic images to challenge the 'power of supernatural and religious cosomology' which has kept them different from 'mainstream [i.e.mainland] Scotland'.[8]

The central Highlands seem now, to the present writer, to be too closely annexed to mainstream British ideology, their past themeparked into conformity with the tastes and cultural preferences of middle England. (Even to speak of the 'central Highlands' is itself problematic, as the topographical 'highlands' are not coextensive with the political 'Highland Region', a creation of the 1975 local government restructuring.) In contrast to the relentlessly commodified central (Middle?!) Highlands, where it can be difficult to see the scenery at all for the Forest Enterprise plantations and the visitor centres (no need for the real thing if it is available ready-interpreted in a monologic and intellectually unchallenging form, if it can always be simulated in good weather and quality souvenirs are on sale), the geographically more peripheral Highland environments are becoming the subject of a very different multi-disciplinary creative response in the approach to the twenty-first century. In poetry, music and the visual arts, through explorations of the anti-sentimental, practitioners are working towards a reinstatement of what Norman MacCaig called 'the mind / Behind the eye, within the passion'.[9] This creates a new subjectivity for the Highlands, which is the product of minds seeking ways of representing them in a non-colonialist manner, challenging the hegemony of the sight by positing a fuller range of bodily responses. It does not seek to deny either the atrocities of their history or their present status as the product of this history, but refuses to be limited exclusively by or to it, and is equally concerned to look to new possibilities in the future.

In Mainland Orkney, a flourishing arts scene exists in Stromness (sometimes known as 'the St Ives of the North'), whilst in remoter islands, Sir Peter Maxwell Davies works both intellect and emotion into abstract 'readings' of the sea's motions and moods in his symphonies. Orkney, however, seems proud primarily to be Orcadian; fertile, relatively prosperous, tolerant, ambiguously Highland: perhaps more like Fife transported three degrees North than other parts of the region with which it is administratively and politically linked. The Western seaboard is undergoing a more surprising and difficult renaissance. The far North-West, and much of the Hebrides, the horizons towards which the eighteenth-century traveller pushed in search of new sensory experience and old cultures, are, literally, 'spaces', defined physically by the clearances, and spiritually and intellectually by evangelical Protestantism. Nonetheless, gestures towards new

---

[8] John Agnew, 'Liminal Travellers: Hebrideans at Home and Away', *Scotlands* 3:1 (1996), pp. 32–41 (pp. 35–6). That Hebrideans tend to define themselves in relation to (difference from) mainland Scots, rather than Lowlanders, or the English, for example, has been noted by Agnew (p. 40), and Berthold Schoene, 'A Passage to Scotland', *Scotlands* 2:1 (1995), pp. 107–22 (p. 110).

[9] 'A man in Assynt', *Collected Poems* (London: Chatto and Windus, 1993), pp. 224–31 (p. 231).

readings of these regions, their topography, culture and history are being made. The most blatantly political of these is probably a 1998 touring exhibition, 'Mactotem', 'featuring 30 artists' amendments, interferences and interventions to the statue of the first Duke of Sutherland, the architect of the Highland clearances', in which the infamous Duke is variously replaced by a sheep, transported to the new world, etc.[10] Other, more subtle, visual renegotiations of the human subject's relationship to the landscape and language of the North West Highlands and Islands are found, for example, in the work of Donald Urquhart.[11] These involve explorations of how non-hierarchical relationships between human and land can be expressed; how alternatives to the Enlightenment aesthetic, founded on the pre-eminence of visual stimulus and the progression from sensation to feeling ('sentiment' – later betrayed into 'sentimentality') to morality, can finally become a possibility. In the work of a growing number of revisionary cultural interventions, the Highlands themselves are (re)cast optimistically as *sujects en process*, in a state of becoming.

The conclusion to Womack's book looks optimistically to this different future: 'the possibility which the myth cherishes and deforms – that beyond the complementary abstractions of Improvement and romance we could discover an authentic way of living together – is not conclusively yet either discredited or achieved' (p. 180). Ten years on, new alternatives are an actuality rather than a possibility, but in the 1980s, many writers were still bound by the 'complementary abstractions of improvement and romance'. I shall use Paul Theroux's chapter 'The Flyer to Cape Wrath' in *The Kingdom by the Sea* (1983) as an example of this stage. And despite the idealism of his closing sentence, Womack's concluding chapter is, as a whole, more cautious, and rightly so, since much creative work in/about the Highlands at the end of the twentieth century departs little from the norms of the early nineteenth century:

> The 'Highlands' (that is, the periphery in mythical form) develop into the privileged home of subjectivity ... hence the proliferation of fictive themes in their representation – folly, imagination, superstition, vision, poetry, holiday. The Gaeltacht becomes, in every sense, an ideal country, until even those who seek to uphold its interests against the core find that they are doing so in the glowing and reverent language which ratifies its oppression. (p. 169)

Womack closes his argument that the Highlands are imaginary, by considering their Utopianism: they are a truly 'imagined community' because they lack state power, and 'the very emptiness of the projected home creates a space for

---

10 Mactotem: Reviewing the Duke of Sutherland Monument (1998). See www.lanntair.com/Exhibitions/default.htm.

11 *Grey Weighted Notes (ComharranThroma Ghlasa)*, An Lanntair, Stornoway (1997).

identification' (p. 179). Rather than becoming a Utopia, it may be more helpful to consider the Highlands (especially as represented in travel writing) as what Foucault has termed a heterotopia, or a counter-site, 'a kind of effectively enacted utopia in which the real sites … are simultaneously represented, contested and inverted'.[12] I find this alternative attractive and productive, because it enables the Highlands to be at once imaginary *and* real: the product of the various subjectivities responding to them, whether present or absent (the emigrant in Nova Scotia, the returned holidaymaker in Nuneaton), *and* an actual physical location. It can, for example, help make sense of the relations between mythic representations and actual lived reality; or between maps and the ground surface of which they form an abstract replication (or distortion). It also offers, as I hope to show, the potential for avoiding hierarchized, gendered binary oppositions. Nor are 'heterotopic readings' inconsistent with recent work on national identity which contests the view (popular at the time Womack's book came out), of the imagined, and therefore unreal, hypothetical, abstract, nature of the nation, and posits instead a belief in the actuality of the place, its inhabitants, and their cultural practices.[13] The heterotopia therefore seems to me to be a most useful model both for the revisionary reading of a number of passages in post-Enlightenment travel writing (from the late-eighteenth to the late-twentieth centuries) and for approaching the most recent experimental representations of the Highlands, as well as for considering continuities between the two. For although I stand by my argument that the new work is taking radical new directions in/to the Highlands, this inevitably does not and cannot involve an entire break from past practices.

I also see the representation of the Highlands 'as fiction' in the late eighteenth and early nineteenth centuries, as symptomatic of a more complex relationship with the move towards self-representation and not, like Womack, just as a direct result or effect of 'Improvement' ideology; a means of allowing their moral superiority whilst prohibiting their reality. He sees the relationship between the fictionalizing of the Highlands and the development of self-representation as one of cause and effect along a temporal continuum; I regard it as more complicated and reciprocal. The 'fictionalizing' of the Highlands is also enabled *by* developments in the understanding of subjectivity, and agency for self-representation.[14]

Travel writing offers an especially useful site for working out these problems. If the Highlands were 'produced' for mass consumption in the novel, to a lesser

---

12 Michel Foucault, 'Of Other Spaces', *Diacritics* (1986), pp. 22–7. This posthumous article is based on a 1967 lecture. Elspeth Probyn gives a critique of the heterotopic model in the introductory chapter of *Outside Belongings* (London: Routledge, 1996): 'heterotopia designates the coexistence of different orders of space, the materiality of different orders of social relations and modes of belonging' (p. 10).

13 See, for example, Slavoj Žižek, *Tarrying with the Negative* (Durham, N. Carolina: Duke UP, 1993).

14 My approach here is closer to that of John Glendening, *The High Road* (Basingstoke: Macmillan, 1997).

extent they were also produced by the travelogue, a genre of potentially greater interest here because of its obvious indeterminacy as 'truth' or 'fiction'. Travel writing in this period is in many ways also the perfect paradigm for autobiography, because the containment of its subject in humanist, centred concepts of self is resisted, and its provisional, shifting nature exploited, at the same time as power is devolved (to varying extents) to the regions represented, and their inhabitants. Self-representation is, for one thing, a very good way of responding to an environment that seems always to have been subject to prior representation, or, conversely, that for which prior representation is unavailable. The post-Enlightenment traveller for leisure typically encounters both these extremes (by visiting the ducal estates at Inveraray and Blair Atholl, and various military sites; and yet also undertaking detours in the pursuit of 'wilderness'; that travellers were invariably aware of the debate surrounding the authenticity of James Macpherson's Ossian poems no doubt contributed to the popularity of this latter practice).[15]

Furthermore, travel writing is also a gendered activity in this period: it was considered suitable for women; but women were also believed to produce a particular kind of travel writing, one which had closer links with fiction, and therefore of less truth-value, than that of men. A practice of valorizing the subjectivity of 'the other' (the Highlands or Highlanders, in this case) is arguably another distinctive feature of the women's travel journal in this period. This is achieved by conferring 'reality' on the Highlander by engaging in an 'interview' in which he or she is granted a speaking part; this is what I mean by 'devolving' power on to the other. This serves to efface the writing subject, but in foregrounding the spoken presence of the native, the writer manages to effect a compromise between self and other, speech and writing, which ultimately and paradoxically serves to reinscribe herself at the centre of the text.

On this point, it should also be said that if the interview format devolved limited powers to the 'native' in the early nineteenth century, the same technique is even more fraught with problems at the end of the twentieth. By identifying herself as a researcher, the visitor/writer is honest about her agenda, but risks forcing or falsifying the response of the 'native'/interviewee. However well-intentioned the subject, it becomes difficult for her to avoid participating in a crudely imperialistic kind of anthropology. On the other hand, in not 'owning up' to her true(?) identity, the writer risks betraying the confidences of the interviewee. The books of Paul Theroux, in common with a large number of popular/journalistic accounts of the Highlands currently in print, draw much of their data from conversation with local

[15] For an introductory summary of the influence of Ossian on representations and readings of the Highlands, see Womack, *Improvement and Romance*, pp. 78–82, 101–9; for more specific discussion of the ramifications for travel writing, see Paul Baines, 'Ossianic Geographies: Fingalian Figures on the Scottish Tour 1760–1830', *Scotlands* 4:1 (1997), pp. 44–61.

people, a technique which can work well, but with which I personally feel uncomfortable. This is not least because texts are now produced and distributed under very different circumstances from nineteenth century travel journals, even those intended for publication. I shall therefore move towards a focus on recent readings of the Highlands which avoid the 'interview' genre.

In non-fiction of the late eighteenth and early nineteenth centuries, which lacks the hindsight, calculated agenda and organized overview of fiction in, say, the form of a Waverley novel, the Highlands are not always unproblematically represented as primitive, but noble. Dorothy Wordsworth utilizes the discourse of romance, of fiction; but the issue here is whether the fictionalizing of otherness merely serves to contain, and erase the specificity of, the Highlands; or whether her use of the fictive can serve a different purpose and signify a different kind of textual response. She wrote two Highland travel journals, after her tours in 1803 (with William Wordsworth and Coleridge) and 1822 (with Joanna Hutchinson), which provide examples of the different characteristics outlined here, including the considerable creative potential afforded to the travel writer by the fictive; and how this paves the way for self-representation.

I have elsewhere examined how women travellers to continental Europe in this period exhibit a self-conscious textuality in which characteristics of artifice and fiction, even comedy, are foregrounded at sites of the conventionally sublime.[16] An example of this occurs almost on the point of entry into the Highlands on the 1803 tour, when Dorothy Wordsworth effectively undermines the military presence at the fortified rock of Dumbarton by deployment of a fictionalizing strategy that was to become characteristic. From the base of the rock, she views a sentinel and some sheep on the top:

> The sheep, I suppose owing to our being accustomed to see them in similar situations, appeared to retain their real size, while, on the contrary, the soldier seemed diminished by the distance till he almost looked like a puppet moved with wires for the pleasure of children, or an eight years' old drummer in his stiff, manly dress beside a company of grenadiers. I had never before, perhaps, thought of sheep and men in soldiers' dresses at the same time, and here they were brought together in a strange fantastic way.[17]

For the twentieth-century reader, there is grim irony in the way soldier and sheep are juxtaposed in a post-Culloden Scotland on the verge of a massive clearance programme, but Dorothy Wordsworth's strategy here is noteworthy for its conscious articulation of 'otherness' in reference to her own cultural norms (sheep in rugged environment: familiar; soldier in ditto: unfamiliar). Also significant is

---

16 'Matrilinear Journalising: Mary and Dorothy Wordsworth's 1820 Continental Tours and the Female Sublime', *Writing Women* 5:3 (1999; forthcoming).

17 Dorothy Wordsworth, *Recollections of a Tour made in Scotland AD 1803*, ed. J.C. Shairp (Edinburgh: Mercat Press, 1981 [1894]), p. 59.

her customization of the common orientalist practice of infantilizing the foreign 'other': by 'fictionalizing' the soldier in addition to comparing him to a child, she also draws attention to the site as a heterotopic interface between fiction and reality (in which the 'natural' inhabitant, the sheep, serves to provide a sense of 'realistic' scale).[18] The rock thus becomes a space in which the writing subject observes the soldier's performance of policing the regional boundary, and hence necessitates an evasive strategy to make a serious political point. That she employs similar tropes (albeit with different results) in a variety of sites, sometimes recycling an old image in new topographic locations, adds a further dimension to her use of the fictive, but is also undoubtedly problematic because of its potential to deny the specificity of particular places, and to imply that, as a woman writer, she is unequipped to respond to the unknown. It is therefore easy to claim that she uses the fictive to make sense of, and make connections between, a range of locations that she does not fully understand. In order to resist this reading, I want to begin to turn now towards what happens when Dorothy Wordsworth the traveller encounters the 'feminine' sector of the domestic interior.

Superficially, Dorothy Wordsworth seems to offer a classic example of how post-Enlightenment domestic space is gendered as feminine, and women's roles spatially fixed. As a woman traveller, she enjoys privileged access to, and knows how to read, the domestic interior. She also seems to read all aspects of the Highlands as interiors, the private domains of femininity, as opposed to using them as a platform for making more 'public' statements about national or regional identity. Certainly gendered segregation exists on the various tours in which she participates, both in Britain and on the Continent: on arrival at a new resting-place, she repeatedly falls into conversation with her female hosts, and sometimes represents their words in her texts. Her mode of representation means that the similarities and continuities between interior and exterior in her journals are actually greater than the difference between them: the interior is just as much a site for the fictive as are open spaces, and open spaces are rendered as enclosing structures; i.e. similar tropes are employed in domestic and open air contexts. This does however enable her to suggest some early possibilities for how space can be manipulated, and in non gender-specific ways. This may be seen in a number of examples.

Sailing on Loch Katrine, she observes how 'on every side of us were bays within bays, often more like tiny lakes or pools than bays, and those not in long succession only, but all around, some almost on the broad breast of the water, the promontories shot out so far' (*Recollections*, p. 99). This is typical of her ascribing

---

18 I employ the terms 'fictionalizing' and 'the fictive' in ways comparative to Womack's use of the term 'imaginary'. In this case it refers to Dorothy Wordsworth's denial of the reality or humanity of the Other – first by likening the soldier to a puppet, and then by emphasizing the theatricality of his function ('men in soldiers' dresses').

interiority to outdoor spaces, and also serves to destabilize the boundary between land and water.[19] In the manuscript she drew sketch maps in a further attempt to achieve representation of the containing effect of these outside enclosures.

The 'region' in which Loch Katrine now lies, the Trossachs (named for the hills at the Eastern end of the loch) is the site of an adventurous detour into 'trackless heath' (p. 86) in 1803: a transgressive itinerary, which while seeking to avoid existent stereotypings, actually contributes to the making of new ones. In her representation of the interior of the hut where they spend a night, Dorothy Wordsworth deploys images of the fictive and of spectacle, just as she does in the open air, at the Dumbarton Rock fortifications:

> I was less occupied by the remembrance of the Trossachs, beautiful as they were, than the vision of the Highland hut, which I could not get out of my head. I thought of the Fairyland of Spenser, and what I had read in romance at other times, and then, what a feast it would be for a London pantomime-maker, could he but transplant it to Drury Lane, with all its beautiful colours! (p. 105)

This 'fictionalizing' could again be read as evidence for her insecurity and unease with aesthetic discourse, and with the unfamiliar location: everywhere that is not Grasmere is essentially the same, and so she takes refuge in a familiar subject matter for the female writer and reader (in 1820 the 'pantomime' image would be recycled in the open air, and on the Continent).[20] However, her reader would also be familiar with new spectacles enabled by stage effects: by making an analogy with an *other* Other, she communicates the strangeness and wonder to her readers at the Grasmere centre. This is as fabulous a world as the London stage, she says, just as much as she belittles it by the pantomime allusions. Although the effect of this particular trope is of course to deny the 'reality' of the site, irrevocably to fictionalize it, it can be read more positively: in comparison with Johnson and Boswell's inexpert handling of their visit to a Highland hut, for example,[21] Dorothy Wordsworth's account demonstrates how this is as fitting a site for representation as the lakes and mountains themselves (and this does occur prior to the greatest exploitative and appropriatative romanticization of the region following the publication of Scott's *The Lady of The Lake* in 1810). This particular domestic space also affords a further example of how she minimizes the

---

19 See also her response to a site on the received itinerary, Inveraray, where the ambient hills serve as walls, enclosing and protecting the Duke of Argyll's centre of benign power (*Recollections*, pp. 126–33).

20 *Journals of Dorothy Wordsworth*, ed. Ernest de Selincourt, 2 vols (London: Macmillan, 1941), ii, pp. 110, 161.

21 Samuel Johnson *A Journey to the Western Isles of Scotland* and James Boswell, *The Journal of a Tour to the Hebrides*, ed. Peter Levi (Harmondsworth: Penguin, 1984), p. 231.

distinction between inside and outside: she notes that by the light from the fire in the next apartment

> the rafters and beams, which crossed each other in almost as intricate and fantastic a manner as I have seen of under-boughs of a large beech-tree withered by the depth of the shade above, produced the most beautiful effect that can be conceived. It was like what I should suppose an underground cave or temple to be, with a dripping or moist roof, and the moonlight entering in by some means or other, and yet the colours were more like melted gems. (pp. 104–5)

Connected by the shafts of light to the family next door, and yet in her own secure enclosure, Dorothy Wordsworth is able to exercise control in an alien environment. The result of this seemingly indiscriminate mixing of discourses can only be to assert the power and centrality of her own literary authority. Where male travellers sometimes achieve this by going a stage further into *self*-fictionalization, actually entering themselves into the fiction, Dorothy Wordsworth creates heterotopic spaces in interior and exterior Highland environments, by remaining herself a *spectator ab extra*, but not just in the conventional manner of the picturesque tourist.[22] Certainly she engages in some feminine communality in the Highlands, but she maintains the heterotopia by refusing to participate fully in the spectacle, or to move from what Elspeth Probyn calls *le dehors*.[23]

Another clear example of this positioning is her visit to Rob Roy's caves on the banks of Loch Lomond in 1822. Having set the scene in which a piper plays amidst 'the grandeur of nature strangely mixed up with Stage effects', she observes how other tourists authenticate themselves by an antifictive strategy: deaestheticising the site, and distancing themselves from the spectacle by refusing to be impressed by it.[24] She, however, considers them to be thereby participating in the spectacle and hence indistinguishable from it: 'We flatter ourselves we made a wiser choice in not entering at all; for they profess to have no motive but to *say* they have been in Rob Roy's Caves because Sir Walter Scott has made them so much talked about; and, when they come out, dashing the dust off their cloths, the best they can say is "Well! there is nothing to be seen; but it is worth while, if only to *say* one has been there!"' (p. 354). Her self-authentication is therefore achieved through anti-deaestheticisation and through refusal to immerse herself in the fictive.

For Womack the twin discourses of improvement and romance bind the Highlands into 'peripheral fastnesses' which 'ensure at once its isolation from and

22 See, for example, in the passage cited above in note 21.

23 For a reading of the Alfoxden and Grasmere Journals in relation to Picturesque theory, see Robert Con Davis, 'The Structure of the Picturesque: Dorothy Wordsworth's Journals', *The Wordsworth Circle* 9 (1978), pp. 45–9. See also my introduction to Dorothy Wordworth, *The Continental Journals* (Bristol: Thoemmes Press, 1995), pp. xx–xxi. Probyn, *Outside Belongings*, p. 11.

24 *Journals of Dorothy Wordsworth*, ii, p. 353.

its subordination to the discourses of power' (*Improvement and Romance*, p. 179). The term 'fastness' seems especially significant in relation to the issues that concern me here, because of its connotations to fixity, and (given the region's profusion of military relics) to siege and warfare. This 'fastness' has nonetheless always been subject to challenge. Dorothy Wordsworth's departures from set itineraries and forays into the, as yet, uncommodified wildernesses exemplify this; they are excursions not at all atypical of travellers of the time, but ones which nonetheless enable her to inscribe her own subjectivity in ways impossible elsewhere on the route. When Paul Theroux confidently proclaims on Cape Wrath 'I felt I had penetrated a fastness', he too is typical of this species of traveller.[25] Theroux is travelling around the peripheries of Britain in search of alternatives to Thatcherism in 1982, and unwittingly ends up in a landscape not dissimilar to that of the Falkland Islands. His prefiguring of Womack's idiom is also ironic because Cape Wrath is a site for Ministry of Defence exercises, although Theroux does not make this connection in his text. He does not find a 'fastness' in the tongues of the inhabitants, and the chapter concludes with him learning about the Clearances in a domestic interior: a typical interview/conversation scenario in service of his own grand narrative.

Dorothy Wordsworth finds her own version of fastness in the the 'unenclosed ground' (*Journals*, ii. p. 386) between Elvanfoot and Moffat on the 1822 tour. The women travellers face potential danger, from male predators, significantly in a location outwith the Highlands, not appropriated as a tourist destination, situated beyond the fertile Clyde Valley and the always-already Romanticized Falls of Clyde. This region is therefore what the 'trackless heath' of the Trossachs detour was on the 1803 tour: the wilderness cast now in opposition to Inveraray in the also ready-Romanticized Argyll Highlands, which are both the farthest and the focal point of this second tour. Taken together, Dorothy Wordsworth's Scottish tours clearly illustrate how wilderness is a shifting locus in this period. As if the Highlands are already too tamed, and contained, in fictionalizing strategies, it is the rural Lowlands that now become a site for danger. This remains a paradoxically central, and yet *border*, site/region: landlocked on the county boundary between Lanarkshire and Dumfries-shire, near the sources of both Clyde and Tweed (typically, there is no brief and incontestible means of locating and naming the site for readers whose familiarity with it cannot be assumed). Always known primarily as a thoroughfare from Highland to Lowland, it is now a trunkroad carrying coachloads of tourists and caravan-towing family saloons to the Highlands and goods containers to the Central belt. Certainly not Highland, but remote and liminal, this is the kind of site that allows me to make connections between newly-Romanticized Scotland and a Scotland 'in rehab' after an overdose of romanticization. Comparatively bereft of familiar landmarks in relation to which

25 Paul Theroux, *The Kingdom by the Sea* (Harmondsworth: Penguin, 1984), p. 284.

traveller and reader can locate themselves, and identified by regional names which have themselves changed (the county names Dorothy Wordsworth would have recognised do not appear in modern road atlases), this place points up the simultaneous fictionality and topographical reality of sites on the Scottish tour. Significantly this is not a wilderness for which Dorothy Wordsworth attempted to produce a sketchmap, and when the focus inevitably moves to the interior and the conversation/interview format, the threat is not neutralized (*Journals*, ii. pp. 392–3). Fears are alternatively raised and allayed for the duration of their overnight stay; gone is the security represented by the Trossachs hut in 1803.

Writing on the Highlands seems to have been marked both by a desire to penetrate their past and present 'fastnesses', and yet simultaneously to discover new sites as yet resistant to this. However, if they are read as heterotopic, these spaces can become instead an 'antifastness', and alternatives to colonialist discourse become a possibility in their interpretation. Yet the post-Enlightenment traveller, though often able to fictionalize the site at the same time as representing its topographic factuality, is still too often limited by a lack of vocabulary for this task other than that of eighteenth-century aesthetics. (I would describe a writer like Theroux as anachronistically inhabiting the literary-historical 'region' of late Enlightenment.)

The eighteenth-century gendering of space is also still apparent for much of the twentieth: for example, in the way female and gay sexuality have remained 'private', nowhere more so than in Highland Scotland. Antecedents are found in the many Gaelic placenames that mark a segregated female space: *Badnaban*, the place of women; *Alltnacaillich*, burn of the old woman. (Handa, off the Sutherland coast, which had its own parliament, like the more famous St Kilda, and also its own queen, could be said to be an early feminine public space.) However, a reimagining is taking place in fiction, with writers such as Ellen Galford and Ali Smith drawing on historical associations between the feminine and Highland topographies, and reversing and channelling in new directions the myths and norms.[26] Although there is a danger of this amounting to little more than positive stereotyping, which (given the history of feminization and fictionalization of the Gaels) 'obfuscates other aspects of power relations, denies other forms of communication', the practice of (re-)representing the 'feminine' Highlands in the novel, as a direct response to prior stereotypings, often seems to work very well.[27]

26 For differing critical views of the feminist use of myth in Scottish literature, see Helen Boden, 'Kathleen Jamie's Semiotic of Scotlands', in Aileen Christianson and Alison Lumsden, eds, *Contemporary Scottish Women's Writing* (Edinburgh: EUP, forthcoming); Adrienne Scullion, 'Feminine Pleasures and Masculine Indignities', in Christopher Whyte, ed., *Gendering the Nation* (Edinburgh: EUP, 1995), pp. 169–204 (pp. 201–3); Sean O'Brien, *The Deregulated Muse* (Newcastle: Bloodaxe, 1998), pp. 266–7.

27 Sabina Sharkey, 'A view of the present state of Irish Studies', in Susan Basnett, ed., *Studying British Cultures* (London: Routledge, 1997), pp. 113–34 (p. 120). Writing in the same volume, David Punter believes 'we can no longer rely either (naturally) on the

Further, with the current popularity of confessional writing, boundaries between fiction and non-fiction are less secure than ever before. Smith's first novel *Like* mixes topographical and imagined locations, and in its form and content tests ideas about truth and factuality. Alan Warner, whose female protagonists inhabit partly-fictionalized Highland settings, has arguably achieved the most successful demonstration to date of how both gender and regional identities, far from being essential, are constructed and contingent.[28]

So, the Highlands are not exhausted as a space for representation, and nor is this representation necessarily limited to obsolete understandings about the human subject's relationship to place. However, it may not (yet) be possible to achieve these 'new understandings' through/in travel writing. Therefore I want to close by returning to the genre for Womack most damningly associated with the Highlands' oppression: poetry. The Highlands become/are made 'poetical', as part of the process of Romantic subjectification.[29] But outwith this function, poetry is not the same as fiction. The task of writing a new poetic for the Highlands is perhaps harder than that of writing fictions which are set in its past and present spaces, fictions which offer a site of resistance to the fictionalizing strategies of earlier poetry and non-fiction. It is also likely that different questions and answers will arise if prose fiction and non-fiction are not used as barometers of national/regional conditions; and if poetry is considered not in isolation, or in relation to other forms of writing, but to visual art .

Into the Oceanic (Dhan Chuan Mhòr) is a collaborative installation commissioned by Taigh Chearasbhagh arts centre in Lochmaddy, North Uist. It replaces with abstractions both the faithful reproductions of actual topography, and imaginary locations, of the past. Elizabeth Ogilvie selected four lines from the text(s) commissioned from Douglas Dunn, and etched them onto 'slender perspex panels suspended over shallow aluminium held pools of water', which 'formed a block, fragmented by gentle undulating movement, dancing light and overlapping reflections'.[30] The photographs and introductory text in the catalogue show how, 'out of the oceanic', in the gallery, the installation has an architectural form whilst alluding to the movement characteristic of the sea. The catalogue goes on to mention further correspondences between the work and the space outside the gallery to which it responds. Not having seen the installation (but remembering other exhibitions in the Western Isles, such as An Lanntair's tenth anniversary

---

stereotype, or, more importantly, on the simple dismantling of stereotype: instead it is axiomatic that we deal seriously in difference' ('Fictional maps of Britain', pp. 65–80 (p. 77)).

28 Ali Smith, *Like* (London: Virago, 1997). See, for example, Alan Warner's *The Sopranos* (London: Jonathan Cape, 1998).

29 Womack, *Improvement and Romance*, pp. 179–80.

30 Douglas Dunn and Elizabeth Ogilvie, *Into the Oceanic* (Lochmaddy: Taigh Chearsabhagh Trust, 1999). Water, dye, aluminium, electric fans, screen-printed text on perspex, 244 × 244 × 610cm, 1998.

Calanais, in which some works used indigenous materials, or images of them; and the work of the sculptor Dorothy Dick in Scourie, Sutherland, which is heavily influenced by local geomorphology), I sensed an ironic but pleasing discontinuity between the ancient natural environment and the modern materials used. Dunn, however, sees the situation in a different light: 'regions as distinctive and relatively remote as the Islands deserve and demand the same contemporaneity in the materials of art as anywhere else'.[31] Ogilivie's practice can then be read as giving something back to the margins, in compensation for the historical trend (still ongoing: witness the plans for the Harris superquarry) of exploiting and depleting such regions' natural resources.

Ogilvie's life and work have been and are constantly influenced by the sea. Her maternal grandfather was from St Kilda, and she now lives in a converted cinema in Fife with a panoramic view over the Forth. Her work develops by repeating techniques and repeatedly working with similar materials (metal, water, text) until, in time, it evolves in new directions. Due to these factors, as well as to its own composition, *Into the Oceanic* could be said to be no more place-specific (to the North Uist topography) than it is gender-specific: it inhabits what might be thought of as a 'post-regionality'. According to Tessa Jackson, writing the foreword to the catalogue of an earlier exhibition, *Island Within*, 'Ogilvie is not interested in the sentimental or social influences of the sea. Her work lies with a de-personalized world of texture, sound, and abstract forms or surfaces'.[32] Ogilvie herself told me that she is not concerned with 'meaning' or 'emotion', or with the viewer's response to her work. Further, despite the tight artistic control she exercises over her material at some stages of production (which can involve considerable physical exertion), some of her pieces assume a post-production life of their own once her part in the creative process is complete. If I did not see *Into the Oceanic* at Taigh Chearsabhagh, I have seen what remained after the installation was dismantled. The evaporation of the water from the aluminium pools has left residual salt crystals, which now resemble something else altogether: an aerial view of the shore at low tide, perhaps. As a viewer of landscape and art, and an academic, I do respond, with intense enjoyment, and intellectual curiosity, and I find it hard to imagine myself responding in a way that does not invoke either meaning or emotion. And by this reaction I am reminded that the members of the local community, too, inevitably have their own valid responses to work produced in and about their environment.

Dunn's writing, which supplements Ogilvie's visual intervention, seems less 'post-personal'. His texts achieve an anti-sentimental reading of a landscape of remote beauty, by questioning the positioning and status of subject and object in what one of the four lines to appear on the installation terms the 'land and water of the broad eye': 'Horizon's all eye. It has nothing to do with / Fingers, ears or nose'.

31 Douglas Dunn, privately, 28 August 1999.

32 Elizabeth Ogilvie, *Island Within* (Bristol: Arnolfini, 1995).

(For Dorothy Wordsworth in the Trossachs, 'the place was all eye', *Recollections*, p. 99). His transformative visuality seems to be a development and abstraction of his concerns in 'St Kilda's Parliament: 1879–1979. The Photographer Revisits his Picture' – 1979 being, of course, the date of the last unsuccessful Scottish referendum. In 1999, with the Scottish Parliament an actuality, *Into the Oceanic* makes a positive and apposite statement about the nation's regional differences and connections, not least because in the publication/catalogue Dunn's texts are also translated into Gaelic by South Uist/Skye poet and Gaelic broadcaster Angus Peter Campbell.[33]

As the poems proceed, by considering the various attributes/features that collectively constitute Dunn's world as 'the colour of water', and the impact on the different senses of the sea, the 'oceanic' becomes a fusion of (internal) sense and (external) element, powerful enough to resist the hegemony of the sight: 'Ocean is elemental fact ... an eye's thought'. Although the sight is quickly augmented by sound, smell, taste and touch, all the sensory stimuli and emotional/intellectual responses are nonetheless unavoidably mediated, through language, of course, but also through his own subjectivity and from his perspective ('my children, my library, my friends / These, too are the colour of water'). Dunn doesn't claim the impossible in his revisionary aesthetic: since the Enlightenment development of the technologies of mapping and aesthetic response it may be impossible (yet?) to view things any other way. And even if the result is to turn to a possessiveness, as Dunn unashamedly does, this is no longer a possession of the landscape itself as metaphor for the more general operations of patriarchy and imperialism; and it permits its objects multiplicity, fluidity, rather than constraining them to fixity: like the ocean they mimic rather than possess, they too can be of any colour. Outwith the Romantic discourse of the sublime and all that that implies of separation, domination, subordination and reunification, an unhierarchized distinction between landscape and human is enabled. The problem of finding a vocabulary for the representation of land/seascape, other than that of eighteenth century aesthetics, is solved: the sight is multifocal and works in collaboration

---

[33] *Into the Oceanic* is a particularly complex 'text'. The installation, described above, was shown in Lochmaddy in July 1998, and afterwards at An Tuireann Art Centre, Skye. It featured four lines by Dunn:

Stare west from here into the oceanic
To describe the Ocean you must write with it
Hold fast to the speech of light, lochs and ocean
Land and water of the broad eye.

The forty-page 1999 publication, which has an indeterminate status between exhibition catalogue and poetry collection, was designed by Ogilvie, and contains over a hundred additional lines by Dunn, with parallel translations into Gaelic by Angus Peter Campbell; three photographs of the installation, and an aerial photograph of Lochmaddy by Patricia Macdonald.

with the other senses, no longer the instrument of tyrannical specularization. The politics of viewing are 'always contextual', never essential.[34]

It should by now be clear that I consider it impossible to write about Highland Scotland and not to encounter the problem of naming, or to avoid making choices between appropriatative, descriptive or imaginative naming. Dunn proclaims that 'the sea says no to names and nationality'. His texts can be read as a search for innovative practices that avoid old associations between naming and possession, not least by reclaiming for the region a history far longer than that inaugurated by the '45 and the battle of Culloden: 'Some call this wilderness / And they are wrong', because evidence of more ancient pasts can be found everywhere in the present, living, environment. 'How can antiquity be so breathable?', he writes of physical objects washed ashore, collapsing distinctions between the corporeal and the linguistic. Repopulating the wilderness, defying its barrenness (a fixity which has helped keep it Romantic, 'cleared'), creatures sing themselves into existence, as along the Aboriginal songlines, claiming 'I am', rather than having names conferred on them; natural history becomes, and articulates itself in, the present. That parallel translations are from English into Gaelic and not *vice versa*, is maybe not unproblematic, but this implicit returning of 'stolen goods' does signal a generosity of exchange rather than an empty tokenism. This is especially evident in the section 'Hebridean Titles', which features the comic invention (in English) of names which, in their form, parody English translations of Gaelic, and which are then translated into Gaelic for the publication, e.g: 'The Loch of the Seven Anoraks' (*Locha nan Seachd Seacaidean*). This is the only text to appear directly under a section heading/title that directly relates to it; the other texts are more arbitrarily interfaced with the 'placenames', 'Loch nam Madadh', 'Atlantic/An Cuan Siar', 'Vallay/Bhàlaigh', 'Solas/Solas', in larger type on coloured pages. These 'Hebridean titles' also seem suggestive of entitlements, title deeds, thereby (like the lines on the viewing subject and the perceived landscape) doing more than merely reversing, yet still maintaining, hierarchized binaries, at the same time as they point to the difficulites of cultural translation. The playful inventiveness makes a compensatory gesture for the post-Culloden practice of renaming which ignores the *dùthchas* (cultural and material inheritance from ancestors), and the Gaelic 'map', on which topography is described according to *use*, representing land encoded with its peoples' culture.

The democratic imperative of *Into the Oceanic* is visible, at a practical level, in the collaborative nature (beyond that between Dunn and Ogilvie) of its production. Together, their work offers some answers to questions such as, 'how are the Highlands imagined, today?' In cultural terms, *Into the Oceanic* suggests that the Highland Scotland finally has moved out of the Ossianic. It represents a decisive break with Enlightenment epistemology and aesthetics; in which

34 Catherine Nash, 'Reclaiming Vision: Looking at Landscape and the Body', *Gender, Place and Culture* 3:2 (1996), pp. 149–69 (p. 167).

the Highlands become again imaginative rather than just imaginary, and this is achieved through an engagement with various versions of the fictive, rather than an absolute rejection of it as oppressive Enlightenment discourse.

The sea is manifestly *not* a region: unlike an onshore region such as Assynt, it could not be the subject of a poem about ownership; it surrounds the UK and links the state's real and imaginary regions. It has always carried associations with the feminine. For Foucault, the boat is the ultimate heterotopia.[35] Even if an area of the North Sea off Scotland falls technically within English fishing boundaries at present; even though the conditions of, and attitudes towards, women in the far North West, though improving, are still out of step with those in more southerly, central or urban regions (the reality of living with alcoholism and drownings does not diminish), recent work in the creative arts and in the development of institutions such as Taigh Chearsabhagh, shows real and enabling possibilities for the future.

Acknowledgements

I am most grateful to Douglas Dunn and Elizabeth Ogilvie for discussing their work with me. Less specific but equally sincere thanks are due to the many people of, from, and travelling to Sutherland and the Outer Hebrides who have influenced and informed the way I read these places; and especially to the late Alasdair Munro of Tarbet, near Scourie.

35 Foucault, 'Of Other Spaces', p. 27.

Chapter 11

Learning to Remember and Remembering to Forget: *Beloved* from Belfast

Eilish Rooney

Introduction: material matters of memory

I was born into a street of poor people. In 'rooms' above a pub, called *The Phoenix*, in Brown Square. My mother told me that, during the war, 'poor prostitutes' used the pub's doorway, and sometimes the snugs, with their American soldier clients. One half of the street comprised poor Protestants, one half poor Catholics. It was what would now be called 'an interface community'. When the Twelfth of July came around the Protestant people stopped talking to their Catholic neighbours.[1] Nothing personal – some may have wished to do otherwise. That's just how it was. One Twelfth, when I was a child of about three, I was attracted by the street bands. I danced away from my mother – to the music. A neighbour lifted me up into the arms of a woman sitting on a donkey. The woman, draped in a blue veil, was being drawn through the parade in mockery of Catholic reverence for the Virgin Mary. The Protestant neighbours thought it a great laugh. I suppose I stood for the baby Jesus in the moving tableau. An appropriate muddle of gender, political and religious mimicry. We moved to Ballymurphy. The Brown Square area has been redeveloped. No Catholics live there any longer.

My name, within the north of Ireland, signals my Catholic upbringing. 'Eilish' is the Ulsterized version of 'Elís', which is variously anglicized as 'Helen' or 'Elizabeth'. Some people, who have recognized that the name is of gaelic derivation, have asked me what does my name 'mean in English'. It is a friendly enquiry. But the request of me to convert my name into something understandable in English is interesting from political and historical perspectives. I usually oblige with the anglicized version.[2] The information carried by my name matters in the

---

1 This is the day when (Protestant) King William's victory over (Catholic) King James, 1698, is commemorated.

2 Introductions are no time to go on about how 'language is not a reflection of the world but produces meaning'. See Avtar Brah, 'The Scent of Memory: Strangers, Our Own and Others', *Feminist Review* 61, Spring (1999), p. 8.

north of Ireland because having Catholic origins has multiple material meanings. I live in a profoundly sectarianized society. Being from a Catholic background fits me into various sets of statistics about the economic outcomes of generations of systemic, sectarian discrimination against Catholics. I am 'counted' in calculations of the relative numbers of Catholic and Protestant employees, in my place of work. My designation of the place that I live as the 'north of Ireland', keeping open the constitutional closure of 'Northern Ireland', suggests that I am some form of nationalist.[3] I want to argue about the assumptions built into the language about my background, my politics, my identifications and me. The language in the north is inflected with sectarian meanings but, as Toni Morrison has said in another context, 'there is no other language to speak'.[4] Like the 'American' usage, to which Morrison here refers, language in the north of Ireland is also inflected with gendered and other power relationships.[5] The most personal uses of language in the north, and the most public, are alike political.

And then, there is the tumult of memories of the conflict, stories that I have gathered, had forced upon me, haven't realized I had until reminded in this year of remembering. I was married the weekend that the civil rights students, Bernadette Devlin famously amongst them, were attacked at Burntollet. Where I came from (in what would now be called a 'sink estate') the protests looked exciting – international – linked to the civil rights protests in the US on TV. But, they also seemed remote – for students and educated 'politicos'. Not for me. I had my first child in the midst of some of the worst riots seen in the north the year that the British Army moved in, 1969. I had my second child six days after the introduction of internment, 9 August 1971, when again the streets were in an uproar of barricades and rioting. A local midwife was contacted to be on standby. Six months later I was amongst the thousands to travel to Derry to walk in the largest civil rights protest against internment that the North had seen; it later became known as Bloody Sunday.[6]

These personal recollections seem strangely at a distance. It is as though to get to them I must ensure that the reader sees some of the wider picture: the context within which individual, vital, personal and collective experiences take place.

---

3 The naming is important for many people who make no identification as nationalist, as well as for nationalists, republicans, and many others who respect the legitimacy of opposition to the setting up of the six county state.

4 Toni Morrison, 'Introduction: Friday on the Potomac', in Toni Morrison, ed. *Engendering Power: Essays on Anita Hill, Clarence Thomas and the Construction of Social Reality* (London: Chatto and Windus, 1993), p. xxviii.

5 Sectarianism and sexism are overtly linked in gender inscribed forms of political agency. See Eilish Rooney, 'Difference Matters: Women in Northern Ireland Politics' in Carmel Royston and Celia Davies, eds, *Gender, Democracy and Inclusion in Northern Ireland Politics* (Basingstoke: Macmillan, forthcoming).

6 Thirteen people were shot dead that day; another died later. A new tribunal of inquiry into events on the day is currently underway.

In Toni Morrison's *Beloved* (1987) there is no dry, political, historical 'context setting'; no tabulation of decisive events in the history of slavery.[7] The story of the novel is woven from the narrative material of re-membering and forgetting. This hyphenated re-membering is used in relation to Morrison's way of setting stories and fragments alongside each other and of seeing in them relationship and community; the present in the past. The record on slavery was not, could not, be 'kept'. But the novel becomes its own meaningful record. It is full of details drawn from the genre of slave narratives. It is a re-membering, in the sense of a reconstruction of slave experience. The language is inflected with a history that is not named in the novel. It is also a novel about remembering and forgetting, and how past acts of remembering and forgetting impact on the present: in the novel and in the worlds of its readers. Remembering and forgetting are important in any place. They are particularly important at times of transition and change. This is the case at this current stage of the political process in the north of Ireland when people are both remembering personal-political experiences and trying to re-member: to find out and put together what happened.

Most of my writing work involves examining issues related to women and politics in the north of Ireland. The closest I get to the inclusion of my own story in this work is an acknowledgement of my 'situatedness' in the politics here. To provide the information is to take the risk that my analysis will be discredited for being 'situated'. I sometimes mention the meanings associated with my name and, perhaps, West Belfast origins (as I do here). I generally provide the information because my analysis is informed by my experience of the conflict. Such experience, however, is not required in order to arrive at similar analysis. Most of the industry of publications on the conflict, academic and otherwise, is 'situated', partial, politically constituted, if not motivated: but few writers, very few academics, see or care to state their own political positioning.

The provision of short-hand, easily misunderstood information about myself, and a use of language that is inflected with sectarian meanings, lays me open to the charge that I have a 'vested interest' in the promotion of my analysis or experience. So be it. Toni Morrison, in her work on 'whiteness' in the American literary tradition, meets the charge that her arguments may be self-serving: 'I have to risk the accusation because the point is too important'.[8] Her point is to investigate the unseen, unanalysed, development of 'whiteness' in what has come to be described as 'American' literature. One reason she cites for the uncritiqued 'whiteness' of 'American' literature is that, 'in matters of race silence and evasion have historically ruled literary discourse':

---

7 Toni Morrison, *Beloved* [1987] (London: Chatto and Windus [Picador], 1988). Further page references to this volume will be given after quotations in the text.

8 Toni Morrison, *Playing in the Dark: Whiteness and the Literary Imagination* (London: Picador, 1990).

> The situation is aggravated by the tremor that breaks into discourse on race. It is further complicated by the fact that the habit of ignoring race is understood to be a graceful, even generous, liberal gesture. To notice is to recognize an already discredited difference. (pp. 9–10)

The 'habit' of ignoring sectarianism in the north of Ireland and of treating it as a problem that the 'two communities' share equally is one of the 'polite' responses in liberal northern Irish society to the socio-economic, cultural, political and sectarian subordination of one group by another. This has resulted in systemic discrimination, materially demonstrated most easily by employment differentials between Catholic and Protestant males. To draw attention to the figures, and to the human consequences, is to disfigure the simple, apolitical equation, and thus to rupture the polite insidious balance in 'two communities'.[9] It is to disallow 'silence and evasion'. To focus on sectarianism as a central feature of our language and our living in the north is to perpetuate the view that people here are locked into a (virtually) meaningless, ancient, conflict around 'constitutional' politics, or a religious war, whilst ignoring the real 'bread and butter' issues. Fundamentally, the conflict has been about the 'bread and butter' issues of democracy, justice, human rights and equality.

Touching on these 'material' matters, and thinking about personal reflections in a text on 'devolving identities', I relate to a concern expressed by Merl Storr in her review of *Black British Feminism: a Reader*.[10] The Reader is a compilation of seminal black British feminist writing from the 1980s and 1990s. Storr notes that the newer contributions to the Reader, 'are products of that paradigm shift from identity to difference in feminist thought' (p. 152). These recent contributors creatively explore subjectivity and the role of memory. Whilst appreciating the strengths of this more recent autobiographical work, Storr also points out that none of the newer articles, 'deals with issues of poverty, of low pay or employment rights for black women workers' (p. 153). Engagement with the material matters of politics and economics is missing in the newer work. Storr identifies this as a general trend in both black and non-black feminist debate. She notes that:

> [Explorations of] subjectivity and autobiography [have] not served these [political and economic] issues well … the refiguring of class within the

---

9 Currently, and after 23 years of fair employment legislation, 16 per cent of Catholic males are unemployed; whilst 6 per cent of Protestant males are unemployed. The differentials are reduced between women, but the marked and powerful differentials between men and women are neither mentioned nor targeted in the British Government's White Paper 'Partnership for Equality' (1998). See Robbie McVeigh, 'Economic Inactivity and Inequality', *Economic Bulletin* 6:3, April/May (1999).

10 Heidi S. Mirza, ed., *Black British Feminism: A Reader* (London and New York: Routledge, 1997); Merl Storr, review of *Black British Feminism: A Reader*, ed. Heidi S. Mirza in *Feminist Review* 61, Spring (1999), p. 152. Further page references to this review article will be given after quotations in the text.

> 'difference' paradigm has tended to present it as a matter solely of one's sense of self, rather than of one's empty purse at the end of the week. (p. 153)

The contemporary issue of 'empty purses' is missing from the Reader. The strike of public sector workers, most of them Asian women, at Hillingdon Hospital, ongoing for over two years at the time of Storr's review, does not feature in the Reader. This contrasts with black feminist writing on the Grunwick strike of the 1980s, which features in the earlier part of the Reader. And no mention is made in the Reader of the worrying incidence of the deaths of black people, the majority of them men, in police custody in London. Yet the personal reflections that feature in the later contributions provide, as one writer says, much needed 'stories to live by'. Storr agrees. We 'need stories to live by', but, she argues, 'stories by themselves are not enough' (p. 153). Storr calls for 'a sustained discussion of matters of physical as well as of spiritual, emotional and intellectual survival' (p. 153). Toni Morrison's *Beloved*, and her work on language, comprise intense explorations of physical, spiritual, emotional, political and intellectual survival.

In the remainder of this chapter, I draw on Morrison's work, and on the work of other writers, to examine re-membering in the north of Ireland, at this stage in the political process. In the next sub-section I explore what Morrison has called the 'necessity for remembering' that traumatized people experience. This re-membering is a dimension of competing political projects and analyses in the north at the moment. I provide examples of creative, and sometimes painful, ways of remembering and celebrating the past. Some of this has involved families of killed relatives campaigning to know the truth about the past. The need to remember is bound up with the competing, survival urge to forget. Morrison deals with this in *Beloved*. Indeed the novel can be read as warning of the failures of forgetting. The next subsection examines how Beloved's story is forgotten, in the novel, by the people who live on Bluestone Road. Nevertheless, the scars of the past are borne into the future. Literally, on the bodies of characters in the novel; and figuratively in the literature that has come to be known as 'American' literature and in racially-inflected language. Language and words are then the focus of the discussion in the following section, 'Knowing words'. Next, under the heading 'Devolving nationalisms,' I relate issues of language, power, feminism to changing understandings of nationalism, drawing on the work of some contemporary Scottish feminists. The brief conclusion is preceded with reflections on 'The politics of memory' where I recall some contemporary attitudes to remembering in the north of Ireland. I ask the reader to consider what media or other 'memories' *s/he* brings to reading the chapter and to figure these into the reflections here. Throughout this chapter, Toni Morrison's insights on language, remembering and racism inform my thinking. Her novels are indeed 'stories to live by'.

'A necessity for remembering' (Morrison)

The political future in the north of Ireland is invested with meanings made in the past and forged anew in the present. In this year of the thirtieth anniversary of the British Army coming on to the streets of Belfast and Derry, people are also 're-membering' events which have been forgotten and ignored. There is a powerful daily moment on local BBC radio each morning, just before the Nine O'Clock News, called 'Legacy', when a person, often nameless, recalls their personal legacy of the conflict. The radio goes quiet, and from the void a voice speaks. Unbearable griefs, broken voices, untold stories, sometimes anger, stoicism, sadness. Political stories of personal experiences.

The neighbourhood I come from is beginning a project building an archive of life in West Belfast 1969–1994.[11] The project is a contribution to the process of peace and reconciliation. It aims to enable local people to 'record their history and experiences, acknowledge their role in the conflict ... explore solutions and contribute to creating a locally based model of conflict resolution' (Duchas: Falls Community Council, 1999). The project cites the Good Friday Agreement's recognition 'that victims have a right to remember as well as to contribute to a changed society'.[12] Who constitutes a legitimate 'victim' is one of the issues currently politicized within unionism in a strategic opposition to the Agreement. Some organizations distinguish between 'innocent' victims (meaning victims of Irish Republican Army violence) and others, mostly Catholic (victims of loyalist and state security force violence).[13]

Toni Morrison talks about the necessity to forget, that traumatised people experience in order that they may go forward from the past to 'make a life'. The phrase occurs in an interview Morrison gave on writing the novel. She was reflecting on those who survived the Middle Passage. *Beloved* is dedicated to the 'Sixty Million and more' who did not make it:

> It was not possible to survive on certain levels and dwell on [those who died *en route*]. People who did dwell on it, it probably killed them, and the

[11] West Belfast includes unionist-loyalist and working class areas. But the 'West Belfast' generally referred to in the media, and by Peter Brooke, the then Secretary of State for Northern Ireland (1989–1992), when he called it 'the terrorist community', consists of the nationalist-republican area west of the city centre.

[12] 'The Good Friday Agreement': hereafter 'The Agreement', government paper printed and distributed in 1998, p. 18.

[13] One of these groups is Families Acting for Innocent Relatives (FAIR). They selectively extend the concept of innocence to relatives of victims of the conflict. In a discussion of the relevance of truth commissions to the northern situation, Bill Rolston notes that: 'almost 400 of the dead in the North, approximately 10 per cent of all victims, were killed by state forces, yet there have only been 21 prosecutions, culminating in 7 convictions for murder and attempted murder'. See Bill Rolston, 'Are the Irish Black?', *Race and Class* 41:1–2 (1999), pp. 95–102.

> people who did not dwell on it probably went forward. They tried to make a life. I think Afro-Americans in rushing away from slavery ... also rushed away from the slaves because it was painful to dwell there, and they may have abandoned some responsibilities in so doing ... there's a necessity for remembering ... in a manner in which the memory is not destructive.[14]

Afro-Americans rushed away from the past, from slavery, as a way to survive. In the novel, 'going forward' compels Sethe and Paul D to bear the wounds of the past literally on their bodies. Sethe's scarred back sprouts a 'chokecherry tree' (p. 16) from being beaten. Paul D, 'collared like a beast' – has 'neck jewelry' (p. 273). George Shulman thus argues that in the novel:

> We witness the act of transfiguring the markings inflicted by history ... in relation to scars we cannot efface or redeem, but whose beauty we can help each other affirm. This is an act of love, and art ... We re-member stories no one of us authors alone; 'community' Paul D suggests, is laying our stories 'next' to each other. But transfiguration by love and art is not transcendence: the novel's last word is Beloved because the plea, be-loved, cannot escape or redeem the pain, loss and longing that name also speaks.[15]

The novel allows Shulman's optimistic interpretation, but there can be no simple or shortcut equation between narrative transfigurations of historical wounds and the legacy of slavery. Sethe no longer has feeling on her back where the scars sprout a vision she will never see. She cannot feel Paul D's affectionate 'cheek pressing into the branches of her chokecherry tree' (p. 17). The impoverished white girl, Amy, is first to see and to name Sethe's 'chokecherry tree'. It is a redemptive moment in the novel when Amy bathes Sethe's swollen feet, tries to heal her wounds and warns: 'It's gonna hurt, now ... Anything dead coming back to life hurts' (p. 35). The warning holds good for re-membering in the novel. And perhaps also in life. When told by Sethe that a white girl helped her, Paul D sceptically corrects Sethe, 'Then she helped herself too, God bless her' (p. 8). In today's sociological parlance, some of which I use here, Amy, poor or no, is a member of the race that has benefited from brutalizing people in slavery. Yet, she acts to help. Morrison refrains from essentializing whiteness. In the end Paul D is drawn back to Sethe because of:

> Her tenderness about his neck jewelry – its three wands, like attentive baby rattlers, curving two feet into the air. How she never mentioned or looked at it, so he did not have to feel the shame of being collared like a beast. (p. 273)

---

[14] Marsha Darling, 'In the Realm of Responsibility: A Conversation with Toni Morrison', *The Women's Review of Books*, V:6, March (1988), pp. 5–6.

[15] George Shulman, 'American Political Culture, Prophetic Narration and Toni Morrison's *Beloved*', *Political Theory*, XXIV:2, May (1996), p. 309.

This is not so much 'beauty affirmed', as Shulman would have it, but respect and knowledge conveyed in silence and in not looking. Sethe does not learn of the origins of Paul D's 'neck jewelry'. There is no need. There is no blueprint in *Beloved* for how the wounds of the past may be transformed to make a future in the world of 'real politics'. But there are moments of insight, and of generosity, that rupture crude identity and belonging boundaries. It is how characters in the novel, and readers in the world, can develop identifications with 'the other' that matters in making the future another and a different country from that of the past. In personal politics, these identifications may be of political solidarity, friendship, generosity: of re-membering the past and accepting responsibility for it.

With respect to the north of Ireland, a practical example of remembering that is being creatively channelled is the transformation of the commemoration of internment (9 August 1971) from an annual, mostly young-male spree of rioting in West Belfast into an annual community festival (Féile an Phobail). The Féile is a productive cultural transformation, whereby the political and personal 'wounds' and achievements of the past are used in music-making and drama, and to debate and display the issues of the day. It is the achievement of hundreds of people in small neighbourhood and interest-based Féile committees. Fifty-seven other Féiles have been established, and have affiliated to Féile an Phobail. It is recognized as one of the most successful community festivals in Europe. It may seem a mundane analogy to make with the nature of the transformations effected in Morrison's novel, but the Féile has become its own powerful transformation of trauma into a celebration of resilience and creativity.

The Féile celebration also involves organized, political and personal remembering. One of this year's events involved an act of re-membering. People from the Springhill neighbourhood in West Belfast gave personal accounts of the 'Springhill Massacre' (9 July 1972) when five people, two of them children and one a priest, were killed in the space of ten minutes' shooting from a nearby timber yard. The British Army had observation posts in the yard and local people believe that the shooting was that of army snipers (Springhill Massacre Committee [SMC], 1999).[16] A local paper, *The Belfast Telegraph*, carried a headline on the evening following the shooting: 'Five Gunmen Shot Dead'. Local people pieced together the events of that day. People I know, whose roles on the day I had never heard told before, publicly remembered their fears, and other people's courage. They also told of being forgotten. Margaret Gargan, a thirteen-year-old girl, was

[16] 'The Springhill Massacre: Belfast's Bloody Sunday', Springhill Massacre Committee Belfast [SMC], 'Relatives for Justice' publication (Belfast: 1999).

The Irish News reported that: 'Mr. Robert Carswell, for the Ministry of Home Affairs ... said that [soldiers'] statements would show that there had been considerable crossfire between them and a number of gunmen ... The soldiers would say that they only shot at identified targets carrying weapons', cited SMC document, p. 5. Lawyers for relatives and the organization 'Relatives for Justice' are calling for an independent inquiry into these events.

shot dead on the day. She had just been talking with some friends. The friends, now women, pieced together the sequence of events: meeting Margaret, who was wearing a leather jacket and dark trousers. It appears that Margaret may have been mistaken for a male. In the report, distributed on the day at the Féile, her mother, Nelly (now dead), recalled: 'She was the type who loved to wear trousers. She just didn't like frocks or dresses. Even when she went to school she used to change out of her uniform in the toilets so she would not have to walk home in a skirt.'[17]

Her clothes were never returned to her family. Margaret Gargan's death is no more and no less important than the deaths of the other 3,637 people who have lost their lives in the conflict. The fact of her gender, of her age, should not matter ... but for the circumstances. The truth about the circumstances of the Springhill deaths has never been told. As I listened to people, many unused to public speaking, tell of their experiences on that day, I realized that I too had forgotten. I vaguely remembered something about a priest being killed on his way to give the last rites to someone else who was shot and dying on the street. I remembered the priest because of the unusualness of a priest's death by shooting.[18] There were so many deaths in the years following internment and Bloody Sunday that I remember little of the detail. In 1972, the year of these killings, 496 people died in the conflict (compared with 26 deaths in 1970 and 186 deaths in 1971).[19] The figures are difficult to make real until a statistic becomes a person with a name, age, gender and a life in the recollections of those that loved them.

My mother told a story from these early years. She was at the shops in the centre of our estate, Ballymurphy. Shots rang out. Everyone dived for cover. When all was quiet, they emerged. There was a soldier lying on the road. Shot and dying. My mother was amongst the group of women who gathered around him. There was a hushed – not knowing what to do – silence. Out of the group stepped a woman whose son had been shot dead by the army the previous year. She kneeled over the soldier, held him, and whispered an act of contrition into his ear. My mother is dead now, but I am sure that I could put together the details of that day. The deaths of the son and of the soldier are equally important. The circumstances matter. I remember my mother's stories and forget events that I lived through. I need to begin to tell my own stories. But first, they have to be 're-membered'.

---

17 SMC document (see note 16), p. 10.

18 I also remember Fr Hugh Mullan who was shot by British troops during internment, 1971, in Springfield Park whilst helping local people who had been shot (see Springfield Massacre Committee, pp. 32–3).

19 See Marie Therese Fay, Mike Morrisey and Marie Smyth, *The Cost of the Troubles: Mapping the Troubles-related deaths in Northern Ireland: 1969–1994* (Derry/Londonderry: INCORE, 1997).

Stories to 'pass on'

Toni Morrison's *Beloved* is the story of Sethe's escape from slavery in Kentucky to freedom (and her children) in Ohio in the 1870s. It is a story of the past literally haunting, or coming to life, in the present in the person of Beloved (Sethe's murdered daughter). The novel is about re-membering and forgetting. It unfolds through the characters' self-preserving ways of looking at, and recalling, the past. Each character is the sum of the memories they can live with, and also those that they manage to keep 'at bay' (p. 42). Some things are actively forgotten – have to be forgotten, because to remember is too painful and dehumanizing. Some things are remembered involuntarily. In the course of the novel the community living on Bluestone Road, Ohio, also learns to forget. The novel closes on this communal learning about forgetting. In the end Beloved is forgotten. About her, the narrator concludes:

> All trace is gone ... The rest is weather. Not the breath of the disremembered and unaccounted for, but wind in the eves, or spring ice thawing too quickly. Just weather. Certainly no clamour for a kiss. (p. 275)

There is a sense of relief. Rest and stillness. Beloved's clamouring, heard in every seasonal sound, has ceased. The call of Beloved – to those in the present – to attend to past wrongs, is quiet. The weather, is just weather: not a call for remembering. Beloved disappears. Perhaps she has become one of 'the disremembered and unaccounted for'. She joins the 'Sixty Million and more' people of the Middle Passage, who died *en route* between Africa and Afro-America, to whom the novel is dedicated. Her 'disappearance', is a necessary, effortful, 'fictional' forgetting for the people in the novel who live on Bluestone Road:

> They forgot her like a bad dream. After they made up their tales, shaped and decorated them, those that saw her that day on the porch quickly and deliberately forgot her. It took longer for those who had spoken to her, lived with her, fallen in love with her, to forget until they realised they couldn't remember or repeat a single thing she said ... So, in the end, they forgot her too.
>
> Remembering seemed unwise. (p. 274)

It is 'unwise' to remember Beloved. Her disappearance, and the community's forgetting, gives them the chance to go forward and 'try to make a life'.[20] For the people in the novel on Bluestone Road, who have lived with the past, the clamouring ceases when Beloved leaves. Weather becomes 'just weather'. It is no longer a restless, agonized communication from the dead, torturing the living: the clamouring of responsibilities abandoned, or, in Sethe's case, the clamouring of a

---

20 Darling, 'Conversation with Morrison', p. 5.

mother-love that entailed killing. Sethe dared do what no slave woman before her could do, and survive – love her children. Paul D saw the dangers:

> Risky, thought Paul D, very risky. For a used-to-be-slave woman to love anything that much was dangerous, especially if it was her children she had settled on to love. The best thing, he knew, was to love just a little bit; everything just a little bit. (p. 45)

Sethe's 'murderous' love claim on her child's future has a history. Her own mother, during the Middle Passage 'threw all [her children] away but [Sethe, to whom] she gave the name of a black man' (p. 62). Sethe carries forward that memory-language and an unwritten history of a language she no longer understands: 'Of that place where she was born ... she remembered only song and dance. Not even her own mother' (p. 30). The men and women of 'that place' danced 'the antelope' (p. 31). Thus, when pregnant and making her escape, Sethe feels the child growing inside her is 'the little antelope' (ibid.) but does not know why: 'She guessed it must have been an invention held on to from before Sweet Home, when she was very young' (p. 30). Sethe intuits, and misplaces, a memory that the reader can connect with her African origins. Sethe's past and present are disconnected by the brutalities of slavery. She murders Beloved to save her from the future, and she raises Denver by 'keeping her from the past'. Re-membering and forgetting.

For those who lived on Bluestone Road the story of Beloved 'was not a story to pass on' (p. 274). The sentence is ambiguous. It occurs three times in the concluding two-page epilogue-like chapter. The words are set off, in paragraph form, for the eye to settle on and the heart to ponder. Is this a story not to be passed by – in the sense of not to be ignored? The people on Bluestone Road manage to 'pass' on this story of a once-slave-woman who made a bid for freedom that allowed her to learn 'mother love': a loving so hard that she kills her child. They manage to forget. But this passing by, through forgetting, means that what might be learned from Sethe's story is also lost. The collective responsibilities for what happened to Sethe are also forgotten. Until, that is, Morrison's narrative retrieval, when she 'passes the story on' by its retelling. As she explains in her interview: 'The act of writing [Beloved] ... is a way of confronting [slavery] in a manner in which the memory is not destructive ... a way of confronting it and making it possible to remember'.[21] The reader reads into the story the responsibilities that are set aside in the act of forgetting and getting on with making a life. The costs of forgetting, of not passing on the story, are disconnections between the past, the present and, by implication, the future. What happened to Beloved? She is heavily pregnant when last seen in the novel. What is her offspring?

21 Ibid., p. 5.

Knowing words

Remembering, and being able to forget, are vital aspects of personal and communal survival for people in the north of Ireland who have endured thirty years of political conflict. Sethe's story, and Morrison's work on language, is about finding right words to tell stories and to re-member. This all seems a very long way – literally, historically and politically – from reflections on devolution in the north of Ireland. Yet it is the right place for me to think about these things. Some of my re-membering, being a woman and a feminist in the north of Ireland entails political analysis; making connections between fragments of the whole complex lived-through-history of the north's conflict. Some of it involves my own 'story'. I am acutely conscious of the process of selection: words, fragments and stories. Of 'passing', in the sense of not telling, certain vital stories. The time for telling is not yet. That is probably the case for many people here. Not telling, and forgetting, are ways of coping. They are ways understood by Morrison. But the novel also warns, through ironies of recognition, and in the appearance and disappearance of Beloved, of the costs to the future, of the comforts of forgetting in the present.

The selection of words is a struggle. Morrison has written incisively about 'racially inflected language'.[22] I imagine I could put together some personal – and, hopefully, revelatory – stories. Revelatory for feminists curious about identification as a feminist within a 'divided society' (and, come to think of it, what society is not 'divided'?). The stories would (this author aspires) offer insights for the kind of person who might take up this book and read this chapter. But the words used already, require deconstruction. 'Devolution' is not the 'right word' to use to describe the process underway in the north of Ireland just now. Devolution, of some powers from Westminster to a local assembly, may be one outcome of the Agreement. It is one element in the Agreement, along with others, about dismantling state sectarianism. These include democratic mechanisms for inclusion, cross-border bodies, human rights, equality, prisoners and victims. There was a devolved one-party parliament at Stormont from 1922 to 1972, when the parliament was prorogued. The prospect of a 'return' to 'devolution' requires cautionary quotation marks and loads of explanation in the context of northern politics.

Similarly, the words 'divided society', in relation to the north of Ireland, fill me with dread. I use the term because it is in common currency in describing the situation. I expect the reader to be familiar with, and possibly to nod agreement in recognition at the phrase. And, to be fair that is where I hope to strike (deconstructively, so to speak) at the familiar assumptions built into the language. The words 'divided society' construct the northern conflict, as they appear

---

22 Toni Morrison, *Playing in the Dark*, p. 13.

to describe it.[23] Hence my bracketed suggestion that all societies are surely 'divided'. The words drain away contextual and political meaning whilst posing as explication. The phrase lacks political nuance or edge. Is racist society 'divided'? What are the implications for raced people if the society that discriminates against them/us is described as 'divided'? I hazard that the implications are a depoliticizing and an ahistorical approach to racism. An exercise in hand washing. A mathematical balancing act emerges under the guise of explication or analysis when 'divided society' (or the friendlier 'divided community') is offered, as both cause and consequence of the conflict in the north. This balancing act involves seeing two sides of an equation wherein one side is 'as bad' as the other (the badness usually consisting of 'evil men' – and none of us likes them). The totalizing conclusion may be derived that the Catholicism of Catholics and the Protestantism of Protestants are the problem. They are not. No more than skin colour is the problem with race. The problem is political, historical, classed and gendered. Historically, religion has a formative role in all of this.

I need to lace my re-membering words with warnings about language. Warnings about the traps there are in the language: fall in and it is hard to see a way out. Morrison has shown a way in her thinking on language. When she was publicizing her latest novel *Paradise* (1998) on BBC radio's 'Start the Week', she responded to a question about black identity and the novel by saying that to know that she is black is to know very little about her.[24] 'In a room full of black people', she said, 'other things matter'. Rereading Morrison, thinking about devolving 'British' and 'Irish' political relationships and identifications, and writing this chapter, the insight bears repetition. To know that I am a northern Irish woman from a Catholic background, brought up in nationalist-republican, working-class West Belfast, is to know very little about me. However, for a reader to be given this information, with the apparently contradictory claim that the information is very little in the line of knowledge, begs a number of questions about words and meanings. Morrison's claim, about her own 'black' identity, questions what listeners may have assumed we 'knew' about her. Listeners to the programme that morning were provoked to examine, or at least to be aware of, our assumptions about what we thought we 'knew' about Morrison by knowing that she is 'black'. Morrison disturbed Monday morning 'Start the Week' certainties by withdrawing any easy assumptions on the listeners' part, that we 'knew' her in some ways, by simply knowing her as 'black'. Did listeners similarly assume to 'know' Melvyn

---

23 See Desmond Bell for his analysis of 'British labourism's' approaches to sectarianism; treating it, variously as 'false consciousness' and 'irredentist "tribalism"': 'Within this perspective the structural relation between class and sectarian division and the mediating role of British imperialism in the north of Ireland cannot even be posed, let alone explained'. Desmond Bell, *Acts of Union: Youth Culture and Sectarianism in Northern Ireland* (London: Macmillan Education Ltd, 1990), p. 65.

24 Toni Morrison, *Paradise* (London: Chatto and Windus, 1998).

Bragg because we know him as white? Or is knowledge of whiteness in an unconscious, unthought of, 'universal' category of meaning? What is the weight of racial meaning carried by 'white' in Britain, and in Ireland, as opposed to the weight of racial meaning in the word 'black'? Morrison has posed the question differently in her study of 'Whiteness and the Literary Imagination' (1992) where her preoccupation is with how language works to 'powerfully evoke and enforce hidden signs of racial superiority, cultural hegemony, and dismissive "othering" of people and language'(p. xii):

> Does racial 'unconsciousness' or awareness of race enrich interpretative language, and when does it impoverish it? What does positing one's writerly self, in the wholly racialised society that is the United States, as unraced and all others as raced entail? What happens to the writerly imagination of a black author who is at some level always conscious of representing one's own race to, or in spite of, a race of readers that understands itself to be 'universal' or race-free? (p. xiv)

'To know that I am black is to know very little about me' ... To know that I am a northern Irish woman ... is to know very little about me. It is to know of my need to state these 'givens' of my 'identity': to offer a reader ways of categorizing me, explaining my perspectives and experiences (explaining me away?). But it is very little in the line of knowledge. The work that Avtar Brah has done on 'constructing ... understanding of identification across "difference"' addresses this business of knowledge, language and identity:

> Knowing is not so much about the assemblage of existing knowledge as it is about recognising our constitution as 'ourselves' within the fragments we possess as knowledge; 'hailing' and being 'hailed' within the discourses that produce us and the narratives we spin.[25]

In this chapter, I am gathering fragments and 'spinning' narratives out of reflections on what it is, what it has been like, to live in the north of Ireland at a time of political crisis and reconstitution and (hopefully of) reconciliation. Language is a vital area for reflections on devolving identities in Britain and the north of Ireland. So many social values, dominant political meanings and historical baggage are packed into the scaffolding of the language and hides inside the words. And, crucially, the actions of the state disappear from view in the two communities' construction.

Morrison's work, as a writer, is, amongst other things, about learning 'how to manoeuver ways to free up the language from its sometimes sinister, frequently lazy, almost always predictable employment of racially informed and determined chains'.[26] The task is undertaken in the knowledge that it is impossible. In the

[25] Avtar Brah, 'The Scent of Memory', p. 5.

[26] Morrsion, *Playing in the Dark*, p. xiii.

absence of radical social change, 'in a wholly racialised society, there is no escape from racially inflected language' (ibid., p. 12–13).

Devolving nationalisms

Conversations amongst some feminists from Scotland in the context of devolution, have drawn attention to how language works to define and marginalize them; to perform disappearing acts. These conversations expose the linguistic scaffolding and bring the 'state' into the picture. From the Scottish perspective, Esther Breitenbach *et al.* argue that the 'United' in the United Kingdom is ironic: 'the apparent unity of Britain is a false imposition that works to marginalize, among others, women in Scotland'.[27] These Scottish feminists see themselves as marginalized within homogenizing 'United Kingdom' mainstream feminism which presumes to 'speak for all' (p. 58). Like other nationalisms, the Scottish variety is generally regarded as a masculinist and misogynist project. To speak out and to defend Scottish nationalism is to risk, at the very least, being misunderstood. But, for Breitenbach *et al.*, the risk has to be taken: 'At the roots of this debate about the state and constitution are arguments about democracy, civil rights and the rule of law (that is to say, a system of justice that commands respect)' (p. 58).

At the time of writing, there is no way of knowing whether or not devolution to a new local assembly will be the outcome of the review of the Agreement. Who could have imagined, when the local devolved parliament in the north was prorogued in 1972, that, before the conflict had reached a process of resolution, Scotland would have a devolved parliament, and that Wales would have a national assembly? It was unimaginable then that questions of nationalism, devolution and local regional identifications would have revived political debate about democracy and accountability in Scotland, England and Wales, and regions therein, at the end of the century. Up until the late 1980s it was commonly argued, particularly in relation to Ireland and the northern conflict, that nationalism was a nineteenth-century anachronism in the modern world. Seamus Deane makes the wry, prescient political point that, until the 1990s imperialism and colonialism were generally characterised in the west as '... myths generated by nationalists, unless, that is, they are spoken of by heroic little republics struggling to free themselves from the Soviet embrace'.[28]

---

27 Esther Breitenbach, Alice Brown and Fiona Myers in 'Understanding Women in Scotland', *Feminist Review*, 58, Spring (1999), p. 50. Further references to this article are given after quotations in the text.

28 Seamus Deane, 'Wherever Green is Red', in Mairin Dhonnchada and Theo Dorgan, *Revising the Rising* (Derry: Field Day, 1991), p. 96.

Interestingly, and not incidentally, given considerations here on the role of remembering and forgetting, Deane's essay occurs in a publication that debates a range of opinions about the 1916 rising. The editors, and others, had originally hoped to have a conference in Dublin on this key event in modern Irish history, to coincide with the 75th anniversary in 1991. Official support was not forthcoming, and given that 'general discussion had been curiously muted, not to say inhibited', the writers settled for a publication, in the belief 'that, as a reaction, amnesia – private or communal – is both unhealthy and dangerous'.[29] For the contributors to *Revising the Rising* 'not looking back' is not an option.

In relation to feminism and the liberation of women, again nationalism has been construed as provincial and backward-looking.[30] Carol Coulter's work on feminism and nationalism challenges simplistic, from-a-safe-distance generalizations:

> The involvement of women is a common feature of nationalist movements. From India to Egypt to Africa to Ireland, the upsurge of nationalism was accompanied by the emergence of women onto the streets in public protest and into public life as organisers, leaders and shock troops. The fact that these societies were often criticised by the imperialist power as repressive of their women, keeping them in thrall to religious and cultural practices redolent of a benighted past, makes this involvement all the more interesting and significant.[31]

Coulter's tone is understandable given the general derision of nationalist movements by many western feminists. However, national liberation movements can no more be generally defended as emancipatory projects without attention to where women's lives feature in the particular context.[32] Listening closely to women and feminists speaking and writing from particular struggles may be valuable in this learning. Which feminists, and which women gain access to voicing their analysis and experience is all part of the politics of struggle. In the north of Ireland, the politics of sectarianism are problematic for feminists who would unite women on the basis of gender identity. These problems have echoes of feminist encounters with race politics. Ignoring race, or ignoring sectarianism (or nationalism) is not an option. But, as Merl Storr's work (cited above) indicates, the

---

29 Mairin Dhonnchada and Theo Dorgan, *Revising the Rising*, p. ix.

30 See for example Carol Coulter, *The Hidden Tradition: Feminism, Women and Nationalism in Ireland* (Cork: Cork University Press, 1993) and Edna Longley *From Cathleen to Anorexia: The Breakdown of Irelands* (Dublin: Attic Press, LIP Pamphlet 1991).

31 Coulter, *Hidden Tradition*, p. 5.

32 Liam O'Dowd's argument about sectarianism and class is relevant for feminist analyses of gender: 'Sectarianism is not a superstructural phenomena floating free of an abstracted economic base, which in turn is divided into classes ... it has a history embedded in colonization ... it cross-cuts politics, ideology and culture'. Cited in Bell, *Acts of Union*, p. 67.

ways of paying attention to race need also to be subjected to critical scrutiny. The question can be posed: what difference does a particular analysis or approach make to the situation? And how is the difference estimated? In this chapter, I hope my reflections and analysis complicate some assumptions about women, devolution and politics in the north of Ireland.

The potential for particular nationalisms to form emancipatory political projects, and to challenge the indifference of global capital, is clear from Noam Chomsky's analysis of recently declassified US post-World War II records.[33] He notes that the prime concern of the US Administration, at this time, was with what was seen as the emerging 'philosophy of new nationalism' (ibid., p. 6). The documents indicate the Administration's concern with a philosophy that embraced 'policies designed to bring about a broader distribution of wealth and to raise the standard of living of the masses' (ibid., p. 6). These emerge from the 'nationalist' principle that 'the first beneficiaries of a country's resources should be the people of that country' (ibid.). This socialist 'potential' within modern Irish republicanism is, arguably, a potential yet to be realized. The politics that may develop, north and south, out of the current peace process allows for hope, but recent history suggests caution. Desmond Bell has argued that the British state's failure to dismantle the structures of sectarianism in the north of Ireland, under direct rule 'has proved the graveyard of British social-democratic illusions about the reforming capacities of the state in capitalist society'.[34] Dismantling sectarian employment practices would require massive state investment. The Agreement is about a process of dismantling sectarian structures, of building inclusive democratic institutions in the north of Ireland and changing political institutions, and institutional thinking, in the south (Republic of Ireland). It is also about changing political relationships between the peoples on these islands. The outcomes of agreements, however, 'are not determined by words, but by the power relations that impose their interpretations'.[35] Women and men are differently entangled in these power relations within and between nationalism and unionism in the north of Ireland.

The politics of memory

In these reflections on the politics of identities in the north of Ireland there may be the assumption that the reflections are about the writer considering her identity, within a particular political context, at a particular moment, whilst the reader absorbs the information and 'freely' interprets it. The act of providing this

33 Noam Chomsky, 'Power in the Global Arena', *New Left Review*, 230, July/August, 1998, p. 6. Further references to this article are given after quotations in the text.

34 Bell, *Acts of Union*, p. 67.

35 Chomsky, p. 26.

information can be a strangely intimate interaction with an unknown reader. However, the meaningfulness of the reflection is as much about the reader's 'identity' as it is about the writer's. The reader's interpretation of the reflections – what the reader reads it to mean – is meaningful both for how *s/he* approaches this chapter, and for the insights that may result. The conflict in the north of Ireland is arguably one of the most contentious and well known political conflicts in Europe; perhaps, given its longevity, in the world. Plotting a personal 'identity' from a place that has attracted the occasional and erratic gaze of the inter/national media has its problems, but also its opportunities. Few people will be indifferent to the story of being a woman and a feminist in the northern Irish 'war'. Many will have certain, competing, complex expectations – and there's the rub. The reader is not a blank page. Writer and reader enter an already constructed space with particular historical and political contours.

Most, if not all, readers of this chapter will have 'memories' of 'Belfast', in the dictionary sense of the word 'memory': being able to 'recall past sensations, thoughts, knowledge, etc'.[36] They are unlikely to be 'beloved' memories, as my title suggests mine are. The city, and the media images of the war, have become twentieth-century icons of 'sectarian state brutality', 'urban guerrilla warfare' ... supply the icon of your choice and analysis. The conflict in the north of Ireland is frequently an irritant to some influential people in the Republic of Ireland who wish the north would forget the past and get on with the present.[37] As though it were that simple. The remembering of the past that goes on in the north seems to be an irritant to some influential people who hail from Britain. On the day he delivered his committee's report on policing, Sir Chris Patten answered a journalist's question about how the committee's 175 recommendations on the Royal Ulster Constabulary, would be received. He answered with a note of irritation: 'The political class, and everybody else in Northern Ireland, have to learn to live in the future rather than living in the past' (BBC local live broadcast, 9 September 1999). A week later, the forensic evidence provided to the Widgery Tribunal (1972), which claimed that some of the people shot dead on Bloody Sunday in Derry had been handling arms, was discredited. In an article entitled, 'Shooting the Irish' (*The Guardian*, 18 September, 1999) Jeremy Hardy claimed that, 'The truth about Bloody Sunday is emerging now. It could not be suppressed forever'; the evidence had already been comprehensively discredited in 1972 by a US forensic expert. I want to believe Hardy: that the 'truth' cannot be suppressed forever. I do believe that for people here to 'live in the future' what happened in the past needs to be faced. The past is no place to live. The trouble is, so much remains hidden and the power to reveal is not the prerogative of those seeking to know what happened.

---

36 *Collins Concise Dictionary* (London: Collins, 1989).

37 Deane, 'Wherever Green is Red', pp. 91–105.

Irritation with the northern conflict spilled over into anger and hurt at a recent conference panel on women in the conflicts in the north of Ireland and Israel/Palestine.[38] One member of the audience said that she passed by Horseguard's Parade, in London, on her way to work each morning. She thought of the dead soldiers each time. On 20 July 1982 the Irish Republican Army (IRA) killed eight members of the Household Cavalry. I remember television images of the hulking, huge, injured and dead horses. How should I have responded? I felt that the people on the panel were being asked to account for the awful deaths. And, whilst I could not do that, neither could I gain refuge by 'hand-washing'.[39]

In some ways, I think that the woman was courageous. How many people have memories from the northern Irish conflict about which they would wish to question people from the place? The summer before the Cavalry deaths, the West Belfast neighbourhood I come from was plunged into grief and anger by the deaths of hunger striker after hunger striker. The Thatcher government refused to move. Eventually, the strike was called off. It could not have been seen at the time, but the hunger strikes, and parallel adventitious Sinn Fein electoral success, have proved to be a watershed in the political and military conflict – leading to the current peace process. Eight Household Cavalry, ten hunger strikers. Two summers. All men, dead.[40]

One set of memories is intimately and politically involved for me. The other is televisual and remote … until a person recalls the memory's meaning for her. I have no way of resolving this, other than to step back into 'history' and witness the deaths, the events and the memories as dimensions of the failure of politics to resolve the colonial relationships between the British and Irish states and peoples. Even then, the concept of history also requires cautionary quotes because, like memory, it too is a politically constituted construction.[41] All of this is little or no consolation to a grieving individual, remembering.

---

38 International Studies Association Annual Convention: 'Feminist Theory and Gender Studies' Round Table, Washington D.C., 1998.

39 I responded by relating my experience of being in Derry on Bloody Sunday and of its impact on me; and by arguing that violence in the conflict needs to be critically and fully analysed.

40 In 1982, 112 people were killed in the conflict. Some 3,637 people have died altogether. This works out at around 2,425 people per million of population. In a country the size of Britain (approximately 56 million) this would convert to around 135,800 people dead over thirty years. Over 90 per cent of the deaths in the conflict here have been men. No work that I know of has been done here on gendered forms of political agency. My current work is on women's gendered forms of political agency in a sectarian society. See Eilish Rooney, *Women in Northern Irish Politics: Difference Matters* (forthcoming).

41 Avtar Brah goes further: 'What is history if not an on-going contestation of the very terms whereby the term itself emerged as a technology of the eurocentric gaze. So that … Hegel could assert … that Africa had no "history"?' Brah, 'The Scent of Memory', p. 6.

The story goes on

The prospect of a resolution to the violent political conflict in the north of Ireland, and a return to local political accountability, entails facing the 'clamouring' of the past: seeing and revisiting the grief-strewn and courageous distances travelled since the last 'experiment' with devolution in the north of Ireland failed everyone. It has so far also involved coping with public and private refusals to face the past – and to live with it.[42] The peace process has brought about public acts of remembering, and it has involved the politicization of private grief. It seems safer to remember now, in ways that were not safe before – to put together, listen to, and to discuss, for the first time, some of the events of the past thirty years: re-membering in order not to forget.

---

[42] Depending on the outcome, in particular for the families of the dead, the ongoing Bloody Sunday Inquiry may be the first of many enquiries relating to state involvement in political violence.

Notes on Contributors

Flora Alexander is a Senior Lecturer in English at the University of Aberdeen, where she also contributes to Women's Studies. Her main research interest is in Canadian women's writing. Recent publications include 'Contemporary Fiction III: The Anglo-Scots', in Douglas Gifford and Dorothy McMillan, eds, *A History of Scottish Women's Writing* (1997) and 'Prisons, Traps and Escape Routes' in Lynne Pearce and Gina Wisker, eds, *Fatal Attractions* (1998).

Helen Boden is a Lecturer in English Literature at the University of Edinburgh. Her research interests include: late eighteenth- and early nineteenth-century English and Scottish literature; travel writing and autobiography; and contemporary Scottish writing and culture. She is currently working on a book entitled *Travel Writing in the Post-Enlightenment Age*.

Rachel Dyer works as a Teaching Assistant in the English Department at Lancaster University where she has just completed her PhD ('Reading and Writing in Collaboration: Dialogues with Scottish and Canadian Women Writers'). Her research interests include: theories of collaboration and new narrative strategies; postcolonial and British studies; children's literature; contemporary poetry; women's writing and literature in hypertext.

Alison Easton is Senior Lecturer in English and a member of the Institute for Women's Studies at Lancaster University. She is the author of *The Making of the Hawthorne Subject* (1996) and essays on nineteenth-century women writers and class, and editor of the Penguin edition of Sarah Orne Jewett's *The Country of the Pointed Firs and Other Stories* (1995). She has also edited the Macmillan New Casebook, *Angela Carter* (2000), and is co-editor with Tess Cosslett and Penny Summerfield of *Woman, Power and Resistance: An Introduction to Women's Studies* (1996). She is presently engaged on a study of Jewett's negotiation of class relations.

Hilary Hinds is a Lecturer in English at Cheltenham and Gloucester College of Higher Education. Her main research interest is in seventeenth-century women's writing, but she likes to make occasional forays, as here, into the twentieth century.

Sinead McDermott is a Lecturer in the Department of English at the Free University of Amsterdam. She has previously held teaching posts at the University of Strathclyde and University College, Scarborough. Her current research addresses the relationship between memory, place and female subjectivity in contemporary women's writing.

Ruth McElroy completed her doctorate on African-American and Latin American women's writing in 1997 (Institute for Women's Studies, Lancaster). Since then, she has lectured at Cheltenham and Gloucester College of Higher Education and currently teaches English, Media Studies and Welsh Studies at Trinity College, Carmarthen. She has published work on Welsh women's writing and feminist approaches to autobiography. Her other research interests include post-colonial literature and film. She is currently working on a book on literary and filmic version of British belongings entitled *Un/homely Britons*.

Lynne Pearce (Editor) is a Senior Lecturer in the English Department at Lancaster University where she teaches mostly in the area of women's writing and feminist theory. She has also been centrally involved in Lancaster's Institute for Women's Studies over the past ten years. Her principal publications include: *Woman/Image/Text: Readings in Pre-Raphaelite Art and Literature* (1991), *Reading Dialogics* (1994) and *Feminism and the Politics of Reading* (1997). She is also co-author, with Sara Mills, of *Feminist Readings/Feminists Reading* (second edition, 1996), and co-editor (with Jackie Stacey) of *Romance Revisited* (1995) and (with Gina Wisker) *Fatal Attractions: Rescripting Romance in Contemporary Literature and Film* (1998). She is now embarking on a new project provisionally entitled 'Textual Turns: Rhetorical Innovations in Contemporary Feminist Discourse' and (as will be evident from this collection) has an abiding interest in the erstwhile 'marginalized' literatures, cultures and communities of the British Isles.

Eilish Rooney is a feminist academic in the University of Ulster where she works and publishes in the areas of feminisms and nationalisms, culture and identity. She is Co-Chairperson of 'Women in Politics' and Board Member of the POWER partnership, both of which are involved in political education in Ireland. WiP works with women in both loyalist and republican areas of Belfast; POWER provides a cross-border programme of university accredited courses on women, politics and economics.

Wren Sidhe is an AHRB-funded doctoral student at Cheltenham and Gloucester College of Higher Education. Her research interests are mainly in the links between sexuality, literature and the nation. She has published poetry and articles in little magazines, and has a forthcoming chapter on interwar sailors' reading matter in *Gendering Library History*, edited by Evelyn Kerslake (Liverpool John Moores University Press).

Charlotte Williams is a Lecturer in Social Policy and Women's Studies at the University of Wales, Bangor. Her academic research includes new ethnicities, nation and cultural identity/citizenship in Wales and Europe. She is co-editor of *Social Work and Minorities: European Perspectives* (1998) and is currently researching aspects of devolved governance in Wales. She also writes poetry and short stories.

Select Bibliography

This bibliography is a compilation of what appear to be the most important, and most frequently cited, volumes from all the chapters. It does not include journal articles or individual chapters in books, nor I have reproduced details of the literary texts and/or associated secondary reading dealt with in the individual chapters. Full details of all this material is provided in the footnotes.

Aaron, Jane, Teresa Betts and Moira Vincentelli, eds, *Our Sister's Lands: the Changing Identities of Women in Wales* (Cardiff: Cardiff University Press, 1994)

Anderson, Benedict, *Imagined Communities: Reflections on the Origin and Spread of Nationalism* [1983] (London: Verso, 1998)

Ashcroft, Bill, Gareth Griffiths and Helen Tiffin, *The Empire Writes Back: Theory and Practice in Postcolonial Literature* (Oxford: Oxford University Press, 1995)

Balibar, Etienne and Immanuel Wallerstein, *Race, Nation, Class: Ambiguous Identities*, trans. Chris Turner (London: Verso, 1991)

Bassnett, Susan, ed., *Studying British Cultures* (London: Routledge, 1997)

Bell, Ian A., *Peripheral Visions: Images of Nationhood in Contemporary British Fiction* (Cardiff: University of Wales Press, 1995)

Benson, Susan Potter, Stephen Brier and Roy Rozenzweig, eds, *Presenting the Past: Essays on History and the Public* (Philadelphia: Temple University Press, 1996)

Benstock, Shari, ed., *The Private Self: Theory and Practice of Women's Autobiographical Writings* (London and New York: Routledge, 1988)

Bhabha, Homi, ed., *Nation and Narration* (London: Routledge, 1990)

———, *The Location of Culture* (London and New York: Routledge, 1994)

Bodnor, John, *Remaking America: Public Memory, Commemoration and Patriotism in the Twentieth Century* (Princeton: Princeton University Press, 1992)

Braidotti, Rosi, *Nomadic Subjects* (New York: Columbia University Press, 1994)

Bumstead, J.M., *The People's Clearance: Highland Emigration to British North America, 1770–1815* (Edinburgh: Edinburgh University Press, 1982)

Cartney, Wilfred, *Whispers from the Caribbean: 'I Going Away and I Going Home'* (Los Angeles: Centre for African American Studies, University of California, 1991)

Coulter, Carol, *The Hidden Tradition: Feminism, Women and Nationalism in Ireland* (Cork: Cork University Press, 1993)

Craig, Cairns, *Out of History: Narrative Paradigms in Scottish and British Culture* (Edinburgh: Polygon, 1996)

Crawford, Robert, *Devolving English Literature* (Oxford: Clarendon Press, 1992)

Dhonnchadha, Mairin and Theo Dorgan, *Revising the Rising* (Derry: Field Day, 1991)

Dyer, Richard, *White* (London and New York: Routledge, 1997)

Eagleton, Terry, Jameson, Frederic, and Said, Edward, *Nationalism, Colonialism and Literature* (Minneapolis: University of Minnesota Press, 1990)

Fay, Marie Therese, Mike Morrissey and Marie Smyth, *The Cost of the Troubles: Mapping the Troubles-related Deaths in Northern Ireland: 1969–1994* (Derry: INCORE, 1997)

Felman, Shoshana, *What Does a Woman Want?* (London and New York: Routledge, 1994)

——— and Dori Laub, eds, *Testimony: Crises of Witnessing in Literature, Psychoanalysis and History* (London and New York: Routledge, 1992)

Fuss, Diana, *Identification Papers* (London and New York: Routledge, 1995)

George, Rosemary Marangoly, *The Politics of Home: Postcolonial Relocations and Twentieth-Century Fiction* (Cambridge: Cambridge University Press, 1996)

Gifford, Douglas and Dorothy McMillan, eds, *A History of Scottish Women's Writing* (Edinburgh: Edinburgh University Press, 1997)

Gilroy, Paul, *There Ain't No Black in the Union Jack: The Cultural Politics of Race and Nation* (London: Routledge, 1987)

Harding, Sandra and Merrll B. Hintikka, eds, *Discovering Reality: Feminist Perspectives on Epistemology, Metaphysics and Philosophy of Science* (Boston: D. Reidel, 1983)

Humm, Maggie, *Border Traffic: Strategies of Contemporary Women Writers* (Manchester: Manchester University Press, 1991)

Hunter, James, *A Dance Called America: The Scottish Highlands, the United States and Canada* (Edinburgh and London: Mainstream Press, 1994)

Kaplan, Caren, *Questions of Travel: Postmodern Discourses of Displacement* (Durham and London: Duke University Press, 1996)

Keith, Michael and Steve Pile, eds, *Place and the Politics of Identity* (London: Routledge, 1993)

Kuhn, Annette, *Family Secrets: Acts of Memory and Imagination* (London and New York: Verso, 1995)

Longley, Edna, *From Cathleen to Anorexia: The Breakdown of Irelands* (Dublin: Attic Press, LIP Pamphlet, 1991)

McClintock, Anne, Aamir Mufti and Ella Shoat, eds, *Dangerous Liaisons: Gender, Nation and Postcolonial Perspectives* (London: University of Minnesota Press, 1997)

McCrone, David, Stephen Kendrick and Pat Straw, eds, *The Making of Scotlands: Nation, Culture and Social Change* (Edinburgh: Edinburgh University Press, 1989)

———, Angela Morris and Richard Kiely, *Scotland – the Brand: The Making of Scottish Heritage* (Edinburgh: Edinburgh University Press, 1995)

Macdonald, Sharon, ed., *Inside European Identities* (Oxford: Berg, 1997)

McDowell, Linda, *Gender, Identity and Place* (Cambridge: Polity, 1999)
Massey, Doreen, *Space, Place and Gender* (Oxford: Polity, 1994)
Minh-ha, Trinh T, *When the Moon Waxes Red: Representation, Gender and Cultural Politics* (London and New York: Routledge, 1991)
Mirza, Heidi-Safia, ed., *Black British Feminism* (London: Rouledge, 1997)
Morrsion, Toni, *Playing in the Dark: Whiteness and the Literary Imagination* (London: Picador, 1990)
Nairn, Tom, *The Break-Up of Britain* [1977] (London: Verso, 1981)
Osmond, John, *The Divided Kingdom* (London: Constable, 1988)
Parker, Andrew et al., *Nationalisms and Sexualities* (London: Routledge, 1994)
Paxman, Jeremy, *The English: A Portrait of a People* (London: Michael Joseph, 1998)
Pearce, Lynne, *Reading Dialogics* (London: Edward Arnold, 1994)
———, *Feminism and the Politics of Reading* (London: Arnold, 1997)
Phillips, Richard, David Shuttleton, Diane Watt, eds, *Decentring Sexualities* (London and New York: Routledge, 2000)
Pittock, Murray, *The Invention of Scotland: The Stuart Myth and the Scottish Identity, 1638 to the Present* (London and New York: Routledge, 1991)
Probyn, Elspeth, *Sexing the Self: Gendered Positions in Cultural Studies* (London: Routledge, 1993)
———, *Outside Belongings* (London: Routledge, 1996)
Robertson, George et al., eds, *Travellers Tales: Narratives of Home and Displacement* (London: Routledge, 1994)
Rutherford, Jonathan, ed., *Identity: Community, Culture, Difference* (London: Lawrence and Wishart, 1990)
Said, Edward, *The World, The Text and the Critic* (Cambridge MA: Harvard University Press, 1983)
Samuel, Raphael, *Island Stories: Unravelling Britain* (*Theatres of Memory*, Vol 2) (London: Verso, 1998)
Singh, Amrijit, Joseph T. Skerrett, Jr, and Robert E. Hogan, *Memory, Narrative, and Identity: New Essays in Ethnic American Literature* (Boston: Northeastern University Press, 1994)
Skeggs, Beverley, *Formations of Class and Gender: Becoming Respectable* (London: Sage, 1997)
Todd, Janet ed., *Women Writers Talking* (New York: Holmes and Meier, 1983)
Webster, Wendy, *Imagining Home: Gender, 'Race' and National Identity 1945–64* (London: UCL Press, 1998)
Whyte, Christopher, *Gendering the Nation: Studies in Modern Scottish Literature* (Edinburgh: Edinburgh University Press, 1995)
Williams, Gwyn A., *When Was Wales?* (London: Picador, 1991)
Williams, Raymond, *Border Country* (London: Chatto & Windus, 1978)
———, *Politics and Letters* (London: Verso, 1979)

———, *Towards 2000* (London: Pantheon Books, 1983)
Womack, Peter, *Improvement and Romance: Constructing the Myth of the Highlands* (Basingstoke: Macmillan, 1989)
Yuval-Davis, Nira, *Gender and Nation* (London: Sage, 1997)
——— and Flora Anthias, eds, *Woman-Nation-State* (London: Macmillan, 1989)

Index